TANKS
INSIDE OUT

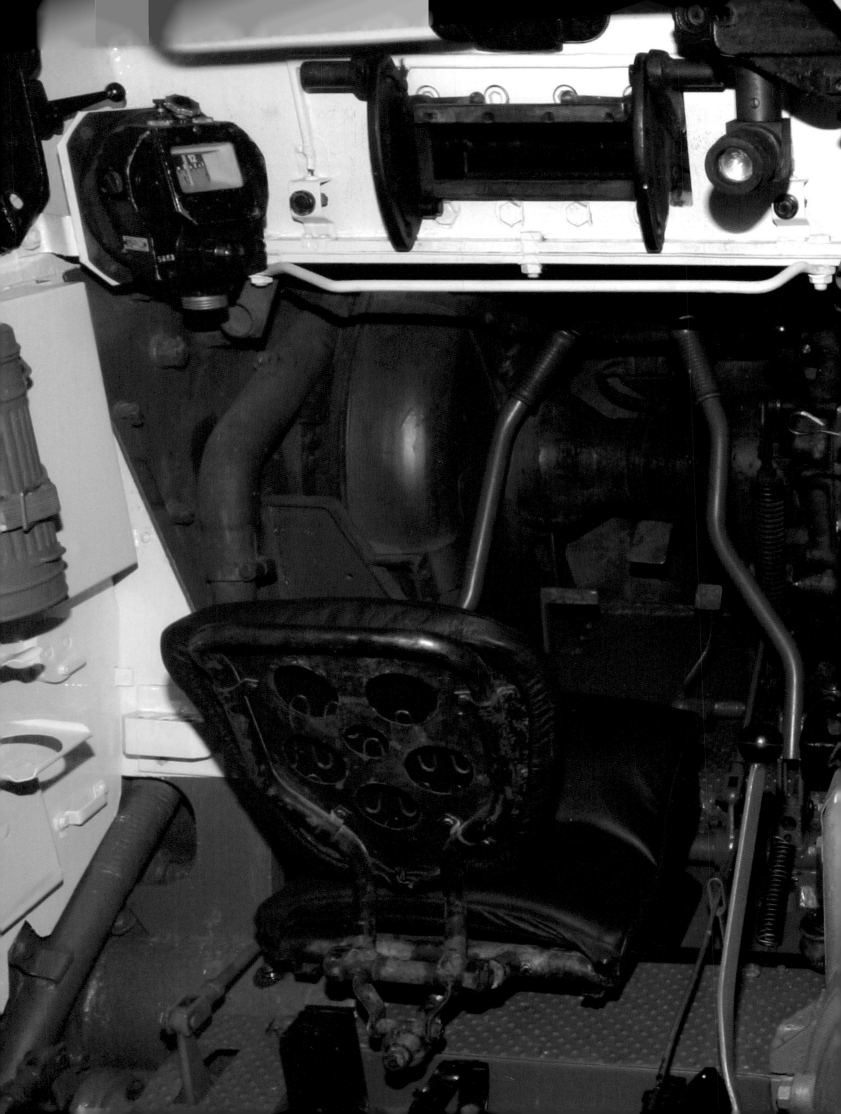

TANKS
INSIDE OUT

Michael E. Haskew

amber
BOOKS

First published in 2010 by Amber Books Ltd
Bradley's Close
74–77 White Lion Street
London N1 9PF
United Kingdom
www.amberbooks.co.uk

ISBN: 978-1-907446-18-4

Project Editor: Sarah Uttridge
Editorial Assistant: Kieron Connolly
Design: Zöe Mellors
Picture Research: Terry Forshaw

Printed and bound in Thailand

Contents

Classic Tanks 1918–60

Modern Tanks 1961–Present

Classic Tanks 1918–1960

The tank debuted and matured rapidly on the battlefield, asserting firepower, mobility, and armour protection like no other land warfare system in history. From design to reality, it revolutionized the way in which wars have been fought.

A British Centurion tank, painted in a European camouflage scheme, awaits orders during exercises. Note the armour skirting for protection of the tracks and wheels against projectiles and land mines.

The concept of the tank, a virtually irresistible, indestructible, and intimidating engine of war, may be credited to Leonardo da Vinci and his fifteenth-century vision of a mobile, well-protected fortress. However, considering the sweep of history, it may also be asserted that the Greek phalanx, with hoplites grouped tightly together, their shields interlocked and bristling with spear points, is nothing short of a "human" tank.

TRENCHES TORN

Its origin notwithstanding, the tank came into its own during the recent, war-ravaged past. While the aircraft has reigned supreme in the skies and the battleship, aircraft carrier, and submarine have held sway on and beneath the sea, the tank has proven itself the mailed fist of the land battle.

The appearance of British tanks on the battlefield during World War I proved a shock to the German military establishment, and the response was swift. In a relatively short period of time, both the Allies and the Central Powers were assailing the enemy's lines in primitive tanks, belching bullets from machine guns or firing heavier cannon. Although the tank may have exhibited plenty of firepower, its most innovative aspect was that of mobility.

Static warfare, theorists reasoned, might well become a thing of the past should tanks be introduced in significant numbers. A modern war of speed and manoeuvre could result, placing an enemy's fixed defences in peril. Perhaps more than its direct impact on the outcome of World War I, the earliest operational tanks such as the British Mark V and Whippet and the German A7V proved to be harbingers of things to come.

TANKS IN TRANSITION

British soldier and military strategist J.F.C. Fuller was among the earliest advocates of armoured warfare during the twentieth century. His influence was reported to have spread and directly impacted the developing battlefield tactics which would define the tank in World War II.

A Churchill tank stirs up a cloud of dust along a dirt road. One of the most versatile chassis designs ever conceived, the Churchill served as the basis for a variety of specialized vehicles.

One tale of Fuller's armoured perspective relates that the British officer attended a review of the burgeoning German army on April 20, 1939, the occasion of Hitler's 50th birthday. Fuller was said to have commented that for hours "a completely mechanized and motorized army roared past the Führer." Hitler supposedly remarked to Fuller as the review ended, "I hope you were pleased with your children." Fuller was reported to have responded, "Your excellency, they have grown up so quickly that I no longer recognize them."

Although this story may be apocryphal, it nevertheless illustrates the breadth of Fuller's influence on the strategy and tactics of modern armoured warfare. A generation after the first steel monsters edged slowly across no-man's-land, the panzers of Heinz Guderian rolled across France to the English Channel, Erwin Rommel's Afrika Korps gained lasting fame, Bernard Montgomery's Desert Rats were victorious at El Alamein, George S. Patton's armoured spearheads relieved Bastogne, and Georgi Zhukov's T-34s rolled through the streets of Berlin.

POST-WAR PROLIFERATION

During the Cold War, the world's great powers continued the development of tanks and complementary armoured fighting vehicles which were capable of transporting combat infantrymen into action, delivering direct fire support, fording streams, removing the wounded and dead from the battlefield, providing anti-aircraft defence, and other supporting roles. The tank itself evolved during its first half century, serving as armoured cavalry, a primary weapon of breakthrough and decision in battle, and the powerful projector of military might on land.

The T-34 medium tank, and those of the KV and Josef Stalin series, manufactured by the Soviet Union during World War II, were exported in

A column of M4 Sherman tanks pauses along a city street during an advance. The second tank in line has been upgunned with the 76.2-mm (3-in) 17-pounder, while the first mounts the original 75-mm (2.95-in) cannon.

Festooned with camouflage branches, an M113 armoured personnel carrier rolls along as its crew focuses forward. The M113 has served as a troop transport and fighting vehicle for nearly half a century.

numbers to client states of the Soviet Bloc, nations of the Middle East, the People's Republic of China, and North Korea. These were followed by the export versions of the T-54/55 and others. In the West, Great Britain, France, and the United States developed powerful tanks based on their experiences during the war. The ubiquitous American Sherman and the British cruiser tanks, whose sheer numbers had overwhelmed the Tigers and Panthers of Hitler's panzer divisions, gave way to heavier designs of the late 1940s and early 1950s, such as the Centurion, Patton, and the AMX-13 light tank.

Through more than 40 years of alternating war and peace, the armoured formation and its accompanying mechanized infantry developed into the modern war machine which was capable of decisive victory on land. A relative few future military operations on the ground, whether offensive or defensive in nature, would result in victory without the involvement of armoured forces.

Eventually, the mere presence of tanks and armoured fighting vehicles would dictate the course of most military ground operations.

"The fact that the tanks had now been raised to such a pitch of technical perfection that they could cross our undamaged trenches and obstacles did not fail to have a marked effect on our troops."

German Field Marshal Paul von Hindenburg
on British tanks during World War I

9

Sturmpanzerwagen A7V

Shocked by the appearance of Allied tanks on the battlefields of World War I, Germany hastened to develop an armoured fighting vehicle of its own. The result was the Sturmpanzerwagen A7V, an ungainly steel fortress made mobile by a tractor chassis.

MAIN ARMAMENT
The main weapon aboard the Sturmpanzerwagen A7V was the Russian Sokol or Belgian-made Maxim Nordenfel 57-mm (2.24-in) short recoil gun, which was fired by a crew of two, a gunner and a loader.

SUSPENSION
The basic suspension system of the Sturmpanzerwagen A7V was that of the Holt tractor, an agricultural vehicle that included 30 small wheels. Components of the suspension system were produced in Austria.

SECONDARY WEAPONS
Six 7.92-mm (0.31-in) Maxim machine guns were situated in the rear and along the sides of the tank. A single "Female" variant, possibly chassis No. 501, was reportedly produced with an additional two machine guns forward and no heavier weapon.

DRIVERS
Two crewmen, positioned inside a noticeable bulge atop the centre of the tank, were required to drive the Sturmpanzerwagen A7V, operating a steering wheel and a system of levers.

ENGINE
Two four-cylinder Daimler engines, mounted in the lower centre of the Sturmpanzerwagen A7V, powered the vehicle, which weighed at least 30 tons, at a top road speed of 9.32 mph (15 km/h) with 74.6 kW (100 hp).

ARMOUR
The armoured protection of the Sturmpanzerwagen A7V was 30 mm (1.2 in) to the front and 20 mm (0.8 in) on each side; however, the steel was not tempered and could not withstand large-calibre shells.

The A7V was designed by committee, meaning that everyone involved had a say as to the overall end product. A weapon designed by a committee usually tends to fall excessively short of expectations, as was the case with the gangly looking Sturmpanzerwagen A7V.

STURMPANZERWAGEN A7V

STURMPANZERWAGEN A7V – SPECIFICATION

Country of Origin: Germany
Crew: 18
Designer: Joseph Vollmer
Designed: 1916
In Service: March–October 1918
Manufacturer: Allgemeines Kriegsdepartement, 7. Abteilung, Verkehrswesen (German army)
Number Built: 21
Produced: October 1917–October 1918
Weight: 32.5 tonnes (35.8 tons)

Dimensions:
Length: 8 m (26.25 ft)
Width: 3.2 m (10.5 ft)
Overall Height: 3.5 m (11.5 ft)

Performance:
Speed: 8 km/h (5 mph)
Range, Road: 80 km (50 miles)
Range, Cross-country: 30 km (18 miles)
Power/Weight Ratio: 6.15 bhp/tonne 1800 rpms
Ground Pressure: n/a
Fording Capacity: 0.65 m (2 ft)
Maximum Gradient: 30 degrees
Maximum Trench Width: 2.2 m (7.25 ft)
Maximum Vertical Obstacle: 0.46 m (1.5 ft)
Suspension Type: Coil-sprung bogies

Engine:
Powerplant: 2 x Daimler-Benz 4 cylinder in-line 165204 petrol engines each developing 74.6 kW (100 hp) @ 1800 rpms
Fuel capacity: n/a

Armour & Armament:
Armour: 20–30 mm (0.8–1.2 in)
Main Armament: 1 x 57-mm L/12 Maxim-Nordenfelt short recoil gun. 500 rounds
Secondary Armament: 6 (or more) x 7.92 mm (0.31 in) MG08/15 machine guns in flexible mounts. 18,000 rounds

Variants:
Sturmpanzerwagen A7V: Basic series designation.
Überlandwagen: Unarmoured, open-top supply vehicle.
A7V/U: Proposed redesign with sponson-type all-around tracks.
A7V/U2: Proposed model based on the A7V/U, this one having slightly smaller track sponsons.
A7V/U3: Proposed "Female" version of the A7V/U2, having only machine guns as armament.

RIVAL: SCHNEIDER CHAR D'ASSAULT

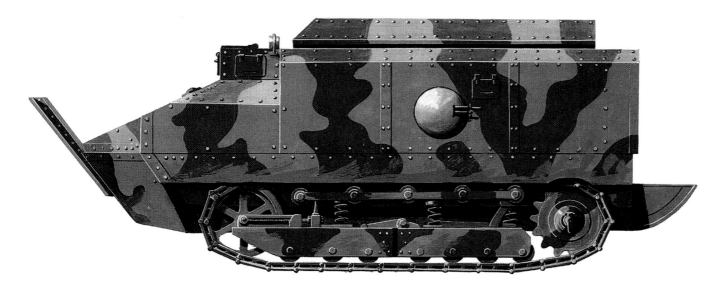

STURMPANZERWAGEN A7V

A captain in the German army and an engineer by profession, Joseph Vollmer headed the design committee that developed the Sturmpanzerwagen A7V. Although German tank design efforts had begun as early as 1911, the hurriedly produced A7V exhibited several notable flaws. At 3.3 m (10 ft 10 in) in height, its silhouette was quite conspicuous, while its ground clearance was only 40 mm (1.6 in). Traversing trenches or even depressions of any depth was virtually impossible. Its full complement of 18 crewmen included a commander, two drivers, machine gunners, and ammunition suppliers, as well as a gunner and loader for the 57-mm (2.24-in) cannon.

The first French tank, the Schneider (above) was designed by Colonel Jean-Baptiste Eugene Estienne and mounted a 75-mm (2.95-in) petard mortar. A second French tank, the St. Chamond (below), appeared months later and proved to be a disappointment.

RIVAL: CHAR D'ASSAULT ST CHAMOND

Crewmen prepare three German Sturmpanzerwagen A7V tanks for deployment to the battlefield. Only 20 of these behemoths were actually delivered to the Western Front. A single example survives and is displayed at a military museum in Australia.

On 13 November, 1916, Germany decided to build tanks. The new vehicle provided a universal platform, to be used as a base for both a tank and a cargo carrier. The first pre-production A7V was built in September 1917.

In the month following the initiation of Operation Michael, Germany's desperate offensive in the West launched on 21 March, 1918, the first confirmed engagement in history between opposing tanks occurred near the French village of Villers-Bretonneux. Here, three German Sturmpanzerwagen A7Vs met three British Mark IVs, one of them the upgunned Male variant mounting a pair of six-pounder cannon. During the initial exchange of gunfire, the Female Mark IVs, armed only with machine guns, were damaged and fell back. The lone Mark IV pressed on, disabling one German tank, commanded by Lieutenant Wilhelm Biltz, and killing five of its crew as they exited the burning A7V.

Second Lieutenant Frank Mitchell, commanding the remaining Mark IV, began to withdraw. However, his tank was heavily damaged by a German mortar round. Seven British Whippet light tanks then advanced, but four of these

were quickly put out of action. It is unclear whether the remaining A7Vs engaged the Whippets or the light tanks fell victim to other German fire. The damaged A7V was later salvaged by the Germans, and it proved to be one of those that had entered combat on 21 March. Of these, two were damaged when they fell into shellholes, three were captured by Allied troops, and others suffered mechanical difficulties.

OUTSIDE THE BOX

Designed and constructed as a box on a tractor, the Sturmpanzerwagen A7V performed best in stationary positions on level ground. Because these ideal conditions were seldom found on the Western Front in 1918, and only 20 A7Vs are known to have become operational before the end of the war, the tank failed to provide an adequate response to the British designs.

The thick steel plating of the A7V provided greater protection for its crew than that of its British counterparts. However, the vehicle's cramped quarters and limited manoeuvrability often left German crewmen preferring to enter combat in captured British tanks. Two variants, an open-topped supply vehicle, the Überlandwagen, and the A7V/U, similar in design to British types with all-around tracks and two 57-mm (2.24-in) guns, were built. A mere 75 of the Überlandwagen were completed, and the A7V/U reached only the prototype stage. The A7V was last employed in combat in October 1918.

IMPROVED DESIGNS UNAVAILABLE
Several improved German tank designs were in various stages of development at the war's end, but none were available before the armistice. The Treaty of Versailles compelled the Germans to research and develop new tank designs in secret in the interwar years.

In a note of supreme irony, the Sturmpanzerwagen A7V appears to have been conceived and constructed with its primary emphasis on firepower rather than manoeuvrability. As the progenitor of the highly mobile German panzer divisions of World War II, the A7V is hardly recognizable as the ancestor of the mailed fist of Hitler's Blitzkrieg a generation later. The only intact Sturmpanzerwagen A7V, No. 506, which was nicknamed Mephisto, is on display today at the Queensland Museum in Brisbane, Australia. Mephisto was one of the three Sturmpanzerwagen A7Vs captured at Villers-Bretonneux on 24 April, 1918.

Interior view

The Sturmpanzerwagen A7V had space for up to 18 crewmen. The compartment housing the driver and the commander was centred on a raised platform above the fighting compartment.

(1) **Steering Wheel:** The driver's seat was positioned to the left in the upper compartment, surrounded by controls.

(2) **Clutch Pedals:** Two clutch pedals were used to engage the gears of the transmission located below. These were located below and forward of the driver's seat.

(3) **Speed Control Selector:** This was set for three optimal speeds, 3, 6, and 12 km/h (2, 4, and 7.5 mph).

(4) **Starter Hand Wheel:** This was used to crank the two four-cylinder Daimler engines that powered the ponderous tank.

(5) **Drive Levers:** Two drive levers were operated independently, one for each track, to initiate forwards and reverse motion. A speed control wheel assisted with wide turns.

(6) **Brake Levers:** These operated independently, each track controlled by a separate system, and assisted in halting the vehicle.

Mark V Male

Late in 1917, Great Britain began producing the Mark V Male tank. It saw limited service during World War I, primarily at the Battle of Hamel in the summer of 1918. The Mark V was a progression from the Mark I, the world's first combat tank.

DRIVER
The first tank that required only a single driver, the Mark V had a Wilson epicyclic gear-box. Seated at left, the driver manipulated levers to control the movement of the Mark V.

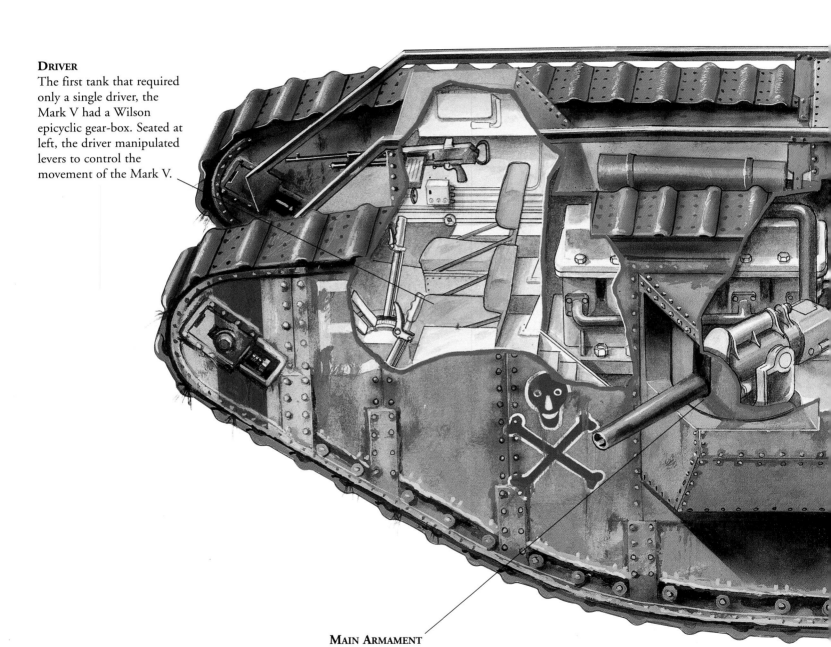

MAIN ARMAMENT
The heavy armament of the Mark V Male tank consisted of two 6-pounder artillery pieces mounted in sponsons on either side of the armoured vehicle, while secondary armament included four Hotchkiss machine guns. The Female version of the Mark V was armed with four Vickers machine guns and two Hotchkiss instead of the cannon.

UNDITCHING BEAM
Carried on top of the rear of the Mark V was an unditching beam, similar to a railway tie. Chaining the beam to the tracks enabled the driver to extricate the vehicle from muddy terrain.

MACHINE GUN MOUNTS
The Mark V incorporated the Skeens ball machine gun mount, which improved the traverse of the weapon from 60 to 90 degrees and offered increased protection from enemy fire.

LENGTH
The length of the Mark V was eventually increased more than 2 m (6 ft) beyond that of its predecessor, the Mark IV, to nearly 8.5 m (27 ft). This was to facilitate the crossing of German trenches, which were sometimes more than 1 m (3 ft) wide.

The Mark V Male tank was deployed late in
World War I and so was involved in combat on a
limited basis, serving with the British, French,
Canadian, and American armies. Its actual
length of service spanned the interwar years.

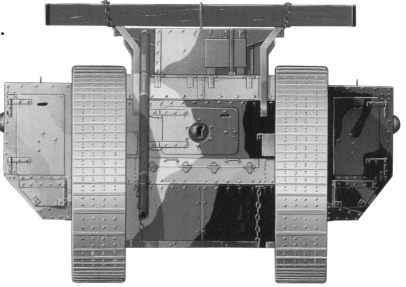

MARK V MALE – SPECIFICATION

Country of Origin: United Kingdom
Crew: Eight (commander, driver, two gearsmen, and four
    gunners)
Designer: Major Wilson
Designed: 1917
In Service: 1918
Manufacturer: Metropolitan Carriage
Number Built: 400
Produced: 1917–June 1918
Weight: 29.5 tonnes (32.5 tons)

Dimensions:
Length: 8.5 m (27 ft)
Width: 4.11 m (13.48 ft)
Height: 2.64 m (8.66 ft)

Performance:
Speed: 7.4 km/h (5 mph)
Range: 72 km (45 miles)
Power/weight Ratio: 5.2 hp/ton
Operational range: 72 km (45 miles), about 10
    hours endurance

Engine:
Powerplant: 1 x Ricardo petrol engine delivering 110kW
    (150 hp)
Transmission: 4 forward, 1 reverse, Wilson epicyclic in final
    drive
Fuel Capacity: 450 l (100 imperial gallons)

Armour & Armament:
Armour: 6–14 mm (0.24–0.55 in)
Main Armament: 2 x 6 pounder guns in side sponsons
Secondary Armament: 4 x 7.7mm (0.303-in) Hotchkiss
    Mk 1 machine guns

Mark V Variants:
Mark V (Male): 2 x 6-pdr guns; 4 x Hotchkiss machine guns
Mark V (Female): 4 x 7.7-mm (0.303-in) Vickers machine guns
Mark V*: Personnel Carrier; transport for up to 25 personnel;
    Male and Female variants available
Mark V:** Improved Tank Mk V* model; Male and Female
    variants available
Mark V:** (Tank RE)

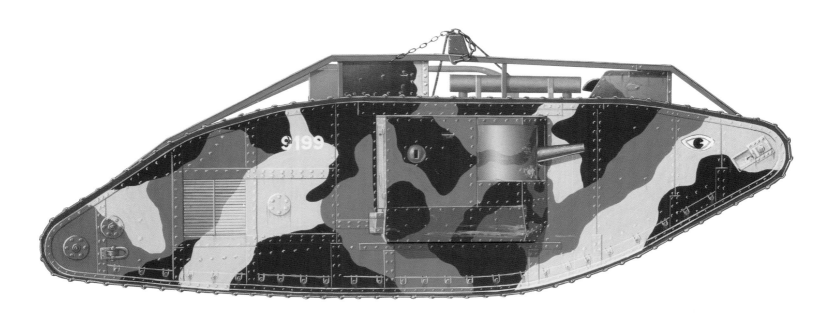

MARK V MALE

The Mark V Male tank provided added firepower with its two sponson-mounted 6-pounder cannon and four Hotchkiss machine guns, but its heavy weight of nearly 26 tonnes (29 tons) and ponderous track arrangement limited its operational range to 72 km (45 miles) and its single engagement timespan to about 10 hours. The 110 kW (150 bhp) Ricardo engine was difficult to start, requiring four men to crank manually while another pressed a magneto switch. In cold weather, personnel had to prime each of the six cylinders and warm the spark plugs. The Mark V crew of eight included a driver, two gearsmen, four gunners, and a commander.

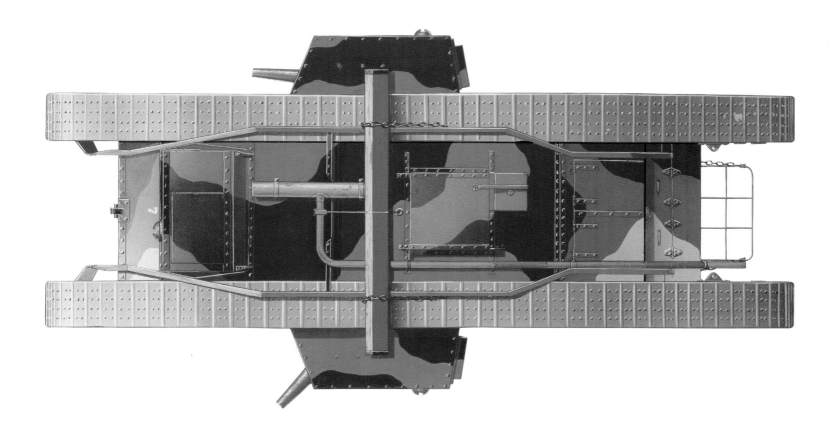

The Mark V Male opened ways through barbed wire and crossed trenches easily. Tanks and infantry adapted to each other's tactics. Infantrymen understood it was not essential for them to gather behind tanks because they could deploy in skirmishing order close to the tanks.

Although it was initially conceived as a completely new design, both the Male and Female variants of the British Mark V combat tanks actually developed as a vast improvement over their predecessor, the Mark IV. Following the debut of the tank on the battlefield at Flers-Courcelette in September 1916, the pace of armoured vehicle development increased rapidly. By the end of World War I, no fewer than nine variants of the original Mark I tank participated in Allied operations on the Western Front.

The Mark V incorporated a number of improvements over the Mark IV, including the Wilson epicyclic gearbox,

Interior view

The British Mark V was the first tank that required only a single soldier as a driver. Seated forward, he viewed the battlefield through a slit in the armoured hull.

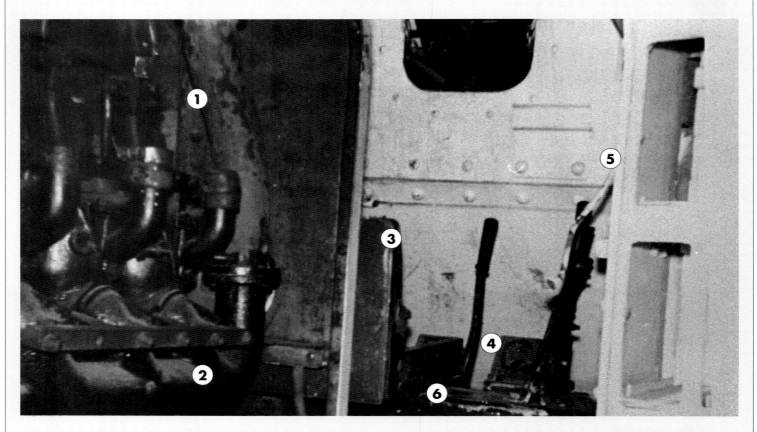

1. **The Engine Compartment:** Here the 110-kW (150-hp) Ricardo petrol engine, the first powerplant specifically designed for a tank, was housed.

2. **Exhaust Manifolds:** These evacuated fumes to the outside. Crew were often overcome by the gases produced by enclosed engines.

3. **Driver's Seat:** Located forwards and to the left with a machine gunner to his right. A gearsman was not needed in the Mark V.

4. **Clutch Pedal:** This was operated to change the four forwards or single reverse gears of the Wilson epicyclic transmission.

5. **Steering Tillers:** The driver operated the Mark V with tillers in forwards or reverse motion, as well as manoeuvring through turns and cross-country.

6. **Foot Brake:** This was readily accessible to the driver and responsive in halting the Mark V and assisting in changing direction.

British infantrymen inspect a curiosity of war, the Mark V Male tank, which represented a major advance in armoured vehicle design and deployment. The Male version of the Mark V mounted heavier firepower than its Female counterpart.

which required only one crewman rather than two to steer the nearly 30-tonne (33-ton) fighting vehicle. While the Male variant included a pair of sponson-mounted 6-pounder guns along with a complement of four 7.7-mm (0.303-in) Hotchkiss machine guns, the slightly lighter-weight Female Mark V was armed with four 7.7-mm (0.303-in) Vickers machine guns. These were fired by single crewmen from Skeens ball mounts, which improved the firing arc from 60 to 90 degrees and provided greater protection for the gunner than the earlier loophole or firing slit configuration of the Mark IV. The 110-kW (150-bhp) engine designed by Harry Ricardo generated greater speed than the Mark IV, and the addition of an undITCHING beam assisted in navigating soft terrain.

IN ACTION

The combat debut of the Mark V took place on 4 July, 1918, as Australian and American troops assaulted a salient in the German line at Le Hamel. Sixty Mark Vs of the 5th Brigade, Royal Tank Corps, supported by four supply tanks, attacked with the infantry. One Australian soldier commented that the presence of the tanks did not relieve them of their sense of obligation to fight and that the soldiers did take immediate advantage of every opening created by the advance of the tanks.

The Allied thrust achieved its objective in a mere 93 minutes, and General J.F.C. Fuller, an early advocate of the use of armour in combat and planner of the major tank assault at Cambrai in late 1917, commented that Le Hamel stood alone among other battles of World War I in the rapidity, brevity, and thoroughness of its success. Australian historian Charles Bean commented that Le Hamel "furnished the model for almost every attack afterwards made by British infantry with tanks during the remainder of that war."

INTERWAR ACTIVITY

After World War I, the Mark V served extensively with White Russian forces during the Russian Civil War, as well as with British troops during their campaign in northern Russia. Active with the Soviet Red Army until the 1930s, the Mark V was reported to have been in service as late as 1941, and an example, long previously captured, was even said to have been used by the Germans as a fixed fortification during the defence of Berlin in 1945.

Two notable variants of the Mark V were introduced late in the war. The Mark V* included a lengthened hull to facilitate the crossing of enemy trench lines, and the Mark V** included a more functional length-width ratio for the longer tank. Four hundred Mark V tanks, 200 each of the Male and Female variants, were produced, while nearly 600 Mark V* tanks were built and only 25 of the Mark V**.

PzKpfw III

During the era of German rearmament in the 1930s, the Panzerkampfwagen III was developed as a lighter medium tank to operate in company with the heavier PzKpfw IV. Soon, however, the PzKpfw III developed a much broader role in the field.

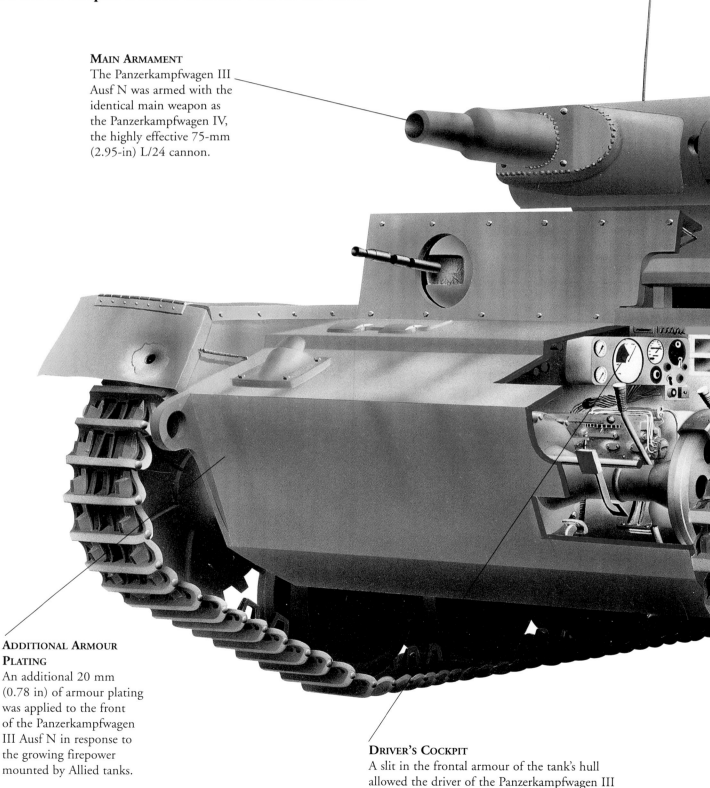

MAIN ARMAMENT
The Panzerkampfwagen III Ausf N was armed with the identical main weapon as the Panzerkampfwagen IV, the highly effective 75-mm (2.95-in) L/24 cannon.

ADDITIONAL ARMOUR PLATING
An additional 20 mm (0.78 in) of armour plating was applied to the front of the Panzerkampfwagen III Ausf N in response to the growing firepower mounted by Allied tanks.

DRIVER'S COCKPIT
A slit in the frontal armour of the tank's hull allowed the driver of the Panzerkampfwagen III only a limited field of vision. He operated the vehicle with a system of levers and pedals.

TURRET ARMOUR
On later versions of the Panzerkampfwagen III, additional side armour was placed around the turret, as shown. Some models were also constructed with armour plating on the sides, added during the spring of 1943. Even with the additional side armour, the tank remained vulnerable to most Allied guns.

FACTS

- Numerous variants of the PzKpfw III were built, each with improved armour or performance.

- More than 1500 PzKpfw chassis were built for fighting vehicles before and during World War II.

- The PzKpfw III Ausf N was an upgunned version with a 75-mm (2.95-in) cannon.

ENGINE
Later versions of the Panzerkampfwagen III were powered by a 186-kW (250-hp), 12-cylinder Maybach HL 120 TRM engine, which generated a top speed of about 40 km/h (24.85 mph).

SUSPENSION
A torsion bar suspension system was standardized on the Ausf E and later versions of the Panzerkampfwagen III, replacing a leaf spring suspension that had proved unsatisfactory.

In late 1942 and early in 1943, the Panzerkampfwagen III Ausf N was out of the factory carrying the 75-mm (2.9-in) gun and intended for an anti-infantry role. Some were assigned to heavy Tiger tank battalions.

PZKPFW III AUSF N – SPECIFICATION

Country of Origin: Germany
Crew: 5
Designer: Daimler-Benz
Designed: 1935 (Panzer III)
In Service: 1942–45
Manufacturer: Daimler-Benz
Number Built: 5774 (all Panzer IIIs, excluding StuG III)
Produced: mid 1942–44
Gross Weight: 23 tonnes (25.4 tons)

Dimensions:
Hull Length: 5.78 m (19 ft)
Length (gun forward): 5.78 m (19 ft)
Width: 2.97 m (9.75 ft)
Overall Height: 2.5 m (8.2 ft)

Performance:
Maximum Speed: 42 km/h (26 mph)
Range, Road: 145 km (90 miles)
Range, Cross-country: 85 km (53 miles)
Power/Weight Ratio: 11.5 bhp/tonne
Ground Pressure: 0.04 kg/cm^2
Fording Capacity: 0.8 m (2.6 ft)
Maximum Gradient: 30 degrees
Maximum Trench Width: 2.2 m (7.2 ft)
Maximum Vertical Obstacle: 0.6 m (2 ft)
Suspension Type: Torsion bars

Engine:
Powerplant: 1 x Maybach HL120TRM 12-cylinder in-line water-cooled petrol engine
Capacity: 11.9 l (2.6 gallons)
Output: 186 kW (250 bhp)

Fuel Capacity: 320 l (71 gallons)

Armour and Armament:
Armour Type: Homogeneous rolled/welded nickel steel with additional appliqué panels 15–50 mm (0.59 in–1.97 in)
Main Armament: 1 x 75-mm (2.95-in) KwK L/24
Secondary Armament: 2 x 7.92-mm (0.31-in) MG34

Other Variants
Ausf A, B, C, D: Pre-production models in 1937–38. 75 produced.
Ausf E, F: Production models 1939–40. Armed with 37-mm (1.45-in) KwK 36 L/46.5 (later 50-mm [1.97-in] KwK 38 L/42) guns. 531 produced.
Ausf G: More armour on gun mantlet. Armed with 50-mm (1.97-in) KwK 38 L/42 gun. 600 produced in 1940–41.
Ausf H: Minor modifications. Bolt-on armour added to front and rear hull (30-mm + 30-mm [1.18-in] plates). 308 produced in 1940–41.
Ausf I: Variant mentioned in Allied intelligence reports but not an existing vehicle.
Ausf J: Hull lengthened. Front armour increased to 50-mm (1.97-in) plate. 482 produced in 1941.
Ausf J¹: Equipped with the longer and more powerful 50-mm (1.97-in) KwK 39 L/60 gun. 1067 produced in 1941–42.
Ausf K: Panzerbefehlswagen command tank variant with modified turret carrying a main armament rather than a dummy gun as on other command versions.
Ausf L: Uparmoured to 50-mm (1.97-in) + 20-mm (0.79-in) plates. 653 produced in 1942.
Ausf M: Minor modifications such as deep-wading exhaust and Schurzen. 250 produced in 1942–43.

PZKPFW III AUSF H

The PzKpfw III Ausf H incorporated minor variations to the original design of the versatile PzKpfw series, including the changes in earlier versions, such as upgunning from the original 37-mm (1.45-in) weapon to a 50-mm (1.97-in) cannon. The PzKpfw III Ausf H was primarily recognized via the addition of bolted-on 30-mm (1.18-in) armour plates to the front and rear of the hull. Later variants, including the J, L, M, and N, which was equipped with a 75-mm (2.95-in) cannon. The first PzKpfw III rolled off the assembly line in late 1939, and by mid-1943 production of the tank had ceased, although the chassis continued in various roles.

The rugged Panzerkampfwagen III was used in all theatres by the German army in World War II. However, the size limitations of the tank's chassis meant that armament upgrades were limited. Its usefulness as a battle tank diminished as the Allies produced more advanced and powerful tanks.

Originally conceived as a complement to the heavier Panzerkampfwagen IV, the PzKpfw III was in service with the German army at the beginning of World War II, its earliest variant participating in the invasion of Poland. During the course of the war, no fewer than 11 versions of the tank were fielded. Notable among these are the A, B, and C models, which were produced in relatively few numbers, with the significant changes to each involving the torsion bar suspension system.

The D and F variants included heavier armour and improvements to the commander's cupola and a higher-

Interior view

The interior of the PzKpfw III was spacious by the standards of early World War II tanks. The larger weapons of later versions decreased available space within the turret.

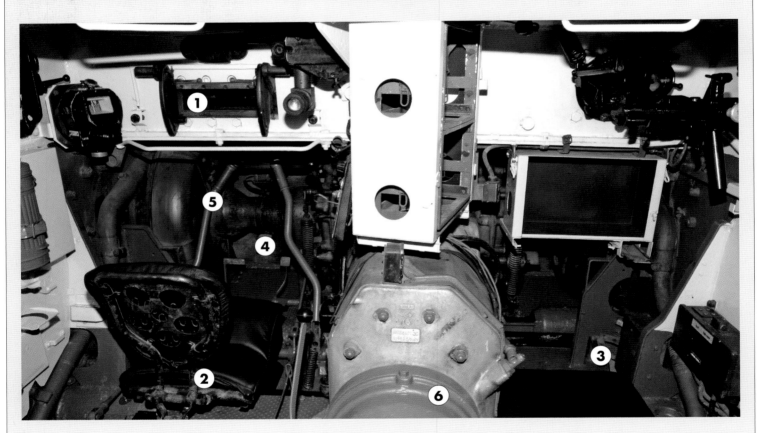

① **Driver's Vision:** The driver was positioned forwards and to the left in the hull. In later models a sliding shutter was provided to improve his range of vision.

② **Driver's Seat:** The driver's seat was slightly inclined for better vision and control while traversing cross country or rugged terrain.

③ **Radio Operator/Machine Gunner:** Vision was improved in later models of the PzKpfw III. Crew communicated within the tank through an intercom system.

④ **Clutch Pedal:** This was engaged to facilitate the changing of gears. The drive train of the tank extended the full length of the chassis.

⑤ **Control Lever:** The driver steered the PzKpfw III with a system of levers, which provided responsive handling in all types of terrain on all fronts.

⑥ **Gearbox:** The variants of the Maybach transmission gearbox were housed in the front compartment between the driver and radio operator/machine gunner.

Equipped with a 50-mm (1.97-in) main cannon, a Panzerkampfwagen III of the legendary Afrika Korps advances across the North African desert in company with supporting infantry. The tank commander has emerged from his turret cupola to observe the landscape.

performing engine respectively. By 1940, the F variant was the first to include the heavier 50-mm (1.97-in) cannon, replacing the original 37-mm (1.45-in), which was ineffective against the armour of most Allied tanks. The G version incorporated a more powerful engine, while the H included wider tracks for greater stability and improved handling.

In the spring of 1942, the PzKpfw Ausf J was introduced in response to the appearance of the superb Soviet T-34 medium tank on the Eastern Front. The original 50-mm (1.97-in) gun was replaced by a long-barrelled weapon of the same calibre with a higher muzzle velocity. By the time the L model made its appearance, further increases in armour protection had nearly doubled the weight of the original PzKpfw III to more than 22.7 tonnes (25 tons). The M variant featured improvements to the chassis and still more armour protection. Two 7.92-mm (0.31-in) MG 34 machine guns provided secondary armament throughout production.

While the PzKpfw III was one of the primary tanks in the German army at the time of the invasion of the Soviet Union on 22 June, 1941, its viability as a main battle tank had begun to wane as Allied designs improved in armour protection and heavier-calibre weapons. Purposely modified as an infantry support vehicle, the PzKpfw III N utilized the short-barrelled 75-mm (2.95-in) cannon, which had originally been installed

on early versions of the PzKpfw IV. Carrying 64 rounds of ammunition, the N variant was routinely assigned to independent panzer battalions as escorts for Tiger tanks. In the spring of 1943, additional external armour plating, called Schurzen, was added to many PzKpfw IIIs.

MULTIPLE ROLES

The PzKpfw III chassis earned a reputation for versatility and reliability. Its rugged torsion bar suspension was greatly improved in the F version and supported the steady gun platform not only in the tank role, but also that of the highly successful Sturmgeschütz 75-mm (2.95-in) self-propelled assault gun. The five-man crew of the PzKpfw III included a three-man turret capacity, which housed the commander, gunner, and loader while the driver and radio operator (or forward machine gunner) rode in the chassis. With two crew serving the main weapon, the commander was better able to control the tank in combat, providing a distinct advantage over several Allied types in which the commander was also obliged to function as a gunner.

The Panzerkampfwagen III proved to be a sound design, serving throughout World War II in a variety of roles. When production of the tank was terminated in 1943, nearly 5800 had been produced, 700 of these in the upgunned Ausf N.

Sturmgeschütz III

During the course of World War I, a glaring deficiency in German infantry tactics grew apparent. The ponderous weight of artillery prevented it from supporting advancing infantry once the foot soldiers had moved beyond effective range. However, a mobile assault gun would remedy the situation.

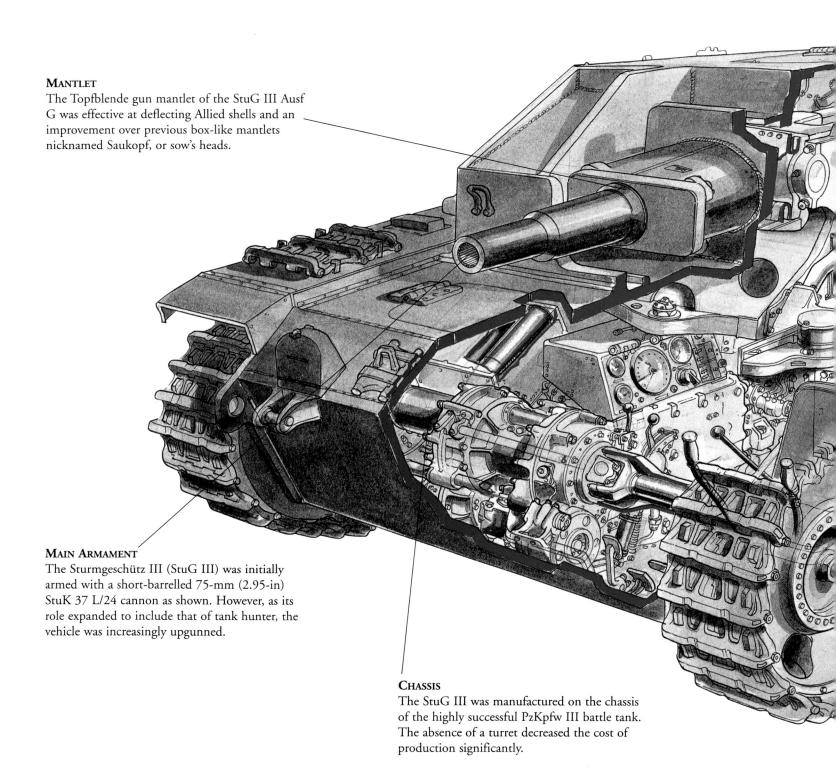

MANTLET
The Topfblende gun mantlet of the StuG III Ausf G was effective at deflecting Allied shells and an improvement over previous box-like mantlets nicknamed Saukopf, or sow's heads.

MAIN ARMAMENT
The Sturmgeschütz III (StuG III) was initially armed with a short-barrelled 75-mm (2.95-in) StuK 37 L/24 cannon as shown. However, as its role expanded to include that of tank hunter, the vehicle was increasingly upgunned.

CHASSIS
The StuG III was manufactured on the chassis of the highly successful PzKpfw III battle tank. The absence of a turret decreased the cost of production significantly.

CREW COMPARTMENT
The four-man crew of the StuG III was situated primarily along the left side of the vehicle with later variants carrying a hull-mounted 7.92-mm (0.31-in) MG 34 machine gun. The Ausf G was armed with a shielded coaxial MG 34 as well.

ENGINE
The V-12, 221-kW (296-hp) Maybach HL 120 TRM engine powered the StuG III Ausf G at a top speed of 40 km/h (25 mph) with a range of 155 km (96 miles).

SILHOUETTE
The low profile of the StuG III made the vehicle easy to conceal, while the addition of armour plating was effective against hollow charge shells.

Sturmgeschütz crews were considered to be the elite of the artillery units of the German army and were issued special grey field uniforms. Overall, the Sturmgeschütz series proved highly successful and served on all fronts as assault guns and tank destroyers.

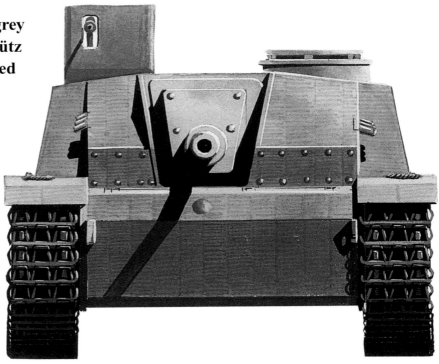

STURMGESCHÜTZ III – SPECIFICATION

Country of Origin: Germany
Crew: 4
Designer: Daimler-Benz
Designed: 1936
In Service: 1940–67
Manufacturer: Alkett, MIAG
Number Built: 9408
Produced: 1940
Gross Weight: 19.6 tonnes (21 tons)

Dimensions:
Hull Length: 5.4 m (17.7 ft)
Length (gun forward): 5.4 m (17.7 ft)
Width: 2.9 m (9.5 ft)
Overall Height: 1.98 m (6.5 ft)

Performance:
Maximum Speed: 40 km/h (25 mph)
Range, Road: 155 km (96 miles)
Range, Cross-country: 85 km (53 miles)
Ground Pressure: 1.04 kg/cm²
Fording Capacity: 0.8 m (2.6 ft)
Maximum Gradient: 30 degrees
Maximum Trench Width: 2.2 m (7.2 ft)
Maximum Vertical Obstacle: 0.6 m (2 ft)
Suspension Type: Torsion bars

Engine:
Powerplant: 1 x Maybach HL120TRM 6-cylinder
    in-line water-cooled petrol engine
Capacity: 11.9 l (2.6 gallons)
Output: 221 kW (296hp) @ 2600 rpm
Power/Weight Ratio: 13.1 bhp/tonne

Fuel Capacity: 320 l (71 gallons)

Armament and Armour:
Main Armament: 1 x 75-mm (2.95-in) StuK 37 L/24
Secondary Armament: 1 x 7.92-mm (0.31-in) MG34
    machine gun (unmounted)
Armour Type: Homogeneous rolled/welded nickel steel
Hull Front: 50 mm (1.97 in)
Hull Sides: 30 mm (1.18 in)
Hull Rear: 30 mm (1.18 in)
Hull Top: 17 mm (0.67 in)
Hull Bottom: 17 mm (0.67 in)
Superstructure Front: 50 mm (1.97 in)
Superstructure Sides: 30 mm (1.18 in)
Superstructure Rear: 30 mm (1.18 in)
Superstructure Top: 16 mm (0.63 in)

Variants:
Ausf A: 30 examples produced; fitted with L/24 main gun.
Ausf B: 320 examples produced; fitted with L/24 main gun.
Ausf C: 50 examples produced.
Ausf D: 150 examples produced.
Ausf E: 272 examples produced.
Ausf F: 336 examples produced with L/43 main gun; later
    models with L/48 type main gun; improved armour protection
    and commander visibility.
Ausf G: 7720 examples produced
"Sturmhaubitze 42": 105-mm (4.1-in) howitzer mated to the
    existing StuG III hull design.
SU-76: Soviet modified assault guns of captured StuG IIIs; fitted
    with Soviet 76.2-mm (3-in) main gun.
SG122A: Soviet modified assault guns of captured StuG IIIs;
    fitted with 122-mm (4.8-in) main gun.

STURMGESCHÜTZ III AUSF G

The short-barrelled 75-mm (2.95-in) StuK 37 L/24 gun mounted on the StuG III Ausf A was effective against fixed fortifications such as pillboxes and bunkers, which could slow the progress of German infantry. However, as World War II progressed, the Sturmgeschütz's low muzzle velocity proved problematic against Allied armour. As the role of the StuG III evolved to one of tank destroyer and at times a main battle tank, its armament was upgunned to higher-velocity, long-barrelled 75-mm (2.95-in) L/43 and L/48 cannon. The StuG III was not well suited to the tank role, primarily because of the lack of a turret, which restricted the traverse of the weapon.

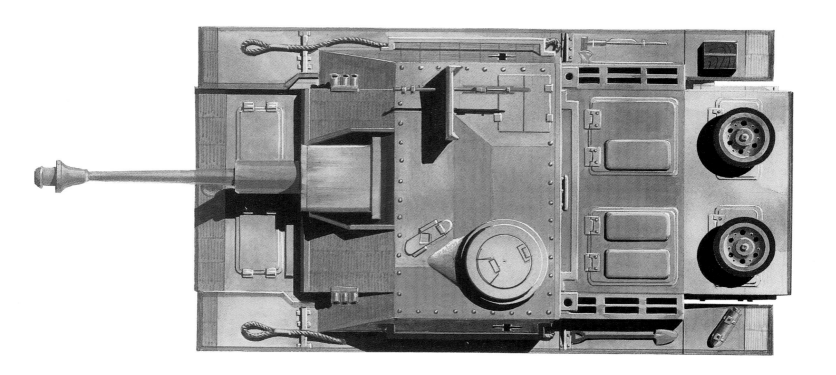

In the autumn of 1944, the Department of Weaponry of the Red Army suggested that the Soviet armed forces use such captured German weapons as the StuG III because of its reliability and the availability of spare parts.

During the 1930s, General Erich von Manstein, then a colonel, suggested developing an infantry assault vehicle that mounted weaponry heavy enough to deal with the enemy fortifications that confronted advancing German infantry. Artillery was effective in support of infantry but lacked the mobility to keep up with the advance. Manstein envisioned a mobile fighting vehicle capable of destroying pillboxes, bunkers, and machine-gun nests with direct fire. The concept led to the formation of the Sturmartillerie, or assault artillery.

By 1936, engineers with Daimler-Benz had been charged with developing such an assault vehicle, and a year later the

Interior view

The interior of the Sturmgeschütz III was cramped with a crew orientation towards the left side of the vehicle caused, in part, by the absence of a turret.

(1) **Breech Block:** The breech block of the 75-mm (2.95-in) heavy weapon occupied much of the interior of the fighting compartment of the turretless Sturmgeschütz III.

(2) **Gun Cradle:** The cradle of a series of 75-mm (2.95-in) cannon served to stabilize the weapons during operation.

(3) **Loader Position:** Next to the 75-mm (2.95-in) gun breech, the loader used a square hatch over his shoulder to exit the vehicle or to operate a top-mounted machine gun.

(4) **Ammunition Ready Area:** Shells for the 75-mm (2.95-in) gun were stored within easy reach of the loader. One of these was held in a single position by a clasp.

(5) **Ammunition Racks:** Various types of ammunition were stored in racks within the hull of the Sturmgeschütz III.

(6) **Hull Floor:** The floor of the fighting compartment was slightly raised to assist in maximizing the elevation and depression of the turretless 75-mm (2.95-in) weapon.

Weary German infantrymen pause for a moment as they hitch a ride aboard an early variant of the Sturmgeschütz III self-propelled assault gun. This Sturmgeschütz III is armed with the short-barrelled 75-mm (2.95-in) StuK 37 L/24 gun.

prototype of the Sturmgeschütz III rolled off the assembly line. During World War II, eight variants of the original design, Ausf A, were introduced with improvements to the superstructure, increased armour protection, and higher-velocity 75-mm (2.95-in) main armament. The first major variation to the StuG III came in 1942 with the installation of the 75-mm (2.95-in) L/43 cannon and the addition of frontal armour and side armour skirts on the Ausf F.

AUSF G VARIANT

The Ausf G was by far the variant produced in largest number, incorporating an improved gun mantlet known as the Topfblende, which was more effective at deflecting enemy shells than previous types, along with a cupola and periscope for the commander's use. Starting late in 1942 through to the end of the war, nearly 8000 StuG III Ausf G assault vehicles were produced.

Because the StuG III was considered mobile artillery, there was initial debate as to whether the vehicle would be controlled by the panzer or artillery administration within the German army. Eventually, it was determined that a manpower shortage among the panzer troops precluded its formation of assault vehicle battalions. Thus, the StuG III formations were controlled by the artillery and became the elite of the arm.

During the war, nearly 11,000 of the StuG III and StuH 42, a heavier variant mounting a 105-mm (4.1-in) cannon, were manufactured. Cost was a contributing factor to the proliferation of the StuG III, which served on all fronts during the conflict. Because a turret was not required for the weapon, Germany saved a substantial amount of money in the production of a StuG III compared to what it had cost to build the Panzer III Ausf M.

By the spring of 1944, StuG III crews had been credited with at least 20,000 Allied tanks destroyed, and the design holds the distinction of being built in the largest numbers of any German armoured vehicle of World War II. A relative few StuG III examples were modified to carry flamethrowers or an even heavier 150-mm (5.9-in) cannon. Only 10 of the flamethrower-equipped StuG III were built, making use of the chassis of StuGs that been damaged in battle. None saw combat. Of the 24 vehicles upgunned to 150-mm (5.9-in) weapons, 12 were deployed during the Battle of Stalingrad, and Soviet forces destroyed or captured all of them.

Under the direction of a seasoned commander, the StuG III was an intimidating adversary, as Oberwachtmeister Kurt Pfreundtner proved on 18 September, 1942. Pfreundtner's StuG III destroyed nine Soviet tanks in the span of only 20 minutes, and he was subsequently awarded the Knight's Cross.

PzKpfw IV

Developed in the mid-1930s, the Panzerkampfwagen IV went on to become the stalwart of the German armoured forces of World War II. The design holds the distinction of being the only German tank in continuous production throughout the war.

ASYMMETRICAL CONSTRUCTION
The turret of the Panzerkampfwagen IV was offset 66.5 mm (2.6 in) from the tank's centreline to allow the torque shaft to clear the rotary base junction. Therefore, the main stowage capacity was on the right side of the tank. The Ausf F2 variant is shown here.

ENGINE
The Panzerkampfwagen IV was powered by a 12-cylinder Maybach HL 120 TRM engine, generating 220 kW (296 hp) and a top road speed of 42 km/h (26 mph).

SUSPENSION
A double bogey leaf spring suspension was installed on the Panzerkampfwagen IV chassis, replacing the preferred torsion bar suspension due to time limitations for the production of a new tank.

FACTS

- More than 8500 of the PzKpfw IV were produced from 1936–45.

- The Syrian army deployed the PzKpfw IV during the 1967 Six-Day War.

- During 1943–44, PzKpfw IV production peaked with more than 6000 rolling off of the factory floors.

MAIN ARMAMENT
Although the initial Panzerkampfwagen IV Ausf F was equipped with the standard 75-mm (2.95-in) L/24 cannon, the Ausf F2, shown here, mounted the longer-barrelled 75-mm (2.95-in) L/43. The change significantly increased the weapon's muzzle velocity and its ability to penetrate the armour of Allied tanks.

MOBILITY
Wider tracks, along with a modified front sprocket and rear idler wheel, improved the handling of the Panzerkampfwagen IV in difficult terrain. Ice sprags were fitted for winter weather.

RADIO OPERATOR'S POSITION
The radio operator, seated in the forward section on the right side, doubled as the hull machine gunner, firing a 7.92-mm (0.31-in) MG 34.

Initially designed as an infantry support medium tank to work in conjunction with the PzKpfw III, which was intended to engage enemy tanks, the PzKpfw IV was later fitted with more armour and guns to enable it to take over the tank fighting role.

PZKPFW IV AUSF F2 – SPECIFICATION

Country of Origin: Germany
Crew: 5
Designer: Krupp
Designed: 1936
In Service: 1939–67 (all Panzer IVs)
Manufacturer: Krupp, Steyr-Daimler-Puch
Number Built: 8800 (estimated, total Panzer IVs)
Produced: 1936–45
Gross Weight: 22 tonnes (24.3 tons)

Dimensions:
Hull Length: 5.91 m (19.4 ft)
Length (gun forward): 7.02 m (23 ft)
Width: 2.88 m (9.45 ft)
Overall Height: 2.68 m (8.8 ft)

Performance:
Maximum Speed: 42 km/h (26 mph)
Range, Road: 240 km (150 miles)
Range, Cross-country: 120 km (75 miles)
Power/Weight Ratio: 10.6 bhp/tonne
Ground Pressure: 0.89 kg/cm²
Fording Capacity: 0.8m (2.6ft)
Maximum Gradient: 29 degrees
Maximum Trench Width: 2.3 m (7.55 ft)
Maximum Vertical Obstacle: 0.6 m (2.0 ft)
Suspension Type: Leaf spring

Engine:
Powerplant: Maybach HL120 12-cylinder in-line water-cooled petrol
Transmission: 6 forward, 1 reverse speed
Capacity: 11.9 l (2.6 gallons)

Output: 220 kW (296 hp) @ 3000 rpm
Fuel Capacity: 470 l (103.5 gallons)

Armour & Armament:
Armour Type: Homogeneous rolled/welded nickel-steel
Hull Front: 60 mm (2.36 in)
Hull Sides: 30 mm (1.18 in)
Hull Rear: 20 mm (0.78 in)
Hull Top: 10 mm (0.34 in)
Hull Bottom: 10 mm (0.34 in)
Turret Front: 50 mm (1.97 in)
Turret Sides: 30 mm (1.18 in)
Turret Rear: 30 mm (1.18 in)
Turret Top: 15–25 mm (0.59–0.98 in)
Main: 1 x 75-mm (2.95-in) L/43 or L/48 KwK 40. 87 rounds
Secondary: 2 x 7.92-mm (0.31-in) MG34 MG. 3150 rounds

Panzer IV Numbers produced

Date	Number of Vehicles	Variant
1937–39	262	Ausf A–D
1940	386	Ausf E
1941	769	
1942	880	Ausf E–G
1943	3013	Ausf H
1944	3125	Ausf J
1945	est. 435	

PZKPFW IV AUSF F1

In March 1941, production of the PzKpfw IV Ausf F, with increased hull, turret, and chassis armour, began. The weight of the Ausf F increased to 22 tonnes (24.3 tons), and its tracks were widened. The main Ausf F weapon was initially the same 75-mm (2.95-in) L/24 cannon of the earlier Ausf E. However, the F version was soon rearmed with the long-barrelled 75-mm (2.95–in) L/43 cannon. The L/24 version was designated F1, while those mounting the L/43 were designated F2. By June 1942, all PzKpfw IV tanks mounting the long-barrelled L/43 were reclassified as the Ausf G.

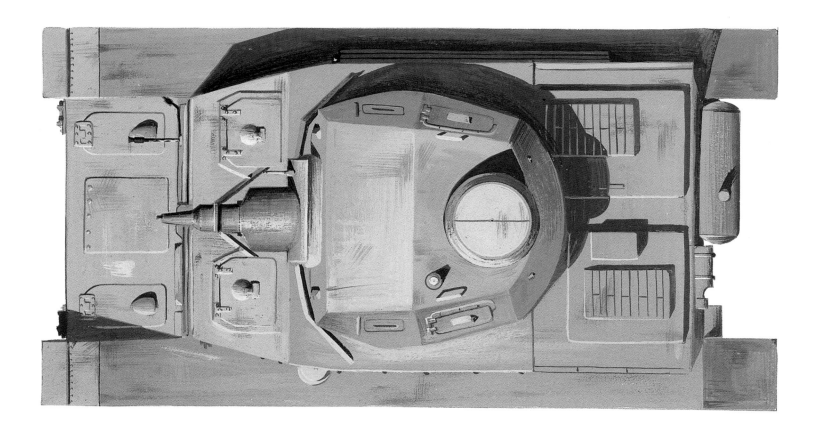

The PzKpfw IV was a mainstay of the German armoured forces in World War II, and open ground proved to be ideal for such tanks. Here, German tanks advance on a broad front through waist-high winter wheat.

The Panzerkampfwagen IV, the workhorse of the German tank corps, was the most widely manufactured and deployed German tank of World War II. It was used as the base for many other fighting vehicles, including tank destroyers and self-propelled anti-aircraft guns.

The Panzerkampfwagen IV served in every theatre of battle where German land forces were engaged during World War II. In continuous production – which began in 1936 and continued until the end of the war – more than 8500 Pzkpfw IV tanks were constructed, and the basic design was the only German tank that was in production throughout the duration of the conflict.

Conceived as an infantry support weapon, while the concurrently developed PzKpfw III was intended to engage enemy armoured units, the PzKpfw IV was developed following specifications issued in January 1934 with a short-barrelled 75-mm (2.96-in) cannon and a pair of 7.92-mm (0.31-in) MG 34 machine guns. The new tank housed a crew of five, including a commander, gunner, loader, driver, and radio operator/forward machine gunner.

While the PzKpfw III was initially armed with a 37-mm (1.4-in) main gun, the heavier weapon on the PzKpfw IV was intended to deal with fixed fortifications, gun emplacements, and enemy troop concentrations that might impede the progress of German troops. General Heinz Guderian (a foremost proponent of the Blitzkrieg tactics that won Germany swift territorial gains in the early months of World War II) put forward the notion of a heavier medium tank.

RAPID SUCCESSION

The PzKpfw Ausf A entered service in 1936, and less than a year later a few B variants were produced with improvements to the engines and transmissions. By 1938, the PzKpfw Ausf C increased the turret armour to 30 mm (1.18 in). Nearly 500 of the F variant were produced starting in April 1941 and continuing to March 1942 as the role of the PzKpfw IV evolved to that of both a main battle tank and an infantry support weapon.

The Ausf F improved upon the E variant with several design alterations, including up to 60 mm (2.36 in) of hull armour and 50 mm (1.96 in) of armour protection in the turret, a ball-mounted hull machine gun, and wider tracks. The most significant modification to the Ausf F was in its main armament. The original F variant included the short-barrelled 75-mm (2.96-in) L/24 cannon. However, the high velocity, long-barrelled 75-mm (2.96-in) L/43 cannon was subsequently installed in numerous tanks, leading to the redesignation of the original as Ausf F1 and the latter as F2.

CONSTRUCTED AT SPEED

The upgunned F2 proved more than a match for British and American tanks in North Africa, but it was in short supply there. In the East, the F2 was, for a time, the mightiest tank in the German arsenal that was available in any numbers.

Later versions of the PzKpfw IV were heavily engaged on the Western Front but sustained serious losses at Falaise and during the Battle of the Bulge.

The last version of the tank, the PzKpfw IV Ausf J, was deployed in the spring of 1944. Its simplified construction meant it could be built quickly to urgently replace battlefield losses, yet its chassis could still serve as a platform for tank destroyers and mobile anti-aircraft weapons. Germany exported several hundred PzKpfw IVs to their Axis partners and other countries, and many of these remained in service long after the end of World War II.

Interior view

Manufactured in great numbers, the functional layout of the PzKpfw IV included space for both gunner and loader in the turret, on either side of the 75-mm (2.96-in) gun breech.

1. **Turret Interior:** This was largely occupied by the operating system of the tank's heavy 75-mm (2.95-in) cannon.

2. **Ammunition Racks:** These provided a ready supply of shells within the turret. Additional supplies of ammunition were stored in the hull of the PzKpfw IV.

3. **Gun Cradle:** This provided a degree of stability for laying and firing the weapon, as well as support while the vehicle itself was in motion.

4. **Breech Block:** The breech block of the turret-mounted 75-mm (2.95-in) cannon is shown. Early PzKpfw IV variants were armed with the short-barrelled L/24 cannon.

5. **Machine Gun:** A turret-mounted 7.62-mm (0.31-in) machine gun was positioned to the right of the breech of the main weapon and fired through the turret mantlet.

6. **Electrical Conduit:** The turret of the PzKpfw IV was capable of 360° traverse. This was accomplished primarily through electricity.

Char B1 bis

The final production model of the Char B1 heavy tank, the Char B1 bis was manufactured by Renault and several other producers. Its increased armour protection, more powerful engine, and reconfigured turret constituted the most advanced French heavy tank design in production and service from 1937.

TURRET ARMAMENT
The cramped turret of the Char B1 bis mounted a 47-mm (1.85-in) L/32 SA 35 cannon with a longer barrel than the 47-mm (1.85-in) gun of its predecessor. Although effective initially, heavy weaponry substantially eclipsed its firepower later in World War II.

HULL ARMAMENT
The effectiveness of the heavy 75-mm (2.95-in) ABS SA 35 howitzer mounted in the hull of the Char B1 bis was limited due to its lack of traverse capability. However, a highly manoeuvrable steering system compensated somewhat for the narrow field of fire.

ENGINE
The 229-kW (307-bhp) Renault 6-cylinder petrol engine of the Char B1 bis could propel the tank forward at up to 25 km/h (15.5 mph).

COMMUNICATIONS
With the four-man crew of the Char B1 bis spread throughout the interior of the vehicle, communications were difficult, hampering combat effectiveness.

FACTS

- The Char B1 bis was produced for a short time from 1937–40.

- The tank carried 72 rounds of 47-mm (1.85-in) ammunition and 74 rounds for its 75-mm (2.95-in) gun.

- The tank's effectiveness was limited by the tactics of senior commanders.

SILHOUETTE
At first glance, the Char B1 bis resembled the tanks of World War I, its high profile presenting a conspicuous target to enemy gunners.

AIR INTAKE
The air-cooled engine required a large intake positioned on the left side of the Char B1 bis. Its armoured plating was deemed sufficiently protective. Standard side armour plating was 55 mm (2.2 in) thick.

The **Char B1 bis** was the main battle tank of the French army in 1940. Considered one of the most powerful and advanced tanks in the world at that time, it was hampered by its low speed and high cost of production.

CHAR B1 BIS – SPECIFICATION

Country of Origin: France
Crew: 4
Designer: Origins began with General Jean-Baptiste Eugène Estienne
Designed: 1921–34 (Char B1)
In Service: 1929–45 (Char B1)
Manufacturer: Renault (and other companies)
Number Built: 369
Produced: 1937–40
Gross Weight: 31.5 tonnes (34.7 tons)

Dimensions:
Hull Length: 6.63 m (21.75 ft)
Length (gun forward): n/a
Width: 2.52 m (8.25 ft)
Overall Height: 2.84 m (9.33 ft)

Performance:
Maximum Speed (road): 28 km/h (17.5 mph)
Maximum Speed (off road): 21 km/h (13 mph)
Range, Road: 135 km (85 miles)
Range, Cross-country: About 100 km (60 miles)
Fording Capacity: n/a
Maximum Gradient: 26 degrees
Maximum Trench Width: 2.75 m (9 ft)
Maximum Vertical Obstacle: 0.9 m (3 ft)
Suspension Type: Independently (coil) sprung road wheels

Engine:
Powerplant: 1 x Renault 6-cylinder in-line petrol engine
Capacity: 14.4 l (3.2 gallons)
Output: 229 kW/307 bhp
Power/Weight Ratio: 8 bhp/tonne

Armour and Armament:
Homogeneous rolled/riveted and welded nickel-steel plate; cast elements. 14–60 mm (0.6-2.4 in)
Main Armament: 1 x 75-mm (2.95-in) ABS SA35 L/17 fixed in azimuth in hull front
Secondary Armament: 1 x 47-mm (1.85-in) SA35 L/32 in fully traversing turret
Ancillary Armament: 1 x coaxially mounted 7.5-mm (0.3-in) Châtellerault Mle.31 MG; 1 x flexibly mounted 7.5-mm (0.3-in) Châtellerault Mle 31 MG

Principal World War II German units of captured Char B1:
Panzer-Brigade 100
Panzer-Regimente 100
Panzer-Ersatz-Abteilung 100
Panzer-Abteilung (F) 102
Panzer-Abteilung 213
SS-Panzer-Abteilung "Prinz Eugen"
Panzer-Kompanie z.b.V. 12
Panzer-Abteilung 223
Beutepanzer-Kompanie 223
I./Artillerie-Regiment 93 of 26. Panzer-Division
II./Panzer-Regiment 1 of 1. Panzer-Division
Panzer-Regiment 2 of 16. Panzer-Division
I./Panzer-Regiment 36 of 14. Panzer-Division
Panzer-Abteilung 205
Panzer-Kompanie 206
Panzer-Kompanie C (ND) 224
Panzerjäger-Abteilung 657 (PK 224)

CHAR B1 BIS

The powerful Char B1 bis was the most advanced version of the Char B1 French heavy tank, the design of which was the result of specifications put forward by a commission set up in 1921. Production of the Char B1 began in 1935, and introduced numerous modern elements, such as an electric starter and self-sealing fuel tanks. Heavily armed, the Char B1 fielded a turret-mounted 47-mm (1.85-in) cannon, a hull-mounted 75-mm (2.95-in) howitzer, and a pair of 7.5-mm (0.3-in) Reibel machine guns. The Char B1 bis entered production in 1937. It had an improved turret design, increased armour protection, and a 307 bhp (229 kW) six-cylinder Renault engine, upgrades from the standard Char B1.

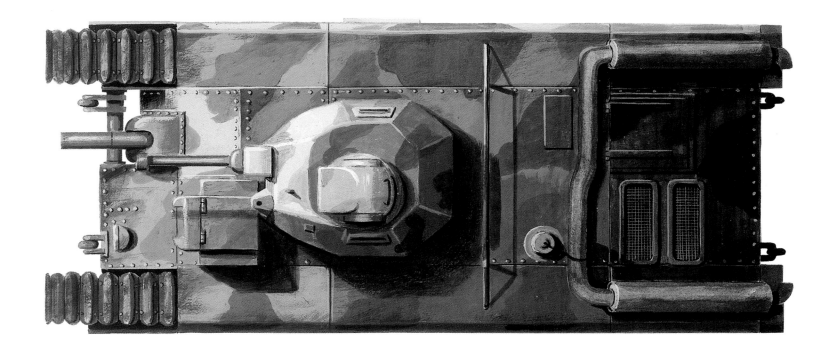

Well armed and armoured, the Char B1 and Char B1 bis were intended to punch a hole in the enemy's defensive line swiftly and decisively. Unfortunately, their high fuel consumption hampered their suitability for the purpose.

On the eve of World War II, the French army appeared to be the most formidable in the world. One element of its considerable perceived strength was the presence of approximately 400 Char B1 and Char B1 bis heavy tanks distributed among three Divisions Cuirassées de Réserve (armoured divisions). Following the outbreak of hostilities, a fourth armoured division received heavy tanks.

The production span of the Char B1 bis was relatively short, and it was never available in the numbers envisioned by the French high command. In fact, from April 1937 through June 1940, only 369 of the heavy tanks were

Interior view

The interior of the Char B1 bis was detrimental to communication among crew members. The commander sat alone in the cramped turret and operated the 47-mm (1.85-in) cannon unassisted.

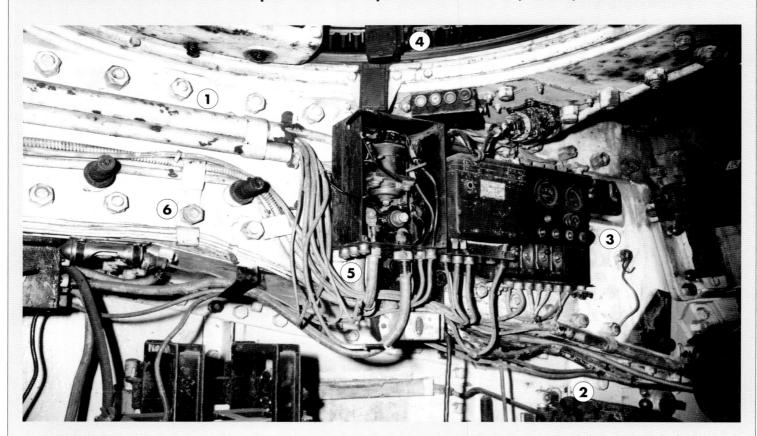

(1) **Hull Compartment:** Here the loader served the 75-mm (2.95-in) cannon and passed 47 mm (1.85 in) shells to the commander.

(2) **Driver's Position:** Placed forwards to the left, it was beside the hull-mounted 75-mm (2.95-in) cannon, directly under an entry hatch.

(3) **Bulkhead Cabling:** Equipment for laying guns, communications, and hydraulics was situated near the driver, along the bulkhead of the loader's compartment.

(4) **Turret Traversing Gear:** This allowed the commander to acquire targets and observe the battlefield. The heavy 75-mm (2.95-in) cannon could not be traversed laterally.

(5) **Hydraulic Lines:** These enabled heavy equipment to function throughout the Char B1 bis. A compressed air hose was also installed above the breech of the main gun.

(6) **Hull Construction:** Heavy bolts and rivets held the steel hull of the tank together.

The Char B1 bis easily stood up to the German panzers during the early months of World War II. However, its agility cross country and heavy firepower were diminished by hull and crew compartment design flaws.

delivered on an order for 1144. A mere 129 were in service at the outbreak of World War II.

During their offensive against France and the Low Countries in the spring of 1940, the Germans maintained a healthy respect for the Char B1 bis, whose 75-mm (2.95-in) cannon was capable of destroying the most modern German fighting vehicles. But the French tanks required considerable field maintenance and were prone to mechanical failure, while trained tank crews were in short supply. Perhaps the greatest shortcoming of the Char B1 bis was its limited range. High fuel consumption could deplete its three fuel tanks' 400-litre (90-gallon) capacity in about six hours.

Further complicating the situation for the French was the penchant of its field commanders to commit the heavy tanks piecemeal rather than in formations large enough to contain rapid German advances. When engaged in combat, the four-man crew was further handicapped by the fact that the tank commander was also required to serve the turret gun.

CHAR B1 BIS AT STONNE

Nevertheless, the Char B1 bis was a combat tank worthy of its reputation as a capable fighting vehicle. On 16 May, 1940, Capitain Pierre Billotte of the 1/41e BCC (Bataillon de

Chars de Combat) reached the town of Stonne, near the Belgian frontier, and advanced into its narrow streets. There, he destroyed 13 German tanks, including 11 Panzer IIIs and two Panzer IVs, along with a pair of 37-mm (1.45-in) Pak anti-tank guns. Billotte's tank, nicknamed "Eure," was hit 140 times. However, no German round penetrated the armour of the Char B1 bis, which was 60 mm (2.3 in) thick to the front and 55 mm (2 in) on its sides.

FALL OF FRANCE

Following the capitulation of France, more than 160 Char B1 tanks were pressed into service by the Germans. The Char B1 bis was renamed the PzKpfw B1 bis 740(f) and was used in a variety of roles, such as garrison duty with occupation forces in the Channel Islands, training vehicles, conversion to self-propelled artillery, and even as a flamethrower.

While the Char B1 bis possessed some notable drawbacks and was seldom employed en masse, it proved to be a dangerous opponent in single combat. The Char B1 ter, a variant with heavier sloped armour and an upgraded engine, was to have gone into production in the summer of 1940. However, by that time the swastika was flying over Paris.

T-34/85

The most influential and successful tank of World War II, the T-34 combined elements of Soviet and Western design. It was produced in overwhelming numbers, becoming symbolic of the Red Army's victory on the Eastern Front.

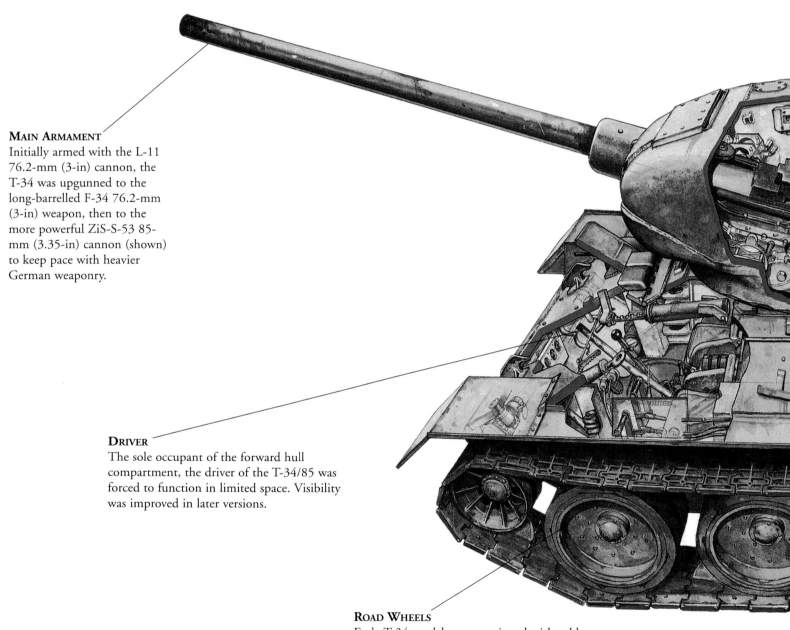

MAIN ARMAMENT
Initially armed with the L-11 76.2-mm (3-in) cannon, the T-34 was upgunned to the long-barrelled F-34 76.2-mm (3-in) weapon, then to the more powerful ZiS-S-53 85-mm (3.35-in) cannon (shown) to keep pace with heavier German weaponry.

DRIVER
The sole occupant of the forward hull compartment, the driver of the T-34/85 was forced to function in limited space. Visibility was improved in later versions.

ROAD WHEELS
Early T-34 models were equipped with rubber road wheels. However, shortages of the material resulted in the adoption of steel rims.

- The T-34 was developed from the BT series of fast tanks.

- In early 1944, the improved T-34/85 was introduced with a more powerful 85-mm (3.35-in) gun and a three-man turret design.

- Over 84,000 were built between 1944–58.

CUPOLA
Beginning in 1942, improvements to the T-34 included the addition of a commander's cupola for an improved field of vision.

TURRET
The original T-34 turret was cramped and accommodated only two crewmen. Later versions included a hexagonal configuration, and then a more spacious three-crew compartment.

RADIO
The radio of the T-34/85 was moved from the hull to the turret for better functionality. Initially, only the tanks of commanders were equipped with a radio.

SUSPENSION
The T-34 incorporated a coil spring suspension developed by American engineer Walter Christie and first used in the earlier BT tank series.

ENGINE
The 12-cylinder V-2 diesel engine of the T-34 generated 375 kW (500 hp). Shortages of the engine resulted in the first production run being equipped with the MT-17 petrol engine.

The tank's effectiveness in the battlefield suffered from the unsatisfactory ergonomic layout of its crew compartment. The two-man turret meant the commander also had to serve as gunner. Three-crew turrets, which accommodated a commander, gunner, and loader, proved superior.

T-34/85 – SPECIFICATION

Country of Origin: USSR
Crew: 5
Designer: Kharkiv Morozov Machine Building Design Bureau
Designed: 1937–40
In Service: 1940–present
Manufacturers: Various
Number Built: 84,070
Produced: 1940–58
Gross Weight: 32 tonnes (35.2 tons)

Dimensions:
Hull Length: 6 m (19.7 ft)
Length (gun forward): 7.5 m (24.6 ft)
Width: 2.92 m (9.6 ft)
Overall Height: 2.39 m (7.85 ft)

Performance:
Maximum Speed: 55 km/h (34 mph)
Range, Road: 300 km (188 miles)
Range, Cross-country: 160 km (100 miles)
Power/Weight Ratio: 16 bhp/tonne
Ground Pressure: 0.087 kg/cm²
Fording Capacity: 0.9 m (3.3 ft)
Maximum Gradient: 30 degrees
Maximum Trench Width: 2.5 m (8.2 ft)
Max Vertical Obstacle: 0.8 m (2.6 ft)
Suspension: Trailing arm/coil spring

Engine:
Powerplant: 1 x V-2-34 V-12 water-cooled diesel engine

Capacity: 38.9 l (8.5 gallons)
Output: 375 kW (500 bhp) @ 2000 rpm
Fuel Capacity: 635 l (140 gallons)

Armour and Armaments:
Armour Type: Homogeneous rolled/welded nickel steel
Hull Front: 45 mm (1.8 in)
Hull Sides: 45 mm (1.8 in)
Hull Rear: 40–45 mm (1.6–1.8 in)
Hull Top: 30 mm (1.2 in)
Hull Bottom: 20 mm (0.8 in)
Turret Front: 45–55 mm (1.8–2.2 in)
Turret Sides: 50–55 mm (2–2.2 in)
Turret Rear: 50 mm (2 in)
Turret Top: 20 m (0.8 in)
Main Armament: 85-mm (3.35-in) ZiS-S-53 cannon
Secondary Armament: 2 x 7.62-mm (0.3-in) MG34 machine guns

Operators:
USSR
Albania
Austria
Bulgaria
Cyprus
Czechoslovakia
Cuba
Finland
East Germany
Hungary
Poland
Romania
Yugoslavia
Afghanistan
Egypt
Indonesia
Iraq
Laos
Lebanon
Libya
Mongolia
North Korea
Palestine (12 operated by the PLO in Lebanon, passed on to the Al-Murabitun)
People's Republic of China
Syria
Vietnam
South Yemen (PDRY)
North Yemen (YAR)
Algeria
Angola
Republic of the Congo
Equatorial Guinea
Ethiopia
Guinea
Guinea-Bissau
Mali
Mozambique
Somalia
Sudan
Togo
Zimbabwe

T-34/85

The T-34/85 improved the original T-34 design with a three-man turret compartment. This enabled the commander to direct the tank in combat more efficiently, relieving him of the requirement to serve the main cannon. It also incorporated a heavier 85-mm (3.35-in) main weapon, which was capable of penetrating the armour of the wartime generation of German tanks at moderate distances. Early T-34s, based on the BT series originally conceived by American engineer Walter Christie (1865–1944), introduced sloped armour but were limited in their combat effectiveness because of the poor layout of the crew compartment and the installation of radios only in commanders' tanks, which hampered communications.

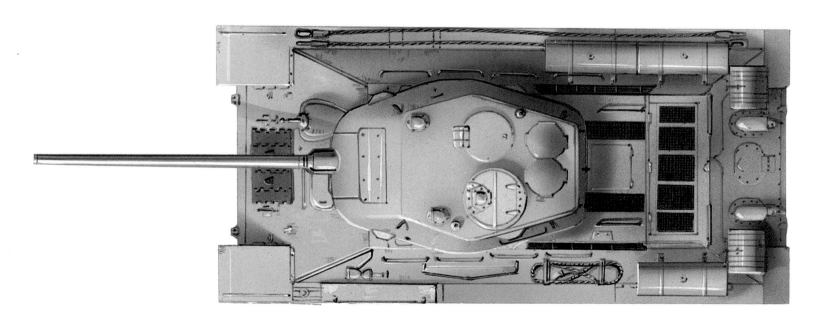

A column of T-34 tanks halts along a snowy road on the Eastern Front as Red Army soldiers clamber aboard during the advance towards the German frontier in the winter of 1944.

The T-34/85 of early 1944 gave the Red Army a tank with better armour and mobility than the German PzKpfw IV and Sturmgeschütz III, but it could not match the Panther in gun or armour protection. However, the T-34/85 was good enough to allow skilled crews to tip the balance.

General Heinz Guderian's Panzergruppe II met the Red Army's T-34 medium tank in combat for the first time in November 1941. At that point, it became readily apparent that German armoured forces were confronting a Soviet tank capable of holding its own ferociously on the battlefield.

"Numerous Russian T-34s went into action and inflicted heavy losses on the German tanks at Mzensk in 1941," wrote Guderian after the war. "Up to this time we had enjoyed tank superiority, but from now on the situation was reversed. The prospect of rapid decisive victories was fading in consequence. I made a report on this situation, which for us was a new one, and sent it to the Army Group. In this report, I described in plain terms the marked superiority of the T-34 to our PzKpfw IV and drew the relevant conclusion as that must affect our future tank production."

Although the appearance of the T-34 came as a shock to the Germans, the tank itself had been in design since the mid-1930s, and the prototype for the new Soviet medium battle tank, replacing the earlier BT series and T-26 vehicles, had been developed by 1940. The combination of rapid mobility, increasingly effective firepower, sloping armour, and deployment in large numbers established the T-34 as the pivotal weapon on the Eastern Front during World War II.

DARING DESIGN

From the beginning, the T-34 was a platform for innovation. It could reach a top road speed of 55 km/h (34 mph) powered by its 12-cylinder V-2 engine. Its sloped armour, on average 52 mm (2 in) thick, provided greater protection against enemy fire through increased thickness without added weight. More often, incoming shells tended to deflect. However, early versions of the T-34 were hampered by the requirement that the commander serve the main 76.2-mm (3-in) cannon. In addition, communications were limited because radios were only installed in commanders' tanks.

By the spring of 1944, the T-34/85 had incorporated numerous design improvements, among them the addition of the ZiS-S-53 85-mm (3.35-in) cannon, which was effective against German armour at moderate distances, and a larger three-man turret, which could accommodate a loader and gunner to service the main weapon. More than 57,000 T-34 variants were constructed throughout World War II, an astonishing feat considering that the bulk of Soviet industrial production had been relocated to the east of the Ural

Mountains following the German invasion of the Soviet Union on 22 June, 1941. A total of 22,500 T-34/85 tanks were constructed, and during the course of the war production time was cut in half while unit cost was substantially reduced as well.

STAGGERING LOSSES REPLACED

In combat, the performance of the T-34 suffered because crews lacked thorough training, and their battlefield tactics evolved only slowly. To nullify the advantage of 75-mm (2.95-in) and 88-mm (3.5-in) weapons on the German heavy tanks, which were capable of destroying a T-34 at a distance of more than 1 mile (1.6 km), the Soviets attempted to close rapidly with the enemy, charging en masse and often without coordination. Losses were staggering, yet Soviet factories were more than able to compensate. Ultimately, the T-34 stood up to the costly and over-engineered German tanks, which were available only in limited numbers.

World War II variants of the T-34 included self-propelled assault guns, a flamethrower version, and recovery and bridging tanks. Improvements continued into the 1960s, and examples of the tank remain in service to this day.

Interior view

The interior of the early T-34 medium tank was not built with comfort in mind. Primitive by Western standards, the design underwent steady improvement during and after World War II.

1. **Gun Laying Equipment:** The main 85-mm (3.35-in) cannon of the T-34/85 tank was sighted with optical tools from inside the turret and adjacent to the weapon itself.

2. **Turret Traverse Mechanism:** The turret was traversed electrically, distinguished by a slight bulge in the turret.

3. **Breech Block:** The upgunned T-34/85 mounted the powerful ZiS-S-53 85-mm (3.34-in) cannon, which was capable of penetrating most German armour.

4. **Gun Cradle:** The cradle of the ZiS-S-53 85-mm (3.35-in) cannon supported the weapon during operation and absorbed some of the recoil of the powerful weapon.

5. **Turret Armour:** The turret was cast to up to 75 mm (2.95 in) thick on the front and sides and 20 mm (0.78 in) on its roof.

6. **Turret Floor:** The lack of a rotating turret basket on which the gunner and loader could stand during combat hampered the T-34/85.

M3A3 Stuart

Developed as a fast infantry support vehicle, the American-built Light Tank M3 was deployed extensively with the U.S., British, and Soviet armed forces. It saw action in both the European and Pacific theatres during World War II.

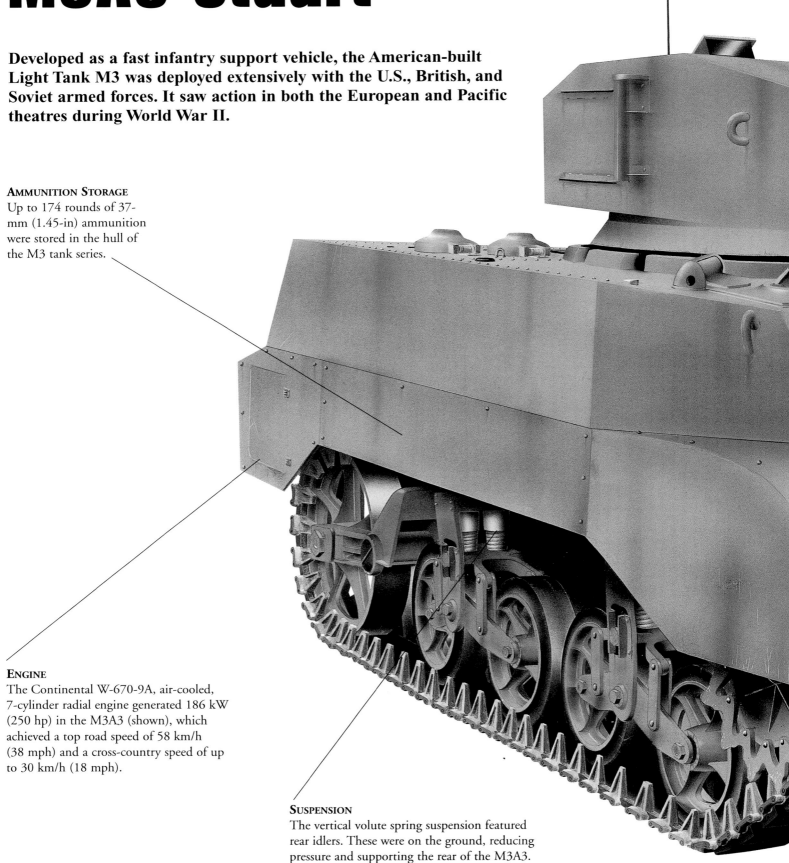

AMMUNITION STORAGE
Up to 174 rounds of 37-mm (1.45-in) ammunition were stored in the hull of the M3 tank series.

ENGINE
The Continental W-670-9A, air-cooled, 7-cylinder radial engine generated 186 kW (250 hp) in the M3A3 (shown), which achieved a top road speed of 58 km/h (38 mph) and a cross-country speed of up to 30 km/h (18 mph).

SUSPENSION
The vertical volute spring suspension featured rear idlers. These were on the ground, reducing pressure and supporting the rear of the M3A3.

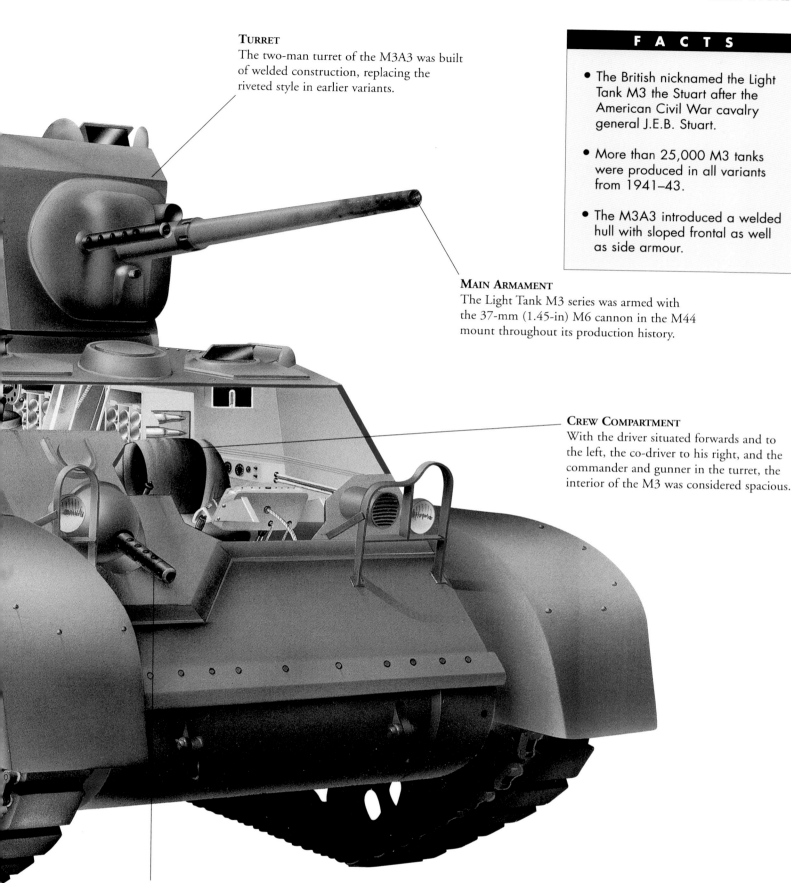

TURRET
The two-man turret of the M3A3 was built of welded construction, replacing the riveted style in earlier variants.

MAIN ARMAMENT
The Light Tank M3 series was armed with the 37-mm (1.45-in) M6 cannon in the M44 mount throughout its production history.

CREW COMPARTMENT
With the driver situated forwards and to the left, the co-driver to his right, and the commander and gunner in the turret, the interior of the M3 was considered spacious.

SECONDARY ARMAMENT
The M3 carried up to five 7.7-mm (0.3-in) Browning M1919A4 machine guns, mounted coaxially in the turret, forwards in the hull. Two were operated by the driver in combat and placed in hull sponsons, and another was mounted on the turret roof for defence against enemy aircraft.

The Light Tank M3 was used wherever the U.S. Army was involved. It proved to be a thoroughly reliable vehicle, greatly liked by its crews. To the British, the Stuart was large for a light tank, but crews soon learnt to appreciate its reliability.

M3A3 STUART – SPECIFICATION

Country of Origin: USA
Crew: 4
Produced: 1941–43
Manufacturer: American Car and Foundry
In Service: 1941–90s
Number Built: 3427
Gross Weight: 14.7 tonnes (16 tons)

Dimensions:
Hull Length: 4.53 m (14.9 ft)
Length (gun forward): 4.53 m (14.9 ft)
Width: 2.23 m (7.33 ft)
Overall Height: 2.52 m (8.25 ft)

Performance:
Range, Road: 120 km (75 miles)
Range, Cross-country: 60 km (40 miles)
Maximum Speed: 58 km/h (35 mph)
Ground Pressure: n/a
Fording Capacity: 0.91 m (3 ft)
Maximum Gradient: 30 degrees
Maximum Trench Width: 1.83 m (6 ft)
Maximum Vertical Obstacle: 0.6 m (2 ft)
Suspension Type: Paired wheels in coil-sprung bogies

Engine:
Powerplant: 1 x Continental W-670-9A radial petrol engine
Capacity: n/a
Output: 250 bhp (186 kW)

Power/Weight Ratio: 17.35 bhp/tonne
Fuel Capacity: 212 l (46.7 gallons)

Armour and Armament:
Armour Type: Homogeneous rolled/welded nickel-steel
Minimum Thickness: 10 mm (0.4 in)
Maximum Thickness: 65 mm (2.6 in)
Main Armament: 1 x 7-mm (0.26-in) M5 L/50 or 37-mm (1.45-in) M6 L/55.103 rounds.
Secondary Armament: 2 x 7.7-mm (0.3-in) M1919A4 air-cooled Browning MGs. Up to 8000 rounds.

Gun Control Equipment:
Turret Traverse: Manual
Elevation Range: -10 to +20 degrees
Stabilisation: Elevation and azimuth

Operators:
Australia
Belgium
Brazil
Canada
Chile
Colombia
Cuba
Dominican Republic
Ecuador
El Salvador
France
Greece
India
Indonesia
Italy
Mexico
Netherlands
New Zealand
Nicaragua
Paraguay
Philippines
Poland
Portugal
Republic of China (Taiwan)
Turkey
UK
Uruguay
USA
USSR
Venezuela
Yugoslavia

M3A3 STUART

The Light Tank M3A3, or Stuart V as it was known to the British, featured a larger driver compartment, sloped frontal and side armour with a thickness increased from 43 to 51 mm (1.7–2 in) in critical areas, a fully welded hull, and an extension at the rear of the multi-sided turret to house radio equipment. The sponson mounted 7.7-mm (0.3-in) machine guns were also removed. A total of 3427 of the M3A3 were built during the war, incorporating improvements made to previous variants of the series. The M3A3 weighed slightly more than 14.5 tonnes (16 tons), and its range was nearly 120 km (75 miles).

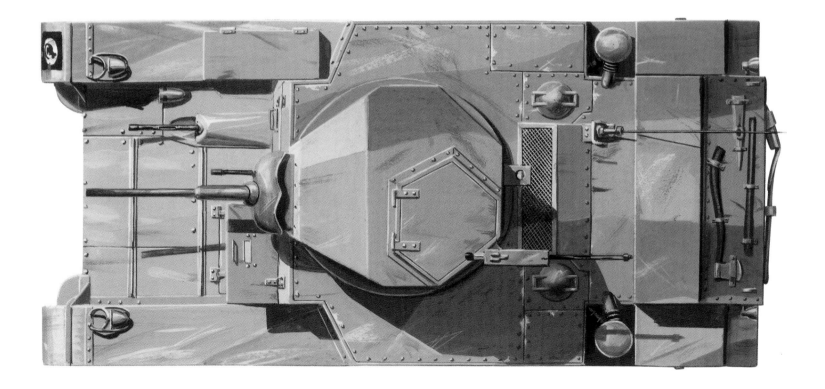

An M3A3 Stuart light tank pauses in a small village in northwest France. Lightly armed and armoured, the Stuart was the embodiment of American armoured doctrine between World Wars I and II, which was one of speed, mobility, and infantry support.

By 1944, the M3 had very little combat value, and many served with reconnaissance units through to the end of the war. The turrets had been removed from some of them and additional machine guns mounted. Others were put to use as command vehicles for armoured formations.

As events unfolded in Europe, American tank designers realized that their Light Tank M2 series was growing obsolescent. By the spring of 1941, they began producing the M3, a new generation of light tank. The main armament, the 37-mm (1.45-in) M6 cannon, was ineffective against the enemy armour of World War II. Even so, the 37-mm (1.45-in) remained constant in all M3 variants. But by the autumn of 1944, the successor to the M3, the M24 Chaffee, was mounting a 75-mm (2.95-in) cannon.

Thousands of M3s were deployed through Lend Lease by Great Britain and the Soviet Union. Under combat conditions, the tank received mixed reviews. It was speedy and ruggedly dependable, but it was undergunned and only thinly armoured. Its shortcomings in tank-versus-tank

action were laid bare in the desert of North Africa and on the Eastern Front. Both the British and the Soviets tended to employ the M3 in reconnaissance, observation, and infantry support roles, as did the Americans later in the war in the European theatre. Crews were fond enough of the tanks to give the tank a pair of nicknames, calling them the "Stuart" and the "Honey."

In the Pacific, the Japanese lagged far behind in the development of armoured fighting vehicles. The M3 proved effective and reasonably operational against machine gun emplacements, troop concentrations, and fixed fortifications during island and jungle fighting. Japanese tanks were few, but the inhospitable terrain often prevented heavier American armour from manoeuvring effectively.

REFINEMENTS AND VARIATIONS
The M3 series was powered primarily by the 186-kW (250-hp) Continental W-670-9A radial engine, which was in high demand. The Guibertson T-1020 diesel engine was also used, to relieve pressure on production of the Continental. In a third powerplant configuration, twin Cadillac V-8 engines were installed in a hull with raised decking. This was

designated the M5 or, to the British, the Stuart VI.

Major variants to the M3 included the M3A1, known as the Stuart III or IV to the British depending on its petrol or diesel powerplant, and the M3A3, or Stuart V. The M3A1 incorporated a gyro-stabilized main weapon mounted in a power traverse turret complete with turret basket. The M3A3 included thicker armour protection and an enlarged driver compartment. A pair of sponson mounts were removed on this variant, resulting in the tank's five Browning 7.7-mm (0.3-in) machine guns being reduced to three. Several specialized M3 designs were never placed in service. These

included a relative few that mounted a 75-mm (2.95-in) howitzer, a flamethrower version, and an anti-aircraft variant armed with 12.7-mm (0.5-in) machine guns.

The Light Tank M3 remained in service with the armed forces of numerous countries after World War II, and some were reported as still being active into the 1990s. The M3 may have lacked substantial firepower and its thin armour protection made the vehicle vulnerable under combat conditions, yet it was still valuable in the reconnaissance and basic infantry support roles. More than 25,000 were produced between March 1941 and October 1943.

Close-up

The M3 Stuart light tank was a pre-World War II design intended for infantry support. Widely used in the war, it was rapidly outclassed by heavier vehicles and grew ineffective against enemy armour.

(1) **Turret Manufacture:** Originally of riveted construction, it was later changed to welded and then to rolled homogeneous steel.

(2) **Suspension:** The vertical volute spring suspension of the early M3 Stuart tanks included two bogies per track, two wheels per bogie, and three return rollers per track.

(3) **Co-Driver:** The co-driver was seated forwards and to the right in the turret. He viewed the terrain ahead through a slit in the upper hull.

(4) **Main Weapon:** The primary armament was inadequate against enemy armour and primarily used in a defensive posture.

(5) **Pistol Ports:** The turret of the M3 Stuart contained three pistol ports for close defence against attacking infantry. Hull and turret-mounted machine guns were also utilized.

(6) **Hull Armour:** The top road speed, up to 58 km/h (38 mph), was facilitated by light, 3.8-cm (1.5-in) armour on the upper hull.

M3A3 General Lee

Reports from the battlefields of Europe prompted American armour designers to quickly adapt an existing chassis to carry heavier armament. The hybrid Medium Tank M3 was the result, and it was deployed extensively with American armoured divisions and Allied formations through Lend Lease.

SECONDARY ARMAMENT
Depending on the M3 variant, secondary armament included up to four 7.62-mm (0.3-in) Browning M1919A machine guns, one in the commander's cupola, one coaxial in the turret, and two located in the hull.

MAIN ARMAMENT
The sponson-mounted 75-mm (2.95-in) cannon was capable of limited traverse, while the 37-mm (1.45-in) turret gun was ineffective in tank-versus-tank combat.

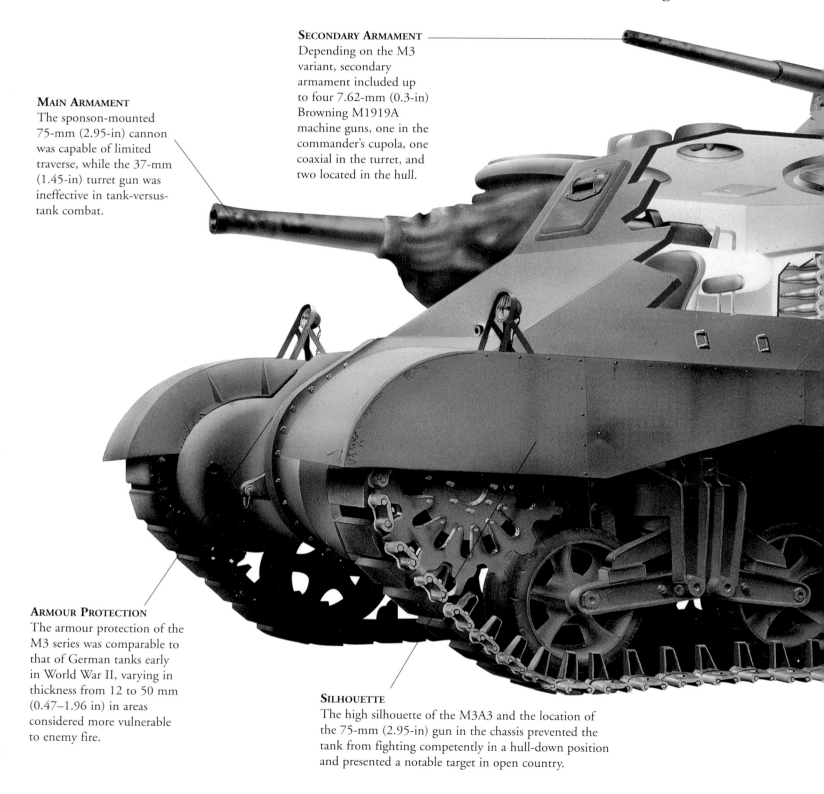

ARMOUR PROTECTION
The armour protection of the M3 series was comparable to that of German tanks early in World War II, varying in thickness from 12 to 50 mm (0.47–1.96 in) in areas considered more vulnerable to enemy fire.

SILHOUETTE
The high silhouette of the M3A3 and the location of the 75-mm (2.95-in) gun in the chassis prevented the tank from fighting competently in a hull-down position and presented a notable target in open country.

TURRET
The small M3 turret could not accommodate a larger gun than the 37 mm (1.45 in). Modifications to those tanks delivered to Great Britain included the removal of the commander's cupola and lengthening of the turret rear to accommodate radio equipment.

FACTS

- Nearly 6300 M3 medium tanks were produced from August 1941 to December 1942.

- Designers were aware of the M3's deficiencies, but the need for tanks was critical.

- When the M3 entered production, no American-built turret could hold a gun larger than 37 mm (1.45 in).

SUSPENSION
The vertical volute suspension of the M3 was improved in later models with the addition of heavy bogies rather than springs.

ENGINE
Initially, the 253-kW (340-hp) Wright Continental R975 EC2 engine, originally intended for aircraft, powered the M3 series of medium tanks. Later M3s were powered by the General Motors 6046 diesel engine, combining two GM 6-71 engines, which could operate independently, and the Chrysler A57 engine.

The design of the M3 was peculiar in that it was a tank caught between two eras of warfare. The profile was unquestionably high, nearly one and a half times the height of an average man.

M3A3 GENERAL LEE – SPECIFICATION

Country of Origin: USA
Crew: 6/7
Designer: N/A
Designed: 1940–41
In Production: August 1941–December 1942
Manufacturer: Baldwin Locomotive Works
In Service: 1942–45
Number Produced: 6258
Gross Weight: 27 tonnes (29.7 tons)

Dimensions:
Hull Length: 5.64 m (18.5 ft)
Length (gun forward): 5.46 m (18.5 ft)
Width: 2.72 m (8.9 ft)
Overall Height: 3 m (10 ft)

Performance:
Maximum Speed: 40 km/h (25 mph)
Range, Road: 240 km (160 miles)
Range, Cross-country: 150 km (90 miles)
Ground Pressure: 0.91 kg/cm^2
Fording Capacity: 0.92 m (3 ft)
Maximum Gradient: 31 degrees
Maximum Trench Width: 2.3 m (7.5 ft)
Maximum Vertical Obstacle: 0.6 m (2 ft)
Suspension Type: Vertical volute sprung two-wheel bogies

Engine:
Powerplant: 1 x General Motors 6046 Twin-Six, 2-cycle 12-cylinder twin in-line diesel
Capacity: 13.9 l (3.1 gallons)
Output: 253 kW (340 hp) @ 2900 rpm
Transmission: Synchromesh, 5 speeds forward, 1 reverse

Power/Weight Ratio: 13 bhp/tonne
Fuel Capacity: 560 l (123 gallons)

Armour Armament:
Armour Type: Homogeneous rolled/welded hull, cast turret
Hull Front: 38–50 mm (1.5–2 in)
Hull Sides: 38 mm (1.5 in)
Hull Rear: 38 mm (1.5 in)
Hull Top: 12.5 mm (0.5 in)
Hull Bottom: 12.5–25 mm (0.5–1 in)
Turret Front: 50–76 mm (2–3 in)
Turret Sides: 50 mm (2 in)
Turret Rear: 50 mm (2 in)
Turret Top: 32 mm (1.3 in)
Main Armament: 1 x 75-mm (2.95-in) M2 L/31 in sponson
Secondary Armament: 1 x 37-mm (1.45-in) M6 in M24 mount in 360-degree traverse turret
Ancillary Armament: 3 x 7.62-mm (0.3-in) M1919A4

American Variants:
M3: Riveted hull, high-profile turret, petrol engine. 4724 built.
M3A1: Cast (rounded) upper hull. 300 built.
M3A2: Welded (sharp-edged) hull. Only 12 vehicles produced.
M3A3: Twin GM 6-71 diesel variant of welded hull.
M3A4: 5 x Chrysler A-57 engines. Side doors eliminated.
M3A5: Twin GM 6-71 diesel variant of riveted hull M3.
M31 Tank Recovery Vehicle: With dummy turret.
M31B1 Tank Recovery Vehicle: Based on M3A3.
M31B2 Tank Recovery Vehicle: Based on M3A5.
M33 Prime Mover: M31 TRV converted to artillery tractor role.
105-mm (4-in) Howitzer Motor Carriage M7
155-mm (6-in) Gun Motor Carriage M12: Howitzer on M3 chassis.

M3A3 GENERAL LEE

The design of the American Medium Tank M3 was inherently flawed, but the tank did still provide an urgently needed interim solution to the shortage of Allied armour facing the might of German panzer divisions. The M3, utilizing the suspension and power train of the earlier M2, stood roughly 3 m (10 ft) tall, including a crew compartment that was raised to accommodate the angle of the drive train, a small turret, and a commander's cupola on top of the earlier variants. Its high silhouette and lumbering cross-country speed of 26 km/h (16 mph) made the M3 vulnerable to enemy tanks with guns in full traversing turrets and to anti-tank weapons.

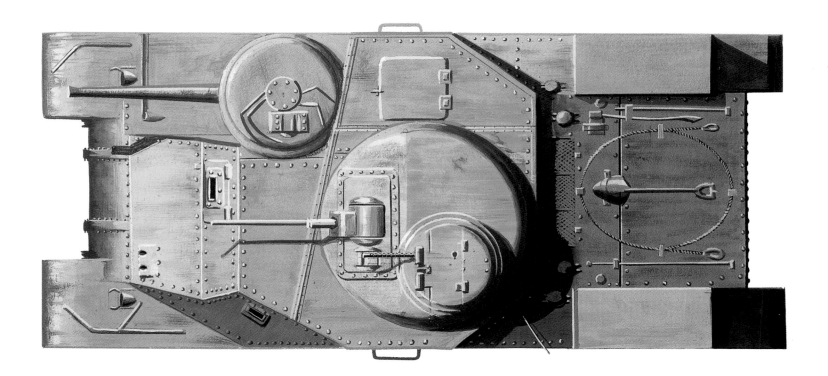

An M3A3 General Lee tank throws up a cloud of dust as it rolls down a dirt road in North Africa. The distinctive silhouette of the General Lee made it particularly vulnerable to enemy anti-tank fire.

In the event, the M3 proved to be a reliable and hard-wearing vehicle. Perhaps the main lesson to be learned from it was the latent power of American industry, which could deliver such a vehicle from scratch in such a short time.

British tank losses reached extreme levels on the battlefields of North Africa. However, the United States rejected an appeal to build British armour designs in American factories. The availability of the Medium Tank M3 emerged as an expedient. It was somewhat workable, yet obviously an imperfect solution to a critical Allied shortage in armoured fighting vehicles.

The American M3 series may best be described as a bridge between the old and new. Clearly influenced by the tank designs of World War I, the M3 carried significant firepower with its 75-mm (2.95-in) cannon mounted in a sponson on the right side of the hull, its 37-mm (1.45-in) turret gun, and up to four .30-06 Browning M1919A4 machine guns. One significant advantage of the 75 mm (2.95 in) was its ability to fire both armour-piercing and high-explosive, anti-personnel shells, while earlier 75s could fire only one or the other. Its hull configuration was

the result of the pressing fact that time was of the essence and no U.S.-built turret able to mount anything heavier than the 37-mm (1.45-in) gun was available in quantity.

However, even as production of the M3 series began in earnest, its replacement, the M4 Sherman, was being rapidly developed. While a total of 6258 M3 tanks were produced in a 17-month period from August 1941 through December 1942, Allied designers were well aware of its inherent flaws. The silhouette, approximately 3 m (10 ft) high, exposed it to enemy armour and mobile anti-tank weapons at great distances. The hull-mounted 75-mm (2.95-in) gun was limited in its traverse and prevented the tank from fighting effectively in the hull-down position. The M3 was slow, with a maximum cross-country speed of just over 26 km/h (16 mph), and early versions were particularly underpowered by the 253 kW (340 hp) Wright Continental R975 EC2 engine, originally intended for aircraft.

MODIFICATIONS AND IMPROVEMENTS

A staple of Lend Lease and purchased in quantity by the British, some M3s were modified to remove the commander's cupola and elongate the turret to hold radio equipment. Those modified M3s delivered to the British were named the General Grant, while later shipments of unmodified M3s were designated the General Lee, both after prominent American Civil War commanders, as was the British custom.

Variants of the M3 included the M3A1, of welded rather than riveted construction, the M3A3, with improved armour protection and two 3678-kW (375-hp) General Motors 6046 diesel engines, the M3A4 with a 3678-kW (370-hp) Chrysler A57 engine, configured of multiple automobile engines, and the M3A5, virtually identical to the M3A3 but with riveted construction. More than 1300 of the M3A3 and M3A5 were delivered to the Soviet Union through Lend Lease, and a number of support vehicles and self-propelled guns utilized the M3 chassis.

COFFIN FOR SEVEN BROTHERS

When the M3 debuted in North Africa, the Germans were shocked by the appearance of a heavily-armed Allied tank. The Soviets, however, nicknamed the tank the "coffin for seven brothers." In truth, despite its pronounced weaknesses, the M3 was a sturdy opponent to the superior German armour until the M4 arrived in quantity.

Interior view

The M3A3 General Lee tank made its combat debut in North Africa and proved a surprise to German and Italian forces. It was heavily armed, but its value in combat was limited by several design flaws.

(1) **Cannon:** The 75-mm (2.95-in) hull-mounted cannon was a deadly weapon limited only by its inability to independently traverse.

(2) **Cannon Elevation:** Traversing the hull-mounted cannon from side to side required the reorientation of the vehicle chassis, but the weapon was elevated independently.

(3) **Driver Position:** Located in the centre of the hull, the driver used a hinged port when not in combat.

(4) **Secondary Cannon:** The 37-mm (1.45-in) cannon mounted in the turret was a potent weapon against lighter armoured vehicles.

(5) **Commander's Cupola:** Lend Lease M3 tanks delivered to the British were often modified with the removal of the commander's cupola to add radio equipment.

(6) **Silhouette:** The M3A3 General Lee stood more than 3 m (10 ft) high, limiting its ability to fight in the hull-down position.

Churchill

Initially envisioned as a tank that would support infantry engaged in the kind of trench-style fighting seen in World War I, the Infantry Tank Mark IV Churchill evolved into a lighter, well-armoured fighting vehicle, variants of which were deployed throughout World War II.

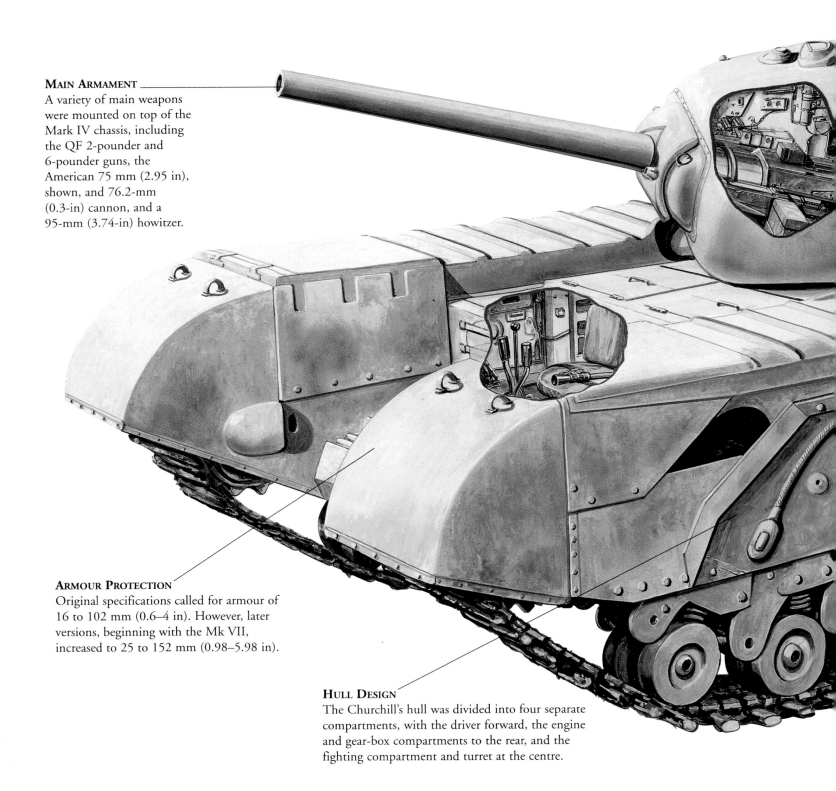

MAIN ARMAMENT
A variety of main weapons were mounted on top of the Mark IV chassis, including the QF 2-pounder and 6-pounder guns, the American 75 mm (2.95 in), shown, and 76.2-mm (0.3-in) cannon, and a 95-mm (3.74-in) howitzer.

ARMOUR PROTECTION
Original specifications called for armour of 16 to 102 mm (0.6–4 in). However, later versions, beginning with the Mk VII, increased to 25 to 152 mm (0.98–5.98 in).

HULL DESIGN
The Churchill's hull was divided into four separate compartments, with the driver forward, the engine and gear-box compartments to the rear, and the fighting compartment and turret at the centre.

TURRET
Both welded and cast construction were used in the production of Churchill Mark IV turrets. The 75-mm (2.95-in) cannon fitted later required a 90-degree rotation for loading from the left because of the crew configuration inside the turret.

FACTS

- A total of 13 Marks or variants of the Churchill Mark IV were produced, along with numerous specialized vehicles.

- Nearly 7400 Churchill variants were constructed during the course of World War II.

- The Churchill saw action first during the disastrous Dieppe raid in 1942.

ENGINES
A pair of 261-kW (350-hp) horizontally opposed Bedford twin-six petrol engines remained in service with the Churchill even after heavier armament and armour protection caused greater weight and slowed the tank from its relative top speed of 24 km/h (15 mph).

SUSPENSION
The coiled spring suspension was contained under panniers on each side with 11 bogeys carrying a pair of 25.4-cm (10-in) wheels. The configuration allowed the tank to traverse difficult terrain with relative ease.

"All those things which we know are not as they should be will be put right. Fighting vehicles are urgently required, and instructions have been received to proceed with the vehicle as it is rather than hold up production."
– Churchill Tank manufacturer, Vauxhall Motors

CHURCHILL MARK IV – SPECIFICATION

Country of Origin: United Kingdom
Crew: 5
Designers: Harland and Wolff (A20)/Vauxhall Motors (A22)
Designed: 1939–42
In Service: 1941–52
Manufacturer: Vauxhall Motors
Number Built: 7368 (all variants)
Produced: 1941–45
Gross Weight: 40.6 tonnes (44.7 tons)

Dimensions:
Hull Length: 7.65 m (25.2 ft)
Length (gun forward): 7.65 m (25.2 ft)
Width: 3.25 m (10.66 ft)
Overall Height: 2.5 m (8.2 ft)

Performance:
Maximum Speed: 25 km/h (15 mph)
Range, Road: 195 km (120 miles)
Range, Cross-country: 100 km (60 miles)
Ground Pressure: 0.92 kg/cm^2
Fording Capacity: 1 m (3.3 ft)
Maximum Gradient: 30 degrees
Maximum Trench Width: 3.05 m (10 ft)
Maximum Vertical Obstacle: 0.75 m (2.5 ft)
Suspension Type: Independently (coil) sprung road wheels

Engine:
Powerplant: 1 x Bedford Twin-Six horizontally opposed 12-cylinder petrol engine
Capacity: 21.3 l (4.7 gallons)
Output: 261 kW (350 bhp) @ 2200rpm
Power/Weight Ratio: 8.85 bhp/tonne
Fuel Capacity: 680 l (149.8 gallons)

Armament and Armour:
Main Armament: 1 x 75-mm (2.95-in) M2/M3 L/37.5

Secondary Armament: 1 x 7.62-mm (0.3-in) M1919A4 coaxial MG
Ancillary Armament: 1 x 7.92-mm (0.31-in) Besa flexibly mounted MG; 1 x 7.7-mm (0.303-in) Bren LMG (optional)
Armour Type: Homogeneous cast and rolled/welded nickel-steel
Hull Front: 102 mm (4 in)
Hull Sides: 76 mm (3 in)
Hull Rear: 50 mm (2 in)
Hull Top: 19 mm (0.8 in)
Hull Bottom: 19 mm (0.8 in)
Turret Front: 89 mm (3.6 in)
Turret Sides: 76 mm (3 in)
Turret Rear: 76 mm (3 in)
Turret Top: 19 mm (0.8 in)

Variants:
Mark I: 2-pounder main gun.
Mark II: 2-pounder main gun with hull-based howitzer.
Mark III: 6-pounder main gun.
Mark IV (NA 75): 75-mm (2.95-in) main gun and cast turret.
Mark V: 25-pounder (95-mm [3.74-in] main gun).
Mark VI (NA 75): 75-mm (2.95-in) main gun.
Mark VII: 75-mm (2.95-in) main gun and 152-mm (5.98-in) frontal armour.
Mark VIII: 95-mm (3.74-in) main gun.
AVRE: Armoured Vehicle Royal Engineers.
Crocodile: Flamethrower Variant.
Bridgelayer
Ark
Plough: Mine Warfare Vehicle.
Snake: Bangalore Torpedo Vehicle.
Light Carrot: Special wall demolition charges.
AVRE/CIRD: Special mine-clearing wheels.
AVRE Carpetlayer: For boggy ground.
ARV: Armoured Recovery Vehicle.

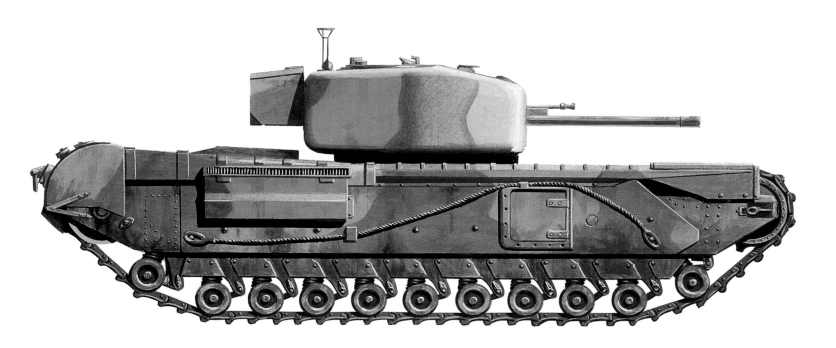

CHURCHILL MARK IV

Early Churchill tanks were rushed into production and deployed without adequate field testing because a German invasion of Britain appeared imminent. Despite its hasty beginnings, the design eventually proved to be versatile as a platform for numerous, more heavily armed Marks and for specialized vehicles, which included such innovations as the flamethrower, bridging, personnel carrier, recovery, AVRE (290-mm [11.4-in] spigot mortar), and others. The Churchill Mark IV (NA 75) began in North Africa as a field experiment, where the 75-mm (2.95–in) gun and mantlet of disabled American M4 Sherman tanks were installed directly into the hull of the Churchill. This proved successful and by the summer of 1944, more than 200 conversions were completed, many of these serving in Italy.

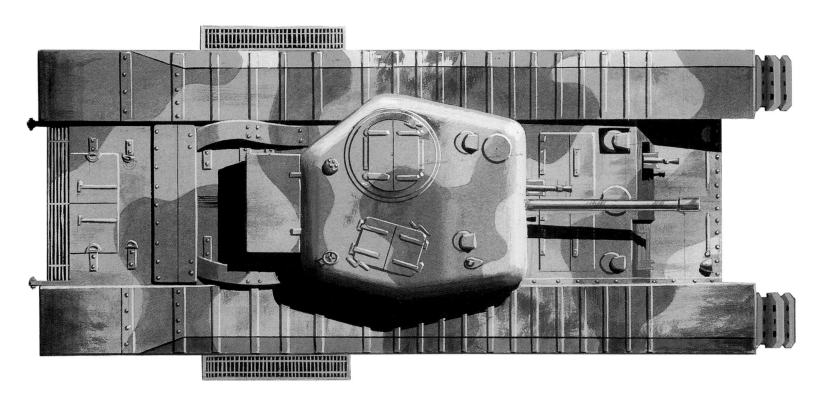

British heavy tanks were developed with the sole intention of supporting infantry in attack. The Churchill was designed to move at the same pace as the soldiers, to cross ground that had been cratered by shells and scarred by trenches, and to climb over other common obstacles.

Undoubtedly, the most enduring legacy of the Infantry Tank Mk IV Churchill is its specialized vehicle role, particularly as it was seen in action during the D-Day invasion of Normandy on 6 June, 1944, and the ensuing campaign in the West. The Churchill served as the platform for numerous such vehicles, including the flamethrower-equipped Crocodile, the Kangaroo personnel carrier, the 290-mm (11.4-in) spigot mortar-carrying AVRE, and the ARK (Armoured Ramp Karrier) bridging tank.

Each of these evolved from a design intended to respond to the unique requirements of trench warfare. Specifications

Close-up

The Churchill Mark IV was based on a post-World War I design which had originally been intended for trench warfare. Poor initial performance nearly ended production but upgrades were promising.

(1) **Turret Extension:** Storage was at a premium, and often extensions or additions of storage bins were added to the exterior.

(2) **All-around Tracks:** The Churchill was known for its lack of speed but all-around tracks and multiple bogeys enhanced platform stability.

(3) **Side Armour:** The Churchill was well known for its distinctive side armour, designed to protect the tracks and wheels.

(4) **Turret Profile:** The distinctive box-like design of the Churchill Mk IV turret did not incorporate sloped armour.

(5) **Main Armament:** The main weapon of the early Churchill was the QF 2-pounder gun. This was upgraded several times including to an American 75-mm (2.95-in) cannon.

(6) **Riveted Construction:** The hull of the early Churchill tanks was of riveted construction, and armour plating was attached with bolts.

An advancing column of Churchill tanks passes a line of Mark 4 Shermans while advancing toward the front line in northwest Europe. The Churchill was produced in great numbers and gave rise to numerous variants.

for the A20 infantry support tank had been undertaken by Harland and Wolff, which created four prototypes by 1940. However, the fall of France made trench warfare unlikely, and a subsequent design, the A22, also known as the Infantry Tank Mark IV, went into production in 1941. In a somewhat confusing progression, the variants of the 34.9-tonne (38.5-ton) Mark IV, later named in honour of Prime Minister Winston Churchill, were labelled with Marks of their own.

INAUSPICIOUS COMBAT DEBUT

Undoubtedly the cross-country capability of the Churchill, facilitated by its multiple-bogeyed, coiled-spring suspension, contributed to its success on the battlefield. However, the combat debut of the Churchill Mark IV was anything but auspicious. During the abortive Dieppe Raid in August 1942, most of the supporting Churchill Mark Is and IIs failed to get off the beach. Mechanical failures, an inadequate powerplant, and initially poor armament due in part to the relatively small size of the turret, added to the misery.

The Churchill had been rushed into service in great haste because of the exigencies of war, and the first 1000 delivered required extensive modifications to bring them up to even minimum viability in the field. Still, the tank proved

excellent in its originally conceived role of infantry support, crossing mountains in North Africa and Italy, and negotiating the rough bocage country in France. Its armour protection, up to 125 mm (4.9 in) in later Marks, also increased survivability. Although the disaster at Dieppe almost led to the early demise of the Churchill, nearly 7400 Marks were built during the course of World War II.

The most notable of these variants were the Mark I, armed with a turret-mounted 2-pounder gun and a 76.2-mm (3-in) howitzer in the chassis; the Mark II, which replaced the limited-functioning howitzer with a hull-mounted 7.92-mm (0.31-in) Besa machine gun (a second machine gun was located in the turret); the Mark III, which was upgunned to the 6-pounder cannon; the Mark IV, which reverted to a cast turret from a welded design and was produced in greater numbers (1622) than any other variant; and the Mark IV NA75, which incorporated the American 75-mm (2.95-in) gun and mantlet. These successive upgrades in armament improved the Churchill's performance in tank-versus-tank combat, a purpose for which it was not originally intended.

Production of the Infantry Tank Mark IV Churchill continued through the end of the war, and in various configurations the tank remained in service until 1952.

M4A4 Sherman

Developed, manufactured, and deployed at great speed, the ubiquitous Medium Tank M4, popularly known as the Sherman, was produced in great numbers. Successfully countering the heavier armour and armament of contemporary German armoured fighting vehicles, the M4 became a symbol of Allied victory.

SILHOUETTE
The high silhouette of the M4 Sherman was protected against direct fire by sloped armour, but its distinct profile presented an inviting target in open country.

ENGINE
While its powerplant was changed in variants, the M4A4 was powered by the 317-kW (425-hp), five-bank Chrysler A57 engine.

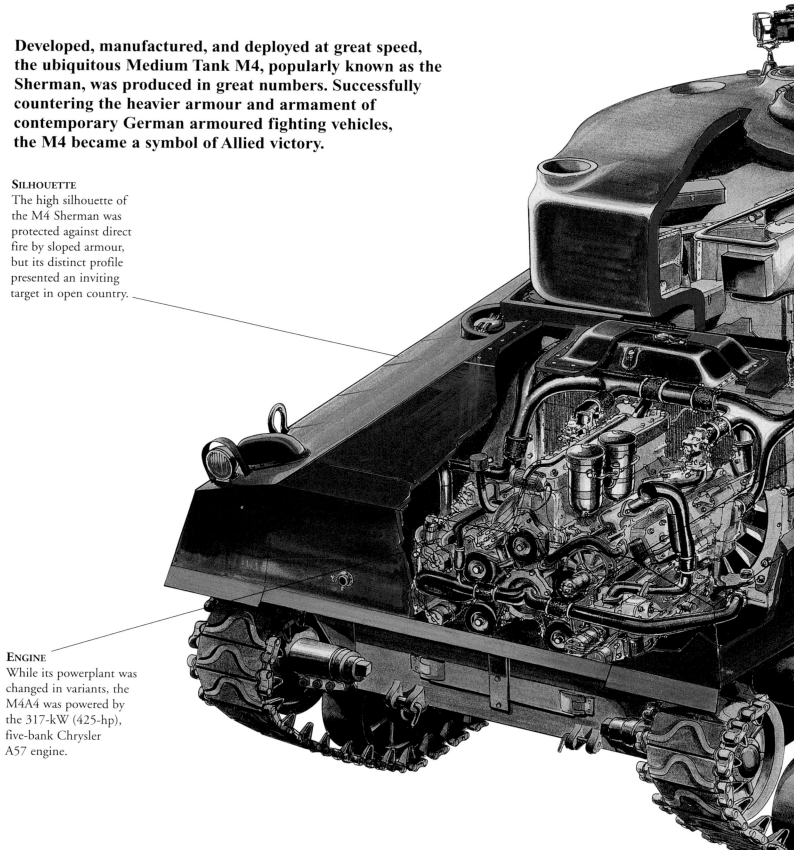

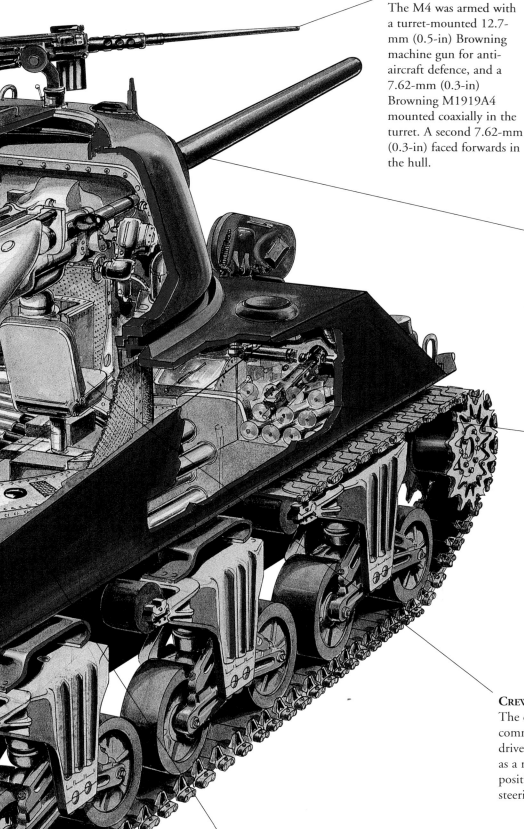

SECONDARY ARMAMENT
The M4 was armed with a turret-mounted 12.7-mm (0.5-in) Browning machine gun for anti-aircraft defence, and a 7.62-mm (0.3-in) Browning M1919A4 mounted coaxially in the turret. A second 7.62-mm (0.3-in) faced forwards in the hull.

MAIN ARMAMENT
The Medium Tank M4 was originally armed with a 75-mm (2.95-in) M3 L/40 cannon, as depicted in the M4A4. Other variants were armed with a 76-mm (3-in) cannon, a 105-mm (4-in) howitzer, and the British QF 17-pounder anti-tank gun.

AMMUNITION STORAGE
The M4 allowed for wet storage of up to 90 rounds of 75-mm (2.95-in) ammunition, reducing the risk of explosion.

CREW
The crew of the M4 Sherman included a commander, ammunition loader, gunner, driver, and an assistant driver who doubled as a machine gunner. The driver was positioned left and forwards, operating two steering levers and foot pedals.

ARMOUR PROTECTION
The M4A4 Sherman's armour protection ranged in thickness from 20 to 85 mm (0.78–3.34 in) in more vulnerable areas.

The M4 was renowned as "the tank that won World War II." The aim of its existence had been to build a tank to correct many of the deficiencies of the M3 mediums but still use as many of the components of the M3 as possible.

M4A4 SHERMAN – SPECIFICATION

Country of Origin: USA
Crew: 5
Designer: U.S. Army Ordnance Department
Designed: 1940
Manufacturer: Detroit Tank Arsenal (Chrysler)
In Production: 1941–50s
In Service: 1942–55
Number Produced: 50,000+
Gross Weight: 31.62 tonnes (34.8 tons)

Dimensions:
Hull Length: 6.06 m (19.8 ft)
Length (gun forward): 6.06 m (19.8 ft)
Width: 2.9 m (9.5 ft)
Overall Height: 2.84 m (9.33 ft)

Performance:
Maximum Speed: 47 km/h (29 mph)
Range, Road: 160 km (100 miles)
Range, Cross-country: 100 km (60 miles)
Ground Pressure: 0.92 kg/cm^2
Fording Capacity: 1.1 m (3.5 ft)
Maximum Gradient: 30 degrees
Maximum Trench Width: 2.44 m (8 ft)
Maximum Vertical Obstacle: 0.6 m (2 ft)
Suspension Type: Vertical volute sprung two-wheel bogies

Engine:
Powerplant: 1 x Chrysler A57 30 cylinder multibank petrol engine
Capacity: 20.5 l (4.5 gallons)
Output: 317 kW (425 hp) @ 2850 rpm
Power/Weight Ratio: 12.2 bhp/tonne
Fuel Capacity: 605 l (133.3 gallons)

Armament and Armour:
Main Armament: 1 x 75-mm (2.95-in) M3 L/40 in M4A4 Mount
Secondary Armament: 2 x 7.62-mm (0.3-in) M1919A4 Browning MG
Ancillary Armament: 12.7-mm (0.5-in) M2HB MG in AA mount
Armour Type: Homogeneous rolled/welded; cast hull, cast turret
Hull Front: 50 mm (2 in)
Hull Sides: 38 mm (1.5 in)
Hull Rear: 38 mm (1.5 in)
Hull Top: 9 mm (0.75 in)
Hull Bottom: 12.5–25 mm (0.5–1 in)
Turret Front: 50–85 mm (2–3.3 in)
Turret Sides: 50 mm (2 in)
Turret Rear: 50 mm (2 in)
Turret Top: 25 mm (1 in)

Variants:
76.2-mm (3-in) Gun Motor Carriage M10: Tank Destroyer.
90-mm (3.54-in) Gun Motor Carriage M36: Tank Destroyer.
105-mm (4-in) Howitzer Motor Carriage M7: Self-propelled artillery (Priest).
155-mm (6-in) Gun Motor Carriage M12: GMC M12 with Cargo Carrier M30.
Flame Tank Sherman: M4A3R3 Zippo, M4 Crocodile, and other flame-throwing Shermans.
Rocket Artillery Sherman: T34 Calliope, T40 Whizbang, and other Sherman rocket launchers.
Amphibious tanks: Duplex Drive (DD) swimming Sherman.
Engineer tanks: Including D-8, M1, and M1A1 dozers, M4 Doozit, Mobile Assault Bridge, and Aunt Jemima.
Recovery tanks: M32 and M74 TRVs.
Artillery tractors: M34 and M35 prime movers.

M4A4 SHERMAN FIREFLY

A multitude of Medium Tank M4 variants were produced during World War II. The distinguishing features of the M4A4 were its Chrysler A57 engine and the modifications to its hull that enabled the tank to accommodate its increased size. The 30-cylinder, five-bank 317-kW (425-hp) Chrysler A57 was introduced on the M4A4 to increase its power. In turn, the welded upper hull, which was used in all Shermans, was lengthened 28 cm (11 in) over other variants. The road wheels on the M4A4 were spaced about 25 cm (10 in) apart, considerably more than the 9 cm (3.5 in) seen on other models. The variant shown here is the M4A4 Sherman Firefly with a 7.62-mm (0.3-in) gun.

Illustrating the sheer weight of numbers that tipped the balance of armoured warfare in favour of the Allies during World War II, a formation of M4A4 Sherman tanks are seen here coming to a halt in the desert.

The Sherman proved to be an excellent fighting platform and went on to be constructed in the thousands. It suffered a wide range of drawbacks but, ultimately, the numerical superiority of the M4 made it a war winner.

An icon of the Allied victory in World War II, the Medium Tank M4, nicknamed Sherman by the British who used it in large numbers through Lend Lease, was built in greater quantity than any other Allied tank except the Soviet T-34. Even as its predecessor, the M3, was on American assembly lines and deploying to the battlefields of North Africa, the M4 was hurriedly being developed. By September 1941, the prototype, designated T6, was completed.

The Sherman made its combat debut with British forces during the pivotal Battle of El Alamein in October 1942 and easily withstood the onslaughts of earlier German armour, like the PzKpfw III and IV. However, with the introduction of the heavier Panther and Tiger tanks, the pronounced shortcomings of the Sherman became apparent. Its main gun, the 75-mm (2.95-in) M3 L/40, was woefully inadequate against the heavy armour of the later German tanks, while the high-velocity German guns were capable of penetrating the Sherman's armour at distances of a mile or more.

STRENGTH IN NUMBERS

In combat, a platoon of four Shermans would often be required to take on a single Tiger tank, and losses were a virtual certainty. However, the might of American industry, which churned out nearly 50,000 Shermans through numerous manufacturers during the war years, made good on the heavy losses. This enabled the Allied Shermans to overwhelm their enemy numerically. If the Sherman had a tactical advantage, it was its maximum road speed of 47 km/h (29 mph) and manoeuvrability.

The primary variants of the M4 included the M4A1, M4A2, M4A3, and M4A4, distinguished mainly by their varying powerplants. Some later models were equipped with a larger turret and a high-velocity 76-mm (3-in) gun. The British substituted the QF 17-pounder anti-tank gun on top of the M4A4 chassis to create a more powerful variant called the Firefly. Some M4s were also upgunned with a 105-mm (4-in) howitzer. The various designations did not necessarily indicate improvements over time, but often modifications in concurrent production models.

The M4A4 hull was lengthened to accommodate its Chrysler A57 engine. Other engines included the 263 kW (353 hp) Wright Whirlwind, 298-kW (400-hp) Continental R975, 335-kW (450-hp) Caterpillar 9-cylinder diesel, 313-kW (420-hp) General Motors 6-71 diesel, and 372-kW (500-hp) Ford GAA III. The M4A1 hull was fully cast, and not simply a combination of cast and welded construction, while the vertical volute spring suspension was replaced with a horizontal configuration on the M4A3.

During World War II, the M4 chassis was modified to perform a number of functions, such as a flail tank for clearing mines, rocket launcher, ammunition carrier, bulldozer, recovery vehicle, and flamethrower. Perhaps the most famous of these variants was the DD (Duplex Drive) tank. This had a canvas screen for flotation and was intended to provide fire support for Allied troops directly on the invasion beaches during the D-Day landings on 6 June, 1944. The Sherman was also deployed in the Pacific and outclassed any armour the Japanese fielded.

The Medium Tank M4 Sherman was arguably one of the most significant weapons of World War II. Despite its shortcomings, it enabled the Allies to win the war.

Interior view

The M4A4 Sherman tank was fast and manoeuvrable, though its armour protection was inadequate against high-calibre German shells. Its interior was functional but felt compact with a crew of five.

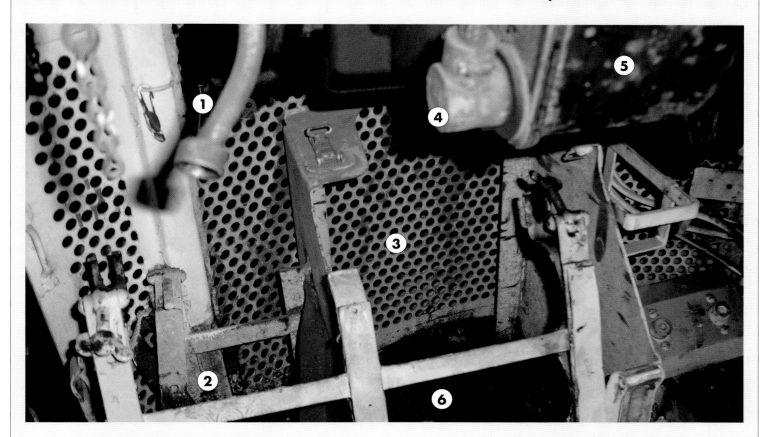

(1) **Electrical Circuitry:** Internally, the M4A4 Sherman relied largely on electricity in order to function.

(2) **Ammunition Storage:** High-explosive and armour-piercing shells were stored near the 75-mm (2.95-in) cannon and also in "wet" storage areas within the hull.

(3) **Mesh Screen:** Operational areas within the M4A4 Sherman were separated by mesh screens. This avoided obstruction during combat but allowed efficient communication.

(4) **Air Cleaner:** An air-cleaning apparatus was connected to the engine and located at the rear of the crew compartment.

(5) **Engine Access:** The 317-kW (425-hp) five-bank Chrysler A57 engine produced a maximum road speed of 47 km/h (29 mph).

(6) **Crew Compartment:** The five-man crew of the M4A4 Sherman tank included three in the turret and crew compartment with a driver and assistant driver/machine gunner forwards in the hull.

PzKpfw V Panther

The capture of a Soviet T-34 medium tank on the Eastern Front led directly to the development of the German Panzerkampfwagen V Panther, which incorporated a number of the design elements of the T-34 and became an exceptional armoured weapon in its own right.

MAIN ARMAMENT
The primary weapon mounted by the Panzerkampfwagen V Panther was the 75-mm (2.95-in) KwK 42 L/70 high-velocity cannon manufactured by Rheinmetall-Borsig.

ARMOUR PROTECTION
The Panther's frontal armour was up to 80 mm (3.2 in) thick. Its 55-degree slope effectively increased the protection afforded the five-man crew. Side armour, which varied from 40 mm (1.6 in) to 50 mm (2 in), could be considered a defensive weakness.

AMMUNITION STORAGE
No ammunition was stored in the Panther's turret. However, up to 48 rounds of 75-mm (2.95-in) ammunition were carried in sponsons on either side of the hull.

TURRET

The Panther tank incorporated an existing three-man turret design that underwent several modifications. Later versions included a cast commander's cupola rather than an early drum-like configuration and a bracket for an MG 34 anti-aircraft machine gun.

F A C T S

- The high-velocity 75-mm (2.95-in) cannon gave the Panther a main armament which was initially superior to most Allied guns.

- Daimler-Benz and Maschinenfabrik Augsburg-Nürnberg AG (MAN) competed for the contract to manufacture the Panther.

- The debut of the Panther at the Battle of Kursk was inauspicious because of mechanical failures.

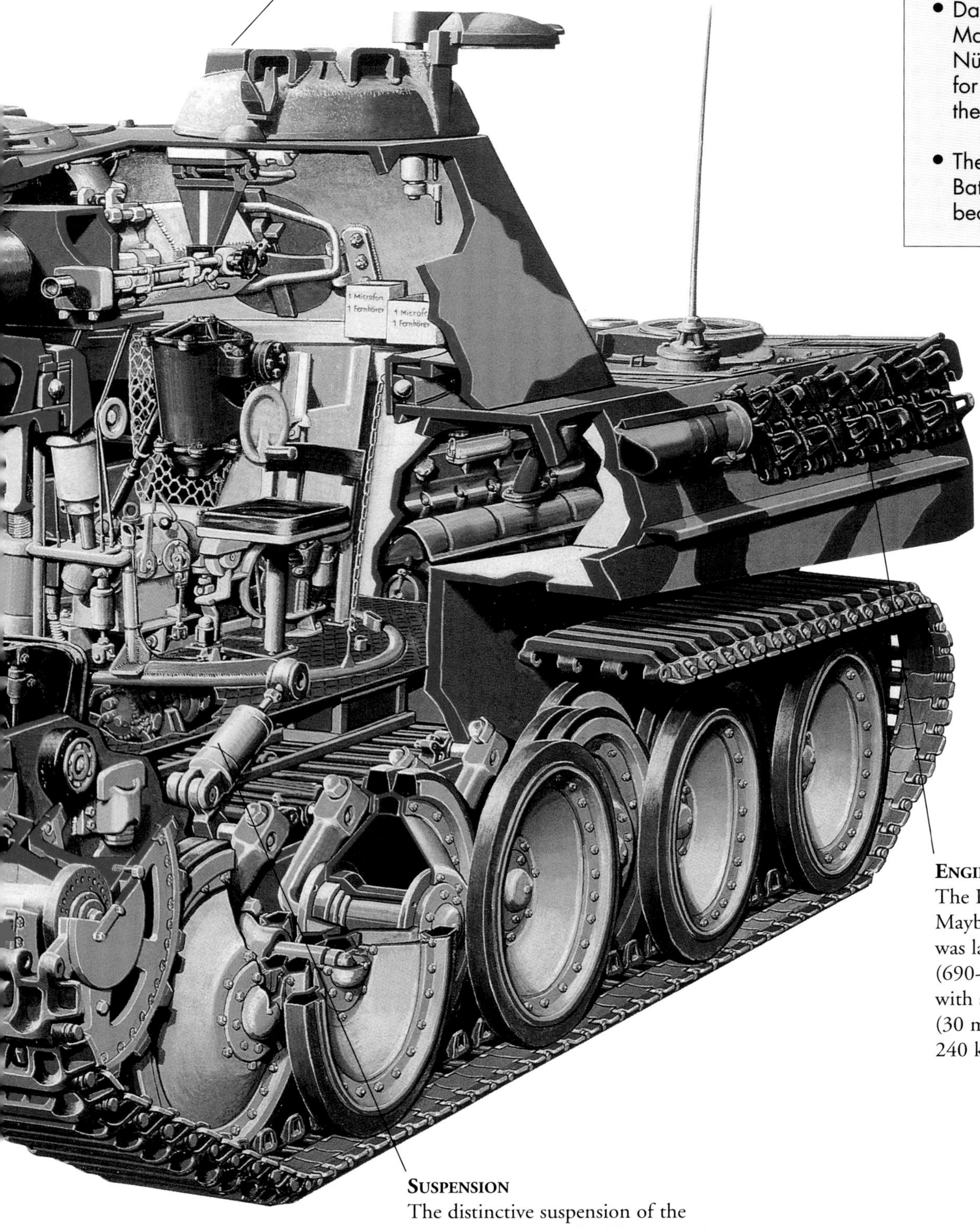

ENGINE

The Panther's 485-kW (650-hp) Maybach HL 210 P 45 petrol engine was later improved to a 514.5-kW (690-hp) V-12 Maybach HL230 P30 with a top speed in excess of 48 km/h (30 mph) and a range of more than 240 km (150 miles).

SUSPENSION

The distinctive suspension of the Panther included a double torsion bar arrangement with interwoven road wheels. This allowed the vehicle to traverse difficult terrain more easily. Wide tracks offered greater stability.

The Panther was sent to frontline units in the spring of 1943 and first saw major combat at Kursk. With the correction of the production-related mechanical difficulties, the Panther became highly popular with German tankers and a fearsome weapon on the battlefield.

PZKPFW V PANTHER AUSF A – SPECIFICATION

Country of Origin: Germany
Crew: 5
Designer: MAN AG
Designed: 1942
In Service: 1943–45
Manufacturers: MAN, Daimler-Benz, Maschinenfabrik Niedersachsen-Hannover (MNH), Henschel & Sohn
Number Built: 6000
Produced: 1942–45
Gross Weight: 45.5 tonnes (50.1 tons)

Dimensions:
Hull Length: 6.9 m (22.6 ft)
Length (gun forward): 8.86 m (29 ft)
Width: 3.27 m (10.75 ft)
Width (with skirts): 3.42 m (11.25 ft)
Overall Height: 3 m (9.9 ft)

Performance:
Maximum Speed: 48 km/h (30 mph)
Range, Road: 200 km (120 miles)
Range, Cross-country: 100 km (60 miles)
Ground Pressure: 0.75 kg/cm^2
Fording Capacity: 1.9 m (6.2 ft)
Maximum Gradient: 36 degrees
Maximum Trench Width: 2.45 m (8 ft)
Maximum Vertical Obstacle: 0.9 m (3 ft)
Suspension Type: Torsion bar

Engine:
Powerplant: 1 x Maybach HL230 P30 V-12 water-cooled petrol engine
Capacity: 23 l (5 gallons)

Output: 690 hp (514.5 kW) @ 3000 rpm
Power/Weight Ratio: 15.5 bhp/tonne
Fuel Capacity: 730 l (160.6 gallons)

Armour and Armament:
Armour Type: Homogenous rolled/welded nickel-steel
Hull Front: 50–80 mm (2–3.2 in)
Hull Sides: 40–50 mm (1.6–2 in)
Hull Rear: 40 mm (1.6 in)
Hull Top: 16 mm (0.6 in)
Hull Bottom: 16 mm (0.6 in)
Turret Front: 100 mm (4 in)
Turret Sides: 45 mm (1.8 in)
Turret Rear: 45 mm (1.8 in)
Turret Top: 16 mm (0.6 in)
Main Armament: 1 x 75-mm (2.95-in) KwK42 L/70. 82 rounds.
Secondary Armament: 2 x 7.92-mm (0.31-in) MG34 machine guns. 4800 rounds.
Ancillary Armament: 92-mm (3.6-in) bomb/grenade launcher

Derived Vehicles:
Jagdpanther: Heavy tank destroyer with the 88-mm (3.45-in) L/71 gun.
Befehlspanzer Panther: Command tank with additional radio equipment.
Beobachtungspanzer Panther: Observation tank for artillery spotters; dummy gun; armed with only two MG34.
Bergepanther: Armoured recovery vehicle.

PZKPFW V PANTHER AUSF D

In the summer of 1942, the Panzerkampfwagen V medium tank, known popularly as the Panther, was rushed into production to counter the superiority of the Soviet-made T-34 on the Eastern Front. The Panther design included several elements of the T-34, such as sloping armour and wider road wheels. Incorporating an existing turret design, the Panther mounted a high-velocity 75-mm (2.95-in) L/70 cannon, which was capable of penetrating up to 150 mm (6 in) of armour at a distance of 1000 m (3280 ft). Unlike the cramped turret of the T-34, the Panther turret accommodated three crewmen and provided for better command and control in battle. The Ausf D variant is shown here.

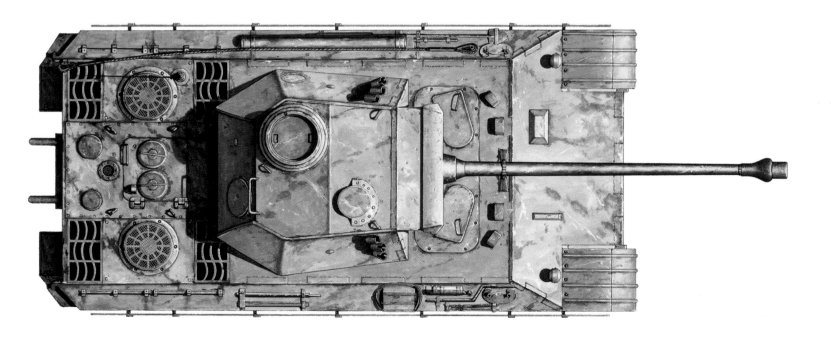

To destroy a Panther, a tank destroyer with a 76-mm (3-in) gun would have to aim for the side or rear of the turret (the opening through which the hull-mounted machine gun projected), or target the underside of the gun shield.

In one single day of combat in late July 1944, SS Oberscharführer (Technical Sergeant) Ernst Barkmann wrote the most famous chapter of his combat career on the Western Front. Near the French village of Le Lorey, Barkmann placed his Panther medium tank among a thick stand of oak trees and waited for an advancing Allied armoured formation.

As a column of 15 American Sherman tanks came into view, the lone Panther quickly knocked out the two leading vehicles as well as a tanker truck attached to the column. Barkmann then hit and disabled two more Shermans

Interior view

The turret of the Panther tank was adapted from a previous design and improved in later variants. Its distinctively sloped armour is apparent from the interior, yet the space accommodated three crewmen.

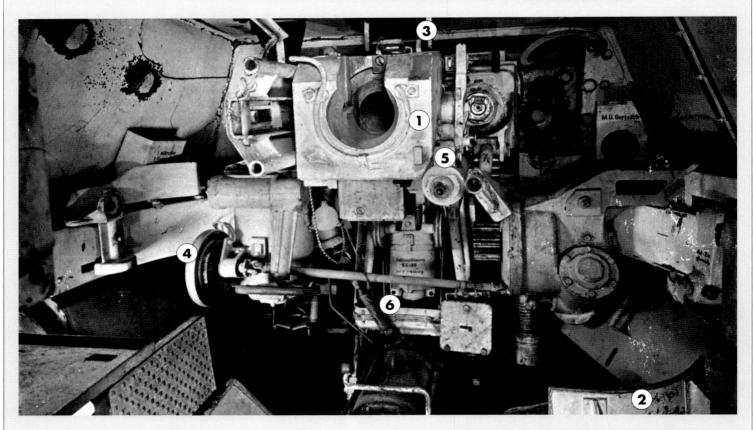

① **Breech Block:** The breech block of the 75-mm (2.9-in) cannon dominates this image of the turret interior. Its high muzzle velocity made an effective long-range weapon.

② **Loader's Seat:** The loader sat to the right of the breech block, able to supply 75-mm (2.9-in) ammunition easily within reach.

③ **Turret Hatch:** Access to and from the Panther's turret was easily accomplished through a hatch mounted on the roof.

④ **Traversing Gear:** The manual traversing gear was used to operate the turret of the PzKpfw V in the event of an electrical failure or damage sustained in battle.

⑤ **Sighting and Recoil Equipment:** Recoil and sighting mechanisms were utilized to visually acquire a target.

⑥ **Elevation Apparatus:** The Panther's 75-mm (2.9-in) L70 cannon was raised or lowered using powered or manual controls.

A column of Panther tanks rolls towards the front during bitter winter fighting. Early Panthers were plagued by mechanical and design flaws yet, ultimately, the PzKpfw V responded ferociously to the Soviet T-34.

attempting to skirt around the wreckage of the earlier victims. As the Americans regrouped, they called for tactical air support, and the Panther was damaged during the ensuing attack. Still, Barkmann defended his ground, knocking out two further Shermans as they closed in. Finally, he was able to coax his damaged tank to safety in the town of Neufbourg.

Against long odds, Barkmann had destroyed nine Sherman tanks and several support vehicles. For this and other exploits in combat, the leading Panther ace of the war received the Knight's Cross of the Iron Cross. He also further enhanced the reputation of the Panzerkampfwagen V Panther as a rugged and formidable foe.

Although the Panther earned a fearsome reputation, the swiftness of its development and deployment resulted in numerous mechanical failures, particularly during the Battle of Kursk. General Heinz Guderian, a famed panzer commander, further stated, "They burnt too easily, the fuel and oil systems were insufficiently protected, and the crews were lost due to lack of training."

RAPID MATURITY

Nevertheless, the Panther's superb long-barrelled 75-mm (2.95-in) cannon and its overall design fostered the development of the tank into one of the finest fighting vehicles of World War II. Following a design competition, which was fought principally between Daimler-Benz and Maschinenfabrik Augsburg Nürnberg (MAN), the MAN design was placed in production. In the summer of 1942, MAN produced two prototypes, and a small production run of only 20 tanks was supplanted by the Ausf D, approximately 250 of which entered service beginning in January 1943. It was this version that took part in the Battle of Kursk. A number of these broke down or were lost because of problems with the transmission or suspension and there were even engine compartment fires. A further 850 improved Ausf D models, with larger engines and redesigned turrets and armour skirts, were manufactured until September 1943.

AUSF G

Curiously designated Ausf A, another variant was placed in production in August 1943, and during the following 10 months more than 2100 were manufactured by MAN, Henschel, Daimler-Benz, and Demag. However, the greatest production version of the Panther was the Ausf G, which incorporated several improvements to the exhaust system, tapered armour on the upper hull, and a rotating driver's periscope. Starting in the spring of 1944 until the end of the war, production of the Ausf G neared 3000 tanks.

PzKpfw VI Tiger

Perhaps the most famous tank of World War II, the Tiger epitomized the German penchant for quality over quantity. Its engineering requirements and high cost precluded the Tiger from being produced in large numbers. However, the prowess of the Tiger on the battlefield was incontestable.

MAIN ARMAMENT
The formidable 88-mm (3.5-in) KwK 36 L/56 cannon, modified to fit the Tiger turret, had already proven itself in the anti-aircraft and anti-tank roles. Complemented with precision optics, its flat trajectory and range were deadly to enemy tanks.

ARMOUR PROTECTION
The frontal hull and turret armour of the Tiger, at 100 mm (4 in) and 120 mm (4.8 in) respectively, were substantially thicker than those of the PzKpfw IV.

MOBILITY
The twin radius steering system, hydraulically controlled pre-selector gearbox, and semi-automatic transmission were state of the art but prone to mechanical difficulties.

SUSPENSION
The torsion bar suspension of the Tiger was divided equally with eight bars on each side, while its interwoven wheels proved problematic in the field.

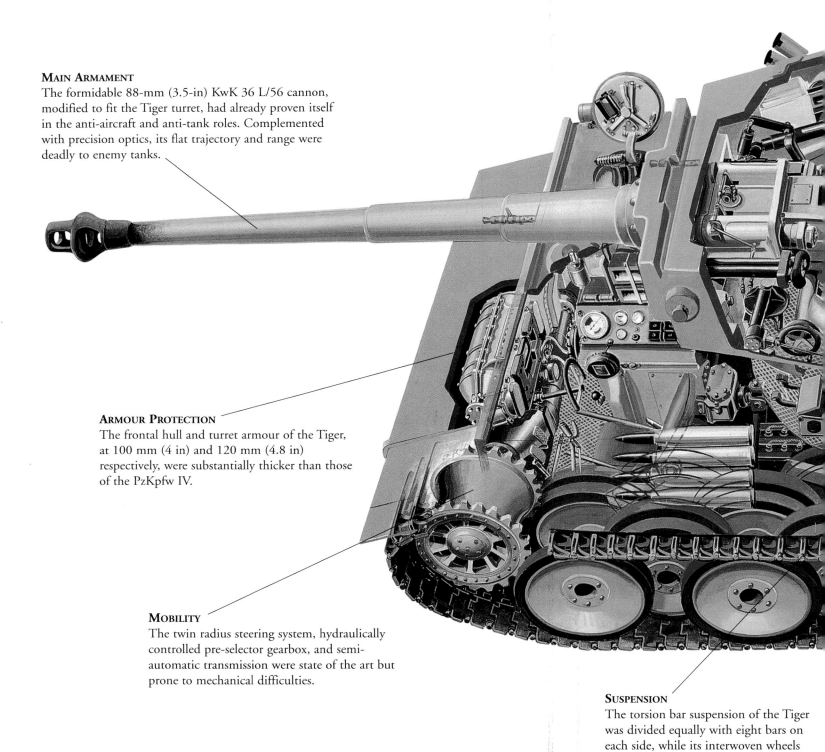

TURRET
With a 360-degree circular floor, the turret of the Tiger tank weighed 9.9 tonnes (11 tons). The gunner sat to the left with the commander at his rear, and the loader occupying a folding seat.

FACTS

- Only 1347 Tigers were produced between 1942 and 1944, while lighter Allied tanks were manufactured in great quantity.

- Following a demonstration on Hitler's birthday, Henschel received the contract for the Tiger.

- The cost to build a Tiger was twice that of the PzKpfw IV.

CREW COMPARTMENT
The driver and radio operator were situated to the left and right of the large gearbox respectively.

ENGINE
After 250 Tigers were produced, the original 479-kW (642-hp), 12-cylinder Maybach HL 210 P45 engine was deemed inadequate for the 52-tonne (57-ton) behemoth and replaced by the 514.5-kW (690-hp) V-12 HL 230 P45.

With five men in a very small area, the interior of the Tiger was somewhat dark and fairly cramped. In addition to that, the crewmen had to make room for at least 92 of the big gun's 88-mm (3.5-in) shells.

TIGER – SPECIFICATION

Country of Origin: Germany
Crew: 5
Designer: Henschel & Son
Designed: 1942
In Service: 1942–45
Manufacturer: Henschel
Number Built: 1347
Produced: 1942–44
Gross Weight: 52 tonnes (57 tons)

Dimensions:
Hull Length: 6.32 m (20.75 ft)
Length (gun forward): 8.46 m (27.75 ft)
Width: 3.73 m (12.25 ft)
Overall Height: 2.9 m (9.5 ft)

Performance:
Maximum Speed:
  Max speed 1st gear 2.8 km/h (1.8 mph)
  Max speed 2nd gear 4.3 km/h (2.7 mph)
  Max speed 3rd gear 6.2 km/h (3.8 mph)
  Max speed 4th gear 9.2 km/h (5.7 mph)
  Max speed 5th gear 14.1 km/h (8.7 mph)
  Max speed 6th gear 20.9 km/h (13 mph)
  Max speed 7th gear 30.5 km/h (18.9 mph)
  Max speed 8th gear 45.4 km/h (28 mph)
  Max speed 1st reverse gear 2.8 km/h (1.8 mph)
  Max speed 2nd reverse gear 4.3 km/h (2.7 mph)
  Max speed 3rd reverse gear 6.2 km/h (3.8 mph)
  Max speed 4th reverse gear 9.2 km/h (5.7 mph)
Range, Road: 195 km (120 miles)
Range, Cross-country: 110 km (65 miles)
Power/Weight Ratio: 12.3 bhp/tonne

Ground Pressure: 0.074 kg/cm²
Fording Capacity: 1.6 m (3.3 ft)
Maximum Gradient: 36 degrees
Maximum Trench Width: 2.3 m (7.55 ft)
Maximum Vertical Obstacle: 0.8 m (2.6 ft)
Suspension Type: Torsion bar

Engine:
Powerplant: 1 x Maybach HL230P45 V-12 water-cooled
  petrol engine
Capacity: 23 l (5.1 gallons)
Output: 479 kW (642 bhp) @ 3000 rpm
Fuel Capacity: 540 l (119 gallons)

Armour and Armament:
Armour Type: Homogeneous rolled/welded nickel steel
Hull Front: 100 mm (4 in)
Hull Sides: 60–80 mm (2.4–3.32 in)
Hull Rear: 80 mm (3.2 in)
Hull Top: 25 mm (1 in)
Hull Bottom: 5 mm (0.2 in)
Turret Front: 100–120 mm (4–4.8 in)
Turret Sides: 80 mm (3.2 in)
Turret Rear: 80 mm (3.2 in)
Turret Top: 25 m (1 in)
Main Armament: 1 x 88-mM (3.05-in) KwK 36 L/56
Secondary Armament: 2 x 7.92-mm (0.31-in) MG34
  machine guns
Ancillary Armament: Grenade/bomb launchers

TIGER

Both Henschel and Porsche submitted prototype designs for the Tiger, and in August 1942, Henschel began production of the 52-tonne (57-ton) tank. Although its capabilities as a fighting vehicle were readily apparent, the Tiger was placed in service following limited trials because of time constraints, while numerous design innovations made production slow and costly and created performance issues in the field. The Tiger's low clearance restricted manoeuvrability in rugged terrain, and its overlapping wheel configuration was difficult to maintain and prone to break down because of icing, heavy mud, or rocks lodging between components. The tank's heavy weight made it a tremendous task to transport it by rail or to tow and recover a damaged Tiger.

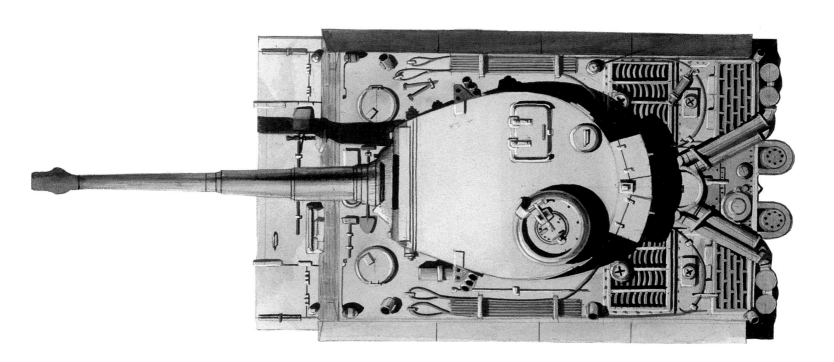

"I had no time to assemble my company; instead I had to act quickly, as I had to assume that the enemy had already spotted me. I set off with one tank and passed the order to the others not to retreat."

On 13 July, 1944, SS Hauptsturmführer (Captain) Michael Wittmann rolled forwards in his Tiger, engaging a column of the British 7th Armoured Division in the French town of Villers-Bocage. Within minutes, his Tiger had wreaked havoc and, by the time other tanks of his SS Heavy Panzer Battalion 101 had finished their work, at least 13 British tanks, two anti-tank guns, and up to 15 troop carriers and support vehicles had been destroyed. Accounts of the action at Villers-Bocage vary, but the conclusion is obvious. As a fighting vehicle, the Tiger was supreme on the battlefields of World War II.

Interior view

The interior of the Tiger tank included several notable revisions from earlier German tank designs, including a reorientation of the famed 88-mm (3.5-in) multi-purpose cannon to fit within the turret.

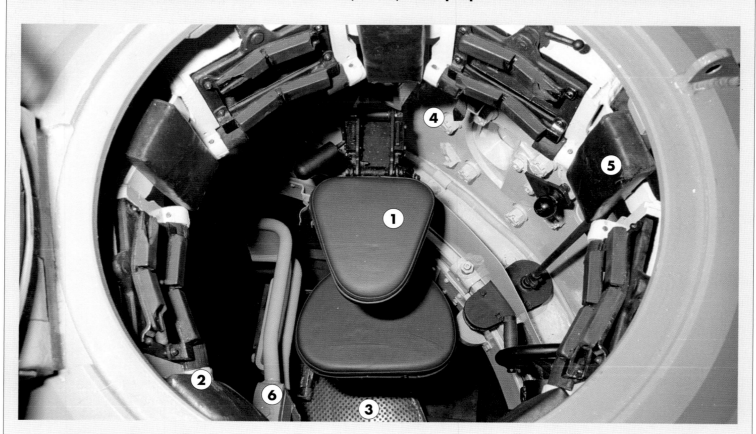

1. **Commander's Seat:** The commander's seat, which folded to allow extra space during combat operations, was located on the left side of the 88-mm (3.5-in) cannon breech.

2. **Ammunition Storage:** 92 rounds of armour-piercing and high-explosive 88-mm (3.5-in) shells were stored beneath the turret floor and passed to the loader as needed.

3. **Turret Basket:** The 360 degree circular floor of the Tiger's 9.9-tonne (11-ton) turret had only cramped space for three crewmen.

4. **Armour Plating:** Heavy armour protection throughout the vehicle made the Tiger virtually impervious to most ordnance.

5. **Optical and Communications Equipment:** The commander of the Tiger tank used advanced optics and communications equipment to acquire targets.

6. **Weapon Configuration:** The bulk of the 88-mm (3.5-in) cannon took up a great deal of space within the turret, protruding to the rear of the compartment.

Covered with anti-mine Zimmerit paste, a Tiger tank pauses on a dirt road on the Western Front. Two crewmen have emerged from their hatches. The main drawback of this powerful tank was that there were never enough of them for the German army to deploy.

Among Allied troops, the Tiger, first deployed in North Africa in late 1942, gained a fearsome reputation. To many British and American soldiers, every German tank they observed on the battlefield was thought to be a Tiger. Allied tank crewmen respected the Tiger as well. "All you saw in your imagination was the muzzle of an 88 behind each leaf," recalled British tank commander Andrew Wilson.

VIRTUALLY UNBEATABLE

The mere presence of the Henschel-designed Tiger tank could alter the course of a battle. It is estimated that the Tiger achieved a kill ratio approaching six to one against Allied tanks. Its 88-mm (3.5-in) cannon, with a muzzle velocity of up to 930 m (3051 ft) per second, could penetrate the frontal armour of an U.S. Sherman or British Churchill IV tank at a distance of more than a mile and the Soviet T-34 at slightly closer range. Its zeiss optics, improved steering and transmission, and heavier armour protection were a huge leap forward in tank design. Favouring firepower and armour over manoeuvrability, the Tiger was virtually unbeatable in single combat on suitable terrain in ideal weather conditions, but rarely were such circumstances assured.

For all its combat capabilities, particularly in the hands of a seasoned commander, the Tiger suffered from numerous mechanical problems, particularly with its overlapping wheels and suspension system, and an initially inadequate powerplant. Its sheer weight made transport, deployment, and routine maintenance challenging. Rushed into production, the Tiger was put through its paces during trials in a cursory manner at best. Further, the complexity of the vehicle resulted in prohibitive cost per unit, roughly equal to that of four PzKpfw III assault guns. Limited production capability meant that slightly fewer than 1350 were built before production ceased in 1944 in favour of the Tiger II. In contrast, more than 40,000 U.S. Sherman tanks and nearly 60,000 Soviet T-34s were produced in that time period.

In addition to Wittmann – a holder of the Knights Cross with Oak Leaves and Swords who was killed in action two months after his stand at Villers-Bocage – numerous Tiger tank commanders racked up impressive scores of enemy vehicles destroyed. At least a dozen claimed to have more than 100 kills. Considering that it was rarely available in large numbers, the combat record of the Tiger tank is all the more impressive and deservedly legendary.

A27M Cromwell Mark VIII

Combining speed, armament, and armour protection, this was the best all-around British-designed battle tank in service in 1943. The Cromwell was intended to replace the outmoded Crusader, and represented a great leap forward in British tank development.

TURRET
The box-like turret of the Cromwell accommodated three crew – the commander, gunner, and loader – while the driver and co-driver occupied positions in the hull.

ENGINE
The 447-kW (600-hp) Rolls Royce Meteor V-12 engine powered the A27M Cromwell Mark VIII, improving performance significantly over the Liberty engine in the related Centaur. With a top speed of 61 km/h (38 mph), the Cromwell was the fastest of the British tanks.

SUSPENSION
The proven Christie suspension provided the basis for the good cross-country characteristics of the Cromwell chassis.

PERISCOPES
The Cromwell's commander, driver, co-driver, and gunner were provided with periscopes but had only a limited view of the terrain ahead.

MAIN ARMAMENT
The QF 75-mm (2.95-in) cannon was deadly against enemy troop concentrations. It replaced the 6-pounder mounted on earlier Cromwells, in spite of the fact that the 6-pounder had been considered more effective against enemy armour.

SECONDARY ARMAMENT
Two 7.92-mm (0.31-in) Besa machine guns, mounted in the turret and the hull, provided defence against enemy infantry.

ARMOUR PROTECTION
Initially, the Cromwell's armour protection ranged from 8 mm to 76 mm (0.31–3 in). In later Marks, however, areas that were especially vulnerable to enemy fire were augmented with welded plates up to 102 mm (4 in) thick.

TRACKS
Wide, reliable tracks gave the Cromwell added stability and facilitated rapid manoeuvre across country.

FACTS

- More than 4000 Cromwell variants were built during World War II.

- The Cromwell was the predecessor of the Comet, the last British-designed tank to see action in the war.

- Only the British 7th Armoured Division was fully equipped with the Cromwell.

Perhaps the principal value of the Cromwell to the British armoured regiments during 1943 was as a training tank: at last the troops had a tank that was something of a match for its German counterparts.

A27M CROMWELL MARK VIII – SPECIFICATION

Country of Origin: United Kingdom
Crew: 5
Designer: Leyland, then Birmingham Railway Carriage and Wagon Company
Designed: 1941
Manufacturer: Nuffield Organisation
Number Built: 4016
In Service: 1943–50
Weight: 28 tonnes (31 tons)

Dimensions:
Length: 6.35 m (20 ft 10 in)
Width: 2.908 m (9 ft 6 in)
Height: 2.832 m (9 ft 3 in)

Performance:
Max Speed: 61 km/h (38 mph)
Range, Road: 270 km (170 miles)
Range, Cross-country: 129 km (80 miles)
Fording: 1.22 m (4 ft)
Vertical Obstacle: 0.91 m (3 ft)
Trench: 2.29 m (7 ft 6 in)

Engine:
Powerplant: 1 x Rolls Royce Meteor V12 petrol 447 kW (600 bhp)
Power/weight: 203 kW (21.4 hp)/tonne
Suspension: Improved Christie
Fuel Capacity: 416 l (110 gallons)

Armour and Armament:
Armour Type: Homogeneous rolled and riveted/welded nickel-steel

Hull Front: 100 mm (3.98 in)
Hull Sides: 32 mm (1.25 in)
Hull Rear: 32 mm (1.25 in)
Hull Top: 19 mm (0.75 in)
Hull Bottom: 7–10 mm (0.25–0.4 in)
Turret Front: 76 mm (3 in)
Turret Sides: 63 mm (2.5 in)
Turret Rear: 57 mm (2.25 in)
Turret Top: 19 mm (0.75 in)

Primary armament: 1 x OQF 75 mm (2.95 in) with 64 rounds
Secondary Armament: 2 x 7.92-mm (0.31-in) Besa machine gun

Variants
Cromwell I: Meteor engine. Only 357 produced.
Cromwell II: Increased track width and removal of the hull machine gun to increase stowage. None produced.
Cromwell III: Centaur I upgraded with Meteor V12 engine. Only about 200 produced due to scarcity of Centaur Is.
Cromwell IV: Centaur III upgraded with Meteor engine. The most numerous variant with more than 1935 units produced.
Cromwell IVw: Meteor engine, and all-welded hull.
Cromwell Vw: Cromwell built from the start with the 75-mm (2.95-in) gun. Used a welded instead of riveted hull.
Cromwell VI: Cromwell armed with 95-mm (3.74-in) howitzer. 341 produced.
Cromwell VII: Cromwell IV and V upgraded with additional armour, wider tracks, and additional gearbox. 1500 produced.
Cromwell VIIw: Cromwell Vw reworked to Cromwell VII standard.
Cromwell VIII: Cromwell VI with same upgrades as VII.

A27M CROMWELL MARK VII

Replacing the obsolete Crusader, the A27 Cromwell advanced British tank design substantially, combining the elements of speed, increased armament, improved armour, and reliability to the greatest extent yet seen by the time it reached full production in the autumn of 1942. Nonetheless, its armoured protection and main weapon were still inferior to those of most front-line German tanks. Early versions of the Cromwell were armed with the QF 6-pounder (57-mm) cannon, while later versions were upgunned to the British QF 75 mm (2.95 in). The Cromwell Mark VI, shown, mounted a 95-mm (3.74-in) howitzer, and nearly 350 of this variant were built.

Early cruiser designs had highlighted the drawbacks of producing a lightly armed and armoured main battle tank, which continued to be used even when a replacement for the Crusader was being sought. Finally, it seems the British began to realize that more armour and a bigger gun were essential.

Throughout World War II, British armoured doctrine differed from that of most other combatants. Light tanks were used for reconnaissance, while heavy tanks supported infantry, and the medium, or "cruiser," tanks were actually envisioned as combat tanks capable of taking on enemy armour. It was here that such armoured theory fell furthest short.

Early British cruiser tanks were inferior to German armour in tank-versus-tank action, as was shown on a limited basis in north-west Europe in 1940 and emphatically in the deserts of North Africa. As it grew more and more apparent that a replacement for the outclassed Crusader was needed,

Interior view

The Cromwell tank replaced the obsolescent Crusader at the height of World War II. Combining speed, firepower, and armour protection, it was the best all-around tank built by the British up to that time.

1. **Breech Block:** The breech block of the QF 75-mm (2.95-in) cannon rests within the Cromwell turret.

2. **Ammunition Storage:** Shells for the 75-mm (2.95-in) cannon were often stored in close proximity to the weapon and within easy reach of the loader.

3. **Turret Basket:** The floor of the turret rotated with the turret in traverse and provided the loader and gunner with clearance to operate the 75-mm (2.95-in) weapon.

4. **Circuitry:** Electrical circuitry connected to a traversing motor enabled the turret to rotate in a 360-degree arc.

5. **Support Structure:** The weight of the heavy QF 75-mm (2.95-in) cannon needed structural support within the turret in order to stabilize the weapon and improve accuracy.

6. **Turret armour:** The Cromwell tank was protected by armour plating from 8–76 mm (0.31–3 in) thick. The turret armour was characterized by pronounced rivets.

A British Cromwell tank grinds to a halt on the desert sands of North Africa. The Cromwell did signal an improvement in overall British tank design. In overall performance, however, it fell short of contemporary German opponents.

specifications for a new cruiser design were issued in 1941. By 1943, two primary candidates had been selected. Heavier armament and armoured protection were prerequisites, so the A27L Centaur, built by Leyland and equipped with the Liberty engine, gave way to the A27M Cromwell, which was fitted with a powerplant based on the legendary Rolls Royce Merlin aircraft engine. Known as the Meteor, this engine was a 447 kW (600 hp), V-12 configuration. This adjustment virtually doubled the performance of the Liberty.

MANUFACTURE

Several companies, including Leyland, Morris Motors, LMS Railway, Birmingham Railway Carriage and Wagon Company, English Electric, and Metro-Cammell, contributed to the manufacture of the A27M Cruiser Tank Cromwell Mark VIII, and more than 4000 rolled off assembly lines by the end of World War II. Some conflicting reports exist raising questions as to whether a portion of these started off as Centaur models that were later converted to Cromwells or were manufactured as the Cromwell from start to finish.

For its part, the Cromwell served as a bridge between the outdated Crusader and the improved Comet, which was the last British-designed tank introduced to combat during the war. The Cromwell provided for increased armour protection, at 8–76 mm (0.31–3 in) over more exposed areas, and this

was later increased 102 mm (4 in) with welded plates. Further, it offered a better-performing main armament in the QF 6-pounder (57 mm) and later the 75-mm (2.95-in) cannon. Perhaps most notable, the Cromwell was speedy and manoeuvrable, known for rugged reliability, and popular with those who served as crew.

CROMWELL VARIANTS

As the war progressed, as many as 10 variants of the original A27M Cromwell Mark VIII were produced, often incorporating such design changes as welded rather than riveted hull or turret construction. More than 340 Cromwell Mark VI tanks were produced with a heavy 95-mm (3.74-in) howitzer main armament, while the Cromwell Mark VII included wider tracks, an additional gearbox, and more armour plating. The chassis proved useful for an updated observation post tank and numerous other variants.

The Cromwell was an improvement over the Crusader in many respects, yet it remained vulnerable to German armoured vehicles under combat conditions. It was never available in numbers approaching those of the American-made M4 Sherman. This meant that it was deployed piecemeal across the British armoured force, with the Sherman providing the bulk of Allied tank strength. The 7th Armoured was the only British division fully equipped with the Cromwell.

Tiger II

Even while the original Tiger tank was in development, the Henschel and Porsche companies were in competition for the contract to construct the next generation of German heavy tanks. By October 1943, Henschel had once again prevailed, and the result was the mighty Tiger II, or King Tiger.

ENGINE
Powered by the 514-kW (690-hp), 12-cylinder Maybach HL 230 P30 engine, which also powered late-production Panther medium tanks, the Tiger II was slowed considerably by its near 63.5-tonne (70-ton) weight.

AMMUNITION STOWAGE
At least 80 rounds of 88-mm (3.5-in) high-explosive and armour-piercing ammunition were carried in the turret and the hull of the Tiger II, with the armour-piercing achieving a much higher muzzle velocity than the same round fired by the 88-mm (3.5-in) L/56 gun of the Tiger I.

TURRET
Two turrets, both designed by Krupp, were fitted onto the Tiger chassis. One of these was known somewhat erroneously as the Porsche turret, while the production turret was labelled the Henschel.

ARMOUR PROTECTION
The frontal armour of the Tiger II was 150 mm (6 in) thick and sloped at an angle of 50 degrees, similar to the armour of the Panther. Side armour was 80 mm (3.2 in) thick and sloped at an angle of 25 degrees.

SECONDARY ARMAMENT
A pair of 7.92-mm (0.31-in) MG34 machine guns were carried on the Tiger II, one with a coaxial configuration in the welded turret, and the second ball mounted on the right front hull and fired by the radio operator/gunner.

MAIN ARMAMENT
The main armament of the Tiger II was the superb 88-mm (3.5-in) KwK 43 L/71 cannon, with its long barrel extending more than 6 m (20 ft).

"On the edge of the village itself were around 120–150 enemy tanks being refuelled and rearmed. I opened fire and destroyed the first and last of the 11 Stalin tanks on the road ... My own personal score of enemy tanks destroyed in this action was 39."
– SS Hauptscharführer (Master Sergeant) Karl Körner

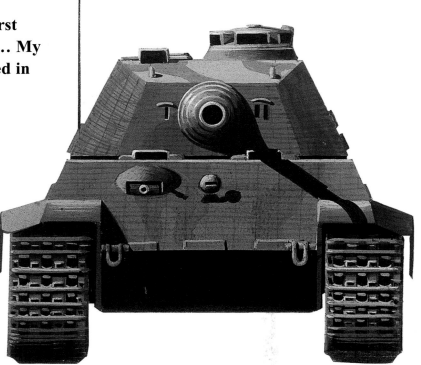

TIGER II (HENSCHEL TURRET) – SPECIFICATION

Country of Origin: Germany
Crew: 5
Designer: Henschel & Son, Krupp
Designed: 1943
In Service: 1944–45
Manufacturer: Henschel & Son, Krupp
Number Built: 492
Produced: 1943–45
Gross Weight: 63.5 tonnes (70 tons)

Dimensions:
Hull Length: 7.25 m (23.8 ft)
Length (gun forward): 10.43 m (34.2 ft)
Width: 3.72 m (12.2 ft)
Overall Height: 3.27 m (10.75 ft)

Performance:
Maximum Speed: 38 km/h (24 mph)
Range, Road: 170 km (105 miles)
Range, Cross-country: 120 km (70 miles)
Power/Weight Ratio: 10 bhp/tonne
Ground Pressure: 0.078 kg/cm²
Fording Capacity: 1.6 m (3.3 ft)
Maximum Gradient: 36 degrees
Maximum Trench Width: 2.5 m (8.2 ft)
Maximum Vertical Obstacle: 0.85 m (2.8 ft)
Suspension Type: Torsion bar

Engine:
Powerplant: 1 x Maybach HL230 P30 V-12 water-cooled petrol engine
Capacity: 23 l (5 gallons)
Output: 690 bhp/514 kW @ 3000 rpm
Fuel Capacity: 860 l (189 gallons)

Armour and Armament:
Armour Type: Homogeneous rolled/welded nickel steel
Hull Front: 100–150 mm (4–6 in)
Hull Sides: 80 mm (3.2 in)
Hull Rear: 80 mm (3.2 in)
Hull Top: 40 mm (1.6 in)
Hull Bottom: 25–40 mm (1–1.6 in)
Turret Front: 180 mm (7.2 in)
Turret Sides: 80 mm (3.2 in)
Turret Rear: 80 mm (3.2 in)
Turret Top: 40 mm (1.6 in)

Main Armament: 1 x 8.8 cm (3.5 in) KwK43 L/71
Secondary Armament: 2 x 7.92-mm (0.31-in) MG34 machine guns

TIGER II

The 88-mm (3.5-in) cannon of the Tiger II, with a muzzle velocity of up to 1000 m (3280 ft) per second, was capable of destroying most Allied tanks at distances of up to 2.4 km (1.5 miles). However, the vehicle was plagued by mechanical problems and tremendous petrol consumption, which caused a number of the heavy vehicles to be destroyed by their crews or abandoned in the field because of lack of fuel. Its 514-kW (690-hp) Maybach HL 230 P30 engine was insufficient to operate the heaviest tank in service during World War II, resulting in numerous drive train failures, while the torsion bar suspension was also too weak to sustain the vehicle's extreme weight.

The imposing barrel of the 88-mm (3.5-in) cannon of the Tiger II extended more than 6 m (20 ft). Powerful though it was, the tank was beset by an insufficient powerplant and an inadequate suspension system.

"The Tiger was for me the best tank that existed. It had its flaws, which you got to know, but you could live with that. Life in a Tiger crew commanding a Tiger company was for me the highlight of my time as a soldier."
– Michael Wittman, the great Tiger tank ace

Only a relative handful of the Tiger II, or King Tiger, tanks were produced from 1943–45. However, the impact of the Tiger II, the heaviest tank deployed during World War II, cannot be overestimated.

"During the Battle of the Bulge when the King Tiger was used against American troops it panicked them. They had never seen anything that big, so they were caught completely by surprise. Here they are supposed to be on a quiet front, and the next thing you know they have this monstrous, huge King Tiger rolling down on top of them, and it shocked them. It was hard to recover from this initial panic," according to Dr. William Atwater, director of the U.S. Army Ordnance Museum.

The high-velocity 88-mm (3.5-in) cannon of the Tiger II dominated the battlefield when in open country with clear fields of fire and manoeuvre. Its Achilles' heel, though, lay in its unreliability and propensity for drive train breakdowns because of an insufficient powerplant and suspension, its tremendous fuel consumption, and its difficulty in moving across natural barriers, such as rivers and rugged terrain.

OVER-ENGINEERED
Ahead of its time in many respects, the Tiger II was over-engineered, and its reliability issues were exacerbated by the necessities of war, which accelerated the development phase from prototype to deployment. The Tiger II required 300,000 man-hours to build, and the cost per unit was prohibitive. However, the design contained some elements that were to be found in numerous tanks of the postwar era.

The Tiger II's welded turret provided space for three of the five crewmen. While the driver and radio operator/ machine gunner were housed forwards in the hull on either side of the gearbox, the commander sat left of centre in the turret, with the gunner slightly below and in front of him. The loader sat to the right of the main weapon. The elongated rear compartment of the turret counterbalanced the weight and recoil of the 88-mm (3.5-in) L/71 gun, the barrel of which extended more than 6 m (20 ft).

SUPERIOR BUT OUTNUMBERED

One Tiger II veteran officer recalled, "I wouldn't have wanted to go into battle in any other tank but the Tiger because it was superior in every aspect to any other tank that we had. The Tiger was for me the best tank that existed."

The Tiger II first saw action on the Eastern Front in the spring of 1944 and was deployed in the defence of Berlin the next year. In the West, it saw action during the Normandy campaign, the Battle of the Bulge, and Operation Market Garden. Superior to Allied armour in many respects, it was in such short supply and fielded so late in the conflict that it was unable to counter the sheer numbers of Allied tanks.

The highest-scoring tank ace of the war with 168 confirmed kills, Feldwebel (Warrant Officer) Kurt Knispel lost his life at the age of 23 while in command of a Tiger II on the Eastern Front.

Interior view

Space was at a premium, with 88-mm (3.5-in) shells stored in the elongated turret as well as in the hull and crewmen, particularly the driver and hull gunner, wedged alongside large equipment.

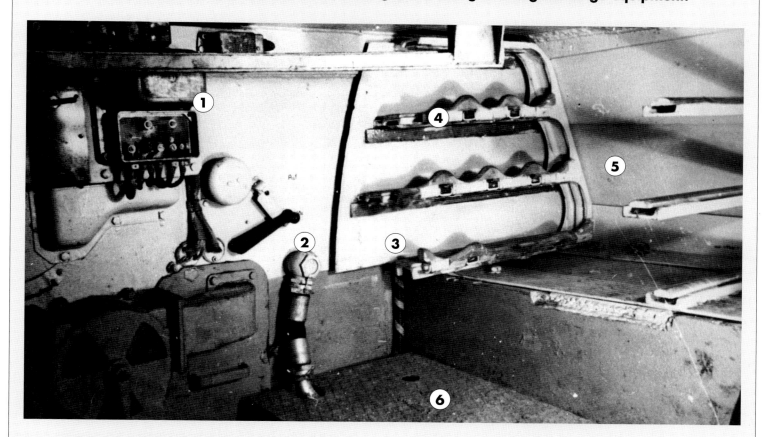

(1) **Electric Circuitry:** The Tiger II depended on such advanced features as new electrical equipment. It may, in part, have fallen victim to the ambitions of its engineers.

(2) **Conduit:** This carried electrical wiring throughout the interior of the Tiger II and provided access to these components.

(3) **Heavy Armour:** While the heavy armour of this tank protected the crew from shot and shell, it also contributed to the Tiger II's tremendous weight and limited its mobility.

(4) **Storage Racks:** Ammunition was often stored in the turret and hull, while every available space was exploited to the fullest possible extent.

(5) **Welded Armour:** The welded armour of the Tiger II was often of inferior quality, as steel was difficult to obtain late in the war.

(6) **Hull and Turret Floor:** The floors of the hull and turret were manufactured of steel plating and provided some protection for the crewmen against land mines.

IS-3 Josef Stalin

The Josef Stalin series of heavy tanks was intended to maintain a perceived Soviet superiority in tank design on the Eastern Front during World War II. The IS-3, developed late in the war, was the world's most powerful tank during the early years of the Cold War.

TURRET
The rounded, cast turret of the IS-3 resembled an overturned soup bowl. It was meant to minimize the tank's silhouette, but it restricted crew movement.

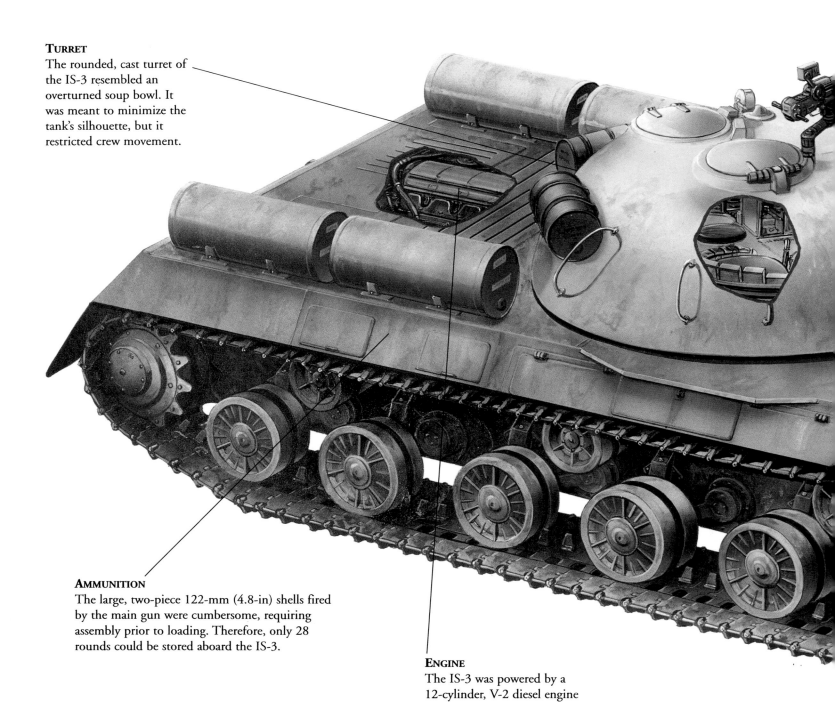

AMMUNITION
The large, two-piece 122-mm (4.8-in) shells fired by the main gun were cumbersome, requiring assembly prior to loading. Therefore, only 28 rounds could be stored aboard the IS-3.

ENGINE
The IS-3 was powered by a 12-cylinder, V-2 diesel engine generating 447 kW (600 hp).

SECONDARY ARMAMENT
The IS-3 was further armed with 12.7-mm
(0.5-in) or 7.62-mm (0.3-in) machine guns.

BREECH
Unable to pivot fully on its vertical axis, the
breech of the main gun limited the ability
to depress the weapon completely.

MAIN ARMAMENT
The heavy D25-T 122-mm (4.8-in)
cannon was capable of destroying German
Panther and Tiger tanks with high-
explosive shells. The 122-mm (4.8-in) was
chosen over a 100-mm (3.94-in) weapon,
which had been shown to have better
armour penetration but was not in full
production.

DRIVER
The driver compartment of the IS-3 hull
was typical of Soviet designs, offering
little comfort or space for storage. The
remainder of the four-man crew was
restricted inside the turret by a
pronounced lack of headroom.

FACTS

- The IS-3 was developed too
  late for deployment during
  World War II.

- Crewmen nicknamed the IS-3
  the Pike thanks to its distinctively
  pointed hull design.

- The IS-3 formed the basis for
  Soviet tank designs of the Cold
  War era.

A special commission was formed in 1943 to analyze the reasons for the horrendous losses suffered by Soviet military tank units in the Battle of Kursk. A total of 6064 machines had been lost during the 38 days of battle. In response, a new heavy tank, the IS-3, was designed.

IS-3 JOSEF STALIN – SPECIFICATION

Country of origin: USSR
Crew: 4
Designer: Zh. Kotin, N. Dukhov
Designed: 1944
In service: 1943–1970s
Manufacturer: Kirov Factory, UZTM
Number built: 2311
Produced: 1943–47
Gross Weight: 45.8 tonnes (50.4 tons)

Dimensions:
Hull Length: 6.77 m (22.2 ft)
Length (gun forward): 9.83 m (32.25 ft)
Width: 3.07 m (10.1 ft)
Overall Height: 2.44 m (8 ft)

Performance:
Maximum Speed: 37 km/hr (23 mph)
Range, Road: 160 km (100 miles)
Range, Cross-country: 120 km (75 miles)
Ground Pressure: 0.83 kg/cm^2
Fording Capacity: 1.3 m (4.3 ft)
Maximum Gradient: 30 degrees
Maximum Trench Width: 2.5 m (8.2 ft)
Maximum Vertical Obstacle: 1 m (3.3 ft)
Suspension Type: Torsion bars

Engine:
Powerplant: V-2-IS V-12 water-cooled diesel
Capacity: 38.9 l (8.6 gallons)
Output: 447 kW (600 bhp)
Power/Weight Ratio: 11.35 bhp/tonne
Fuel Capacity: 520 l (114 gallons); +300 l (66 gallons)

Armament and Armour:
Main Armament: 1 x 122-mm (4.8-in) L/43 D-25 (M1943)
Secondary Armament: 2 x 7.62-mm (0.3-in) DT or DTM MG
Ancillary Armament: 12.7-mm (0.5-in) DShK MG on AA mount
Armour Type: Homogeneous rolled/welded and cast nickel-steel
Hull Front: 90–120 mm (3.6–4.7 in)
Hull Sides: 95 mm (3.8 in)
Hull Rear: 60 mm (2.4 in)
Hull Top: 20–30 mm (0.8–1.2 in)
Hull Bottom: 20–30 mm (0.8–1.2 in)
Turret Front: 230 mm (9 in)
Turret Sides: 100–160 mm (3.9–6.3 in)
Turret Rear: 90 mm (3.6 in)
Turret Top: 30 mm (1.2 in)

Other Variants:
IS-85 (IS-1): 1943 model armed with an 85-mm (3.35-in) gun.
IS-100: A prototype version armed with a 100-mm (3.94-in) gun.
IS-122 (IS-2 model 1943): Production model with A-19 122-mm (4.8-in) gun.
IS-2 model 1944 (sometimes "IS-2m"): 1944 improvement with D25-T 122-mm (4.8-in) gun.
IS-2M: 1950s modernization of IS-2 tanks.
IS-3M: (1952) Modernized version of IS-3.
IS-4: 1944 design, in competition against the IS-3. Longer hull and thicker armour than IS-2.
IS-7 model 1948: 1946 prototype, only three built. Crew of five.
IS-10: 1952 improvement with a longer hull, seven pairs of road wheels instead of six, a larger turret mounting a new gun with fume extractor, an improved diesel engine, and increased armour. Renamed T-10.

IS-3 JOSEF STALIN

Incorporating a heavy 122-mm (4.8-in) cannon, the IS-3 was the latest Soviet tank design of World War II. However, it was not deployed during the war. A welded hull of rolled steel plating was sloped to the maximum degree, and the frontal area of the tank was substantially reduced from its predecessor, the IS-2. The thickness of the frontal hull armour was increased to 120 mm (4.7 in), while the turret thickness was raised to 230 mm (9 in). The turret was dramatically rounded and flattened, reducing the silhouette at the expense of crew space and the ability of the main weapon to fully depress.

The IS-3 heavy tank was the final Soviet design of the World War II era. It was not deployed during the war, but served as a symbol of excellence in Soviet Cold War tank design.

In late 1944, the IS-2 design was upgraded to the IS-3. This tank had improved armour layout and a hemispherical cast turret, resembling an overturned soup bowl, which was to be the hallmark of postwar Soviet tanks.

Some reports indicate that the Soviet IS-3 heavy tank may have been deployed in quite limited numbers during World War II, possibly against the Japanese in Manchuria in 1945. However, no official documentation of such an event is known to exist. Nevertheless, the IS-3, named in honour of Soviet premier Josef Stalin, represented the pinnacle of Soviet armoured design during the war and provided a foretaste of a design philosophy that would go on to dominate Eastern bloc production throughout the Cold War.

The Soviet T-34 medium and KV-1 heavy tanks had, by 1943, enabled the Red Army to seize the initiative on the Eastern Front. While the T-34 became a combat legend, the KV-1 and its later variant, the KV-85, were the subjects of

considerable modification. A retooling of the transmission and suspension, coupled with a redesigned turret and hull configuration, evolved the tank into more than a new variant of the KV-1. The new armoured fighting vehicle was designated the IS-1, mounting an 85-mm (3.35-in) main cannon identical to that of the KV-85. As the new tank developed, it was apparent that it could accommodate a heavier gun, and trials were conducted with a 100-mm (3.94-in) and a 122-mm (4.8-in) gun. The former offered better armour penetration capability, but the latter was chosen because of the explosive power of its round and ready availability. In time, the 122-mm (4.8-in) proved to be a deadly efficient anti-personnel round.

MORE ARMOUR, REDUCED WEIGHT

By 1944, the IS-2 had entered service, mounting the 122-mm (4.8-in) cannon and introducing reconfigured armour plating, which provided virtually the same protection for tank and crew but reduced the overall weight. However, the two components of the heavy 122-mm (4.8-in) shell had to be assembled prior to loading, significantly slowing the rate of fire. The original 122-mm (4.8-in) gun, the A-19, was replaced subsequently by the D25-T, with a double baffle muzzle brake, which had a better rate of fire and improved fire control and coordination. Additional improvements to later IS-2 models included a turret-mounted anti-aircraft machine gun and a hull configuration without a step-up to the front.

FUTURE SHAPE

Production of the IS-3 began in May 1945 under the direction of M.F. Balzha at Soviet Experimental Plant No. 100 and concluded a year later. By the end of World War II, fewer than 30 IS-3s had been built, but by mid-1946, IS-3s in service totalled more than 2300. The tank control system enabled the commander to rotate the turret, and its flattened design and bow-shaped forward hull looked sleek, yet it was less able to take advantage of hull-down tactics as a result.

The IS-3 did not participate in operations during World War II, but a regiment was paraded through Moscow on 7 September, 1945. The IS-3 was considered the world's most powerful tank for years to come, and its initial appearance gave Western military leaders reason to pause.

Close-up

The design of the IS-3 Josef Stalin heavy tank did little to improve internal ergonomics or the comfort of its crew. The distinctive turret offered little headroom for three crewmen.

1. **Handle Assists:** Handles on the turret allowed infantrymen and maintenance personnel to enter and exit the tank easily.

2. **Rear Hatches:** A pair of circular hatches allowed access to and from the IS-3 hull at the rear of the tank and facilitated the loading of ammunition and supplies.

3. **Top Hatches:** Two rectangular hatches on top of the rear hull, sited just behind the turret, allowed crewmen rapid entry and exit.

4. **Commander's Cupola:** This was often equipped with either a 12.7-mm (0.5-in) or 7.62-mm (0.3-in) ring-mounted machine gun.

5. **Fuel Barrels:** In keeping with tanks of the Soviet Red Army deployed previously, the IS-3 Josef Stalin carried fuel barrels secured externally to its elongated hull.

6. **Sloped Armour:** The hull and turret armour of this heavy tank featured a pronounced slope, increasing protective thickness.

Centurion A41

Britain drew upon its experience of having had to fight against superior armour during World War II when it created the Centurion A41 main battle tank. More than a dozen variants, or Marks, were produced during a post-war length of service that spanned more than 50 years.

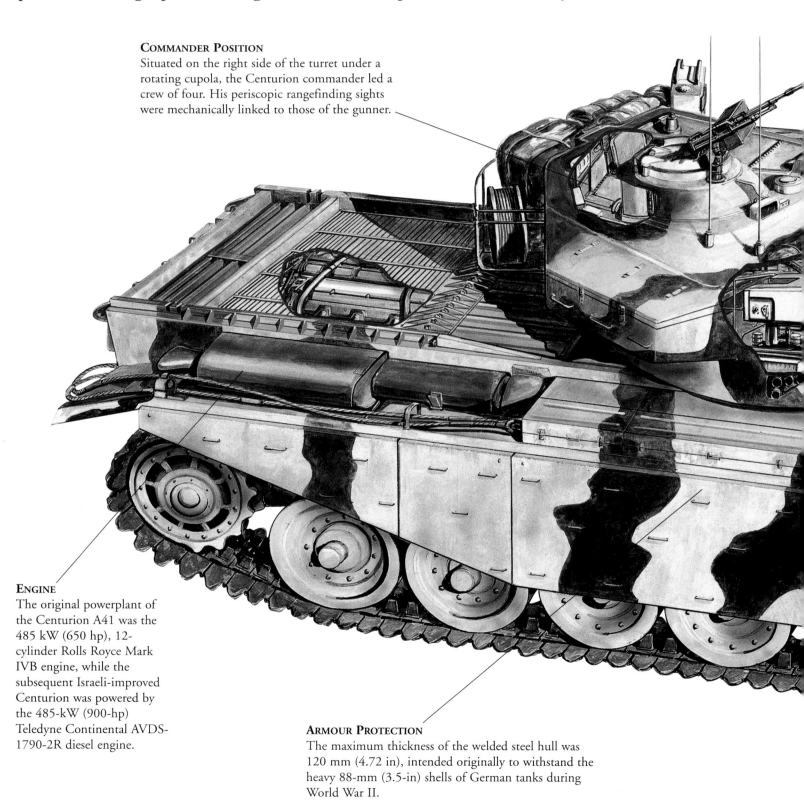

COMMANDER POSITION
Situated on the right side of the turret under a rotating cupola, the Centurion commander led a crew of four. His periscopic rangefinding sights were mechanically linked to those of the gunner.

ENGINE
The original powerplant of the Centurion A41 was the 485 kW (650 hp), 12-cylinder Rolls Royce Mark IVB engine, while the subsequent Israeli-improved Centurion was powered by the 485-kW (900-hp) Teledyne Continental AVDS-1790-2R diesel engine.

ARMOUR PROTECTION
The maximum thickness of the welded steel hull was 120 mm (4.72 in), intended originally to withstand the heavy 88-mm (3.5-in) shells of German tanks during World War II.

SECONDARY ARMAMENT
A 7.62-mm (0.3-in) calibre Browning machine gun was mounted coaxially in the turret. A second 7.62-mm (0.3-in) calibre machine gun was mounted in the hull, and a 12.7-mm (0.5-in) calibre Browning M2 anti-aircraft machine gun was situated on top of the turret. Other options included an early 20-mm (0.78-in) cannon and smoke grenade launchers.

DRIVER COMPARTMENT
The driver compartment, forwards and to the right, was equipped with two periscopes for forwards observation. Ammunition was stored to the driver's left.

MAIN ARMAMENT
Early versions of the Centurion tank were armed with the QF 17-pounder cannon, and later variants were upgunned to the 105-mm (4.1-in) L7A2 rifled cannon, as shown.

The Centurion was replaced by the Chieftain in the British Army itself, but at least 2400 are still in service. The Centurion's longevity is a tribute to the soundness of the basic design, including its ability to incorporate a host of modifications.

CENTURION A41 – SPECIFICATION

Country of Origin: United Kingdom
Crew: 4
Designer: Department of Tank Design
Designed: 1943–45
Manufacturers: Leyland, Royal Ordnance Factories, Vickers
In Production: 1945–62
In Service: 1946–90s (derivatives still in service)
Number Produced: 4423
Weight: 52 tonnes (57 tons)

Dimensions:
Hull Length: 7.6 m (25 ft)
Length (gun forward): 9.85 m (32 ft 4 in)
Width: 3.38 m (11 ft 1 in)
Height: 3.01 m (9 ft 10.5 in)

Performance:
Speed: 34 km/h (21 mph)
Operational range: 450 km (280 miles)
Gradient: 60 degrees
Maximum Vertical Obstacle: 0.91 m (3 ft)
Maximum Trench Width: 3.35 m (11 ft)

Engine:
Powerplant: 1 x Rolls-Royce Meteor 485 kW (650 hp)
Power/Weight Ratio: 13 hp/tonne
Suspension: Horstmann suspension

Armour and Armament:
Armour: 150 mm (6 in)
Main Armament: 105-mm (4.1-in) L7A2 rifled gun
   17-pounder, 20-pounder
Secondary Armament: 7.62-mm (0.3-in) Browning machine gun

Major UK variants:
Mark 1: 17-pounder armed version.
Mark 2: Fully cast turret.
Mark 3: Fitted with 20-pounder, 2 stowage positions for track links.
Mark 4: Projected close-support version with 95-mm (3.74-in) CS howitzer.
Mark 5: Browning machine guns fitted to coaxial and commander's cupola mounts, stowage bin on glacis.
Mark 6: Upgunned and uparmoured Mark 5.
Mark 7 aka FV 4007: Revised engine decks.
Mark 8: Resilient mantlet and new commander's cupola.
Mark 9 (aka FV 4015): Upgunned and uparmoured Mark 7.
Mark 10 (aka FV 4017): Upgunned and uparmoured Mark 8.
Mark 11: Mark 6 fitted with IR equipment and ranging gun.
Mark 12: Mark 9 fitted with IR equipment and ranging gun.
AVRE 105: Combat Engineer Version with 105-mm (4.1-in) gun.
AVRE 165: Combat Engineer Version with 165-mm (6.5-in) gun.
BARV: Beach Armoured Recovery Vehicle.
Bridgelayer aka FV 4002: Class 80 bridgelayer.

CENTURION SHO'T

The Centurion design is considered one of the best of the post–World War II era, and the Israeli Sho't variant (shown) remained in service into the 1990s. Armed with the 105-mm (4.13-in) L7 cannon, the Sho't gained fame during the Yom Kippur War of 1973, battling Syrian T-54/55 and T-62 tanks. The Centurion incorporated a Horstmann suspension of external horizontal springs, a welded hull of sloped armour, and turret armour of 152 mm (6 in). The driver was seated in the bow with the commander in the turret above the fighting compartment at centre, and the engine compartment to the rear. The gunner was situated below and in front of the commander, while the loader served the main weapon from his left.

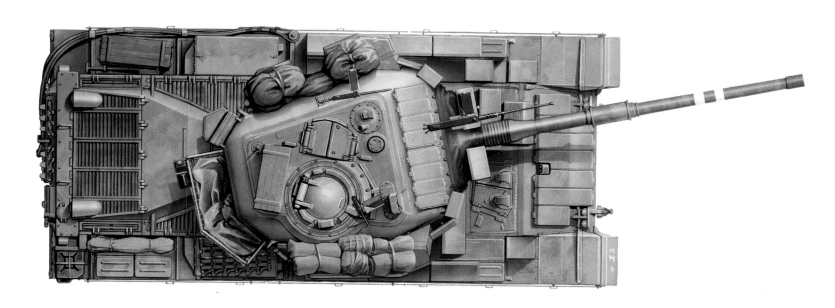

In one of the few instances on record, the War Ministry decided it would be a better idea to build new trailers than hamper a superb design. Even before prototypes of the original 36-tonne (40-ton) design were completed, a heavier version was well under way.

The eventual weight of the British Centurion A41 main battle tank was to reach 45 tonnes (52 tons) but the need for heavier trailers to transport the behemoth was considered a reasonable tradeoff by the Department of Tank Design. The Centurion measured up so well to its other specifications that it was considered by many to be the "universal tank."

Initially, the Centurion A41 was the response to the War Ministry's 1943 requirement for a British tank that could take on heavy German armour on the battlefields of World War II. In the event, it reached the continent of Europe in May 1945, only days after the conflict had ended. All the

Interior view

The turret's mechanical apparatus and power generation systems were located below the turret basket and crew areas, making them easily accessible for routine maintenance or repairs.

1. **Electric Transversing Motor:** The electric transversing motor and transmission supplied power to the broad shaft in the background.

2. **Air Collection:** The collection and filtering of air within the turret reduced the possible build-up of noxious fumes.

3. **Hydraulic Lines:** Hydraulics and electrical lines powered the turret and were used to adjust the elevation of the main weapon, and operate other systems.

4. **Armour Protection:** The hull of the Centurion tank was made of welded steel up to 120 mm (4 in) thick to defend against the high velocity German 88-mm (3.46-in) shell.

5. **Transversing Gears:** The teeth of the transversing gears are visible in a circular pattern at the base of the turret.

6. **Elevation Apparatus:** The elevation of the main weapon was controlled by the apparatus shown in the foreground.

Crewmen of a Centurion tank change one of the armoured vehicle's drive sprockets in the field. The Centurion was developed during World War II but arrived too late to see action. However, it became a tank of great standing in the Cold War era.

effort in its creation did not go to waste, though, because the Centurion went on to become one of the most enduring tank designs of the Cold War era.

During nearly two decades of production by the Royal Ordnance Factory, Leyland, Vickers, and other companies, no fewer than 12 variants of the original Centurion were produced. A total of 4423 were manufactured, and the Israeli Defence Force became the largest single user with more than 1100 in service.

Early Centurions were armed with the QF 17-pounder anti-tank gun, while a relative few mounted the 20-pounder, and later the 105-mm (4-in) L7A2 rifled gun became the standard. Through the years, armoured protection increased from 76 mm (3 in) in the Mark 1 to 120 mm (4.7 in) in the welded steel plate hull and more than 150 mm (5.9 in) in the turret. Prominent among the variants were the Centurion Mark 2, which included better armour protection, and the Mark 3, fitted with an automated gun stabilizer. The Mark 5 was the first to mount the 105-mm (4-in) main armament.

Although the all-round performance of the Centurion exceeded expectations, its limited range, relatively low road speed of 34 km/h (21 mph), and merely average cross-country capabilities were its most prominent drawbacks. The Israelis actually improved the Centurion's performance by fitting the tank with a larger Teledyne Continental diesel engine, which gave it greater fuel and ammunition capacity. They also fitted the tank with superior fire-control equipment.

COLD WAR VETERAN

The combat record of the Centurion A41 can justifiably be considered superb. During the Korean War, the 8th King's Royal Irish Hussars covered the retreat of the outnumbered 29th Infantry Brigade at the Battle of the Imjin River and earned high praise from General John O'Daniel, commander of the U.S. I Corps, who commented that the "8th Hussars have evolved a new type of tank warfare. They taught us that anywhere a tank can go is tank country – even the tops of mountains."

During the Vietnam War, the Royal Australian Armoured Corps deployed 58 Centurion tanks, while the Centurions of the Indian army outclassed American tanks supplied to Pakistani forces during the wars of 1965 and 1971. The Israelis deployed Centurions during the Six-Day War of 1967, the Yom Kippur War of 1973, and later incursions into Lebanon. In Korea and Southeast Asia, however, the Centurion was limited in its deployment because of its weight, which was too great for most bridges.

The longevity of the Centurion A41, along with its proven combat effectiveness, make the design one of the best of the latter half of the twentieth century.

T-54/55

Produced in greater numbers than any other tank in history, the Soviet T-54/55 series was developed as a successor to the T-44, which had been a disappointing attempt to improve the famed T-34 of World War II. The service life of the T-54/55 exceeds half a century.

FIRE CONTROL
Early models of the T-54/55 were equipped with manual target-acquisition systems. These were replaced with automated systems on later models, but even these were not as good as contemporary NATO aiming devices.

MAIN ARMAMENT
The original armament of the T-54/55 series was the D-10T 100-mm (3.94-in) rifled cannon. This gun eventually proved inferior to more modern weapons and was replaced by the D-10T2S with a bore evacuator located near the muzzle.

ARMOUR PROTECTION
Even though it was relatively lightly armoured, the T-54/55 provided turret crew with the protection of 203-mm (8-in) armour, while the front glacis was 100 mm (3.94 in) thick and the sides 70 mm (2.75 in) thick.

TURRET
The low silhouette of the T-54/55 was made possible by the turret design, resembling an overturned frying pan. However, the confined space inside, along with the absence of a turret basket in earlier models, made operating the tank exhausting for three of the four crewmen.

SUSPENSION
The modified Christie suspension did not provide return rollers, while tracks were replaced twice as often as those of contemporary Western tanks. The tracks were also prone to being thrown at higher speeds.

ENGINE
The 388-kW (520-hp) V-2-54 diesel engine of the early T-54 was prone to failure and catching fire because of metal filings clogging oil lines. Built primarily of magnesium alloy, it was replaced with a larger V-12 engine in the T-55.

Its armament, design, and construction are often considered inferior to the tanks of other nations, yet the T-54/55 was always available in large numbers. Its production was nearly three times that of U.S. tanks manufactured from 1945–80.

T-54

T-54/55 – SPECIFICATION

Country of Origin: Soviet Union
Crew: 4
Designer: Not Specified
Designed: Not Specified
In Production: 1948–78
Manufacturers: Various
In Service: 1948–present
Number Built: 95,000
Gross Weight: 36 tonnes (39.6 tons)

Dimensions:
Hull Length: 6.45 m (21.15 ft)
Length (gun forward): 9 m (29.5 ft)
Width: 3.27 m (10.7 ft)
Overall Height: 2.4 m (7.85 ft)

Performance:
Range, Road: 500 km (300 miles)
Range, Cross-country: 300 km (180 miles)
Maximum Speed: 50 km/h (30 mph)
Ground Pressure: 0.81 kg/cm²
Fording Capacity: 1.4 m (4.6 ft) (Submersible to 5.5 m [18 ft] with preparation)
Maximum Gradient: 30 degrees
Maximum Trench Width: 2.7 m (8.9 ft)
Maximum Vertical Obstacle: 0.8 m (2.6 ft)
Suspension Type: Torsion bar

Engine:
Powerplant: 1 x Type V-54 V-12 water-cooled diesel
Capacity: n/a
Output: 388 kW (520 hp) @ 2000 rpm

Power/Weight Ratio: 16.1 bhp/tonne
Fuel Capacity: 960 l (211.5 gallons)

Armament and Armour:
Main Armament: 1 x 100-mm (3.94-in) D-10T2S L/54 gun
Secondary Armament: 7.62-mm (0.3-in) PKT MG in coaxial mount
Ancillary Armament: 12.7-mm (0.5-in) DShKM MG in AA mount
Armour Type: Homogeneous rolled/welded with cast turret
Hull Front: 100 mm (4 in)
Hull Sides: 70 mm (2.8 in)
Hull Rear: 60 mm (2.4 in)
Hull Top: 30 mm (1.2 in)
Hull Bottom: 20 mm (0.8 in)
Turret Front: 100–170 mm (4–6.8 in)
Turret Sides: 100 mm (4 in)
Turret Rear: 100 mm (4 in)
Turret Top: 70 mm (2.8 in)

Variants:
T-54A: Fitted with 100-mm (3.94-in) main gun with fume extractor, deep water equipment, and gun stabilizer on vertical plane.
T-54AK: Command tank.
T-54M: T-54 models upgraded to T-55 standard.
T-54B: With infra-red night vision equipment.
T-54C: Some sans AA gun; later retrofitted.
T-55M: Sans loader's cupola.
T-54K: Command vehicle.
T-54 ARV: Armoured Recovery Vehicle utilizing T-54 chassis.
T-54 AVLB: Bridge layer variant utilizing T-54 chassis.
T-54 IMR: Combat engineer vehicle utilizing T-54 chassis.
Type 59: Chinese production model designation.
TI-67: Israeli conversion model.
T-54AD: Polish designation of T-54AK command tank.

VARIANT: T-55

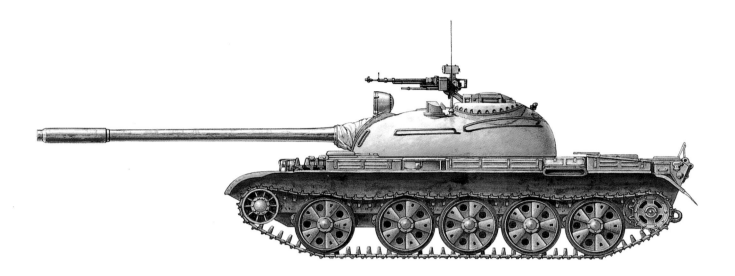

T-54/55

When the T-44 proved an unworthy late wartime successor to the legendary T-34/85 medium tank, its hull was topped with a sleek, dome-shaped turret and a 100-mm (4-in) cannon in the prototype of the T-54 main battle tank. By the late 1950s, so many modifications had been made that a new designation, T-55, was given to a version with an improved main weapon and more powerful engine. Still, the shortcomings of the T-54/55 design persisted, most notably the confined turret space with three crewmen on the same side and the loader required to perform an exhausting series of movements to service the main gun.

VARIANT: T55

The T-54 and T-55 tanks are outwardly very similar and difficult to distinguish visually. Many T-54s were also updated to T-55 standards, and the distinction is often downplayed with the collective name T-54/55. Numerous variants of both tanks are in service today.

The T-54/55 main battle tank remains the backbone of the armoured forces of many former Warsaw Pact and Third World countries. Since 1949, more than 80,000 have been produced, and the basic design has served in combat in the deserts of the Middle East and the jungles of Africa and Southeast Asia.

At 36 tonnes (39.6 tons), the T-54/55 was lighter than other main battle tanks of the Cold War era, and its armour protection was inferior to that of potential opponents. The effectiveness of the original main gun, the 100-mm (3.94-in) D10T, which was adapted from a dual-purpose naval weapon,

Close-up

The Soviet tank designers' neglect of crew comfort and operational space inside the tank continued with the T-54/55, the first post–World War II tank exported by the Soviet Union.

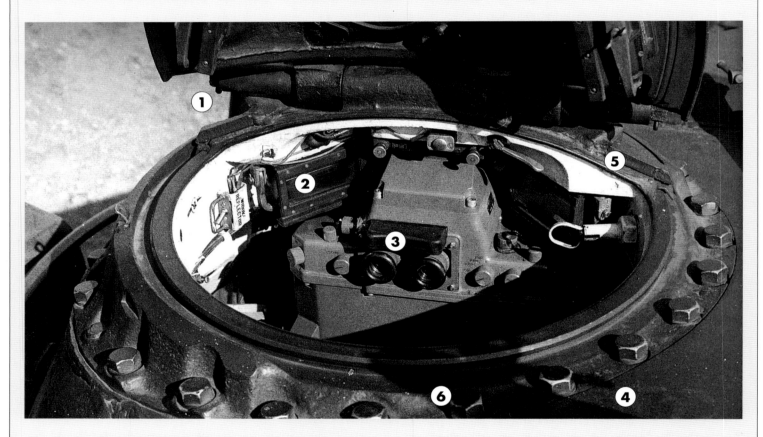

(1) **Turret Hatch:** One of two hatches on top of the turret, the commander's hatch was affixed to a slightly raised cupola.

(2) **Periscopes:** These ringed the turret cupola, allowing the commander a broad view of the field before him.

(3) **Telescopic Sight:** Telescopic sights were used by both the gunner and commander to acquire targets and assess the terrain over which their T-54/55 tank was manoeuvring.

(4) **Turret Armour:** Though the turret armour was thick at 203 mm (8 in) in the front, it measured only 39 mm (1.5 in) on top.

(5) **Turret Seal:** The tight turret seal of later variants of the T-54/55 tank was an essential component of defence against nuclear, chemical, and biological agents.

(6) **Bolted Construction:** Some variants of this tank have bolted, rather than cast, cupolas for both the commander and the gunner.

The pintle-mounted 12.7-mm (0.5-in) anti-aircraft machine gun of the T-54/55 fires rapidly during exercises. More than 80,000 variants of the ubiquitous Soviet main battle tank were built during a period of more than three decades.

was limited due to the lack of a computerized fire-control system. Its top-loading breech was a handicap, seriously reducing its rate of fire. Later, the D-10T2S, with a bore evacuator and improved gun-laying system, were installed. Secondary armament first consisted of a coaxial 7.62-mm (0.3-in) machine gun, a remote-controlled, hull-mounted 7.62-mm (0.3-in) machine gun, as well as a 12.7-mm (0.5-in) pintle-mounted machine gun near the loader's hatch.

The design of the T-54 is similar to other Soviet-era tanks, with an engine compartment to the rear, driver compartment forwards, and low, cramped turret that hampers the traverse of the main cannon. One of the most serious limitations of the T-54 was the design of the turret interior. Three crewmen, the commander, gunner, and loader, were all on the left side and could all be taken out by a single hit. The driver was situated in the centreline of the hull. Fuel and ammunition were in close proximity to each other, also posing an extraordinary danger to vehicle survivability.

STEADY IMPROVEMENT

Further, the seats on the early T-54 were welded to the hull, and the turret floor did not rotate with the turret itself. Therefore, the loader was required to pull rounds from storage while avoiding the breech as the turret rotated. He then had to place a shell into

the breech with his left hand. By the mid-1950s, improvements to the T-54 included a stabilized main gun and a nuclear, biological, and chemical (NBC) defence system. This variant was designated T-54A. In the subsequent T-54B, the 100-mm (3.94-in) D-10T2S gun was stabilized in two planes, and by 1960, the T-54C was notable for the removal of one of the machine guns and a loader's hatch, which was flush with the turret. Certain tanks have been equipped with a snorkel and can traverse up to 5.5 m (18 ft) of water.

In 1958, the T-55 emerged as the latest variant in the T-54 series. The primary distinguishing features of the T-55 included the absence of a loader's cupola and a turret dome ventilator, as well as the removal, in most cases, of the turret-mounted 12.7-mm (0.5-in) machine gun. Its 432-kW (580-hp) V-12 water-cooled V-2-55 diesel engine was an improvement over that of the T-54, but it was still prone to mechanical failure because of inferior manufacture. The T-55 did incorporate a turret basket, greatly improving the main gun's efficiency. Further improvements with the T-55 included a modestly increased ammunition capacity, better fire control with the introduction of a laser rangefinder, and enhanced armour protection.

While the T-54/55 is largely outmoded, its great numbers and adaptability to upgrades have increased its longevity.

M48 Patton

Cold War battles against Soviet tanks in Europe were seen as a real possibility when this tank was conceptualized. The third in the Patton series of U.S. medium tanks, the M48 was designed to be an improvement over its immediate predecessor, the M47.

TURRET

Three crew – the commander, gunner, and loader – sat in the turret. The commander was situated high and to the right with the loader to his left, while the gunner sat below the commander. The turret itself was elliptical in shape, and had a maximum armour protection of 110 mm (4.3 in).

FIRE CONTROL

The fire-control system of the M48A3 was highly specialized for its time in the 1960s. A system of mirrors found range and fed data into a ballistic computer.

HULL CONSTRUCTION

The improved hull of the M48 included a bowl-shaped bottom and sloping top sides. Previous designs had a welded, box-like construction.

SEARCHLIGHT
Sighted with the main gun and gunsights, a xenon searchlight with one million candle power functioned in both infrared and standard modes to illuminate targets.

MAIN ARMAMENT
The 90-mm (3.54-in) M41 gun was mounted in the redesigned turret of the M48A3 (shown) and incorporated a T-shaped muzzle brake. The 105-mm (4-in) M68 cannon was installed on the later model M48A5.

ENGINE
Early petrol engines often caught fire and so were replaced on the M48A3 with the 560-kW (750-hp) Continental AVDS-1790-2A diesel engine.

DRIVER
Seated forward and left in the hull, the driver viewed the field with three M27 observation periscopes and an M24 infrared night scope. An aircraft-style wheel was used for steering. The brake and accelerator pedals were similar to those of an automobile.

With the advent of the M48 series medium tanks, the U.S. Army acquired the combat tank that was to become the mainstay of its armoured fleet for decades. It remains in service with a number of armies around the world to this day.

M48A1 PATTON

M48A3 PATTON – SPECIFICATION

Country of Origin: USA
Crew: 4
Designer: Not specified
Designed: 1951–53
Manufacturer: Chrysler, Fisher Tank Arsenal, Ford Motor Company
In Production: 1952–59
Number Built: 12,000
In Service: 1950s–90s
Gross Weight: 47 tonnes (51.7 tons)

Dimensions:
Hull Length: 6.82 m (22.6 ft)
Length (gun forward): 7.44 m (24.4 ft)
Width: 3.63 m (11.9 ft)
Overall Height: 3.1 m (10.1 ft)

Performance:
Maximum Speed: 48 km/h (30 mph)
Range, Road: 465 km (290 miles)
Range, Cross-country: 300 km (180 miles)
Ground Pressure: 0.83 kg/cm^2
Fording Capacity: 1.2 m (4 ft)
Maximum Gradient: 30 degrees
Maximum Trench Width: 2.6 m (8.5 ft)
Maximum Vertical Obstacle: 0.9 m (3 ft)
Suspension Type: Torsion bar

Engine:
Powerplant: 1 x Continental AVDS-1790-2A supercharged V-12 diesel engine
Capacity: 29.4 l (6.5 gallons)
Output: 750 bhp/559 kW @ 2400 rpm

Power/Weight Ratio: 15.9 bhp/tonne
Fuel Capacity: 1420 l (312.1 gallons)

Armament and Armour:
Main Armament: 1 x 90-mm (3.5-in) gun
Secondary Armament: 7.62-mm (0.3-in) machine gun
Ancillary Armament: 12.7-mm (0.5-in) machine gun
Armour Type: Homogenous cast/welded nickel-steel
Hull Front: 100–120 mm (3.9–4.7 in)
Hull Sides: 50–75 mm (2–2.9 in)
Hull Rear: 45 mm (1.8 in)
Hull Top: 57 mm (2.2 in)
Hull Bottom: 13–63 mm (0.5–2.5 in)
Turret Front: 110 mm (4.3 in)
Turret Sides: 75 mm (2.9 in)
Turret Rear: 50 mm (2 in)
Turret Top: 25 mm (1 in)

Major Variants:
M48: Differed from the M47 in having another new turret design and a redesigned hull.
M48A1: New driver hatch and M1 commander's cupola.
M48A2: Improved powerpack and transmission, redesigned rear plate, and improved turret control.
M48A3: Refit of M48A1s with diesel engines.
M48A3 Mod. B: Additional rear armour and raised commander's cupola.
M48A4: Proposed refit of M48A3s with M60 turrets, scrapped.
M48A5: Upgunned with the 105-mm (4-in) M68 gun.
M48A5PI: M1 cupola replaced by the Israeli Urdan model.
M67 "Zippo": M48 armed with a flamethrower inside a dummy model of the main gun with fake muzzle brake.

M47 PATTON

M48A3 PATTON

A modification of earlier variants of the M48 Patton medium tank, the M48A3 was delivered to the U.S. Army in early 1963 and subsequently deployed for service during the Vietnam War. The 604 kW (810 hp), V-12 Continental AVDS-1790-5B petrol engine, which had been prone to catching fire, was replaced in the M48A3 with the 560 kW (750 hp) Continental AVDS-1790-2 diesel powerplant, which improved fuel consumption. The Allison CD-850-6A cross drive transmission was also installed. In 1967, additions to the M48A3 Mod. B included protective boxes covering the tail lights, more armour around the exhaust door louvres, and an adapter ring that raised the commander's cupola by 12.7 cm (5 in).

M48A5 PATTON

Manning his M48 Patton tank's turret-mounted 12.7-mm (0.5in) machine gun, a commander scans the field and maintains communication with a headset while a crewman emerges from a second hatch. The tank's powerful searchlight is clearly visible.

The M48 has adapted well to improvement and modification, and is still used in large numbers. Because it is reliable, relatively cheap, and available in large quantities, many armies have decided to upgrade their M48s, rather than replace them.

The longevity of the M48, the third and final of the Patton series of tanks, has been remarkable. Named for General George S. Patton, commander of the U.S. Third Army during World War II, the Pattons were designed to battle Soviet-built tanks during the early Cold War period.

During the early 1950s, major modifications were made to the turret and hull of the existing M47 medium tank. The egg-shaped, sloping armour of the M48's turret, cast in a single piece of steel, offered enhanced ballistic protection, strength, and lighter weight, while reducing the angles more susceptible to enemy shells. The hull, with its bowl shape and further rounded edges, proved stronger than the previous box-like hull configuration and was also cast in a single piece. Additional armour plate was often welded to the exterior. The glacis was armoured up to 120 mm (4.7 in) with a 60-degree slope.

The original petrol engine had a bad reputation thanks to its tendency to ignite. A decade after the first M48 was delivered to the U.S. Army, the tank was fitted with a Continental diesel engine to rectify this. Other drawbacks included high fuel consumption and the absence of a stabilization system for the main 90-mm (3.54-in) M41 cannon, which made accurate fire on the move virtually impossible. Secondary armament consisted of a 12.7-mm (0.5-in) turret-mounted machine gun, and a coaxial 7.62-mm (0.3-in) machine gun.

CONTINUOUSLY IMPROVING TECHNOLOGY
Significant technological advances were incorporated into the M48, including a fully enclosed machine-gun mount on the commander's cupola with the M48A1, larger fuel tanks, better fire control, a T-shaped muzzle brake, and a fuel-injected engine with the M48A2, and the installation of the diesel engine. The commander's cupola was raised, and a simplified rangefinder was fitted on the M48A3, of which 1019 were built. The first 600 went to the U.S. Army and the remainder went to the U.S. Marine Corps. Highly

sophisticated for its time, the fire-control system of the M48A3 was comprised of a series of mirrors and a ballistic computer that was operated with cams and gears.

Variants of the M48 were manufactured by the Fisher Tank Arsenal, Chrysler Corporation, and Ford Motor Company, while the modifications of the earlier models to the M48A3 were completed at the army's Anniston and Red River depots. These modifications further included a carbon dioxide fire-extinguishing system and equipment for chemical, biological, and radiologic warfare. Other variations to the M48A1 resulted in the M48A3 Mod B,

with the raised cupola and protection for running lights. The Israeli Defence Force initiated an upgrade of more than 600 M48s beginning in the mid-1960s, improving the standard main armament from 90 mm (3.54 in) to the 105-mm (4-in) L7A1, enhancing the fire-control system, and reducing the cupola profile. The Americans picked up these modifications, designating the improved tanks as M48A5. More than 600 M48s were deployed during the Vietnam War, while the tank was also in action during the Indo-Pakistani wars of 1965 and 1971, and during the Six-Day War of 1967. Thousands of M48s remain in service today.

Close-up

The M48A3 Patton tank has experienced a lengthy service life due to its adaptability and ease of upgrade. Numerous nations have chosen to enhance their standard M48s with more recent systems.

(1) **Commander's Cupola:** The M48 commander was positioned on the left inside the turret.

(2) **Searchlight:** The xenon searchlight, sighted with both the main 90-mm (3.5-in) weapon and gunsights, was capable of operating in standard or infrared modes.

(3) **Turret:** The elliptical shape of the turret was a departure from previous designs and facilitated fighting in the hull-down position.

(4) **Main Armament:** The 90-mm (3.54-in) M41 main cannon was mounted in a slightly redesigned turret on the M48A3 Patton tank.

(5) **Sloped Armour:** The 60-degree slope of the glacis armour on the upper hull of the M48A3 effectively increased its thickness and the protection afforded the crew.

(6) **Lower Hull:** This was cast in a single piece, with additional armour plating often welded on to protect against anti-tank mines.

M41 Walker Bulldog

Implementing lessons learnt in combat during World War II, U.S. engineers developed the M41 Walker Bulldog. This light, air-transportable tank was armed well enough to defend itself and was compatible with parts designed for other armoured vehicles.

INTERNAL CONFIGURATION
Divided into three compartments, with the driver to the front, the fighting compartment at centre, and the engine compartment separated by a firewall to the rear, the M41 interior was highly functional, though American crews complained of limited headroom.

TURRET
The cast and welded turret of the M41 was distinguished by its elongated bustle. It accommodated three crewmen.

DRIVER
The M41 driver sat forwards and to the left in the hull. A drop-out escape hatch was provided through the floor of the hull under the driver's seat.

FACTS

- Intended to be air-transportable, the M41 eventually became too heavy for airlift deployment.
- The Brazilian armed forces upgunned the M41 with a 90-mm (3.54-in) cannon.
- The M41 was named the Walker Bulldog for General Walton H. Walker, who died in a jeep accident in Korea in 1950.

MAIN ARMAMENT
The 76-mm (3-in) M32 main cannon featured an automatic loader, the first to be installed in a U.S.-manufactured tank. The loader was used to select, lift, index, and ram the shell into position, and then to dispense of the empty casings.

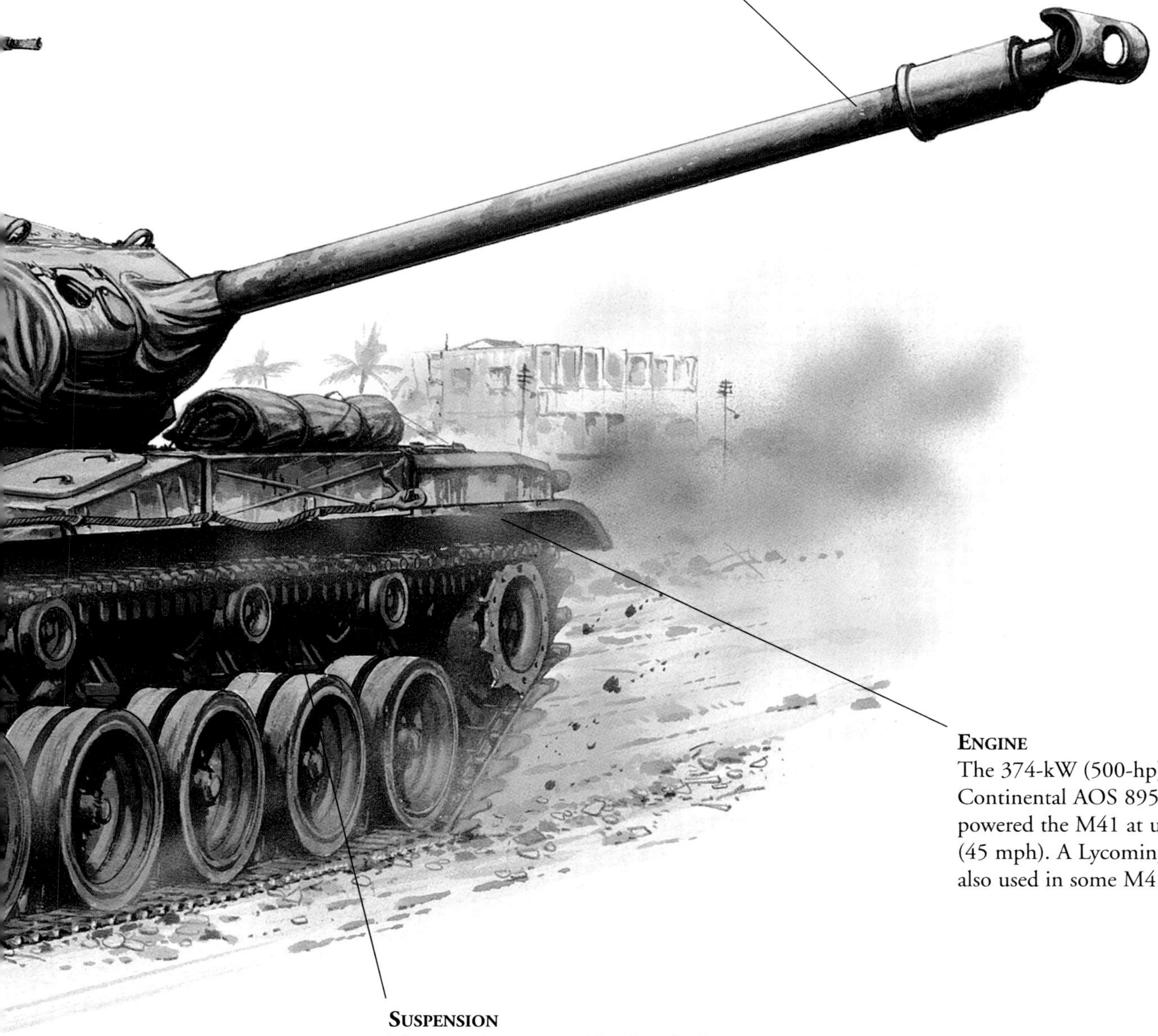

ENGINE
The 374-kW (500-hp), six-cylinder Continental AOS 895-3 engine powered the M41 at up to 72 km/h (45 mph). A Lycoming engine was also used in some M41s.

SUSPENSION
The torsialastic, or rubber-brushed, suspension of the M41 included torsion bars and hydraulic shock absorbers. The drive sprocket was positioned at the rear, with an idler to the front and three return rollers, providing a relatively smooth cross-country ride.

The **T41E1**, which became the **M41**, was fitted with a state-of-the-art power train. This was interchangeable with components in several other vehicles in the army's tactical fleet. Its clean and efficient design made the tank a worthy successor to the M24.

M41 WALKER BULLDOG – SPECIFICATION

Country of Origin: USA
Crew: 4
Designer: Not specified
Designed: Late 1940s
Manufacturer: Cadillac
In Production: 1951–69
In Service: 1953–present
Number Built: 2100
Weight: 23.5 tonnes (25.9 tons)

Dimensions:
Hull Length: 5.8 m (19.1 ft)
Length, gun forward: 8.2 m (27 ft)
Width: 3.2 m (10.5 ft)
Height: 2.71 m (8.9 ft)

Performance:
Speed: 72 km/h (45 mph)
Range, Road: 225 km (140 miles)
Range Cross-country: 100 km (60 miles)
Ground Pressure: 0.72 kg/cm²
Fording Capacity: 1.1 m (3.3 ft)
Maximum Gradient: 31 degrees
Maximum Trench Width: 1.8 m (6 ft)
Maximum Vertical Obstacle: 0.7 m (2.3 ft)

Engine:
Powerplant: 1 x Continental AOS 895-3 6-cylinder petrol 374 kW (500 hp) engine
Capacity: 14.7 l (3.88 gallons)
Power/Weight Ratio: 21.3 hp/tonne
Suspension: Torsion bar

Armament and Armour:
Primary Armament: 1 x 76-mm (3-in) L/52 M32 gun
Secondary Armament: 1 x 7.69-mm (0.3-in) Browning M1919A4E1 machine gun
Ancillary Armament: 1 x 12.7-mm (0.5-in) Browning M2 HB AA machine gun
Armour Type: Homogenous nickel-steel rolled/welded hull, cast/welded turret
Hull Front: 25–32 mm (1–1.3 in)
Hull Sides: 19–25 mm (0.75–1 in)
Hull Rear: 19 mm (0.75 in)
Hull Top: 12–15 mm (0.47–0.59 in)
Hull Bottom: 9–32 mm (0.35–1.3 in)
Turret Front: 25 mm (1 in)
Turret Sides: 25 mm (1 in)
Turret Rear: 25 mm (1 in)
Turret Top: 13 mm (0.51 in)

Variants:
M41A1: (1953) Hydraulic instead of electrical turret traverse.
M41A2: (1956) Production tanks with fuel-injected Continental 6-cylinder petrol engine replacing carburettor fuel system.
M41A3: M41A1 tanks with engines upgraded to fuel injection.
M41 DK-1: Danish upgrade. New engine, thermal sights.
Type 64 (Experimental): Taiwanese development modified. Did not enter mass production and is not to be confused with another M42-based light tank conversion bearing the same designation.
M41D: Taiwanese upgrade.
M42 Duster: (1952) Self-propelled anti-aircraft defence weapon system based on the M41 chassis.

M41 WALKER BULLDOG

The successor to the M24 Chaffee light tank, which was deployed late in 1944 and saw only limited service during World War II, the M41 Walker Bulldog continued to be built on a theme of compatibility among a team of armoured vehicles capable of utilizing the same chassis and common components. The rangefinder, fully enclosed in the cast and welded turret, proved troublesome and delayed production until 1951. While the driver was situated in the hull, the three crew members in the turret were sometimes hampered by limited space. Both commander and loader had access to hatches, which opened to the rear.

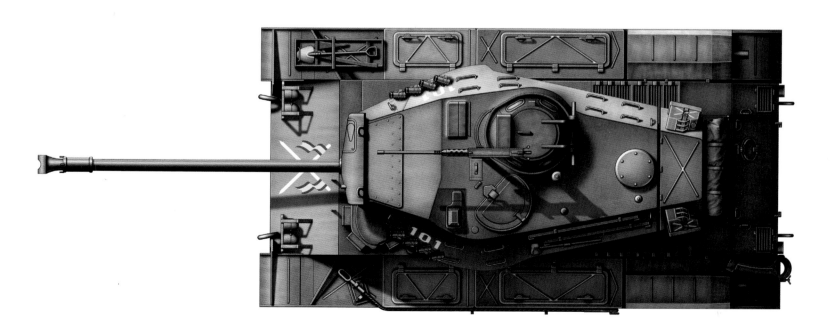

Pausing along a street in a South Vietnamese city, the American crewmen of a Walker Bulldog tank watch traffic move past as infantrymen maintain a continuing cordon of security against Viet Cong infiltrators.

The M41 Walker Bulldog was developed as a fast, agile light tank for close infantry support and cavalry reconnaissance. Carrying a 76-mm (3-in) M32 main gun, it was amply armed to defend itself even against enemy medium tanks.

In the wake of World War II, the U.S. Army was confronted with countering the perceived menace of communism on a global scale. American tank designers had already begun to heed the lessons of armoured warfare gleaned from the battlefields of Europe. Applying these to their own designs and maintaining some adherence to the early U.S. armoured doctrine of infantry support and scouting functions, the M41 Walker Bulldog emerged as the first post-war U.S. light tank to see extensive service around the world.

A relative few of the M41's predecessor, the M24 Chaffee, had seen action during World War II, and although the M24 design appeared to be solid and functional, the U.S. effort to upgrade continued. By 1949, the prototype T41E1 had largely been designed around the proposed powerplant, the 374-kW (500-hp), six-cylinder Continental AOS 895-3 or a comparable Lycoming engine, which had originally been intended for use in aircraft.

In response to the defence demands placed on the U.S. Army, the M41 – named the Walker Bulldog in honour of General Walton H. Walker, who was killed in Korea in 1950 – was intended for rapid deployment, by air if necessary. It was meant to pack enough punch with its 76-mm (3-in) cannon to defend itself against heavier enemy tanks. Its armoured protection ranged from 9.75 to 38 mm (0.38–1.5 in). Its secondary armament was a single hull-mounted Browning 7.62-mm (0.3-in) machine gun and a turret-mounted 12.7-mm (0.5-in) machine gun for anti-aircraft defence.

In the event, at 23.5 tonnes (25.9 tons), the M41 proved too heavy for reasonable air deployment. However, its firepower, top road speed of 72 km/h (45 mph), and range of 225 km (140 miles) proved to be valuable assets. Production began in 1951 at the Cleveland, Ohio, plant operated by the Cadillac division of General Motors, and 1802 were built.

COMPONENTS AND COMBAT
The M41 utilized a CD 500-3 cross-drive transmission with hydraulic torque converters, two forwards speeds, and a single reverse gear. Its innovative suspension included a combination of torsion bars and hydraulic shock absorbers. An automatic loader improved the 76-mm (3-in) cannon's rate of fire significantly, and the original rangefinder was

replaced with a simplified version in production models. Infrared optics and searchlights facilitated nocturnal operations. The M41 was capable of fording just over 1 m (40 in) of still water and climbing a 76-cm (30-in) vertical obstruction. An external telephone was mounted in the hull for communication with infantry.

Even though it was deployed only on a limited basis during the Korean War, the tank was still designated T41. Its single greatest limitation was turret space, with limited headroom for three crewmen, yet the tank was deployed in significant numbers during the Vietnam War, becoming popular among South Vietnamese tank crews, generally of slighter stature than their American allies.

MULTI-NATIONAL USERS

The armed forces of more than 20 nations deployed the M41, and its combat record in Southeast Asia included the first armoured engagement of the Vietnam War. During this incident three of five M41s, along with 25 armoured personnel carriers, were lost. In addition, the South Vietnamese armoured force and supporting air strikes destroyed 22 Soviet-built T-54 and PT-76 tanks.

Interior view

The cramped interior of the M41 made it a relatively unpopular vehicle with American armoured crews. South Vietnamese soldiers who used the tank found the space to be adequate.

1. **Ballistic Unit:** This included a control knob for choosing the right type of ammunition to engage a selected target.

2. **Gun Breech:** The breech of the M41 Walker Bulldog's 76-mm (3-in) main gun was semi-automatic and installed vertically. A bin for spent shell casings was located nearby.

3. **Traverse Mechanism Hand Wheel:** This connected to the commander's hand control through a long crossrod, which ran towards the rear of the turret.

4. **Optics:** The M20 periscope and M79 telescope were the gunner's primary and back-up equipment for sighting targets for the pulsed relay system of the main weapon.

5. **Gun Firing Control Box:** This served as an electric switch panel, powering components of the 76-mm (3-in) gun-laying system.

6. **Gunner's Position:** The gunner was positioned to use the optics and manipulate manual hydraulic equipment to elevate the main weapon.

AMX-13

An early post–World War II French tank design, the AMX-13 was a light, air-mobile fighting vehicle. Its designers were responsible for introducing such innovations as an automatic loading system and oscillating turret. Variants have been exported to at least 25 countries.

TURRET
The oscillating turret of the AMX-13 involves a fixed main weapon while the upper half of the turret pivots on the lower half to change the gun's elevation.

LOADING SYSTEM
The main cannon was loaded with an automatic system of revolver-type magazines, two of which were available and held six shells apiece. After these two magazines were fired, the magazines were refilled manually.

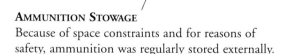

AMMUNITION STOWAGE
Because of space constraints and for reasons of safety, ammunition was regularly stored externally.

ENGINE
The 187-kW (250-hp) SOFAM 8Gxb eight-cylinder petrol engine ran the length of the right side of the AMX-13 hull.

SECONDARY ARMAMENT

In various configurations, the secondary armament of the AMX-13 included a coaxial 7.5-mm (0.29-in) or 7.62-mm (0.3-in) machine gun on the right side of the main cannon and a 7.62-mm (0.3-in) anti-aircraft machine gun.

MAIN ARMAMENT

Originally armed with a 75-mm (2.95-in) cannon patterned after the World War II–vintage German 75-mm (2.95-in) KwK 42 L/70 mounted on the PzKpfw V Panther medium tank, the AMX-13 was upgunned to a 90-mm (3.54-in) weapon and then a 105-mm (4-in) for export.

FACTS

- Production of AMX-13 variants lasted from 1952–87.

- Approximately half of the 7700 AMX-13 variants were exported.

- Early petrol engines were retrofitted with diesel powerplants to minimize the risk of fire and improve range.

DRIVER POSITION

Seated forwards and to the left in the hull, the driver was able to view the field through three periscopes.

ARMOUR PROTECTION

With only 25 mm (1 in) of armour protection, the AMX-13 hull was vulnerable to large-calibre shells and protected only against small arms, splinters, and flash burn.

In 1946, when work on the design of the AMX-13 began, the tank was intended to be used as a tank destroyer and reconnaissance vehicle. As the tank developed, the manufacturer, Atelier de Construction Roanne (ARE), modified the design slightly and produced a true light tank.

AMX-13 – SPECIFICATION

Country of Origin: France
Crew: 3
Designer: Atelier de Construction d'Issy-les-Moulineaux
Designed: 1946
In Production: 1952–87
Manufacturer: Atelier de Construction Roanne
In Service: 1953–present
Number Built: 7700
Gross Weight: 15 tonnes (16.5 tons)

Dimensions:
Hull Length: 4.88 m (16 ft)
Length (gun forward): 6.36 m (20.9 ft)
Width: 2.5 m (8.2 ft)
Overall Height: 2.3 m (7.6 ft) (to cupola top)

Performance:
Maximum Speed: 60 km/h (37 mph)
Range, Road: 400 km (250 miles)
Range, Cross-country: 250 km (150 miles)
Ground Pressure: 0.76 kg/cm²
Fording Capacity: 0.6 m (2 ft)
Maximum Gradient: 30 degrees
Maximum Trench Width: 1.6 m (5.25 ft)
Maximum Vertical Obstacle: 0.65 m (2.2 ft)
Suspension Type: Torsion bars

Engine:
Powerplant: 1 x SOFAM (Saviem) 8GXb V-8 liquid-cooled petrol
Capacity: n/a
Output: 187 kW (250 hp) @ 3200 rpm
Power/Weight Ratio: 16.7 bhp/tonne
Fuel Capacity: 480 l (106 gallons)

Armour and Armament:
Main Armament: 1 x 75-mm (2.95-in) L/57 (1967 replaced by 90 mm [3.54 in])
Secondary Armament: 2 x 7.5-mm (0.29-in) or 7.62-mm (0.3-in) FN1/AAT52 machine guns
Armour Type: Homogeneous rolled/welded nickel-steel with cast turret
Hull Front: 40 mm (1.58 in)
Hull Sides: 20 mm (0.79 in)
Hull Rear: 15 mm (0.59 in)
Hull Top: 10 mm (0.39 in)
Hull Bottom: 10 mm (0.39 in)
Turret Front: 40 mm (1.58 in)
Turret Sides: 20 mm (0.79 in)
Turret Rear: 20 mm (0.79 in)
Turret Top: 10 mm (0.39 in)

Variants:
75 Modèle 51: High-velocity 75-mm (2.95-in) gun in FL-11 turret.
T75 (Char Lance SS-11): Fitted with SS-11 ATGM launchers.
T75 avec TCA: Fitted with electronic missile guidance system.
90 Modèle 52: FL-10 turret refitted with F3 90-mm (3.54-in) gun.
90 LRF: Fitted with laser rangefinder.
105 Modèle 58: Fitted with 105-mm (4-in) gun in FL-12 turret.
13/105: Upgraded export version of the Modele 58.
Model 1987: Late production version.
DCA aka AMX-13/S530: SPAAG version.
DCA 30: (aka Bitube de 30-mm [1.18-in] anti-aérien automoteur, Oeil Noir) SPAAG version with retractable radar.
[Training Tank]: AMX-13 with turret removed.
Modèle 55 (AMX-D): Recovery version.
PDP (Poseur De Pont) Modèle 51: Scissors-type bridgelayer.

VARIANT: AMX 13 DCA ANTI-AIRCRAFT

AMX-13

The interior of the AMX-13 was divided into a forward compartment holding the engine on the right and running the length of the hull, and the driver on the left, along with a fighting compartment accommodating the commander and gunner to the rear. The oscillating turret was fitted towards the rear of the chassis and featured an automatic loading system, which fired six-round magazines. One of the driver's viewing periscopes was often retrofitted with an infrared scope for night vision, while the commander was situated under a domed cupola with 360-degree visibility. Early optics were improved with computers and laser rangefinders.

SUPPORT VEHICLE: PANHARD EBR ARMOURED CAR

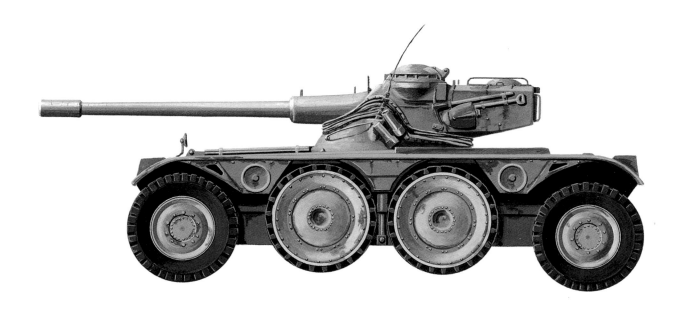

Even though it is now functionally obsolescent, the AMX-13 remains in service with several countries. The Israeli army used the tank in its 1956 and 1967 wars, but found it unsatisfactory. It was phased out of service with the French army in the 1970s.

The innovations of the French-built AMX-13 light tank proved modern in concept but troublesome at times in application. Conceived in the wake of World War II, the tank was named in recognition of its original weight, 13 tonnes (14 tons). Later versions, carrying heavier armament and diesel engines, weighed 15 tonnes (16.5 tons) or more. Intended as a fire support and reconnaissance vehicle for airborne troops, it was deployable by air. However, its air mobile weight was achieved at the expense of adequate armour protection (25 mm [0.98 in]), making the vehicle vulnerable to virtually any anti-tank weapon in service.

Close-up

The AMX-13 was innovative in concept and design, but it proved a disappointment under the rigours of combat. Nevertheless, it was a popular export to other nations, and was produced for 25 years.

(1) **Main Weapon System:** Early AMX-13s were armed with a 75-mm (2.9-in) cannon, but were upgraded to 105 mm (4 in).

(2) **Light Weight:** The tank's light weight made it air-transportable to fulfill its primary role of fire support and reconnaissance for airborne troops.

(3) **Driver Position:** The driver sat in the front of the hull and to the left, with the engine running the length of the right side.

(4) **Oscillating Turret:** Along with an automatic loading system for the main weapon, the oscillating turret was also an innovation.

(5) **Smoke Grenade Launcher:** External smoke grenade launchers were commonly used to provide concealment for the vehicle and infantry units in Cold War era tanks.

(6) **Ammunition Storage:** This was outside the tank, which meant reloading was somewhat problematic.

One of the more than 100 variants of the French AMX-13 light tank rolls down a thoroughfare during parade activities. The AMX-13 was light and manoeuvrable, though limited armour protection made it highly vulnerable to enemy fire.

Further, the AMX-13 introduced a Fives-Gail Babcock oscillating turret, which included a fixed main gun on the upper half of the turret. Pivoting the upper half of the turret on the lower half raised or lowered the main gun's elevation. In certain mountainous terrain, the turret rendered the main gun almost unusable. Although such a turret configuration facilitated the introduction of an automatic loading system, eliminating the need for a fourth crewman, the loading system fired only two six-round magazines. Once these initial 12 shells were fired, the weapon had to be served manually because the magazines were reloaded outside the vehicle. This stretched the effectiveness of the three-man crew heavily in combat, and put them at further risk.

ARMS FOR SALE

Early AMX-13 models were powered by the eight-cylinder SOFAM 8Gxb petrol engine generating 187 kW (250 hp). However, some countries have opted for diesel engines to reduce the potential for fire and increase the vehicle's range. The original turret, designated the FL-10, mounted the German-inspired 75-mm (2.95-in) cannon with a single baffle muzzle brake based on that of the Panther medium tank of World War II. It fired at a rate of one round every five seconds until its magazines were emptied.

By 1966, the 90-mm (3.54-in) AMX-13/90 gun had been introduced in the new FL-12 turret, and many existing tanks were retrofitted with the improved weapon. Along with secondary armament of a 7.5-mm (0.29-in) or 7.62-mm (0.3-in) coaxial machine gun and a 7.62-mm (0.3-in) anti-aircraft machine gun, a third light machine gun could be mounted near the commander's cupola for added infantry support. The original torsion bar suspension was upgraded with a hydro-pneumatic system in 1985 along with the introduction of a fully automatic transmission and a standard diesel engine.

Production of the AMX-13 began at ARE in 1952 following at least five years of research and development and was taken over by Cruesot-Loire in 1964. By the time production ceased in 1987, more than 7700 had been built. Over 3000 of these were exported from France to other countries, and a version specifically for export had been upgunned with a low-velocity 105-mm (4-in) cannon. A number of purchasers improved their AMX-13s with better weapons or added nuclear, biological, and chemical defensive systems along with night fighting technology.

More than 100 variants of the AMX-13 have been developed during five decades of service. These include an armoured personnel carrier and platforms for self-propelled artillery and anti-tank guided missile systems.

PT 76

Developed in the early 1950s, the PT 76 has served as a primary Soviet Bloc amphibious light tank for reconnaissance, infantry support, and troop transportation. Its versatility has been proven in combat in Southeast Asia, the Middle East, and in Afghanistan.

MAIN ARMAMENT
Later production models of the PT 76 were armed with an improved D-56TM, 76.2-mm (3-in) main cannon, which featured a double-baffle muzzle brake and a bore evacuator to release toxic fumes.

HULL CONFIGURATION
The distinctive pontoon-shaped hull is divided into a crew compartment in front, and an engine compartment to the rear.

DRIVER
Seated forwards and to the centre of the vehicle, the driver views the field through three observation periscopes, one of which is interchangeable with an infrared scope.

COMMANDER
Seated in the small turret directly behind the driver and with the gunner to his left, the tank commander has three periscopes and a basic gunsight for observation. The commander serves the main weapon and operates the radio.

ENGINE
A 179-kW (240-hp), V6-B inline water-cooled diesel engine powers the PT 76 at a top speed of 44 km/h (27 mph).

FACTS

- The PT 76 is amphibious without field modification.

- Although largely replaced in the Russian army, the PT 76 is still in use with the armed forces of at least 25 nations.

- Russian naval infantry and Polish marines deployed a later variant for amphibious operations.

ARMOUR PROTECTION
Thinly armoured, the PT 76 is vulnerable to enemy fire of 12.7-mm (0.5-in) calibre or greater. Its frontal armour is 10–14 mm (0.4–0.5 in) thick and sloped at 80.5 degrees, while turret armour is 10–20 mm (0.4–0.78 in) thick.

AMPHIBIOUS PROPULSION
A hydrojet engine pumps water into the system through two intakes and ejects it at high velocity to propel the PT 76 through water at a top speed of 10 km/h (6 mph).

The **PT 76** is designed to enhance its amphibious capability, but this limits the tank as a fighting vehicle in a number of ways. It has a boat-like hull and there are limits to how much it can weigh, meaning its armour protection is reduced.

PT-76

PT 76 – SPECIFICATION

Country of Origin: Soviet Union
Crew: 3
Designers: N. Shashmurin and Zh.Y. Kotin
Designed: 1949–51
Manufacturer: VTZ, Kirov Factory
Produced: 1953–69
Number Built: Around 12,000
In Service: August 1952–present
Weight: 14 tonnes (15.4 tons)

Dimensions:
Hull Length: 6.91 m (22 ft 8 in)
Width: 3.15 m (10 ft 4 in)
Height: 2.325 m (7 ft 5.6 in)

Performance:
Range: 370–400 km (230–248 miles), 480–510 km
(300–317 miles) with external fuel
Speed: 44 km/h (27 mph), 10.2 km/h (6.3 mph) in water

Engine:
Powerplant: 6-cylinder diesel 179 kW (240 hp)
Power/Weight Ratio: 16.4 hp/tonne
Suspension: Torsion-bar
Ground Clearance: 370 mm (14.6 in)
Fuel Capacity: 250 l (66 gallons)

Armour and Armament:
Armour: 20 mm (0.79 in)
Main armament: 1 x 76.2-mm (3-in) D-56T rifled tank gun (40 rounds)
Secondary armament: 7.62-mm (0.3-in) SGMT coaxial machine gun (1000 rounds)

Variants:
PT 76 Model 1: An original PT 76 armed with the D-56T 76.2-mm (3-in) rifled tank gun.
PT 76 Model 2 (1954): PT 76 armed with the D-56TM 76.2-mm (3-in) rifled tank gun.
PT 76B: Armed with the D-56TS or the D-56B 76.2-mm (3-in) rifled tank gun.
PT 71: A PT 76B fitted with 9M14 "Malyutka" (NATO code: AT-3 Sagger) anti-tank guided missile pack on the rear of the turret.
PT 76A: PT 76 and PT 76Bs armed with DShK 1938/46 12.7-mm (0.5-in) anti-aircraft heavy MG on rotating turret mount.
PT 76: Armed with a 57-mm (2.24-in) autocannon.
PT 76K: Command version with an additional antenna on the right-hand side of the turret and a generator at the rear.
PT 76M (Ob'yekt 740M): Improved amphibious features.
PT 90 (Ob'yekt 906): PT 76 armed with 90-mm (3.54-in) rifled tank gun.
Objekt 280: PT 76 fitted with a 16 x 130-mm (5-in) multi-barrel rocket launcher.
PT-76RKh: Converted to a light amphibious reconnaissance tank.
BTR-50: PT 76 converted into an amphibious tracked APC.
Ob'yekt 914: Experimental IFV.
MTP-1: PT 76 converted into a technical support vehicle.
UR-67: (Ustanovka Razminirovaniya) Mine-clearing vehicle equipped with a UR-67 rocket launcher system.
ASU-85: PT 76 converted to 85-mm (3.35-in) airborne assault gun.
FROG-2 "Mars": Tactical missile launch vehicle.
FROG-5 "Luna": Tactical missile launch vehicle.
GM-568: Chassis used for the 1S91 guidance vehicle of 2K12 Kub surface-to-air missile system.
GM-575: Chassis used for the ZSU-23-4 self-propelled anti-aircraft gun.
GM-578: Chassis used for the 2P25 launch vehicle.

SUPPORT VEHICLE: ASU-85

PT 76

An amphibious light tank originally deployed with Soviet Bloc forces in the 1950s, the PT 76 has remained in service on a global scale. Its combat efficiency is limited because the commander must function as gunner and radio operator in the cramped turret. The welded steel hull with sharply sloped front glacis is ideal for flotation, but the amphibious nature of the tank means that its armour protection, up to a maximum of 14 mm (0.5 in), is relatively thin and protective against only small arms, shell fragments, and flash burn. Its 76.2-mm (3-in) cannon is considered light for tank-versus-tank encounters. In an attempt to improve the amphibious characteristics and increase the combat power of their wheeled reconnaissance vehicles, the Soviets produced the BRDM-2 (below), which was introduced into service in 1962. The ASU-85 self-propelled gun was used for light infantry support or assault.

SUPPORT VEHICLE: BRDM-2

Seen here with the Soviet naval insignia emblazoned on its hull, a PT 76 amphibious light tank churns across a snowy landscape. The PT 76 has seen wide deployment with Soviet, Warsaw Pact, and Russian forces.

The PT 76 performed well in Vietnam but poorly in the Arab-Israeli wars. The fact that the Russian army has not introduced a better replacement reflects their almost sacrificial role as fire-drawing precursors for main battle tanks.

The nature of reconnaissance involves vulnerability, and as World War II–era Soviet light tanks become increasingly obsolescent, the PT 76 was developed between 1949 and 1951 to provide amphibious capabilities without field modification, transport troops, and provide close fire support to attacking infantry. The literal translation of the vehicle's name, Plavayushtshiy Tank, is "amphibious tank." Production began in 1953 at the Volgograd Tank Factory, and more than 12,000 of the original model and subsequent variants were produced during the next 20 years.

The low silhouette of the PT 76 is reminiscent of other Soviet tank designs, with the turret positioned forwards and the pronounced slope to the front glacis plate of the hull. Divided into two compartments, the tank is manned by a crew of three, with the driver forward and in the centreline of the hull, the commander and gunner in the confining turret. Seated on the right of the main 76.2-mm (3-in) gun, the commander had access to three observation periscopes and used a simple TshK-2-66 sight for the weapon. In common with previous Soviet designs, the commander was also required to serve as radio operator and to serve the gun in combat. The gunner was positioned to the left of the main cannon, which had an MK-4 sight.

FIRING IN MOTION

Early PT 76s were armed with the unstabilized D-56T cannon, which prohibited the weapon being fired while the tank was on the move. Later versions were equipped with the improved D-56TM, and subsequently, on the PT 76B, which debuted in 1959, the D-56TS. This was stabilized in two planes for firing on the move. Secondary armament consisted of a coaxial 7.62-mm (0.3-in) machine gun. Some later models also mounted a 12.7-mm (0.5-in) machine gun for anti-aircraft defence. The welded hull is rolled thinly from a single sheet of steel, and the V-6 diesel engine generates 179 kW (240 hp). The five-gear transmission is quite similar to that of the venerable T-34/85 medium tank. The primary reconnaissance tank for the Red Army and the forces of the Warsaw Pact for at least a quarter of a century, the original PT 76 entered service in 1954. Maintaining its amphibious capabilities did not require a halt to the vehicle's advance or any major reconfigurations by the crew. A water jet propulsion system was engaged for crossing streams, although the vehicle did have limitations in heavy surf. A snorkel was mounted, and electric bilge pumps were installed to help keep the vehicle afloat in the event that it sustained battle damage.

Major upgrades included the PT 76B, mounting the D-56TS cannon, improved radio communication, better optics, and more advanced electrical equipment. External fuel tanks could also be attached to improve the vehicle's range. The somewhat larger PT 76M was developed for the Soviet navy but dropped in favour of the snorkel-equipped PT 76B. For years, China has manufactured an unlicensed version of the tank, while a Polish variant has also been introduced. The PT 76 chassis has served as a platform for the FROG and SA-6 missile systems, the ASU-85 airborne assault gun, and the BTR-50P armoured personnel carrier.

Interior view

The interior of the PT 76 was cramped and ergonomically inefficient, with the commander required to perform several additional functions, including operating the radio and serving the main weapon.

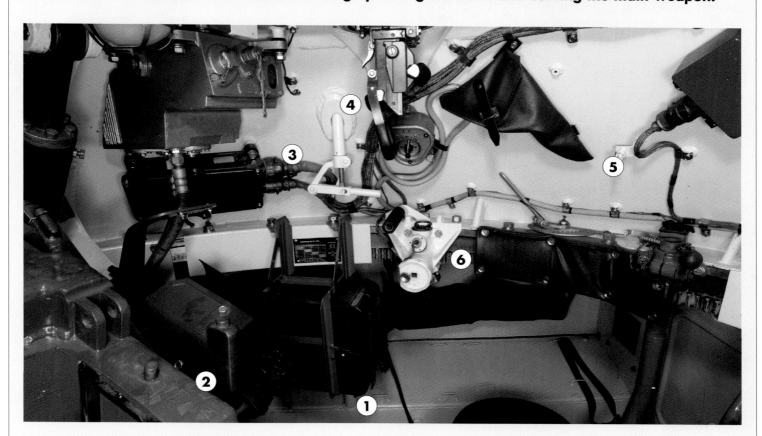

(1) **Commander's Position:** This was inside the low, elliptical turret to the right of the gunner and directly behind the driver.

(2) **Gun Breech:** The main 76.2-mm (3-in) D-56TM cannon mounted on the PT 76 was similar to that of the famed Soviet T-34 medium tank of World War II.

(3) **Rangefinding Equipment:** Target acquisition was accomplished using sights within the turret of the amphibious PT 76.

(4) **Communications:** The commander communicated with the gunner and driver with a headset and module.

(5) **Armour Shield:** The amphibious PT 76 was an adequate scouting and infantry support vehicle. However, the thinly armoured turret and hull were vulnerable to enemy fire.

(6) **Turret Mechanism:** The gears upon which the PT 76 turret rotated are visible here at the centre.

Saladin

The Alvis Saladin armoured car was placed in service with the armed forces of numerous countries during the 1960s and 1970s, as well as with the United Nations. It proved to be extremely well adapted as a patrol and reconnaissance vehicle.

SECONDARY ARMAMENT

For anti-aircraft defence, a 7.62-mm (0.3-in) Browning machine gun is mounted beside the commander's hatch on the turret. A second 7.62-mm (0.3-in) machine gun is mounted coaxially in the turret, and two six-round smoke grenade launchers are located on either side of the hull.

MAIN ARMAMENT

The main armament of the Saladin consists of a low-muzzle-velocity 76.2-mm (3-in) L5 gun. Its maximum effect range is 1000 m (3,280 ft).

DRIVER POSITION

The Saladin driver is allowed a maximum field of vision with the hatch, forwards left of the vehicle, folded back completely. In his enclosed compartment, the driver sees through three periscopes.

F A C T S

- A total of 1177 Saladin armoured cars were produced from 1958–72.

- Manufactured by Alvis, the Saladin is the armoured car in the company's FV 600 series.

- The Saladin replaced the Daimler armoured cars that had served with the British Army in World War II.

COMMANDER POSITION
The commander sees through four periscopes mounted forwards and a fifth swivelling periscope at the rear of the hatch.

ENGINE
The 127-kW (170-hp), eight-cylinder Rolls-Royce B80 Mk.6A engine of the Saladin is enclosed in a rear compartment.

GUNNER POSITION
His periscope divided into two parts, the Saladin gunner sits to the left of the commander inside the turret and scans the horizon for targets using an upper scope with no magnification and a lower scope with 6 x magnification power.

TURRET
The manually traversed, steel turret is of all-welded construction and protected by 32 mm (1.25 in) of armour plating.

The Saladin had been designed in the late 1940s, but it did not enter service until 1958. The armed forces of no fewer than 13 countries and those under the flag of the United Nations used the Saladin over the following two decades.

SUPPORT VEHICLE: SARACEN

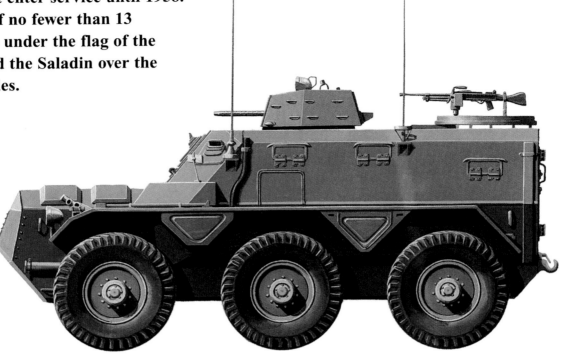

SALADIN – SPECIFICATION

Country of Origin: United Kingdom
Crew: 3
Designer: Alvis
Designed: 1956
Manufacturer: Alvis
In Production: 1958–72
In Service: 1959–today
Number Produced: 1177
Weight: 11.6 tonnes (12.78 tons)

Dimensions:
Hull Length: 4.93 m (16.17 ft)
Length (gun forward): 5.28 m (17 ft 4 in)
Wheelbase: 3.048 m (10 ft)
Width: 2.54 m (8.33 ft)
Height: 2.39 m (7.84 ft)

Performance:
Speed: 72 km/h (45 mph)
Range, Road: 400 km (249 miles)
Fording: 1.07 m (3 ft 6 in)
Gradient: 46 degrees
Vertical Obstacle: 0.46 m (1 ft 6 in)
Trench: 1.52 m (5 ft 0 in)
Ground Pressure: 1.12 kg/cm²

Engine:
Powerplant: 1 x Rolls Royce B80 Mk.6A, 8 cylinder petrol engine producing 1667 kW (170 hp)
Fuel Capacity: 241 l (63.7 gallons)
Power/Weight Ratio: 15.5 hp/tonne
Suspension: 6x6 wheel torsion bars

Armour and Armament:
Armour: Up to 32 mm (1.46 in)
Main Armament: 1 x 76-mm (3-in) L5A1 gun. 43 rounds.
Secondary Armament: 2 x 7.62-mm (0.3-in) coaxial machine guns. 2750 rounds.

Operators:
Australia
Germany
Honduras
Indonesia
Kuwait
Lebanon
Maldives
Mauritania
Oman
Portugal
Sri Lanka
Sudan
Tunisia
United Kingdom
Yemen

SUPPORT VEHICLE: HUMBER PIG

SALADIN

The Saladin FV 601 armoured car is one of a series of vehicles produced by the Alvis Car and Engineering Company Ltd. The FV 600 series also included the Stalwart High Mobility Load Carrier and the Salamander fire tender. The interior of the Saladin is divided into two compartments, with the crew forwards and the engine to the rear. The driver sits in the bow and to the right, while the commander and gunner are seated right and left respectively in the turret. A fireproof bulkhead separates the crew and engine compartments, and air to cool the engine is drawn through louvred covers on top of the compartment, exiting through the rear of the hull.

The Humber Pig was designed to supplement the Saracen; it was intended purely for transport to and from the battlefield rather than for any combat role. The Stalwart comes from the same family as the Saracen and the Saladin and uses many of the same basic components.

VARIANT: STALWART

The Saladin uses many components of the FV 603 armoured personnel carrier, one of the differences being that the Saracen has its engine in the front and the Saladin has its Rolls Royce engine in the rear.

The Alvis FV 601 armoured car, known as the Saladin after the famed Muslim warrior, entered service with the British Army in 1958. However, its design dates back to the mid-1940s as British engineers sought a suitable replacement for the Daimler armoured cars that had served with Commonwealth forces during World War II.

Perhaps best known for its service with a range of countries besides Great Britain and under the banner of the United Nations, the Saladin included numerous components in common with the Saracen armoured personnel carrier. Along with the Stalwart High Mobility load carrier and the

Interior view

The turret of the Alvis Saladin armoured car housed the commander and gunner, who used an array of controls to manually traverse the turret and sight the 76.2-mm (3-in) main armament.

1. **Cabling:** Electrical and hydraulic cabling provided power to the systems within the hull and turret of the Alvis Saladin.

2. **Timepiece:** This was mounted along the hull of the Saladin turret and tracked various intervals, allowing the commander and gunner to manage timetables.

3. **Optics:** The gunner used optics, including an upper periscope without magnification and a lower scope that could magnify targets.

4. **Stowage:** Ammunition for the 76.2-mm (3-in) main gun was stowed in the turret, within easy reach of the gunner and commander.

5. **Gun Breech:** The 76.2-mm (3-in) L5 gun was effective against light armoured vehicles and some stationary targets, including infantry and machine-gun positions.

6. **Gunner's Position:** The gunner sat left of the turret, where he could reach manual turret traverse equipment and the main weapon.

Soldiers spring from the rear of a Saracen armoured personnel vehicle, while the six-wheeled Saladin armoured car powers up an incline. One of the roles of the Saladin was to provide close support for infantry.

Salamander fire tender, it comprised the FV 600 series manufactured by the Alvis Car and Engineering Company until 1972. At that time, production was discontinued because the Saladin was being replaced by the tracked Scorpion reconnaissance vehicle.

DESIGNED FOR MOBILITY

Constructed with an all-welded steel hull, the Saladin is operated by a crew of three – a commander, gunner, and driver. Its interior includes two compartments separated by a fireproof bulkhead. The 1667-kW (170-hp) Rolls Royce engine is situated to the rear, and the crew compartment, including a two-man turret and the driver seat in the hull, is forwards. Each crewman is provided with several periscopes for optimal vision, and the hull is thinly protected by only 8 to 16 mm (0.3–0.6 in) of armour, conceivably enough to counter small-arms fire or shell fragments. The turret is protected by a 32-mm (1.25-in) layer of armour. The top speed of the Saladin is 72 km/h (45 mph) on the road, and its range is 400 km (250 miles). The vehicle's six wheels are each individually powered, and the front four respond to steering.

The main armament of the Saladin is a turret-mounted 76.2-mm (3-in) low-velocity cannon with a range of 1000 m (3,280 ft) and a muzzle velocity of only 533 m (1750 ft) per second. Along with the main weapon, a 7.62-mm (0.3-in) machine gun is mounted coaxially in the Saladin turret, while a second machine gun is pintle-mounted near the commander's hatch. As a result of a pair of serious design flaws, the commander functions as a loader for the main gun and, in order to operate the second machine gun, must stand up in the turret, fully exposing himself to enemy fire.

During the 1970s, the Saladin operated with United Nations forces in Cyprus, protecting the airport at the capital city of Nicosia, as well as with British forces during numerous deployments to hot spots around the world. The Australian army modified a quantity of its M113A1 armoured personnel carriers with Saladin turrets in an effort to develop an infantry support vehicle. When this proved less than satisfactory, the Saladin turret was replaced with that of the Scorpion light tank.

As a scouting, patrol, and reconnaissance vehicle, the Saladin generally performed well, and during the production period 1177 were manufactured. The armed forces of such nations as Australia, Indonesia, Jordan, Kuwait, Lebanon, Oman, and others have deployed the wheeled vehicle, and one of its few variants is an amphibious model.

M60

The initial U.S. main battle tank of the Cold War era, the M60 can be categorized as the fourth incarnation of the post-war Patton series or considered a direct descendant. First developed in response to the improvements made in Soviet armour, the M60 remains in service today.

SECONDARY ARMAMENT
A 12.7-mm (0.5-in) M2 heavy machine gun mounted on the commander's cupola was complemented by at least one 7.62-mm (0.3-in) coaxial machine gun and sometimes a second near the loader's hatch. On each side of the turret, a six-round smoke grenade launcher was attached.

TURRET
The original M60 turret was similar to that of the M48, being elliptical in shape. However, the A1 and A3 variants mounted a needle-nose turret, which presented a reduced frontal area in combat.

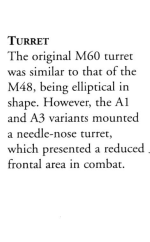

INTERIOR CONFIGURATION
As with the Patton series, the M60 was divided into three compartments: the fighting compartment in the centre, engine and transmission compartment to the rear, and the driver compartment to the front.

MAIN ARMAMENT
The 105-mm (4-in) M68, a license-built version of the British L7A1 cannon, was installed on the M60 and on the tanks of several other countries.

ENGINE
The 12-cylinder, 560-kW (750-hp) AVDS-1790-2A engine powered the M60 at a top road speed of 50 km/h (30 mph).

SUSPENSION
A torsion bar suspension was installed in more than one design in the M60 series. This included the tube over bar system, in which the torsion bar was enclosed in a tube, connected together at one end, and worked as a double suspension.

An external layer of appliqué armour was fitted to some M60A3s to give the tank adequate protection against the improved weapons systems it would encounter in the 1990s. The extra protection centred on the turret and the front glacis plate.

M60

M60

Placed in production in 1977, the M60A3 weighed 52 tonnes (57 tons), nearly the same as the M60A1, but incorporated a number of improvements over the earlier model, including a Hughes integrated laser rangefinding sight and thermal night sight for the commander, a VGS-2 thermal imaging sight and Hughes VVG-2 laser rangefinder for the gunner, and a solid-state ballistic computer with increased accuracy and an operating range of 200–5000 m (656 ft–5500 yards). A previous improvement to the original M60 design moved the main gun forward 12 cm (5 in), providing additional space inside the three-man turret. An Israeli-designed HALON automatic fire extinguisher system was standard on the M60A3.

VARIANT: M728 CEV

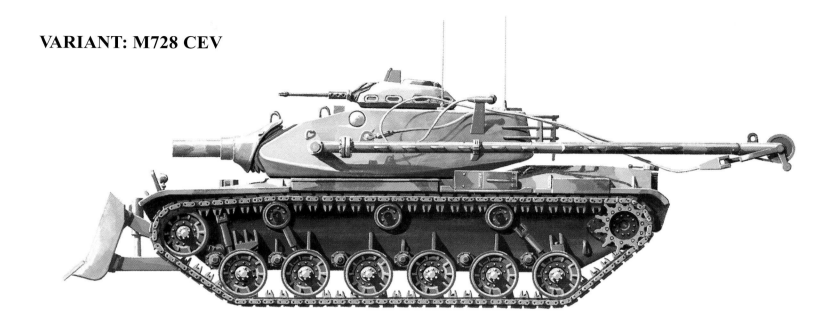

Country of Origin: USA
Crew: 4
Designer: Not specified
Designed: 1957–59
Manufacturer: Detroit Arsenal Tank Plant, Chrysler
In Production: 1959–83
In Service: 1960–97
Numbers Built: More than 15,000
Weight: 45 tons (50 tonnes)

Dimensions:
Length: 6.94 m (22 ft 9 in)
Width: 3.6 m (11 ft)
Height: 3.2 m (10 ft 6 in)

Performance:
Speed: 48 km/h (30 mph)
Operational range: 480 km (300 miles)

Engine:
Powerplant: 1 x Continental AVDS-1790-2 V12, air-cooled
twin-turbo diesel engine 560 kW (750 hp)
Power/weight Ratio: 14.5 hp/ton
Suspension: Torsion bar suspension
Ground clearance: 389 mm (15.3 in)

Armour and Armament:
Armour: 150 mm (5.9 in)
Main armament: 1 x 105-mm (4.1-in) M68 gun (M60/A1/A3);
1 x 152-mm (6-in) M162 Gun/Launcher (M60A2)
Secondary armament: 1 x 12.7-mm (0.50-in) M85;
1 x 7.62-mm (0.3-in) machine gun

Variants:
XM60/M60: Bearing a strong resemblance to the M48, the
M60 also has a wedge-shaped hull, three return rollers, and
aluminium road wheels. Early versions did not have the
commander's cupola.
M60A1: First variant to feature the distinctive needle-nose turret.
M60A1 AOS: Add-On Stabilization introduced in 1972 for the
M68 gun.
M60A1 RISE: Reliability Improvements for Selected Equipment,
featured improvements of almost all the basic systems,
including an upgraded engine design that enabled easier
access to components to allow removing the engine pack in
less time.
M60A1 RISE Passive: RISE, but with a smaller infrared/white
light-capable searchlight and passive night vision equipment.
M60A1E1: Developmental test vehicles fitted with the 152-mm (6-
in) M162 gun-missile launchers.
M60A1E2/M60A2: Turret design finalized, giving the
distinctive "starship" look. A variant was tested with a remote-
controlled 20-mm (0.79-in) cannon as well.
M60A1E3: Prototype M60A1E2 fitted with 105-mm
(4.1-in) gun.
M60A1E4: Experimental type with remote-control weapons.
M60A3: M60A1 fitted with a laser rangefinder.
M60A3 TTS: M60A3s fitted with the AN/VSG-2 thermal sight.
M60 Super/AX: Uparmoured versions with minor
improvements.
M60-2000/120S: M60/Abrams hybrid vehicle developed by
General Dynamics Land Division. Not adopted by the United
States military.
M728 CEV: M60A1-based Combat Engineer Vehicle.
M728A1: Upgraded version of the M728 CEV.

In 1956, intelligence reports regarding tank development in the Soviet Union suggested that a tank more capable than the T-54/T-55 main battle tank was being developed. A design team suggested that there was plenty of room for improving the M48, and upgrade programmes were immediately undertaken.

Production of the M60 main battle tank began at the height of the Cold War. It was based largely on the M48, even though the older design was considered inferior to a coming generation of improved Soviet tanks. The M48 was hampered in combat by its short range and extreme fuel consumption, heavy weight, and comparatively thin armour protection. The improved M60 entered service in 1960 and comprised the bulk of U.S. fighting armour for the next 20 years. Eventually the M1 Abrams largely replaced it, yet production of the M60 did not cease until 1987. Altogether, more than 15,000 M60s were manufactured.

Interior view

The M60 was designed as the first U.S. main battle tank of the Cold War era and is one of the world's most successful main battle tanks, with 15,000 having been produced.

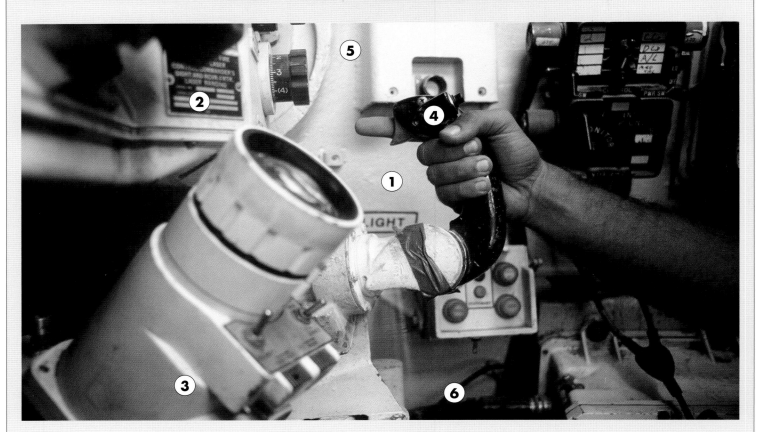

(1) **Commander's Position:** The commander sat in the turret above the gunner. The turret-mounted machine gun fired from the cupola.

(2) **Laser Rangefinder:** The laser rangefinder emits a laser beam that indentifies the target and provides a range, or distance, to the target for the main weapon to fire at.

(3) **105-mm (4-in) Night Sight:** The tank commander's night sight is an extension of the gunner's, enabling him to see what the gunner sees at night or during the day.

(4) **Tank Commander Override:** This allows the commander to elevate, depress, and fire the main cannon, traverse the turret, and follow moving targets.

(5) **Lighting:** The night sight uses ambient light rather than thermal imaging, as does the main gun's night sight.

(6) **Turret Basket:** The turret basket rotates in concert as the turret traverses, allowing the crew to orient themselves immediately to the interior of the M60 tank.

The externally-mounted laser rangefinder and smoke grenade launchers are affixed to the turret of the M60 main battle tank. Note the large searchlight, commander's cupola, and driver positioned in the centre of the hull.

The turret of the original M60 was subsequently replaced in the M60A1 and A3 models as designers opted for a cast needle-nose configuration, which offered a minimal target and improved armour protection in excess of 127 mm (5 in). The commander, gunner, and loader were positioned in the M60 turret, with the gunner in front and on the right, the loader above and to the left, and the commander directly behind and above the gunner. Seated in the left front of the hull and protected by armour up to 150 mm (5.9 in) thick, the driver viewed the surrounding terrain through three periscopes and an infrared scope for night vision. Both the commander and the gunner had good fields of vision. The gunner used a roof-mounted periscope, which could be interchanged with an infrared version, while the commander used eight vision slits circuiting the hand-rotated cupola.

THE "STARSHIP" DISAPPOINTS

The heavy 105-mm (4-in) M68 cannon could be ranged and fired by either the gunner or the commander, both of whom could also traverse the turret. The license-built M68 was a British design, which also equipped the tanks of several other nations, including the German Leopard I and later production models of the British Centurion.

The M60A2 variant was a radical departure from the main battle tank standard and proved to be a disappointment.

Nicknamed the "Starship," the M60A2 incorporated a redesigned turret mounting the Shillelagh weapons system, which proved unreliable. The Shillelagh weighed about half as much as a more conventional main gun, and the complicated 152-mm (6-in) system was capable of firing missiles or conventional high explosive, white phosphorus, or training ammunition rounds. Fewer than 550 of the M60A2 were built, and these were soon placed in storage.

By 1977, the production of the M60A3 and the upgrading of many M60A1 models already in service had begun. Beyond the improved fire control installed on the M60A3, a better track system, with pads that could be replaced by the crewmen, were added. The M60A3 was also given smokescreen capability, along with a snorkel, which allowed the tank to ford water to a depth of almost 4 m (13 ft).

A relative few M60s were deployed to Vietnam, and the tanks entered combat with the Israeli Defence Force during the Yom Kippur War. They were also used during the Iran-Iraq War and in Operation Desert Storm. Reviews of the performance of early M60s were mixed, particulary when confronted with the Soviet Sagger anti-tank missile. However, modifications allowed the M60 to keep pace with the latest in Soviet armour during its tenure. Today, numerous countries continue to field the M60, and the process of upgrading the design goes on.

BTR-60PA

Replacing the BTR-152, a converted truck, the development of the BTR-60 and its later variant, the BTR-60PA, began in 1959. Eventually, more than 25,000 of the vehicles were produced in the Soviet Union, equipping the Red Army and the ground forces of Warsaw Pact and other nations.

ARMAMENT
Either a DshK 12.7-mm (0.5-in) heavy machine gun or a light 7.62-mm (0.3-in) PKT coaxial machine gun was mounted above a single hatch positioned behind the commander and driver hatches. Some BTR-60PA models were fitted with two 7.62-mm (0.3-in) machine guns, one on either side of the hatch.

ARMOUR PROTECTION
Frontal hull armour protection was only 9 mm (0.35 in) thick, while the hull sides varied from 5–7 mm (0.2–0.26 in), which was just enough to protect against shell splinters and small-arms fire.

SUSPENSION
The wheeled eight-by-eight vehicle was supported by a torsion bar suspension with two hydraulic shock absorbers on the first and second road wheels of each side, and a single hydraulic shock absorber for the third and fourth road wheels.

ACCESS

A lone hatch, opening to the right, was provided above the personnel compartment, while three firing ports were installed on each side of the vehicle. No entry access was available along the sides.

CAPACITY

Along with its crew of two – a driver and commander – the BTR-60PA carried up to 14 passengers. Later variants added another crewman – a gunner – to man additional armament.

ENGINE

Twin 67-kW (90-hp), six-cylinder GAZ-40P petrol engines powered the BTR-60 and were prone to catching fire.

The BTR-60 was continuously improved during the 1960s. Numerically, it was the most important vehicle in the Soviet army, issued in quantity to the East German, Bulgarian, and Romanian armies and exported to Yugoslavia. It was the standard armoured personnel carrier of Soviet naval infantry.

BTR-60

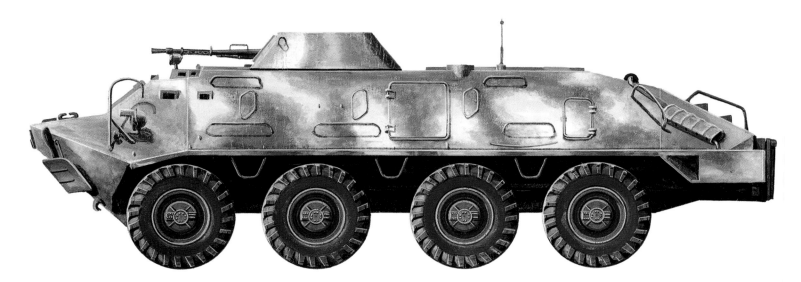

BTR-60PA – SPECIFICATION

Country of Origin: Soviet Union
Crew: 2 + 16 passengers
Designer: V. A. Dedkov
Designed: 1955
Manufacturers: Gorkovsky Avtomobilny Zavod (USSR); Ratmil Regie Automoma (Romania, TAB-71)
Produced: 1960–76
In Service: 1959–present
Number Built: About 25,000 (USSR), +1872 (Romania, TAB-71)
Weight: 10.2 tonnes (11.24 tons)

Dimensions:
Length: 7.56 m (24.8 ft)
Width: 2.825 m (7.5 ft)
Height: 2.06 m (6.76 ft)

Performance:
Speed, Road: 80 km/h (49.7 mph)
Speed, Water: 10 km/h (6.2 mph)
Operational Range: 500 km (311 miles)
Suspension: Wheeled 8 x 8
Ground Clearance: 475 mm (187 in)

Engine:
Powerplant: 2 x GAZ-40P 6-cylinder petrol engines producing 67 kW (90 hp) each and 134 kW (180 hp) combined
Power/weight: 13.1 kW/tonne (17.6 hp/tonne)
Fuel capacity: 290 l (76.6 gallons)

Armour and Armament:
Armour: Welded steel
Hull Upper Front: 7 mm (0.26 in) at 86 degrees

Hull Lower Front: 9 mm (0.35 in) at 47 degrees
Hull Sides: 7 mm (0.26 in)
Hull Upper Rear: 5 mm (0.2 in)
Hull Lower Rear: 7 mm (0.26 in)
Hull Floor: 5 mm (0.2 in)
Hull Roof: 7 mm (0.26 in)
Turret Front: 10 mm (0.39 in)
Turret Sides: 7 mm (0.26 in)
Turret Rear: 7 mm (0.26 in)
Turret Roof: 7 mm (0.26 in)
Main Armament: Early models: 1 x 7.62-mm (0.3-in) PKT, SGMB or PKB tank/medium/general purpose machine gun (2,000 rounds); later models: 1 x 12.7-mm (0.5-in) DShK 1938/46 heavy machine gun (500 rounds).
Secondary Armament: 2 x 7.62-mm (0.3-in) PKT, SGMB or PKB tank/medium/general purpose MGs (3000 rounds) mounted on the sides of the troop compartment (optional).

Major Variants
BTR-60P: Early version. Open roof, various MG arrangements.
BTR-60PA: Second Production Vehicle. Closed roof, NBC system.
BTR-60P: Utilizes the OT-64C(1) turret.
BTR-60PBK: Commander's Vehicle.
BTR-60 1V18: Artillery Observation Vehicle.
BTR-60 1V19: Fire Direction Vehicle.
BTR-60-R-409BM: Communications Vehicle.
BTR-60AVS: Command Post Vehicle.
BTR-60PAU: Artillery Communications Vehicle.
BTR-60PU-12M: Air Defence Command and Control Vehicle.
BTR-60 VVS: Command Post Vehicle.
BTR-60 ACVR M1979(2): Artillery Tow Vehicle.
BTR-60PU: Commander's Vehicle.

REPLACEMENT: BTR-70

BTR-60PA

The BTR-60PA signalled an improvement over the original BTR-60 in that its armoured roof covering for the personnel compartment, thin at only 7 mm (0.26 in), offered some protection against shell fragments and small arms fire from above. However, its complement of up to 14 combat infantrymen were exposed to the enemy while exiting through a top hatch because no exit was possible from the sides. In addition, the BTR-60PA was distinguished from its predecessor by the driver's roof-mounted periscope, heavier machine gun armament, and NBC defences. To assist with ingress and egress, six handrails, grouped in two pairs of three, were attached to the exterior of each side.

REPLACEMENT: BTR-80

Between 1956 and 1957, the Soviets decided to convert all Red Army rifle and mechanized divisions into new motor rifle divisions, and set out to determine the requirements for such new vehicles. The low combat value of the BTR-152 had been exposed during the Suez Crisis.

First noted by Western observers in 1961, the BTR-60 was developed in the late 1950s as a replacement for the unsatisfactory BTR-152 and BTR-40 armoured personnel carriers in service shortly after the end of World War II. Between 1960 and 1976, more than 25,000 were constructed in the Soviet Union, primarily by the Arzamas Machinery plant, and thousands have served with the armed forces of the former Warsaw Pact countries and other purchasers around the world.

The hull of the BTR-60 resembled a boat with a welded construction. It was divided into a crew compartment

Interior view

The spacious crew compartment of the BTR-60PA provided wide fields of vision for the driver and commander while the vehicle was underway. To the rear there was capacity for up to 14 soldiers.

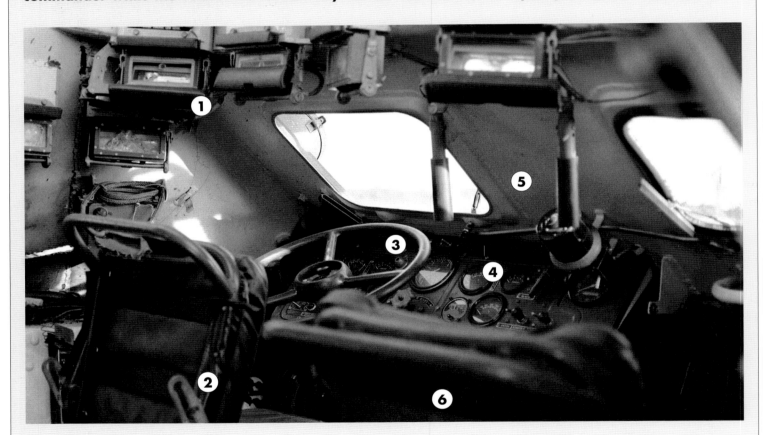

1. **Viewing Ports:** Multiple viewing ports allowed the driver and commander of the vehicle to observe the land before them.

2. **Driver's Seat:** The multi-position driver's seat was functional, although the comfort of the crew was always secondary in the approach of Soviet armoured vehicle design theory.

3. **Steering Wheel:** A steering wheel made the BTR-60PA simpler to operate, which made it relatively easy for new drivers to become familiar with the vehicle.

4. **Engine Gauges:** The simple layout of the driver's position allowed ease of monitoring engine oil pressure and fuel levels.

5. **Exterior Hull:** The light armour of the BTR-60PA, only 9 mm (0.35 in) on the front of the hull, was a concession to achieve higher road and cross-country speed.

6. **Commander's Position:** The commander often also served as the infantry squad leader. This meant his seat was positioned to facilitate his rapid exit from the vehicle.

This BTR-60PA, deployed with a contingent of United Nations peacekeeping forces, demonstrates the multiple positions from which combat infantrymen might engage the enemy with some protection. Later models included a heavy, turret-mounted machine gun.

forwards, a personnel or troop compartment in the centre, and an engine compartment to the rear. Firing ports were located along the sides. The driver was seated to the left and steered the vehicle with a wheel, while the commander was seated to the right. Later variants added a gunner.

DUAL THREAT

The tank's pair of 67-kW (90-hp) six-cylinder petrol engines were prone to catching fire or exploding when the thin hull armour was compromised. The vehicle's top road speed was 80 km/h (50 mph). All eight wheels were powered, with the transmission of the right engine powering the first and third axles and the transmission of the left engine powering the second and fourth. Fully amphibious without preparation, the BTR-60PA was powered through water at 10 km/h (6 mph) by a pair of pump jets. The driver was vulnerable to small-arms fire through the unprotected front wheel wells.

In 1964, the BTR-60PA was introduced with a roof covering over the troop compartment, which gave some protection for the infantry within, along with an NBC system. The troop-carrying capacity of the BTR-60 varied, with the BTR-60PA, the first substantial modification, carrying from 12 to 14 combat-ready infantrymen.

The original BTR-60 was also known as the BTR-60P. Other variants included the BTR-60PBK, a command

version, the BTR-60PU, which was utilized as a mobile command post with communications apparatus, and the BTR-60PB forwards air control vehicle, with a plexiglass window instead of weaponry. The more heavily armed standard BTR-60PB, introduced in 1965, included a machine gun turret mounting a 14.5-mm (0.57-in) KPVT heavy machine gun and a coaxial 7.62-mm (0.3-in) PKT machine gun. Additional modifications to the BTR-60PB included AGS-17 automatic grenade launchers and other turrets capable of housing 30-mm (1.18-in) cannon and incorporating improved target acquisition and ranging equipment. A Czech modification, designated the OT-64 SKOT, also included a machine gun turret, heavier armour, and propellers rather than pump jets.

Although the BTR-60 was fast and reasonably mobile cross country, it remained lightly armed and armoured. Aside from its vulnerable powerplant, its human cargo was quite exposed to enemy fire in the BTR-60PA. Later models lacked exits along the sides, which meant that infantry had to deploy through a roof hatch.

The combat history of the BTR-60 includes service in the Soviet invasion of the former Czechoslovakia in 1968, the Sino-Soviet border conflict the following year, the Yom Kippur War, the Soviet invasion of Afghanistan in 1979, Russia's Chechen wars, and the Persian Gulf.

Modern Tanks 1961–Present

Continuing implementation of rapidly advancing technology has brought about a refinement of the capabilities of the tank. From unprecedented firepower to equipment which pierces the dark of night, tanks and armoured fighting vehicles have transformed the modern battlefield.

The British Challenger II main battle tank was initially armed with the 120-mm (4.7-in) L30 rifled gun. Its innovative design incorporated few of the components of its Challenger I predecessor.

The awesome, deadly firepower of the U.S. 24th Infantry Division, which included more than 200 M1A1 Abrams main battle tanks, electrified the world as its forces stalked and destroyed elements of the Iraqi Republican Guard during Operation Desert Storm. A host of Coalition armour, including the British Challenger, the French AMX-30, and others, demonstrated the

ability of the main battle tank to dominate a hostile landscape.

Opposing the Coalition forces, the Iraqi army had employed primarily export variants of the Soviet-manufactured T-54/55, T-62, and T-72 tanks. Capable when maintained for peak performance or provided with the updated technology necessary to survive on the modern battlefield, the Iraqi armour may indeed have been degraded and at a disadvantage from the beginning. One common thread for both sides, however, is the lineage of these beasts of battle, weighing in excess of 49 tonnes (50 tons) and mounting main weapons of 120 mm (4.7 in) or greater.

DIVISION OF LABOR

At the height of the Cold War, the strategic arms race made headlines as a doctrine of "mutually assured destruction" with nuclear-armed intercontinental ballistic missiles weighed on the collective psyche. At the same time, however, the tank, which would be put to the tactical test in the event of a conventional war, was steadily upgraded. While weaponry was improved, gun platforms

were stabilized, fire control was upgraded with infrared sensors and thermal imaging, a new generation of composite armour provided unprecedented protection, computers became capable of tracking multiple targets simultaneously, and defences against nuclear, biological, and chemical weapons were developed.

Meanwhile, the role of the tank as a light, medium, or heavy armoured vehicle, deployed for scout and reconnaissance missions, tank-versus-tank combat, or long-range fire support, was evaluated by designers and military theorists both East and West. Through trial and error, tinkering and testing, the concept of the main battle tank, capable of a variety of missions, was born. The Soviet T-64 and later variants, the British Chieftain

The M2/M3 Bradley fighting vehicle overcame scandal and difficulties during more than 15 years of development to perform exceptionally well throughout deployments to the Middle East and the Balkans.

and Challenger, the French AMX-30, the Israeli Merkava, the German Leopard, and the tanks of the U.S. Patton series and its successor the Abrams embodied the traditional advantages of the tank – firepower, armour protection, and mobility – while serving as platforms for the latest in military technology.

RAGE AGAINST THE MACHINE

As the prowess of the main battle tank progressed, the defences against it grew more sophisticated as well. Combat conditions revealed shortcomings in certain areas, and while these were exploited by adversaries, they were being addressed by engineers and designers. Given the challenges of difficult terrain, the jungles of Southeast Asia provided a stern test for the deployment of tanks and armoured vehicles against an insurgency and a well-armed and organized enemy. U.S. tanks and armoured personnel carriers regularly faced a

gauntlet of rocket-propelled grenades, particularly the Soviet RPG-7, and anti-tank mines buried along roadways.

During the Yom Kippur War, Israeli tanks, which had performed tremendously during the Six-Day War of 1967, were devastated by squads of Egyptian infantrymen with the portable Soviet-made AT-3 Sagger anti-tank missile. The U.S. developed the LAW (Light Anti-tank Weapon) and the TOW, a wire-guided missile system fired from a platform such as a jeep or armoured personnel carrier. As tank technology improved, the ability to destroy or disable the tank gained greater importance, and a continual contest of technological one-upmanship ensued.

URBAN AND OPEN COUNTRY

While armoured encounters such as those of the Indo-Pakistani wars, the modern wars of the Arab-Israeli conflict, the major battles of the Gulf War,

The German Leopard I main battle tank has been praised as an example of post-war engineering excellence. The Leopard I was widely exported to other countries during the 1980s.

An Iraqi T-72 fires its 125-mm (4.9-in) gun during exercises. Produced in greater numbers than any other tank in history, variants of the T-72 continue in service following numerous upgrade programs.

and the 2003 invasion of Iraq have demonstrated the awesome power of the tank, low-intensity conflict has tested the ability of the heavy vehicles to withstand powerful improvised explosive devices (IEDs) and to function effectively and efficiently in an urban environment where speed and firepower are somewhat nullified by narrow streets and vulnerable civilian populations.

Israeli incursions into Lebanon in the last quarter century, the intervention of the U.S. and British-led Coalition in Iraq, and NATO involvement in Afghanistan have provided graphic evidence of the need to improve tank performance in an urban setting. For example, the Israelis have outfitted their Merkava with urban warfare equipment, and the Americans have fitted many of their Abrams main battle tanks with the TUSK (Tank Urban Survival Kit). Other nations have done the same.

Although close-quarter fighting is as challenging today as it was decades ago, tanks and mechanized infantry continue to excel in open country, where fast-moving mutual support and the combination of survivability, speed, and devastating firepower

remain lethal. The battlefield of tomorrow will undoubtedly pose yet unknown challenges; however, the tank is destined to remain a principal instrument of attack and defence.

"They [Iraqi forces] had Soviet equipment, they had French equipment, they had British equipment… they had three different generations of Soviet tank from a very early rudimentary generation of T-55, all the way up to the T-72 which was a very, very good tank."

General Norman Schwarzkopf, commander

T-62

The Soviet T-62 was developed during the late 1950s, but it was not revealed to the public until 1965. By that time, its shortcomings were evident. A slight improvement to the T-54/55, it remained inferior to Western designs throughout its career as the front-line Soviet tank.

TURRET
The readily identifiable egg-shaped turret was carried over from the T-54/55. It provided good protection but limited the depression of the main weapon.

MAIN ARMAMENT
The 115-mm (4.5-in) smoothbore U-5TS high-velocity cannon was distinguished from the 100-mm (3.9-in) D-10T cannon of the T-54/55 by its greater length and the addition of a bore evacuator.

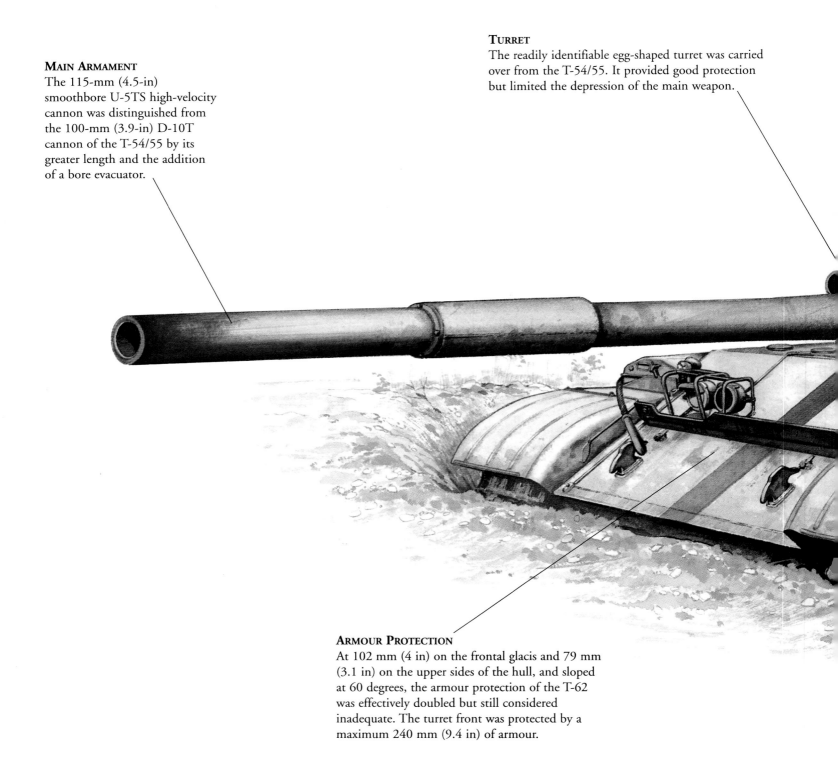

ARMOUR PROTECTION
At 102 mm (4 in) on the frontal glacis and 79 mm (3.1 in) on the upper sides of the hull, and sloped at 60 degrees, the armour protection of the T-62 was effectively doubled but still considered inadequate. The turret front was protected by a maximum 240 mm (9.4 in) of armour.

FACTS

- More than 20,000 T-62 tanks were built in the Soviet Union and Czechoslovakia during the 1960s.

- Long after Soviet production ceased, North Korea continued to build a modified T-62.

- Vehicles utilizing the T-62 chassis included the self-propelled SU-130 assault gun, a flamethrower tank, and a recovery vehicle.

COMMANDER POSITION
Seated to the upper left inside the turret, with the loader to his right and the gunner forwards and below, the commander viewed the field through four periscopes, which were integral with his rotating cupola.

ENGINE
The 12-cylinder, 433-kW (581-hp) V-55-5 diesel engine powered the T-62 at a maximum road speed of 50 km/h (30 mph) with a range of 500 km (310 miles) on the road.

DRIVER COMPARTMENT
Seated forwards and to the left in the hull, the driver had a pair of observation periscopes, which could be changed for infrared vision.

SUSPENSION
The modified Christie suspension included five oversize bogies but lacked return rollers. Its traction was good, but it was prone to throwing tracks at high speed.

Marginally inferior to 1960s vintage Western tanks, the T-62 had all the virtues and vices of the T-54/55. It was fairly easy to maintain, had good mobility, a low silhouette, and an excellent gun. On the other hand, the vehicle was a cramped "ergonomic slum."

RIVAL: T-64

T-62 – SPECIFICATION

Country of Origin: Soviet Union
Crew: 4
Designer: OKB-520 design bureau
Designed: late 1950s–1961
Manufacturer: Uralvagonzavod
Produced: 1961–75 (USSR); 1975–78 (Czechoslovakia); until 1980s (North Korea)
Number Built: More than 22,700
In Service: July 1961–present
Weight: 40 tonnes (44.09 tons)

Dimensions:
Length (with barrel): 9.34 m (30.6 ft)
Length (hull): 6.63 m (21.75 ft)
Width: 3.30 m (10.83 ft)
Height: 2.40 m (7.87 ft)

Performance:
Speed, Road: 50 km/h (31 mph)
Speed, Cross-country: 40 km/h (24.9 mph)
Range, On Road: 450 km (279.6 miles) (650 km [404 miles] with two extra 200 l [52.8 gallon] fuel tanks)
Range, Cross-country: 320 km (199 miles) (450 km [279.6 miles] with two extra 200 l [52.8 gallon] fuel tanks)
Suspension: Torsion bar

Engine:
Powerplant: 1 x V-55 12-cylinder 4-stroke one-chamber 38.88 l (10.2 gallon) water-cooled diesel producing 433 kW (581 hp) at 2,000 rpm
Power/weight: 10.8 kW (14.5 hp) per tonne
Fuel capacity: 960 l (253.6 gallons)

Armour and Armament:
Armour Type: Cast turret
Turret Front: 242 mm (2.53 in)
Turret Sides: 153 mm (6.02 in)
Turret Rear: 97 mm (3.82 in)
Turret Roof: 40 mm (1.56 in)
Hull Front: 102 mm (4.02 in) at 60 degrees
Hull Upper Sides: 79 mm (3.11 in)
Hull Lower Sides: 15 mm (0.59 in)
Hull Rear: 46 mm (1.8 in) at 0 degrees
Hull Bottom: 20 mm (0.79 in)
Hull Roof: 31 mm (1.22 in)
Main Armament: 1 x 115-mm (4.5-in) U-5TS (2A20) smoothbore gun. 40 rounds
Secondary Armament: 1 x 7.62-mm (0.3-in) PKT coaxial general-purpose machine gun (2500 rounds); 1 x 12.7-mm (0.5-in) DShK 1938/46 anti-aircraft heavy MG (Optional until T-62 Obr. 1972)

Variants
T-62: Base production vehicle.
T-62K: Commander's vehicle.
T-62D: Additional armour and specialized anti-tank system.
T-62D-1: Updated T-62D variant with newer powerplant.
T-62M: Modifications including anti-tank defence system and added passive armour.
T-62M1: Updated engine; added passive armour.
T-62M1-1: Sans passive armour and anti-armour defence system.
T-62MV: Features explosive reactive armour.
T-62 Flamethrower Vehicle: Added flamethrower to turret.

T-62

T-62, T64 AND TYPE 69

The T-62A (shown), incorporated a 12.7-mm (0.5-in) DshK anti-aircraft machine gun in addition to the coaxial 7.62-mm (0.3-in) machine gun, which was used for close defence against infantry. Although it also included a stabilized main gun, which theoretically allowed for firing on the move, the 115-mm (4.5-in) cannon could not be loaded while the turret was being traversed, minimizing any advantages it brought. The T-62 has been referred to as a stretched version of the T-55 with a larger hull and turret ring. Such changes were necessary to absorb the recoil of the 115-mm (4.5-in) gun. However, a top-loading breech and other factors limited the rate of fire to a maximum of four rounds per minute.

The T-64 was introduced the the 1960s and was a more advanced version of the T-62; a revolutionary feature of the T-64 was the incorporation of an automatic loader for its 115-mm gun, allowing a crewmember's position to be omitted.

Some of the components of the T-62 were copied in the Chinese Type 69; this was after a Soviet T-62 tank was captured by the PLA in 1969.

CHINESE VARIANT: TYPE 69

Painted in mottled camouflage, this T-62 presents an ominous sight with its 115-mm (4.5-in) U5TS smoothbore main cannon. Note the thermal sleeve on the weapon's barrel and the externally mounted fuel tank.

The T-62 remained the standard Soviet main battle tank from the mid-1960s until the late 1970s, when it was superseded by the T-64 and T-72, which was developed rapidly and purchased by the armed forces of numerous non-Warsaw Pact nations.

At the height of the Cold War, it was apparent to Soviet tank designers that their T-54/55 main battle tank could not penetrate the frontal armour of NATO tanks, such as the U.S. Patton or British Centurion with its 100-mm (3.9-in) main weapon firing armour-piercing shells. When an attempt to upgun the T-55 to a 115-mm (4.5-in) main gun failed, a larger hull and turret ring were engineered to mount the heavier U-5TS cannon. In this way, the T-62 was born.

While the T-62 did provide improvements over the T-54/55, such as better armament, reinforced hull bottom armour to protect against mines, a thermal sleeve for the main gun, and rubber track pads, the tank remained quite similar to its predecessor. The interior was laid out in typical Soviet style, with little consideration for the comfort of the four-man crew. While the T-62 maintained the qualities of low silhouette, good cross-country mobility, and ease of maintenance, its functionality in combat continued to suffer.

FIRING FAILINGS

The entire firing procedure was cumbersome at best. The commander acquired the target through a stadiametric sight, then rotated the turret to the proper position. At that point, the gunner took over, sighting the weapon and then firing. After firing, the gun would go into détente for the spent cartridge to eject, and traversing the turret was not possible while loading. An open driver's hatch prevented the turret from traversing as well, and the low turret ceiling was even more restrictive, particularly when attempting to fire on targets at lower grade than the T-62.

Further, the gunner was required to heave a 23-kg (50-lb) ammunition round into the breech left-handed. The main gun had been stabilized, but the outdated fire controls virtually eliminated this improvement. The low rate of fire resulted in few second-chance successes, and the poor fire control limited the effective range of the 115-mm (4.5-in) gun from its 2000-m (6560-ft) limit to about half that distance.

The turret of the T-62 was lined with leaded foam to protect against radiation, and an NBC (nuclear, biological, chemical) defence filtration system was incorporated. Although such movement was hazardous, the tank was capable of deploying a snorkel and traversing water up to 4 m (13 ft) deep. However, the tank's armour protection was considered inadequate and ammunition storage in the hull near the tank's fuel supply could produce devastating results if the armour was penetrated. The advantage of its low maintenance was tempered by the fact that the components of the T-62, particularly the 433-kW (581-hp), 12-cylinder V-

55-5 diesel engine, transmission, and tracks, were of inferior quality and only half as durable as those of contemporary Western tanks.

The T-62 saw combat during the Iran-Iraq War of the 1980s, the Middle East conflicts, the Soviet invasion of Afghanistan, and in Angola. Antiquated Iraqi T-62s were also destroyed in large numbers during the first Gulf War as a new generation of main battle tanks eclipsed any improvements to the original version. Modernized variants continue to serve with the armies of such nations as Egypt, Iran, Cuba, Libya, Syria, and Vietnam.

Interior view

The turret of the Soviet T-62 heavy tank was cramped and allowed little room for crewmen to reposition themselves. Its low ceiling also restricted the depression of the main armament.

(1) **Interior Lighting:** A small light mounted on the interior of the T-62 turret provided some illumination during operations.

(2) **Electrical Circuitry:** The T-62 depended on electrical current to operate multiple systems within the tank, and circuitry was in several positions throughout the hull and turret.

(3) **Manual Travers Crank:** In the event of a power failure or battle damage, the turret could be traversed manually using this combination of wheel and handle.

(4) **Elevation Equipment:** The angle of elevation of the main cannon was controlled from the gunner's position with powered switches.

(5) **Communication Equipment:** The gunner was provided with his own junction box, which was attached to the hull on his left side next to the AM 1780/VRC radio mount.

(6) **Gunner's Controls:** The gunner controlled the sighting and firing of the main cannon with stabilization, elevation, and traverse controls and a main and back-up trigger system.

M113

Conceived as a battle taxi to deliver infantry to combat zones and then withdraw, the M113 armoured personnel carrier evolved into a fighting vehicle. Its chassis has served as the platform for numerous special-purpose vehicles since the 1960s.

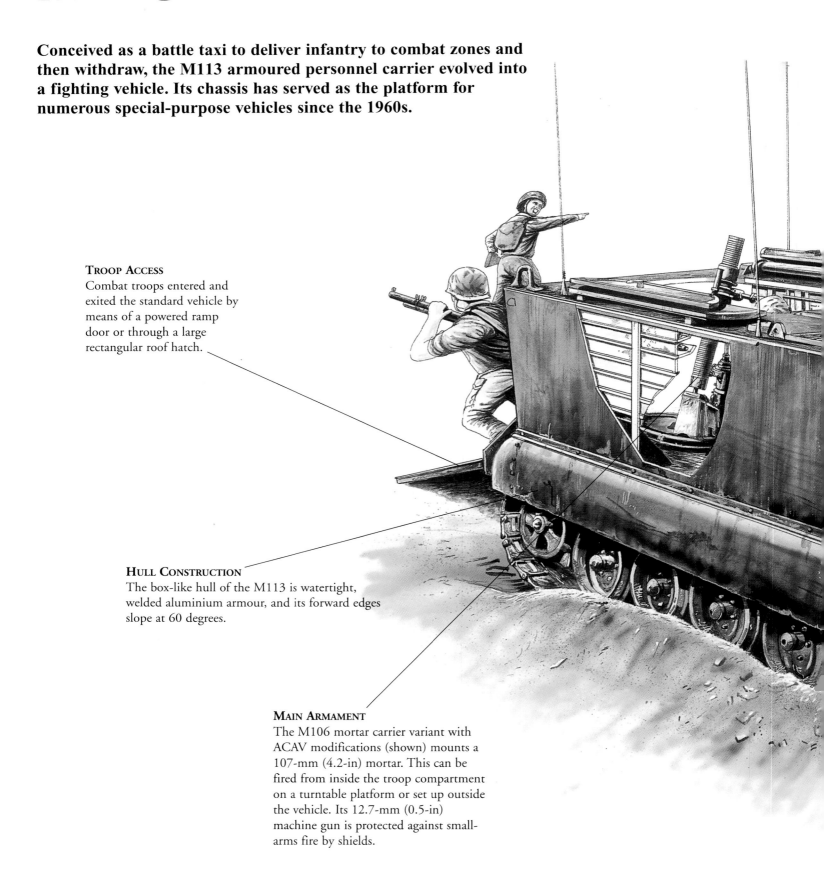

TROOP ACCESS
Combat troops entered and exited the standard vehicle by means of a powered ramp door or through a large rectangular roof hatch.

HULL CONSTRUCTION
The box-like hull of the M113 is watertight, welded aluminium armour, and its forward edges slope at 60 degrees.

MAIN ARMAMENT
The M106 mortar carrier variant with ACAV modifications (shown) mounts a 107-mm (4.2-in) mortar. This can be fired from inside the troop compartment on a turntable platform or set up outside the vehicle. Its 12.7-mm (0.5-in) machine gun is protected against small-arms fire by shields.

TROOP CAPACITY
The interior of the standard M113 armoured personnel carrier is capable of transporting up to 11 combat-ready infantrymen, five seated on benches along either side of the vehicle and another located in an aisle jump seat.

FACTS

- The M113 armoured personnel carrier entered service in 1960 and was deployed to Vietnam.

- The M113 chassis serves as the basis for gun carriers, recovery vehicles, and missile systems.

- More than 4500 M113s have been produced under licence by the Italian manufacturer OTO Melara.

INTERNAL CONFIGURATION
The interior of the standard M113 is divided into two compartments. Forward of the troop compartment, the driver is positioned to the left with the engine on his right. The commander's position is in the centre, slightly behind the driver.

ENGINE
Early M113s were petrol powered. However, these were modified beginning with the M113A1 in favour of a 205-kW (275-hp) Detroit Diesel 6V53T powerplant.

The M113 armoured personnel carrier proved to be a remarkable vehicle both in the versatility of its applications and in the reliability of its design and construction. The M113 family of vehicles has been applied to nearly every major functional combat area of the U.S. Army.

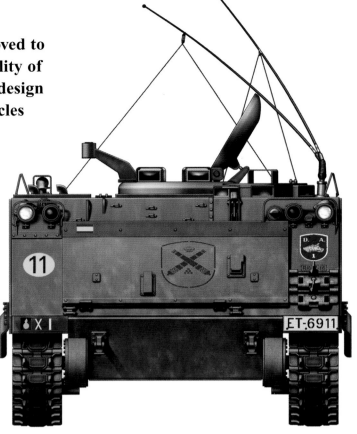

M113 – SPECIFICATION

Country of Origin: USA
Crew: 2 plus 11
Designer: Army Ordnance Tank-Automotive Command (ATAC)
Designed: 1956–60
Manufacturer: Army Ordnance Tank-Automotive Command (ATAC)
In Production: 1960–present
In Service: 1962–present
Numbers Built: 80,000
Weight: 11.3 tonnes (12.43 tons)

Dimensions:
Length: 2.52 m (8 ft 3 in)
Width: 2.69 m (8 ft 10 in)
Height: 1.85 m (6 ft 1 in)

Performance:
Speed, road: 61 km/h (38 mph)
Speed, amphibious: 5 km/h (3 mph)
Operational Range: 480 km (298 miles)

Engine:
Powerplant: 1 x General Motors 6V53 6-cylinder diesel, 205 kW (275 hp)
Power/Weight Ratio: 22.36 hp/tonne
Suspension: Torsion bar, 5 road wheels

Armour and Armament:
Armour: 45 mm (1.77 in)
Main Armament: Various but minimum usually 1 x 12.7-mm (0.5-in) machine gun

Variants:
M113A1: Starting in 1964, the petrol engine was replaced with a diesel engine to take advantage of the better fuel economy and reduced fire hazard of the diesel engine. The suffix A1 was used on all variants to denote a diesel engine.
M113A2: 1979 upgrades including cooling and suspension improvements and smoke grenade launchers on the glacis plate. The suffix A2 is used on all variants to denote upgrade to A2 standard.
M113A3: 1987 further improvements included a yoke for steering instead of laterals, a more powerful engine, external fuel tanks, and internal spall liners for improved protection.
M113 Armoured Cavalry Assault Vehicle (ACAV): The Armoured Cavalry Assault Vehicle (ACAV) was introduced in the Vietnam War after it was found that the commander and cargo hatch positions were extremely exposed and the vehicle's armament was in many ways inadequate. The kit included shields and circular turret armour for the commander's Browning M-2 12.7-mm (0.5-in) machine gun, and two additional 7.62-mm (0.3-in) M60 machine guns, again with shields, fitted on either side of the top cargo hatch.

VARIANT: M113 FITTER

M113

The M113 was not designed as an armoured fighting vehicle, but the exigencies of combat, particularly in Vietnam, caused its role to rapidly evolve and brought about a number of fighting versions. The M106 variant mounts a 107-mm (4.2-in) mortar on a turntable and is distinguished by its three-piece circular hatch above the modified troop compartment rather than the standard single hatch. The mortar may be removed from the vehicle for combat or fired from inside with the large ramp to the rear closed. Other mortar variants of the M113 include the M125, armed with an 81-mm (3-in) mortar, and the M121 with a 120-mm (4.7-in) weapon. A huge range of M113 variants exist, ranging from infantry carriers to nuclear missile carriers.

VARIANT: M113A1 DOZER

The role of the M113 armoured personnel carrier extended beyond that of a battle taxi for delivering personnel during the Vietnam War. The M113 became a fighting vehicle, and numerous variants were produced in response to the particular requirements of combat.

Designed to be smaller, less expensive, lighter, and faster than its predecessor, the M59, the M113 may well be the most highly modified armoured vehicle in history, ranging from troop carrier to fighting vehicle and weapons platform. Its versatility has lengthened its service life substantially.

An icon of U.S. involvement in Vietnam, the M113 armoured personnel carrier was developed as a vehicle to deliver infantry into combat. However, the role of the M113 continued to evolve during the next half-century.

Following a series of trials which had begun in the mid-1950s, the M113, developed by Ford Machinery Corporation (FMC), entered service in 1960 as a lighter, faster APC with amphibious capabilities. It could be deployed by air, and had a suitable capacity for troop transport.

CONSPICUOUS BUT SWIFT

The box-like M113 hull design is built of watertight, welded aluminium armour, considered superior to a similar hull of steel construction, with the glacis sloped at 60 degrees as added protection against anti-tank explosive charges. Early M113s were powered by the 160-kW (215-hp) Chrysler V-8

75M petrol engine. With a height of 2.5 m (8 ft 2 in), the silhouette of the M113 is somewhat conspicuous. However, its ground speed exceeds 64 km/h (40 mph). Its armour protection, ranging from 12–38 mm (0.4–1.5 in), is adequate against small arms and shell fragments. Amphibious track action allows the M113 to travel through water at speeds of nearly 6 km/h (3.5 mph).

The interior of the M113 is divided into two main compartments, with space for 11 combat soldiers seated to the rear. The driver sits forward and to the left with the engine on his right, and the commander sits behind the engine. The commander's cupola has five observation periscopes, while the driver has four, plus an interchangeable infrared night scope. Standard armament includes a single 12.7-mm (0.5-in) M2 machine gun, although a myriad of variants have mounted numerous weapons systems.

In the autumn of 1962, the U.S. Army accepted the M113A1, but replaced the Chrysler engine with the 205-kW (275-hp) General Motors Detroit Diesel 6V53T engine. This reduced the risk of fire substantially and extended the vehicle's range to approximately 480 km (300 miles). In 1979, the M113A2, with a more efficient method of air-cooling the engine, externally mounted fuel tanks, and improvements to the torsion bar suspension, was introduced. By 1987, combat experience had resulted in another principal variant with the M113A3. Bolt holes for the installation of more armour plate were added, as was the RISE (Reliability Improvements for Selected Equipment) package, including the fuel-efficient Allison X200-4 hydraulic transmission, improved steering and power brakes, and a turbocharged engine. Many of the M113A2 vehicles were also upgraded with the RISE package.

The M113 earned its reputation as an efficient combat vehicle during the Vietnam War. Several upgrades included the addition of machine guns, firing ports for infantry from inside the vehicle, and armour shields to protect the roof machine gunner. Further variants to the M113 chassis have mounted mortars, anti-aircraft guns, and missile systems. The most famous modification was the Vietnam-era ACAV (Armoured Cavalry Assault Vehicle). Along with shields for the exposed 12.7-mm (0.5-in) position, the ACAV had a pair of side-mounted shielded 7.62-mm (0.3-in) machine guns. These ACAV kits were manufactured by FMC and the Rock Island Arsenal.

Approximately 80,000 M113 variants have been manufactured and have served with the armed forces of at least 50 nations. Still in use today, the vehicle is expected to remain in service for a number of years to come

Interior view

The spacious interior of the M113 armoured personnel carrier could transport up to 11 combat personnel, while the driver, one of three crew members, was seated forwards and to the left.

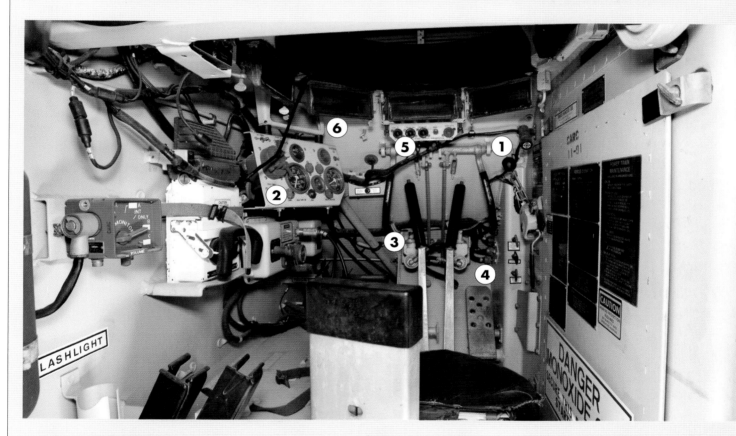

(1) **Transmission Shift Lever:** This was set high and to the right of the driver's seat, within easy reach while the vehicle was in motion.

(2) **Engine Gauges:** The standard gauges measuring speed, oil pressure, temperature, and other vital signs were positioned high and to the left of the M113 driver.

(3) **Steering Levers:** The driver operated the M113 with a pair of steering levers and the transmission shift.

(4) **Accelerator Pedal:** The driver operated the accelerator with his right foot, with the ramp-actuating lever to his right.

(5) **Warning Light Panel:** From the left, the warning lights indicated high temperatures for differential oil, transmission oil, and engine oil.

(6) **Driver Periscopes:** Three of the nine periscopes used by the driver to survey the surrounding terrain are visible here.

Chieftain Mark 5

Although its conceptualization began in the 1940s as a replacement for the Centurion series and a counter to a new generation of Soviet tanks, the Chieftain main battle tank embodied a departure from traditional British design. It did not enter service until the mid-1960s.

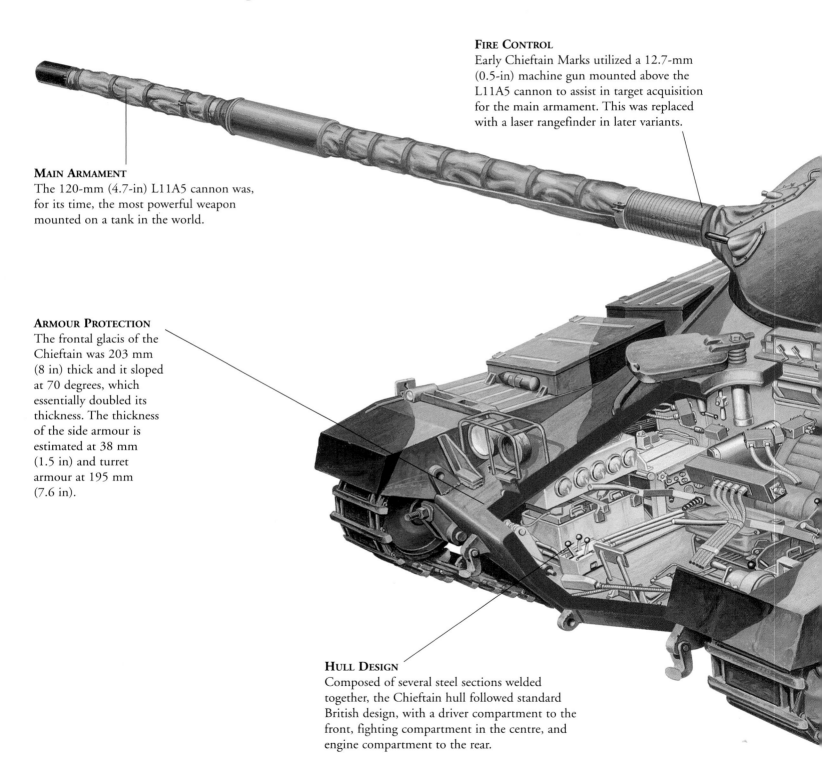

FIRE CONTROL
Early Chieftain Marks utilized a 12.7-mm (0.5-in) machine gun mounted above the L11A5 cannon to assist in target acquisition for the main armament. This was replaced with a laser rangefinder in later variants.

MAIN ARMAMENT
The 120-mm (4.7-in) L11A5 cannon was, for its time, the most powerful weapon mounted on a tank in the world.

ARMOUR PROTECTION
The frontal glacis of the Chieftain was 203 mm (8 in) thick and it sloped at 70 degrees, which essentially doubled its thickness. The thickness of the side armour is estimated at 38 mm (1.5 in) and turret armour at 195 mm (7.6 in).

HULL DESIGN
Composed of several steel sections welded together, the Chieftain hull followed standard British design, with a driver compartment to the front, fighting compartment in the centre, and engine compartment to the rear.

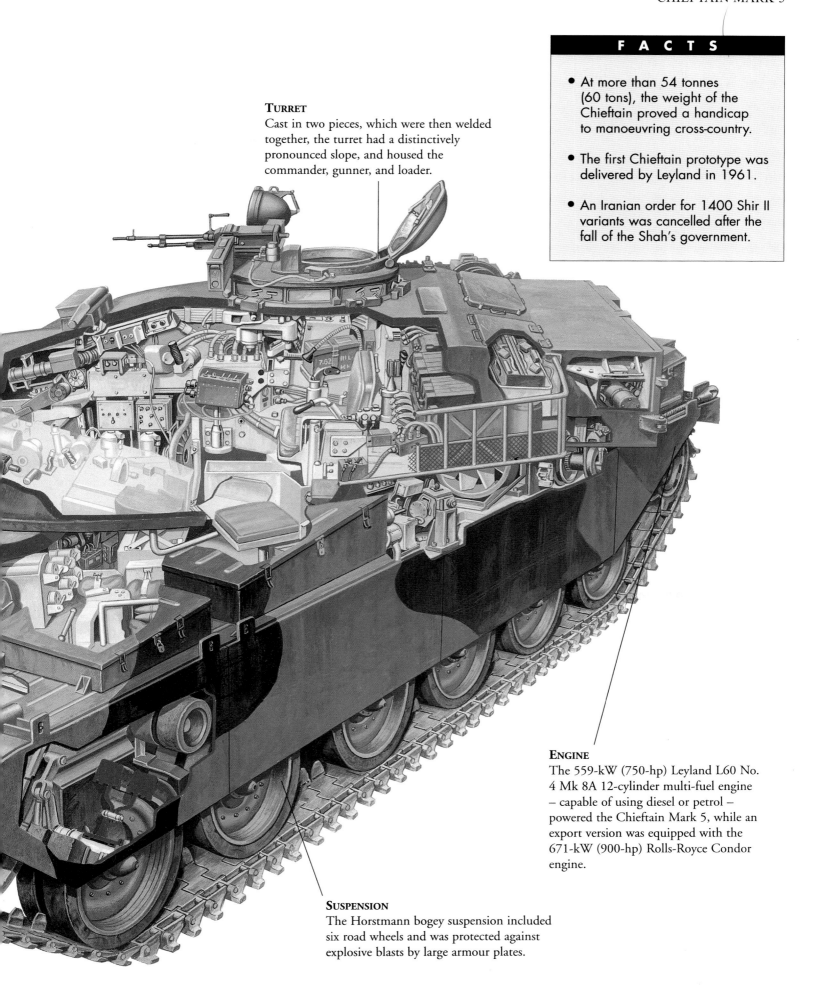

TURRET
Cast in two pieces, which were then welded together, the turret had a distinctively pronounced slope, and housed the commander, gunner, and loader.

FACTS

- At more than 54 tonnes (60 tons), the weight of the Chieftain proved a handicap to manoeuvring cross-country.

- The first Chieftain prototype was delivered by Leyland in 1961.

- An Iranian order for 1400 Shir II variants was cancelled after the fall of the Shah's government.

ENGINE
The 559-kW (750-hp) Leyland L60 No. 4 Mk 8A 12-cylinder multi-fuel engine – capable of using diesel or petrol – powered the Chieftain Mark 5, while an export version was equipped with the 671-kW (900-hp) Rolls-Royce Condor engine.

SUSPENSION
The Horstmann bogey suspension included six road wheels and was protected against explosive blasts by large armour plates.

The Chieftain main battle tank is derived from a long line of tanks that began with the Matilda in 1939. The Matilda's successors evolved from infantry support through cruiser to main battle tank as they were made progressively faster and upgunned.

CHIEFTAIN MARK 5

CHIEFTAIN MARK 5 – SPECIFICATION

Country of Origin: United Kingdom
Crew: 4
Designer: Leyland Motors
Designed: 1956
Manufacturer: Leyland Motors
In Production: 1963–early 1970s
In Service: 1963–96
Number Built: 900
Gross Weight: 55 tonnes (60.5 tons)

Dimensions:
Hull Length: 7.52 m (24.7 ft)
Length (Gun forward): 10.8 m (35.4 ft)
Width: 3.5 m (11.5 ft) (over skirts)
Overall Height: 2.9 m (9.5 ft)

Performance:
Maximum Speed: 50 km/h (30 mph)
Range, Road: 500 km (310 miles)
Range, Cross-country: Approx. 300 km (180 miles)
Ground Pressure: 0.9 kg/cm²
Fording Capacity: 1.07 m (3.5 ft) (4.6 m [15 ft]
     with preparation)
Maximum Gradient: 37 degrees
Maximum Trench Width: 3.15 m (10.3 ft)
Maximum Vertical Obstacle: 0.9 m (3 ft)
Suspension Type: Horstmann

Engine:
Powerplant: 1 x Leyland L60 No.4 Mark 8A vertically opposed
     12 cyl. liquid-cooled compression-ignition 2-stroke multifuel
Capacity: n/a
Output: 750 bhp/560 kW @ 2100 rpm
Power/Weight Ratio: 13.6 bhp/tonne
Fuel Capacity: 955 l (210 gallons)

Armament and Armour:
Main Armament: 1 x 120-mm (4.7-in) L11A5 L/56
Secondary Armament: 1 x 12.7-mm (0.5-in) L21 ranging
     MG; 1 x 7.62-mm (0.3-in) L8 GP MG
Ancillary Armament: 1 x 7.62-mm (0.3-in) L37 GP MG in AA
     mount
Armour Type: Homogeneous cast/welded nickel steel with
     cast/welded turret plus Stillbrew composite steel/ceramic
     appliqué panels

Variants:
Mark 2: Fitted with 484 kW (650 bhp) engine.
Mark 3: Improved Chieftain.
Mark 5: Featured an uprated engine.
Mark 5/2K: Kuwaiti export models; 165 examples delivered.
Mark 6: Standardization of previous production Mark; ranging
     machine gun added to main gun.
Mark 7: Revised engine.
Mark 8: Resilient mantlet and new commander's cupola.
Mark 9: Revised intermediate production Mark; IFCS (Improved
     Fire Control System).
Mark 10: Revised intermediate production Mark; IFCS; night and
     all-weather fighting capability with Thermal Observation and
     Gunnery Sight implementation.
Mark 11: Revised intermediate production Mark; IFCS;
     "Stillbrew" passive armour.
"Shir 1": Modified for Iranian export; later named "Khalid."
"Shir 2": Iranian export; 1225 examples ordered but never
     produced or delivered due to the regime change in 1979.
ARV: Armoured Recovery Vehicle.
AVLB: Armoured Bridgelayer.
AVRE: Armoured Vehicle Royal Engineers.
Chieftain ARRV: Armored Recovery and Repair Vehicle.

VARIANT: CHIEFTAIN 900

CHIEFTAIN MK 5

The interior of the Chieftain, as shown in the Mark 5 which was the final production variant, included a semi-reclining position for the driver. Such a configuration facilitated the tank's low silhouette, while sloping armour contributed to a less conspicuous profile and effectively doubled the protection afforded the crew of four. The commander, gunner, and loader were stationed in the low, sleek turret, which did not include a gun mantlet and allowed greater concealment in the hull-down position. The Mark 5 included improvements to the engine and the introduction of a nuclear, biological, and chemical (NBC) defence system.

VARIANT: CHIEFTAIN AVRE

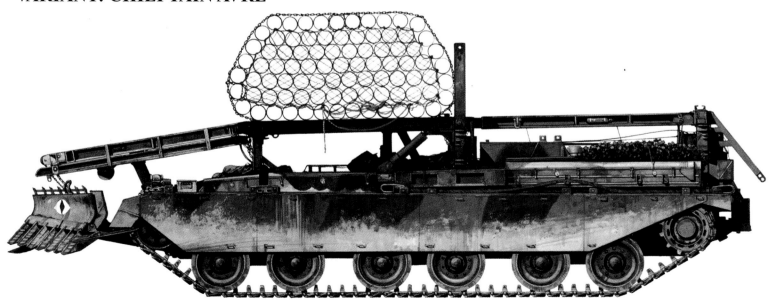

The Chieftain main battle tank is distinguishable by its sloping turret and the imposing 120-mm (4.7-in) L11A5 cannon it mounts. Deployed at the height of the Cold War, the Chieftain was Britain's response to the heavy Soviet tanks of the era.

In the 1960s, the Chieftain main battle tank was, for a time, the most powerful fighting vehicle of its kind in the world. Its 120-mm (4.7-in) L11A5 main cannon was the heaviest weapon then deployed in a tank.

By the time the Chieftain was deployed with the British Army in the 1960s, the Cold War was at its height. By then, the need for a main battle tank that combined maximum firepower with mobility and well protected armour was considered paramount. The Soviet T-54/55 series was well known to military intelligence, and the lessons learned during World War II still resonated among armour engineers.

Conceived as a replacement for the ageing Centurion series, the specifications for the new Chieftain were drawn in 1958. By 1961, Leyland Motors produced the first prototypes. The first operational Chieftain entered service with the British Army two years later. Immediately, the Chieftain was recognized as the most powerfully armed tank then fielded. It remained so until the introduction of the German Leopard series some time later. The 120-mm (4.7-in) L11A5 main gun of the Chieftain was notable for its

power to penetrate armour and for the fact that it fired charges and projectiles that were separate rather than encased in combination. This was a major survivability improvement, reducing the potential for a catastrophic explosion.

The main gun was initially laid with the assistance of a 12.7-mm (0.5-in) ranging machine gun that fired tracers to mark targets. However, this was replaced in later variants with a laser rangefinder. Secondary armament included a coaxial 7.62-mm (0.3-in) machine gun and a second machine gun of the same size situated on top of the turret near the commander's cupola.

Early Chieftains were powered by a 436-kW (585-hp) diesel engine, but this proved inadequate and was updated in 1967 with the 560-kW (750-hp) Leyland L60 No. 4 Mark 8, while an export version utilized the 671-kW (900-hp) Rolls-Royce Condor. Although an upgrade, the L60 was still considered less than adequate to move the 54-tonne (60-ton) vehicle at a reasonable speed, particularly across country. Its reliability was found to be dubious as well, with a breakdown rate approaching 90 per cent. The Horstmann suspension featured six road wheels and heavy armour side plates for added protection against projectiles and to reduce the possibility the vulnerable tracks being disabled.

MOBILITY VERSUS POWER

The interior of the Chieftain followed the standard British layout, with the driver forward, the fighting compartment and the centred turret behind, and the engine compartment in the rear. The driver sat in a semi-reclined position and steered the tank with conventional hydraulic tillers and external disc brakes. The commander sat in the turret to the right beneath the rotating cupola and viewed the field through 360-degree periscopes, while the gunner was below and to his front with the loader on the left, both also in the turret. Infrared sights were available to the commander and

the gunner, while an externally mounted infrared searchlight was attached on the left side of the turret.

The Chieftain's mobility was restricted by its standard powerplant and unremarkable top speed of 48 km/h (30 mph) on the road. The final production model was the Mark 5, and upgrades continued until a total of 12 variants were offered with further enhancements of engine performance, optics, or improved systems. The Middle East was a lucrative market for export versions of the Chieftain, such as the Shir I and II. The armies of Iran, Kuwait, Jordan, and Oman are among the countries that have purchased it

Interior view

The Chieftain Mark 5 main battle tank was a mainstay of British forces in Europe during the Cold War. Its interior was in keeping with previous British designs, but it had significant turret modifications.

(1) **Laser Rangefinding Equipment:** This increases the accuracy of the main 120-mm (4.7-in) L11A5 cannon.

(2) **Electronic Equipment:** Numerous systems converge inside the turret, including equipment for target acquisition, gun laying, various defences, and communications.

(3) **Optics:** Image-intensifying day and night vision equipment are used by the crew of the Chieftain Mark 5.

(4) **Sloped Turret:** This allowed freer movement within the confining area, improved armour protection, and even offered storage space.

(5) **Hatch Opening:** Hatches for the commander and other personnel were located on top of the sloped turret, while the driver assumed a semi-recumbent position in the hull.

(6) **Gunner Position:** The gunner sat in front of the tank commander, while the loader sat to his left.

M109

The primary self-propelled indirect fire support weapon of the U.S. Army over a period of more than 40 years, the M109 mounts a powerful 155-mm (6-in) howitzer and has demonstrated the ability to decimate distant targets while maintaining the pace of rapid advance.

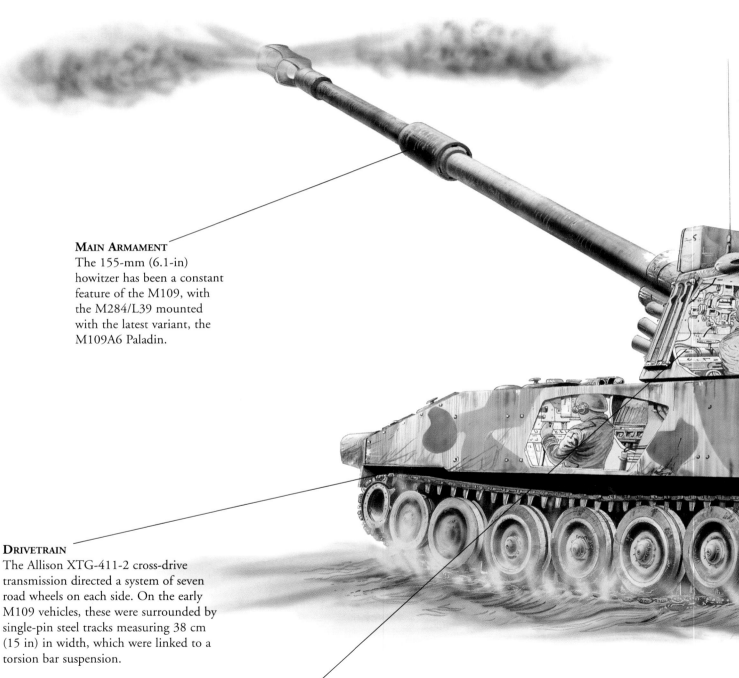

MAIN ARMAMENT
The 155-mm (6.1-in) howitzer has been a constant feature of the M109, with the M284/L39 mounted with the latest variant, the M109A6 Paladin.

DRIVETRAIN
The Allison XTG-411-2 cross-drive transmission directed a system of seven road wheels on each side. On the early M109 vehicles, these were surrounded by single-pin steel tracks measuring 38 cm (15 in) in width, which were linked to a torsion bar suspension.

AMMUNITION
The 155-mm (6.1-in) howitzer is capable of firing conventional ammunition with separately bagged charges of high-explosive, Improved Conventional Munitions (ICM), which scatter bomblets, rocket-assisted projectiles, and tactical nuclear weapons. Its rocket-assisted range is 30 km (18.6 miles).

- The first operational M109 self-propelled howitzers were delivered to U.S. Army units in June 1963.

- The M109 howitzer has been deployed with U.S. forces in combat from Vietnam to Iraq.

- The most recent variant, the M109A6 Paladin, is likely to be the last of its series.

CREW

The M109A6 Paladin crew includes a section chief, driver, gunner, and assistant gunner. Additional ammunition handlers are also sometimes included in the crew.

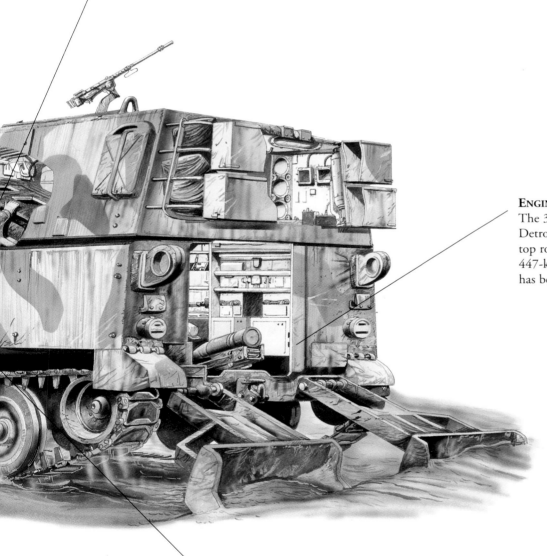

ENGINE

The 328-kW (440-hp) General Motors Detroit Diesel 8V71T engine is capable of a top road speed of 56 km/h (35 mph). A 447-kW (600-hp) Cummins diesel engine has been considered as a possible upgrade.

CHASSIS

The M109 series utilizes the same chassis as the now-retired M108 self-propelled 105-mm (4.1-in) howitzer, which consisted primarily of components from the M113 armoured personnel carrier. Later improvements moved the driver's position from the turret to a more advantageous location in the hull.

The **M109** howitzer provides armoured combat support, is transportable by air, loaded internally, and has excellent ground mobility. It allows firing in a 360-degree circle through its primary armament. The system is capable of both direct and indirect firing.

PREDECESSOR: M108

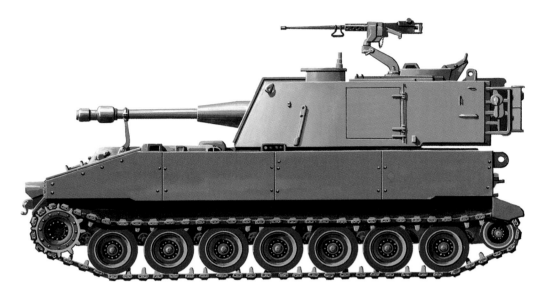

M109 – SPECIFICATION

Country of Origin: United States
Crew: 8
Designer: Not specified
Designed: Not specified
In Production: 1962–present
Manufacturer: United Defense, LP, York, Pennsylvania
In Service: 1963–present
Number Built: Not available
Weight: 24.9 tonnes (27.5 tons)

Dimensions:
Length: 9.1 m (30 ft)
Width: 3.1 m (10.3 ft)
Height: 3.3 m (10.7 ft)

Performance:
Speed: 56 km/h (35 mph)
Operational Range: 350 km (216 miles)

Engine:
Powerplant: 1 x 328-kW (440-hp) General Motors Detroit Diesel 8V71T engine
Power/weight: 13.9kW (18.7hp) per tonne
Suspension: Torsion bar

Armament and Armour
Main Armament: 1 x M126 155-mm (6.1-in) howitzer
Secondary Armament: 1x 12.7-mm (0.5-in) M2 machine gun
Shell: Separate loading, bagged charge
Calibre: 155 mm (6.1 in)
Breech: Interrupted screw
Traverse: 360°
Armour: Classified

Rate of Fire: 4 round/minute maximum, 1 round/minute sustained
Effective Range: 30 km (18.6 miles)

Variants
M109: First production model.
M109A1: Longer main gun barrel; minor overall improvements.
M109A1B: More recent model with improvements. Intended for export.
M109A2: Minor improvements to M109A1.
M109A3: New gun mount and improved RAM-D.
M109A3B: M109A1s and M109A1Bs rebuilt to M109A2 standard respectively.
M109A4: Improved NBC system; covers all updated M109A2 or M109A3 models.
M109A5: Updated M109A4.
M109A5+: Various manufacturers have upgraded the fire control and other components of the M109A5.
M109A6: Latest production model. New turret with automatic fire control system and added armour.
M109A3G: German army export variant known as M109G.
M109 "Kawest": Swiss improvised version with Swiss-designed L47 155-mm (6.1-in) gun with an increased firing range of up to 36 km (22.4 miles).
M109L: Italian army export variant.
M109AL "Doher": Israeli army export variant.
M109L47: United Arab Emirates and Swiss export variant.
M992 FAASV: Field Artillery Ammunition Support Vehicle (ammunition carrier).

M109

M109

The U.S. Army's M109 self-propelled howitzer set the standard for long-range fire support of ground troops and was adopted by the armed forces of a wide variety of nations during the 1960s and 1970s. The reliable 155-mm (6.1-in) howitzer, upgraded on several occasions, has been lengthened to add greater muzzle velocity while its ability to fire more recently developed ammunition, such as rocket-assisted projectiles and tactical nuclear weapons, has also been enhanced. The number of crew has varied through the years, with the M109A6 Paladin fielding a complement of four — a section chief, driver, gunner, and assistant gunner — with the driver located in the hull and the other three in the turret.

HEAVY SUPPORT: M110A2

Variants of the M109 self-propelled howitzer, mounting a 155-mm (6.1-in) weapon, served as the primary mobile artillery of the U.S. armed forces, as well as those of other nations, for approximately half a century.

The Paladin is an upgrade of the 1960s-era M109. While the vehicle includes a new turret, many components, such as the chassis, its automotive capability, and the level of protection it affords, are fundamentally the same as in the earlier versions of the M109.

For nearly half a century, the M109 self-propelled howitzer has been the front-line fire support artillery of its kind for the U.S. Army. While its upgrades pioneered much of the technology now available in the most modern self-propelled howitzers, the latest version of the M109, the M109A6 Paladin, has become something of a bridge vehicle between once-innovative technology, which is now largely common, and the anticipated weapons systems of the future.

PALADIN IMPROVEMENT

During the late 1990s, the Crusader project was undertaken to replace the M109. However, this was cancelled in 2002, breathing new life into the M109. As a result, the Paladin has undergone another upgrade, known as the PIM (Paladin Integrated Management) project. While numerous upgrades have taken place over the years, the PIM specifically includes the introduction of some components common with the M2/M3 Bradley Fighting Vehicle, an automatic loading

system for the main 155-mm (6.1-in) howitzer, new electric controls replacing hydraulics (which had previously been incorporated in the M109A4), and a non-line-of-sight cannon (NLOS-C). Other aspects of the cancelled Crusader programme have been incorporated with the PIM as well.

The Cadillac Division of General Motors was the original producer of the M109, followed by the Chrysler Corporation. Original M109s of the early 1960s fielded a short-barrelled 155-mm (6.1-in) howitzer designated the M126, which had a double-baffle muzzle brake and a pronounced bore evacuator. Successively, the A2, A3, and A4 variants mounted the longer M185 howitzer, and the A5 and A6 have transported the M284. Until the PIM programme, the main weapon has been loaded manually or by a semi-automatic means, limiting its maximum rate of fire to four rounds per minute and its sustained rate to three rounds. Meanwhile, the German PzH2000 and the British AS-90 are automatically loaded with rates of fire nearly twice that of the standard M109A6 Paladin.

The most significant upgrades to the M109 platform include the M109A2, which introduced the M185 howitzer, a turret bustle that increased ammunition storage capacity, and a total of 27 improvements to the original design, while the M109A4 added an improved NBC defence capability and hydraulic controls for the turret. The M109A5 incorporated the M284 howitzer and an improved M182 gun mount.

In the M109A6, loading continued to be primarily performed by hand. However, an improved navigation system, a muzzle reference system, digital communications for coordination with fire director centres, an ergonomically enhanced turret with spall liner, and a Kevlar lining for the chassis were all introduced on this tank.

SHOOT-AND-SCOOT

Capable of firing on the move, and of stationary "shoot-and-scoot" operations, the Paladin can halt, stabilize, and fire its first round in less than one minute. While it remains a viable weapon on today's battlefield, it appears to be nearing its end of service. The NLOS-C, with its first prototype built in 2008, is expected to replace the M109A6 eventually. However, the U.S. Defense Department announced substantial budget cuts in the spring of 2009, which will undoubtedly have an impact on the deployment of NLOS-C.

During its length of service, the M109 series has been purchased and deployed by numerous countries and proven its worthiness in combat during the Vietnam War, the 1973 Yom Kippur War, the 1982 Lebanon conflict, the Iran-Iraq War, the 1991 Gulf War, and the invasion of Iraq in 2003.

Interior view

Up to eight crew, including those responsible for operating the self-propelled armoured vehicle and those who serviced the 155-mm (6.1-in) main weapon, sat within the hull and turret of the M109.

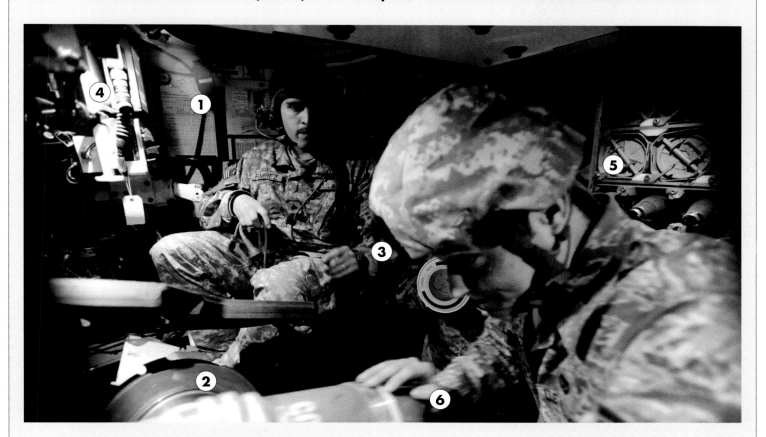

(1) **Turret:** The huge turret housed equipment for servicing the 155-mm (6.1-in) gun, including rangefinding, gun laying, loading, and firing.

(2) **Hydraulic Ramming Assembly:** The heavy shells of the M109 were placed in the breech of the 155-mm (6.1-in) weapon with a hydraulic ramming assembly.

(3) **Hand Controls:** Manual controls were available for loading and firing the main weapon should the M109 lose power or sustain battle damage.

(4) **Optical Instruments:** Rangefinding was sited near the gunner and section commander in order to facilitate the acquisition of targets.

(5) **Ammunition:** This was fed to the howitzer via an automatic system, which placed shells into a trough for movement forwards towards the breech of the weapon.

(6) **Shell Structure:** Bagged charges provided the propellant for the 155-mm (6.1-in) shells fired from the howitzer. The weapon could fire at a sustained rate of one round per minute.

ZSU-23-4

The quadruple-barrelled, self-propelled ZSU-23-4 anti-aircraft system proved a formidable weapon in combination with surface-to-air missile batteries. It served as the primary close-support air defence gun for the Soviet Red Army and numerous other nations for three decades.

RADAR DETECTION
The RPK-2 Tobol radar, referred to as "Gun Dish" in the West, was capable of picking up aircraft at a distance of 20 km (12.4 miles) away.

TURRET
The welded turret was adapted from the T-54 main battle tank and was fully stabilized to allow accurate fire on the move.

ARMOUR PROTECTION
The maximum armour thickness of 9.2 mm (0.36 in) in the hull and 8.3 mm (0.32 in) in the turret was sufficient to withstand only small arms and shell fragments.

MAIN ARMAMENT
Four turret-mounted 23-mm (0.9-in) AZP-23 water-cooled autocannons with a cyclical rate of fire up to 1000 rounds per minute posed a significant threat to helicopters and low-flying aircraft.

INTERIOR
Divided into three compartments, the engine was situated at the rear, with the fighting compartment, housing the commander, gunner, and radar operator, in the centre, and the driver forward. Unlike the other crewmen, the driver benefitted from an electric heating system and better air flow.

ENGINE
The 209-kW (280-hp) six-cylinder V-6R diesel engine was somewhat underpowered for the ZSU-23-4 – which weighed up to 19 tonnes (21 tons) – particularly traversing rugged terrain.

SUSPENSION
The individual torsion bar suspension supported the GM-575 tracked vehicle chassis and included six road wheels with rubber tyres, rear drive sprockets, and one idler wheel on each side.

A self-propelled battlefield air defence system developed in the early 1960s, the ZSU-23-4 has been produced in larger numbers than any other self-propelled anti-aircraft gun. The Soviet army alone had more than 2000, and large numbers have been exported.

ZSU-23-4

ZSU-23-4 – SPECIFICATION

Country of Origin: Soviet Union
Crew: 4
Designer: AG Shipunov
Designed: 1957–62
Manufacturer: Mytishchi Engineering Works (MMZ)
Produced: 1964–82
In Service: 1965–present
Number Built: About 6500
Weight: 19 tonnes (20.9 tons)

Dimensions:
Length: 6.535 m (21.44 ft)
Width: 3.125 m (10.25 ft)
Height: 2.576 m (8.45 ft) (3.572 m [11.72 ft] with elevated radar)

Performance:
Speed, Road: 44 km/h (27 mph)
Speed, Cross-country: 30 km/h (18.6 mph)
Range, Road: 450 km (279.6 miles)
Range, Cross-country: 300 km (186 miles)
Suspension: Individual torsion bar with hydraulic shock absorbers of 1st, 5th left, and 6th right road wheels
Ground Clearance: 400 mm (15.75 in)

Engine:
Powerplant: 1 x V-6R, 6-cylinder 4-stroke airless-injection water-cooled diesel engine producing 209 kW (280 hp) at 2000 rpm
Power/weight: 11 kW (14.7 hp) per tonne
Fuel Capacity: 515 l (136 gallons)

Armour and Armament:
Armour: Welded steel

Turret: 8.3 mm (0.32 in)
Hull: 9.2 mm (0.36 in)
Main Armament: 4 x 23-mm (0.9-in) 2A7 autocannons (AZP-23 "Amur" quad automatic anti-aircraft gun), ammunition 2000 rounds.

Variants
ZSU-23-4V "Shilka" (1968): Modernized variant with enhanced reliability of some details, ventilation system case located on the right side of the hull. Commander vision device added.
ZSU-23-4V1 "Shilka" (1970): Modernized variant with enhanced reliability of radar system and other details, ventilation system cases located on front bilges of the turret.
ZSU-23-4M "Biryusa" (1973): Armed with modernized autocannons 2A7M. Increased autocannon barrel life from 3500 rounds to 4500 rounds.
ZSU-23-4MZ "Biryusa" (1977): Equipped with identification friend-or-foe system "Luk." All ZSU-23-4M were upgraded to ZSU-23-4MZ level. (Z stands for "zaproschik" – enquirer.)
ZSU-23-4M2 (1978): So-called "Afghan" variant. Re-equipment performed during Soviet War in Afghanistan. Radar system removed and night-sight added. Ammunition increased from 2000 to 4000 rounds.
ZSU-23-4M4 (1999): Modernized variant.
Donets (1999): Ukrainian modernization. Improved turret from ZSU-23-4 armed with two additional paired man-portable air-defence systems "Strela-10" was installed on chassis from T-80UD main battle tank.
ZSU-23-4MP "Biala" (2000): Polish upgrade. Grom anti-aircraft missiles, fully digital passive aiming devices.

RIVAL: M163 VULCAN

ZSU-23-4

The highly mobile ZSU-23-4 self-propelled anti-aircraft vehicle was designed to provide defensive support for Red Army troops in the field, moving forwards with infantry and armoured units while working in tandem with surface-to-air missile systems such as the SA-6 GAINFUL and the SA-9 GASKIN. Its four 23-mm (0.9-in) autocannon were water-cooled and belt-fed, and capable of firing different types of ammunition independently. Its GM-575 chassis had many common components with the amphibious PT-76, although the ZSU-23-4 did not have amphibious capabilities. Basic maintenance in the field was relatively easy to perform, but replacing certain electrical and engine components took the tank out of action for a significant time.

RIVAL: FLAKPANZER I GEPARD

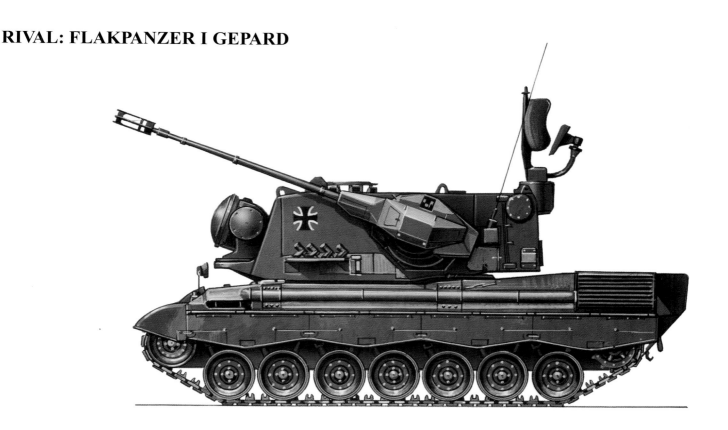

A ZSU-23-4 Shilka sits abandoned on a desert battlefield. The Shilka was an effective weapon against low-flying aircraft as demonstrated during the Yom Kippur War of 1973 when the Israeli Air Force took heavy losses.

The Shilka was the standard anti-aircraft gun in Soviet tank and motorized rifle regiments, with one platoon of four Shilkas attached to every regimental air defence company. In combat, ZSU-23-4s would follow closely behind the lead combat echelons.

The ZSU-23-4 Shilka served as the frontline anti-aircraft support vehicle for Red Army and Warsaw Pact infantry units for nearly 30 years before being replaced by the ZSU-30. It was known for its firepower and accuracy against low-level aircraft, particularly helicopters and fixed-wing planes at a vertical range of 1.5 km (0.9 miles). Developed in the early 1960s and built by the Mytishchi Engineering Works, more than 6500 Shilkas, also known by the nickname "Zeus," were produced from 1964–82. The self-propelled air-defence system has been exported to numerous countries.

The ZSU-23-4 derives its name from the literal Russian designation of "Anti-aircraft Self-Propelled Gun" along with the calibre and number of its quadruple turret-mounted weapons. The four 23-mm (0.9-in) water-cooled AZP-23 autocannons are enclosed in the welded turret with a 360-degree traverse and are capable of firing up to 1000 rounds of belt-fed ammunition per minute for a combined maximum rate of fire of 4000 rounds. Additionally, each gun is capable of firing a different type of ammunition independently of the others.

The GM-575 tracked vehicle chassis is adapted from the amphibious PT-76 armoured personnel carrier, although the ZSU-23-4 is not amphibious. The crew of four (commander, gunner, driver, and radar operator) has the driver housed in a heated compartment forwards and the others in the fighting compartment and turret at the centre. The powerplant consists of the 209-kW (280-hp), six-cylinder V-6R diesel engine with a top road speed of 44 km/h (27 mph), to keep pace with forward infantry and armoured units. However, its engine was not up to the demands of strenuous cross-country operations. The crew was protected against burns by armour plating within the turret, as well as armour of up to 9.2 mm (0.36 in), which was sufficient for protection against small arms or shell fragments.

EYES IN THE SKY
The most distinctive characteristic of the ZSU-23-4 was its RPK-2 Tobol "Gun Dish" radar. It was a prominent feature

when it was deployed for use, but for travelling purposes it was stabilized along with the guns, and folded. The radar system was capable of acquiring targets at a range of 20 km (12.4 miles) and tracking them at nearly 8 km (4.8 miles). Optical tracking and sighting proved more effective against aircraft flying below 60 m (200 ft). Under radar direction, the guns engaged targets at a range of 3500 m (2.2 miles) and altitudes from 60–4875 m (200–16,000 ft). The Shilka was also used in concert with surface-to-air missile systems and to engage light ground targets as direct fire support for infantry.

The ZSU-23-4 service record includes deployment in Vietnam after 1972 and during the Yom Kippur War of 1973, when the system was credited with shooting down a number of Israeli aircraft that had lowered their altitude in order to escape Egyptian surface-to-air missiles and had flown into the Shilka's curtain of fire. U.S. Army evaluations of the system noted the ZSU-23-4 offered a hit probability of 53 per cent with a 40-round burst at 1000 m (0.6 miles). By contrast, the vehicle exhibited pronounced shortcomings in armour protection, cross-country manoeuvrability, cooling of the guns, and enemy jamming of the radar.

Interior view

The combat compartment of the ZSU-23-4 Shilka self-propelled armoured vehicle includes access to the turret area, where a quad-mounted 23-mm (0.9-in) anti-aircraft gun was served by the crew.

(1) Platform: The crew accessed the weapon from the hull and serviced the quad-mounted 23-mm (0.9-in) system from a platform.

(2) Crew Seating: The seats inside the combat compartment were sometimes folded so the vehicle could carry supplies, ammunition, or wounded soldiers.

(3) Electronics: The ZSU-23-4 was equipped with sophisticated radar and other electronic systems, which were monitored by crewmen from within the combat compartment.

(4) Interior Controls: Communications from internal systems to the crew manning the weapon were maintained in the hull.

(5) Combat Compartment Display: Information systems displayed data on target location and acquisition via the advanced radar mounted on the ZSU-23-4 Shilka.

(6) System Circuitry: The interior of the ZSU-23-4 Shilka was filled with sensitive electronic equipment with interlocking circuitry, which ran the length of the combat compartment.

Leopard 1

The first main battle tank developed in post-war West Germany, the Leopard 1 began as a joint venture with France. However, when the combined effort failed, the Germans pursued their own design independently. By 1965, the Leopard 1 was placed in service.

TURRET
The elongated cast turret of the Leopard 1 was modified several times and included an ammunition resupply hatch to the left, a searchlight attached above the 105-mm (4.1-in) gun, and a stowage area to the rear.

MAIN ARMAMENT
A German-built version of the proven 105-mm (4.1-in) British Royal Ordnance L7A3 L/52 rifled cannon served as the primary weapon of the Leopard 1 and many other Western main battle tanks.

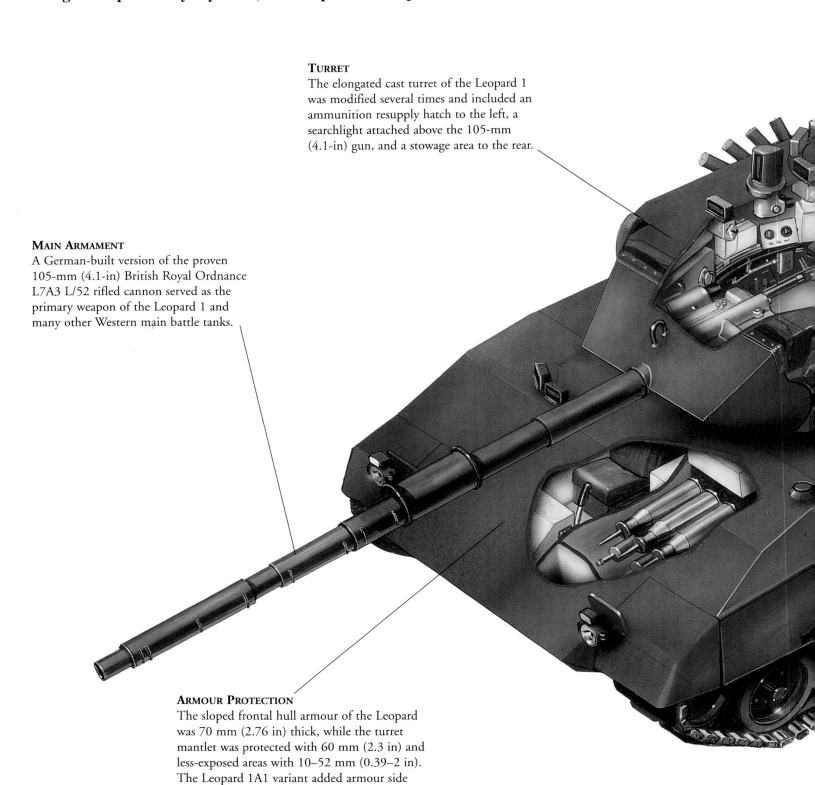

ARMOUR PROTECTION
The sloped frontal hull armour of the Leopard was 70 mm (2.76 in) thick, while the turret mantlet was protected with 60 mm (2.3 in) and less-exposed areas with 10–52 mm (0.39–2 in). The Leopard 1A1 variant added armour side skirts to protect the tracks and wheels.

SECONDARY ARMAMENT
The Leopard 1 secondary armament consisted of one 7.62-mm (0.3-in) Rheinmetall MG3 machine gun mounted coaxially and a second weapon of the same size pintle-mounted on the commander's hatch.

ENGINE
The 619-kW (830-hp), 10-cylinder MTU MB 838 CaM 500 multi-fuel engine was primarily powered by diesel and capable of a top road speed of 65 km/h (40 mph).

SUSPENSION
The torsion bar suspension of the Leopard 1 contributed to the tank's excellent handling during cross-country manoeuvres, while its relative light weight at 39 tonnes (43 tons) enhanced its speed and mobility.

At the time that the Leopard 1 was developed, the emphasis of German armoured warfare doctrine was on mobility and relatively limited armour protection. The glacis plate, however, was sloped at 60 degrees from the vertical, effectively doubling armour protection.

LEOPARD 1 – SPECIFICATION

Country of origin: West Germany
Crew: 4
Designer: Krauss-Maffei
Designed: Early 1960s
Manufacturers: Oto Melara, Italy
In Production: 1965–79
In Service: 1965–present
Number Built: 5816
Weight: 39 tonnes (44 tons), 42.2 tonnes (46.5 tons) on later models

Dimensions:
Length (gun forward): 9.54 m (31.3 ft)
Length (hull): 8.29 m (27.2 ft)
Width: 3.37 m (11.06 ft)
Height (turret roof): 2.39 m (7.84 ft)
Height (absolute): 2.7 m (8.86 ft)

Performance:
Speed: 65 km/h (40 mph)
Range, Road: 600 km (373 miles)
Range, Cross-country: 450 km (280 miles)

Engine:
Powerplant: 1 x MTU MB 838 Ca M500 10-cylinder, 37.4 l (9.9 gallon) multi-fuel engine generating 619 kW (830 hp) at 2200 rpm
Power/weight: 19.6 PS/tonne
Suspension: Torsion bar

Armour and Armament:
Armour: RHA, 10–70 mm (0.39–2.76 in)
Main Armament: 1 x 105-mm (4.1-in) Royal Ordnance L7A3 L/52 rifled gun. 13 rounds in turret, 42 rounds in hull.
Secondary Armament: 2 x 7.62-mm (0.3-in) MG3 or FN MAG (co-axial and commander's hatch). 5500 rounds.

Major Variants
Leopard 1A1A1: Additional turret armour.
Leopard 1A2: Updated turret function and passive night vision equipment installed.
Leopard 1A3: Improved armour and new all-welded turret production.
Leopard 1A4: Integrated fire control system implemented. This was the last variant used by the German army.
Leopard 1A5: Updated night vision equipment, computerized fire control and became upgraded version for all earlier German army models.
Leopard 1 AVLB: Bridgelayer.
Leopard 1 ARV: Armoured Recovery Vehicle.
Leopard 1 AEV: Engineering Vehicle.
Leopard 1 Trainer: Replaced with windowed turret for driver training.
Gepard Flakpanzer: Mobile twin 35-mm (1.38-in) anti-aircraft air defence system (Leopard 1 chassis).

LEOPARD 1

The interior of the Leopard 1 main battle tank was divided into two compartments, with the engine to the rear and separated from the forwards fighting compartment by a firewall. Its crew of four included the driver, positioned in the hull forwards and to the right. The commander and gunner were seated in the cast turret to the right, while the loader was to the left, where he fed shells into the breech of the 105-mm (4.1-in) L7A3 gun by hand. The coaxial 7.62-mm (0.3-in) machine gun was originally utilized for ranging the main weapon. However, this was later upgraded with an optical gunsight.

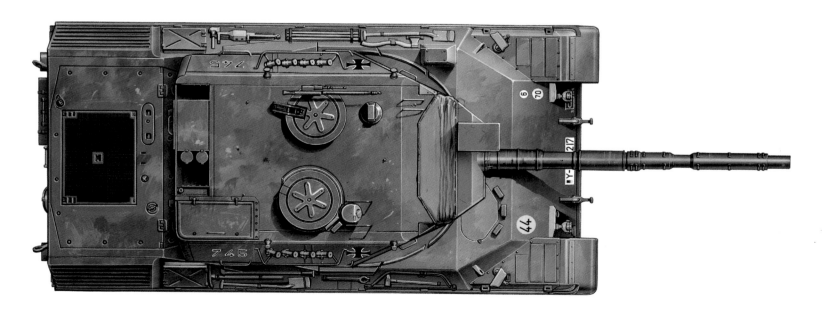

Shown during training exercises, this Leopard 1 main battle tank is painted in winter camouflage. Note the driver's periscope located near the centre of the hull and the coaxial FN MAG machine gun mounted near the commander's hatch. This tank was exported to at least 14 countries.

Beginning in 1971, the Federal Republic of Germany initiated a series of modifications to the Leopard 1, including a gun stabilization system enabling the tank to fire on the move. This rectified the Leopard's greatest deficiency, aside from its inadequate armour protection, which was sacrificed for improved mobility.

When the army of the Fedral Republic of Germany was reconstituted a decade after the end of World War II, its armoured formations were initially equipped with U.S. M48 Patton tanks. Within two years, the government of the German Federal Republic had authorized the development of a new main battle tank, in a joint effort with French designers. The project produced unsatisfactory results, so German engineers pursued their own design, the Leopard 1.

The Leopard 1 prototype was delivered in 1961, and production was initiated by Krauss Maffei of Munich in 1964. The first production Leopard 1 was received by the German army in September, 1965. Nearly 6500 main battle tanks and variants were built in Germany and under licence by the Italian manufacturer OTO-Melara.

Armed with the German-built L7A3 L/52 105-mm (4.1-in) cannon, originally a British design, the Leopard 1 combined firepower and mobility. The compromise was in protective armour. Even though the armour of both the front glacis and turret were sloped, the protection at a maximum of 70 mm (2.75 in) was considered inadequate. At 39 tonnes (43 tons), the tank was comparatively light, and the 619-kW (830-hp), V-10 multi-fuel engine produced the best power-to-weight ratio of contemporary main battle tanks. It could also be replaced in the field in as little as 20 minutes.

EIGHT PERISCOPES

A crew of four manned the Leopard 1, with the driver viewing the field through three periscopes, one of which could be replaced with infrared equipment for night vision. The gunner and loader were provided with a single scope and stereoscopic rangefinder and a pair of scopes respectively, while the commander could look through any of eight periscopes (one of these capable of infrared replacement) incorporated into his hatch on top of the turret.

The rifled 105-mm (4.1-in) cannon was also deployed with British and U.S. main battle tanks, such as the Centurion and M1 Abrams. The weapon was not stabilized in early production Leopards, but this was corrected with a Cadillac Gage system in the 1A1 variant. The loader was required to place each round of ammunition into the breech by hand, but the spent shell casing was automatically ejected.

Prominent variants of the Leopard 1 included the 1A1. It had a stabilized main gun fitted with a thermal sleeve to reduce warping and maintain accuracy, improved tracks, and armoured skirts to protect the tracks and wheels. The 1A1A1, which was upgraded from 1974–77, featured the addition of armour made of reinforced steel plate. This was developed by Blohm and Voss for the turret, gun mantlet, and forward section of the hull. Another notable variant, the 1A1A2, featured a system for intensifying images.

The Leopard 1A2 featured a sturdier cast turret, better night vision equipment, and NBC (nuclear, biological, chemical) defence improvements. The 1A3 introduced a welded turret with a wedge-shaped mantlet and spaced armour. In 1974, the 1A4 was equipped with an upgraded computerized fire control system. Further modifications led to the 1A5 in the early 1980s, and in 1987 the 1A6 introduced a 120-mm (4.7-in) cannon. Other variants included armoured engineering, recovery, anti-aircraft, and bridging vehicles.

By the mid-1980s, the Leopard 2 was being introduced, and the German army subsequently relegated the Leopard 1 to reserve units.

Interior view

The turret interior of the German Leopard 1 main battle tank provided space for three crew – commander, gunner, and loader. The commander and gunner cooperated in the acquisition of targets.

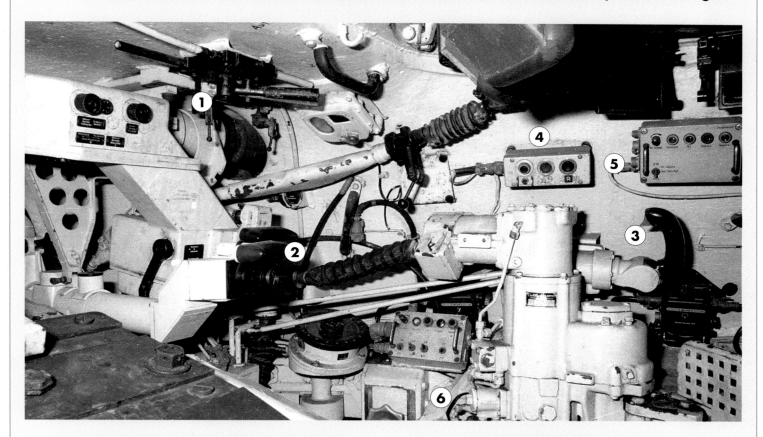

(1) **Gunner's Sights:** The tank's gunner used sophisticated sighting equipment and rangefinding computers to identify targets.

(2) **Gunner's Controls:** At his fingertips, the gunner had controls that traversed the turret and adjusted the elevation of the main weapon to acquire distant targets.

(3) **Commander's Station:** The Leopard 1 commander could also fire the main weapon and used his manual hand station to override the controls when necessary.

(4) **Commander's Control Box:** The commander monitored the systems, several groups of switches, and the gauges.

(5) **Intercom Box:** The commander's intercom box was mounted to the turret hull on the Leopard 1, allowing him to maintain communications with other crew members.

(6) **Gunner's Seat:** This was forwards of the commander's position on the Leopard 1 main battle tank, where he conducted the operation of the 105-mm (4.1-in) cannon.

Stridsvagn 103B

The first main battle tank to be deployed without a turret, the Stridsvagen (Strv) 103 was designed for the Swedish armed forces as a cost-effective armoured vehicle primarily suited for defence. It did offer some advantages, but the entire tank had to be turned in order to engage an enemy.

DRIVE TRAIN
Key elements of laying and firing the main weapon were the fully automated transmission and the hydro-pneumatic suspension system.

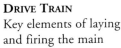

MAIN ARMAMENT
Manufactured by Bofors, the 105-mm (4.1-in) L74 cannon was virtually identical to the famous British-manufactured L7, which armed a number of contemporary main battle tanks.

ENGINE
The dual powerplant concept was innovative, and in the case of the Strv 103B (shown), the 179 kW (240 hp) Rolls-Royce K60 diesel and 365 kW (490 hp) Caterpillar 553 petrol turbine engine were paired.

SECONDARY ARMAMENT
Two 7.62-mm (0.3-in) machine guns were fixed to the left side of the hull, and a third machine gun of the same calibre was pintle-mounted adjacent to the commander's cupola for anti-aircraft defence.

ARMOUR PROTECTION
The absence of a turret allowed for greater armour protection in the hull. The maximum armour thickness ranged from 90–100 mm (3.5–3.9 in) on the sloped front glacis, while horizontal ribs were added to increase deflection of projectiles. The slope effectively doubled the thickness of the armour.

INTERIOR DESIGN
The hull of the Strv 103 included a combination driver and engine compartment forwards, a fighting compartment in the centre accommodating the commander and radio operator to the right, and a magazine to the rear. The driver doubled as gunner.

With the S-Tank, Sweden sought a tank suited to its own particular landscape, which featured rolling farmland in the south and, in the north, high forests and tundra, which are frozen in the winter and soggy in the summer.

SUPPORT VEHICLE: PBV 302 APC

STRIDSVAGN 103B – SPECIFICATION

Country of Origin: Sweden
Crew: 3
Designer: Sven Berge
Designed: Mid-1950s
Manufacturer: Bofors
In Production: 1966–71
In Service: 1966–97
Number Built: 300
Gross Weight: 38.9 tonnes (42.8 tons)

Dimensions:
Hull Length: 7.04 m (23.1 ft)
Overall Length: 8.99 m (29.5 ft)
Width: 3.6 m (11.9 ft)
Overall Height: 2.15 m (7 ft)

Performance:
Maximum Speed: 50 km/h (30 mph)
Range, Road: 390 km (240 miles)
Range, Cross-country: about 200 km (120 miles)
Ground Pressure: 0.9 kg/cm²
Fording Capacity: 1.5 m (5 ft) (amphibious with preparation, by means of flotation screen)
Maximum Gradient: 30 degrees
Maximum Trench Width: 2.3 m (7.5 ft)
Maximum Vertical Obstacle: 0.9 m (3 ft)
Suspension Type: Hydropneumatic, adjustable for fore-and-aft rake

Engine:
Powerplant: 1 x Boeing 553 gas turbine; 1 x Rolls-Royce K60 V-8 multi-fuel engine
Capacity: n/a
Output: 490 bhp/365 kW and 240 bhp/179 kW respectively
Power/Weight Ratio: 18.4 bhp/tonne on both powerplants
Fuel Capacity: 960 l (212 gallons)

Armament and Armour:
Main Armament: 1x 105-mm (4.1-in) Bofors L74 L/62. 50 rounds
Secondary Armament: 3 x 7.62-mm (0.3-in) FFV machine guns, two coaxial, one in AA mount. 2750 rounds
Armour Type: Homogeneous rolled/welded nickel-steel

Upgrades
103C
1986: Improved fire control systems, dozer blades fitted to all tanks.
1987/88: New engine: 216 kW (290 hp) Detroit Diesel, new laser rangefinder.

103D (single prototype upgrade)
1989: Fire-control computer, thermal viewers for gunner and the commander, passive light enhancers for driving, minor changes to the suspension system, minor changes to engine.

SUPPORT VEHICLE: BANDKANON 1

STRIDSVAGN 103B

The defensive perspective with which the Strv 103 was designed carried over to the layout of the tank's interior and the positioning of its crew. The driver, who also functioned as the gunner, was situated forwards and to the left in the hull with an OPS-1 periscope and binocular sight, while the commander was positioned beneath a cupola with controls for both the main weapon and the ability to drive the tank. The radio operator was situated behind the driver and facing to the rear, and also had access to driving controls. In the event that it became necessary, the tank functioned fully in a rearwards orientation, which allowed the main weapon to be brought to bear quickly.

STRIDSVAGN 103B

The low profile made the Strv 103 very difficult to see when it is on the move and almost impossible to find when lying hull-down in ambush. Though tested by several other armies, the S-Tank was not exported, nor has the turretless design been emulated.

Seeking a viable replacement for its ageing British-built Centurion main battle tanks, Sweden solicited a new design for a main battle tank during the mid-1950s. After disqualifying a joint effort by Bofors, Volvo, and Landsverk and considering buying foreign tanks, the decision was made to pursue a radical design put forward by Sven Berge of the Swedish Arms Administration. The tank would be built in Sweden with defensive capabilities tailored to Sweden's terrain, as well as its budget.

The Strv 103, or S-Tank, was a turretless main battle tank incorporating the 105-mm (4.1-in) L74 cannon, quite similar

Interior view

With its turretless construction, the Stridsvagn resembled tank destroyers of World War II. Its interior included space for a radio operator, who faced backwards and could drive the tank in that direction.

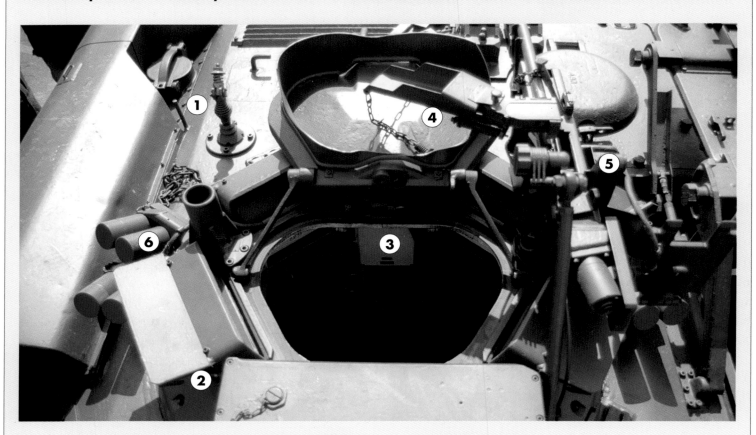

1. **Hull Armour:** The slope of the hull increased the effectiveness of the armour plating, which was up to 100 mm (3.9 in) thick.

2. **Viewing Ports:** Several viewing ports allowed crewmen to see to their immediate front, which was all the more critical without a traversing turret.

3. **Interior Access:** A pair of hatches in the upper hull opened to the interior of the Stridsvagen 103B.

4. **Hatch Cover:** The uniquely shaped hatch cover and hull opening facilitated the easy entry of the three crewmen.

5. **Machine Gun Mounts:** The tank was armed with up to three 7.62-mm (0.3-in) machine guns. One was mounted near the cupola; two others were in the hull.

6. **Smoke Grenade Launchers:** Mounted to the top of the hull, these were fired from inside the tank during combat operations.

A Swedish Stridsvagn 103B negotiates a slight grade during cross-country manoeuvres. Because of the turretless configuration, it presented a low silhouette, but it was unable to function effectively in the hull-down position.

to the British-designed L7 gun. However, the L74 was manufactured by Bofors and incorporated a longer barrel for better muzzle velocity and range. Complementing the L74 were an automatic loading system and twin vertical breech blocks attached to a magazine, which held 50 ready rounds of ammunition. The rate of fire was an outstanding 15 rounds per minute, and the type of ammunition could be changed with the push of a button. The magazines could be replenished in as little as 10 minutes, and empty shell casings were automatically ejected to the rear.

DARING DESIGN

The innovative design of the Strv 103 provided distinct advantages. Because a turret and heavy gun mantlet were not required, more armour protection could be added to the hull. In the hull-down position, the tank did not present a prominent silhouette. Both the commander and driver/gunner were capable of laying and firing the main weapon. The combination of diesel "cruising" and petrol "sprint" engines offered fuel economy and good performance in all weather conditions. The initial S-Tank was thought to be underpowered, though, and so the Strv 103B introduced an upgraded Caterpillar 365-kW (490-hp) 553 petrol engine to complement the Rolls-Royce K60 diesel. In the 103C, a 216-kW (290-hp) General Motors Detroit Diesel engine replaced the Rolls-Royce powerplant.

For all its innovation, the S-Tank required a great deal of manoeuvre before its main weapon could be fired, a potentially fatal drawback in combat. In order to sight and fire on a target, the entire vehicle had to be turned and elevated. This meant that it was impossible for the S-Tank to fire on the move. Berge attempted to compensate for the obvious difficulty in firing the L74 gun with an automated transmission, external crossbar steering mechanism, and a sophisticated hydro-pneumatic suspension, which elevated the pitch of the vehicle. The commander would theoretically sight the target and then override the driver's steering with his own tiller-type equipment, swinging the S-Tank into position and selecting the appropriate ammunition before allowing the driver/gunner to fire.

Aside from the engine upgrades in the 103B and 103C, the 103B introduced an amphibious flotation screen. This enabled the tank to traverse water through track action at nearly 6 km/h (3.6 mph). In the 103C, the S-Tank was fitted with a bulldozer blade, additional fuel tanks, and laser rangefinding equipment. The 103D introduced a fire-control computer and thermal imaging for combat operations at night and in bad weather.

The Strv 103 served with the Swedish armed forces for 25 years and was eventually phased out with the acquisition of the German Leopard 2 main battle tank. The vehicle was never to see combat.

BMP-1

The world's first true infantry fighting vehicle, the BMP-1 was heavily armed with cannon and anti-tank guided missiles. It was intended originally to serve as a protected position for infantry to fight from, in the wake of tactical nuclear weapons.

ANTI-TANK MISSILES
The 9S428 launcher mounted above the 73-mm (2.87-in) cannon fired the AT-3 Sagger, a wire-guided anti-tank missile, with five rounds on board.

MAIN ARMAMENT
The 73-mm (2.87-in) 2A28 Grom smoothbore, semi-automatic cannon was housed inside a one-man turret. It fired at a rate of eight rounds per minute and had 40 rounds stored in the automatic loader and throughout the hull.

ENGINE
The BMP-1 was powered by a 224-kW (300-hp), six-cylinder UTD-20 engine with a maximum range of 500 km (310 miles) cross country or 600 km (370 miles) on the road.

TURRET

Positioned in the centre of the hull, the low, cone-shaped turret housed the 73-mm (2.87-in) cannon, the automatic loader, and a coaxial 7.62-mm (0.3-in) machine gun. When the turret faced backwards, the gun prevented the roof hatches from opening.

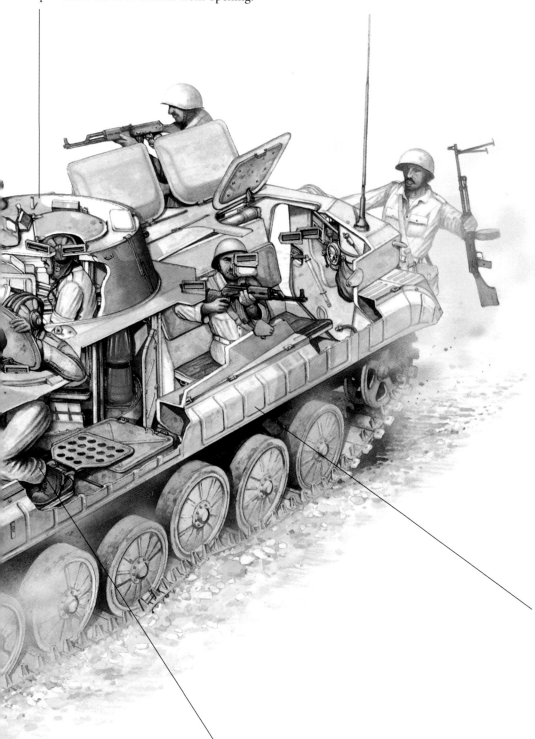

F A C T S

- The vehicle name, Bronevaya Maschina Pekhoty (BMP), translates as "infantry fighting vehicle."

- The BMP-1 was produced in the Soviet Union, Poland, and Czechoslovakia.

- The 73-mm (2.87-in) cannon fired the same ammunition as the vaunted RPG-7 infantry rocket-propelled grenade launcher.

ARMOUR PROTECTION

Ranging from 6–33 mm (0.24–1.3 in) thick, the aluminium alloy armour protection afforded the interior of the vehicle little protection against weapons of heavy calibre.

TROOP COMPLEMENT

The BMP-1 was capable of transporting up to eight combat-ready infantrymen seated back to back in rows of four in the hull's rear compartment. The crew of three included the commander and gunner in the centred fighting compartment, and the driver forwards to the left of the engine.

In service with Soviet and other
Warsaw Pact forces, and also widely
exported, the BMP-1 was a
revolutionary innovation. It was
developed beginning in the early 1960s
for the fast-paced armoured warfare
on the nuclear battlefield with NBC
(nuclear, biological, chemical) defence
and sufficient armament.

BMP-1 – SPECIFICATION

Country of Origin: Soviet Union
Crew: 3 + 8 passengers
Designer: Pavel Isakov (Design Bureau of the ChTZ)
Designed: 1961–65
Manufacturers: Kurgan Engineering Works (KMZ) (USSR);
ZTS Dubnica nad Váhom (Czechoslovakia); Military
Motorization Works No. 5 (Poland)
Produced: 1966–83 (USSR); unknown–1988 (Poland)
In Service: 1966–present
Number Built: More than 20,000 of all variants (USSR); more
than 3000 of all variants (PRC): 1994 (Czechoslovakia); 274
(Poland); 800 (India)
Weight: 13.2 tonnes (14.6 tons)

Dimensions:
Length: 6.735 m (22 ft 1.2 in)
Width: 2.94 m (9 ft 8 in)
Height (to turret top): 2.07 m (6 ft 9.4 in)
Height (base): 1.881 m (6 ft 2.1 in)

Performance:
Speed, Road: 65 km/h (40 mph)
Speed, Cross-country: 45 km/h (28 mph)
Speed, Water: 5 km/h (3 mph)
Range, Road: 600 km (370 miles)
Range, Cross-country: 500 km (310 miles)

Engine:
Powerplant: 1 x UTD-20, 6-cylinder 4-stroke V-shaped airless-
injection water-cooled multi-fuel 15.8 l (4.17 gallon) diesel
producing 224 kW (300 hp) at 2600 rpm
Power/weight: 22.7 hp/tonne (17 kW/tonne)
Suspension: Individual torsion bar with hydraulic shock
absorbers on the 1st and 6th road wheels

Ground Clearance: 370 mm (15 in)
Fuel Capacity: 462 l (122 gallons)

Armament and Armour:
Main Armament: 1x 73-mm (2.87-in) 2A28 Grom low-pressure
smoothbore short-recoil semi-automatic gun (40 rounds);
9S428 ATGM launcher for 9M14 Malyutka (4 + 1 rounds)
Secondary Armament: 7.62-mm (0.3-in) PKT coaxial machine
gun (2000 rounds)
Gun Mantlet: 26–33 mm (0.9–1.3 in)
Turret Front: 23 mm (0.9 in) at 42 degrees
Turret Side: 19 mm (0.75 in) at 36 degrees
Turret Rear: 13 mm (0.51 in) at 30 degrees
Turret Top: 6 mm (0.24 in)
Upper Hull Front: 7 mm (0.28 in) at 80 degrees
Hull Lower Front: 19 mm (0.75 in) at 57 degrees
Hull Upper Side: 16 mm (0.63 in) at 14 degrees
Hull Lower Side: 18 mm (0.7 in) at 0 degrees
Hull Rear: 16 mm (0.63 in) at 19 degrees
Hull Top: 6 mm (0.24 in)

Major Variants
BMP-1F: Reconnaissance vehicle (Hungary).
BMP-1K: Commander's vehicle.
BMP-1P: No Sagger anti-tank weapon system fitted.
BMP-1KShM: Unarmed command vehicle.
BWP: Base BMP-1 (Poland).
BMP-POO: Training Vehicle with raised roof and no turret.
BMP-1G: Export version with no AT Sagger support in turret.
Pbv 501: Base BMP-1 model (Sweden).

REPLACEMENT: BMP-2

Eight combat infantrymen were not only carried into battle by the BMP-1, but could fight from within its protection, firing small arms through three gun ports on each side and two located in the rear doors. Further, the troop compartment was sealed against chemical or nuclear contamination. The infantrymen exited through the rear doors and four roof hatches. The driver viewed the field through three observation periscopes, as did the commander, positioned behind and above the driver on the left of the hull, which was considerably smaller than those of its Western counterparts. The gunner sat inside the rotating turret with four periscopes and sighting equipment for the main weapon.

REPLACEMENT: BMP-3

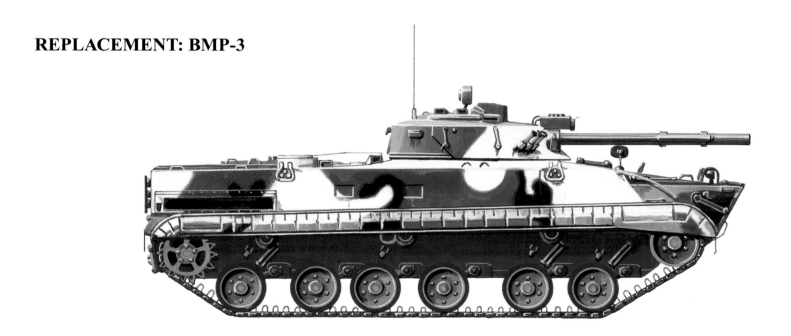

A combination of effective anti-tank firepower, high mobility, and satisfactory protection made the BMP-1 a formidable addition to the inventory of Soviet motorized rifle units. The vehicle was designed to suit the demands of the high-speed offensive in a nuclear war.

The embodiment of Soviet Red Army field tactics in the event of nuclear war, the BMP-1, with its distinctive low silhouette, characteristically sloped armour, and heavy armament, was originally intended to serve as a platform for the destruction of enemy armour with its 73-mm (2.87-in) semi-automatic, smoothbore cannon and anti-tank guided missile launch system.

The vehicle was also designed to protect eight infantrymen, who would engage the enemy from within the pressurized hull, protected from radiation and chemical weapons by an NBC filtration system. Later, Soviet field

Interior view

The Soviet-designed BMP-1 was the world's first AFV to be designed intentionally as an infantry fighting vehicle. Its interior housed a crew of three and up to eight infantrymen.

(1) **Driver's Instrument Panel:** A system of gauges allowed the driver to monitor fuel, pressure, oil, and other levels during operations.

(2) **Hydraulic Lines:** Hydraulic and electrical lines powered the BMP-1 onboard systems, allowing it to function with a high degree of efficiency during field deployment.

(3) **Steering Gear:** The butterfly steering yoke was centred in the driver's position and forwards of the instrument panel.

(4) **Transmission Selector:** This was operated by the driver to engage engine gears to negotiate various types of terrain.

(5) **Armour Protection:** The thin hull of the BMP-1 provided minimal protection, while the engine was separated from the driver's position only by a narrow bulkhead.

(6) **Driver's Pedals:** Clutch, brake, and accelerator pedals were located at the driver's feet and manipulated as necessary.

Emblazoned with the Iraqi flag and painted in desert camouflage, a BMP-1 speeds down a dirt road. Several infantrymen are perched on the hull or posted from hatches in the hull.

doctrine was altered to emphasize non-nuclear combat, which meant the troops were expected to dismount the vehicle. Unlike the difficulty encountered with armoured personnel carriers, such as the BTR-60, egress from the BMP-1 was accomplished quickly via four roof hatches and two rear doors. In that circumstance, the BMP-1 commander would then serve as squad leader.

First seen in 1967 during a military parade in the Red Square, the BMP-1 was the product of a new concept of warfare, which was later adapted to more conventional deployment. Design work began in the late 1950s, and the vehicle entered service in 1966. With armour protection up to 33 mm (1.3 in) thick, the BMP-1 was capable of withstanding small-arms fire and shell splinters, while its 224-kW (300-hp), six-cylinder UTD-20 engine, combined with a suspension of torsion bars and hydraulic shock absorbers, was up to the task of manoeuvring in rugged terrain. Track action powered the amphibious vehicle through water at a top speed of 5 km/h (3 mph).

FIREPOWER AT A PRICE

The performance of the 73-mm (2.87-in) cannon was reduced by a low muzzle velocity and relatively primitive sighting equipment. The cannon's effectiveness was further hampered due to the low turret configuration, which was a

distinct disadvantage in engaging targets from a hull-down position because of the limited ability to depress the weapon. Further, during traverse, the barrel of the gun had to be elevated sufficiently to clear the infrared searchlight sited on top of the commander's cupola. This meant that neither the cannon nor the 7.62-mm (0.3-in) PKT machine gun could be brought to bear between the 10- and 11-o'clock positions. The turret also served as a platform for the AT-3 Sagger missile. This could be fired from inside the vehicle, but a crewman had to exit to reload the launcher from outside.

When the BMP-1 made its combat debut with the Egyptian army during the 1973 Yom Kippur War, a major shortcoming was revealed. The compact hull housed a volatile assortment of ordnance and fuel, and penetration often resulted in a catastrophic explosion. For this reason, it was determined that the BMP-1 was too lightly armoured to fight alongside tanks in the front echelons of an advance.

By 1980, the BMP-2 was introduced with a two-man turret, a 30-mm (1.18-in) automatic cannon replacing the 73-mm (2.87-in) gun, and the AT-5 Spandrel anti-tank missile replacing the Sagger. In the mid-1980s, a radically redesigned vehicle, the BMP-3, was deployed with Red Army units in limited numbers. More than 20,000 BMP-1s were built between 1966–83, and the vehicle remains in service in large numbers today.

M551 Sheridan

Largely a disappointment, the M551 Sheridan Armoured Reconnaissance Airborne Assault Vehicle was developed during a transitional period for the U.S. Army, as the role of the tank was being re-evaluated and a vehicle deployable by air was being sought.

MAIN ARMAMENT
The M81E1 rifled 152-mm (6-in) gun and missile launcher system was capable of firing conventional ammunition at low velocity or the MGM-51 Shillelagh anti-tank guided missile.

HULL
Arranged in standard configuration, the aluminium hull of the M551 Sheridan was divided into an engine compartment to the rear, a centred fighting compartment, and the driver's compartment forwards with the hatch centrally positioned.

ARMOUR PROTECTION
Thin aluminium armour was up to 50 mm (1.97 in) thick and was sloped at 40 degrees. This improved its effectiveness, yet the tank remained vulnerable to mines and some infantry-portable anti-tank weapons.

SECONDARY ARMAMENT
An M240 7.62-mm (0.3-in) coaxial machine gun was set in the turret, while a Browning 12.7-mm (0.5-in) heavy machine gun was ring-mounted on top of the turret beside the commander's cupola.

TURRET
The flattened welded-steel turret housed the commander seated on the right, the gunner below and to the front, and the loader to the left.

ENGINE
The 224-kW (300-hp) General Motors Detroit 6V-53T, six-cylinder turbocharged diesel engine was capable of achieving a top road speed of 68 km/h (42 mph). It was paired with the Allison TG-25–2A powershift cross-drive transmission with four forwards and one reverse gear.

SUSPENSION
The torsion bar suspension supported a light vehicle weighing only 15 tonnes (17 tons) and provided good cross-country mobility.

The **M551 Sheridan Armoured Reconnaissance Airborne Assault Vehicle** represented an unsuccessful attempt to use an excessively advanced missile armament system in order to combine the speed and mobility of a light tank with the firepower of a main battle tank.

M551 SHERIDAN

M551 SHERIDAN – SPECIFICATION

Country of Origin: United States
Crew: 4
Designer: Not specified
Designed: 1959–65
Manufacturer: Not specified
In Production: 1965–70
In Service: 1967–96
Number Built: 1700
Weight: 15.2 tonnes (16.76 tons)

Dimensions:
Length: 6.3 m (20.6 ft)
Width: 2.8 m (9.1 ft)
Height: 2.3 m (7.5 ft)

Performance:
Speed, Road: 68 km/h (42 mph)
Speed, Water: 5.8 km/h (3.6 mph)
Operational Range: 560 km (348 miles)

Engine:
Powerplant: 1 x General Motors 6V53T, six-cylinder, turbocharged diesel 224 kW (300 hp)
Power/weight: 19.7 hp/tonne
Suspension: Torsion bar

Armour and Armament:
Armour Type: Aluminium
Main Armament: 1 x M81E1 Rifled 152-mm (5.9-in) gun/launcher. 20 rounds. 9 x MGM-51 Shillelagh missiles
Secondary Armament: Early models: 1 x 7.62-mm (0.3-in) M73/M219 machine gun. 3000 rounds. 8 smoke grenade dischargers.

Later models: 1 x 7.62-mm (0.3-in) M240C machine gun. 3000 rounds. 1 x 12.7-mm (0.50-in) M2HB machine gun. 1000 rounds. 8 smoke grenade dischargers.

Variants
XM551: Limited pre-production model produced in 1965.
M551: Basic production model beginning production in 1967.
"Two Box" M551: Guidance and fire control of the missiles systems changed to create space for two boxes: one for 7.62 x 51-mm (0.3 x 2-in) NATO ammunition (coaxial machine gun), and one for 12.7 x 99-mm (0.5 x 3.98-in) BMG (.50-calibre) ammunition. Missile stowage redesigned to accept conventional rounds.
M551A1: Upgraded M551 with AN/VVG-1 laser rangefinder.
M551A1 TTS: Tank Thermal Sight, fitted with the AN/VSG-2B thermal sight unit, similar to the unit used on the M60A3 MBT. This later became standard to all M551A1s.
M551 NTC: National Training Center. Using M551 hulls, the NTC created a number of mock vehicles for training exercises resembling common Soviet/Warsaw Pact types. They were also known as "vismods," short for VISually MODified.

SUPPORT VEHICLE: M50 ONTOS

M551 SHERIDAN

The driver of the M551 Sheridan had the use of three periscopes, one of which could be replaced with an infrared scope, as well as a vision slit. The commander's cupola incorporated periscopes for 360-degree viewing with the centre-capable of accepting an infrared night scope. The gunner's optical sights were integrated with laser rangefinding equipment, possibly the first such apparatus in service, and the system was linked to an analog fire-control computer. The interior of the M551 was functional, but because of the lack of sufficient armour protection it was susceptible to enemy fire of any greater calibre than basic small arms, as well as land mines.

SUPPORT VEHICLE: M113

The M551 Sheridan had a patchy development history, characterized by difficulties with the complex electronics gear associated with its MGM-51 Shillelagh anti-tank missile system and problems with the combustible cases for its 152-mm (6-in) rounds for the main gun.

The M551 Sheridan was adopted by the U.S. Army in response to the need to replace its antiquated M41 Walker Bulldog light tanks. At the same time, the army was evaluating its designations of light, medium, and heavy tanks and moving towards a comprehensive primary armoured fighting vehicle that would become the concept of the main battle tank.

During the early 1960s, the U.S. Army realized it needed a light tank that could not only be deployed by air but could provide substantial fire support for cavalry and armoured infantry units. With the development of a new generation of

Interior view

The M551 Sheridan air-mobile tank was intended for deployment with airborne troops and mounted the Shillelagh anti-tank missile system along with a heavy 152-mm (6-in) rifled main gun.

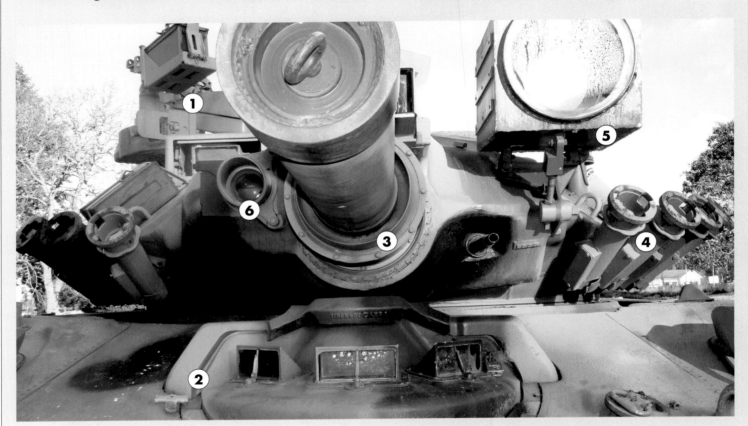

(1) **Laser Rangefinder:** Added onto the exterior of the tank, laser rangefinding equipment assisted in the acquisition of targets.

(2) **Hull Armour:** Designed to be light in weight, the Sheridan has proven susceptible to land mines, direct fire, and improvised explosive devices (IED) during combat situations.

(3) **Main Weapon:** The 152-mm (6-in) rifled gun of the M551 Sheridan was also designed to fire the Shillelagh anti-tank missile.

(4) **Smoke Grenade Launcher:** The turret was fitted with a pair of smoke grenade launchers to provide cover to the vehicle.

(5) **Searchlight:** A powerful searchlight, capable of standard and infrared illumination, enhanced the ability of the tank crew to identify targets.

(6) **Driver's Periscope:** The driver, centred forwards in the hull, viewed the terrain ahead through viewing ports.

An M551 Sheridan tank moves down a street as three of its crewmen survey the surroundings. The U.S. 82nd Airborne Division is the last to use the Sheridan in its air-mobile role.

Soviet vehicles, amphibious capabilities were given a priority as well. The Sheridan was hurried into production at the height of the Vietnam War and deployed to Southeast Asia, where significant deficiencies were soon revealed.

In the great heat and humidity of Vietnam's climate, the turbocharged diesel engine tended to overheat, and its fire-control capability rapidly degraded. Even more problematic was the ineffectiveness of its M81 main armament system. The gun was designed to fire 152-mm (6-in) shells, but its short-barrelled muzzle velocity was so low that armour penetration was severely diminished, while the ammunition itself proved unstable and was hazardous in combat in the event that the thin hull was compromised. The main gun was also designed to fire the MGM-51 Shillelagh anti-tank guided missile, which required the maintenance of a line of sight to the target, reducing its effectiveness.

WHEEL-LIFTING RECOIL
The gun itself was prone to fouling, while its concussion and recoil played havoc with the sensitive electronics required to operate the Shillelagh missile system. Some considered that the chassis was too light for the weapon's recoil, which was reported to have literally lifted the second and third road wheels off the ground at times.

Even though the Shillelagh system was not installed on the Sheridans that had been deployed to Vietnam, the criticism of the vehicle extended to battlefield performance. It proved to be vulnerable to mines and to the lethal rocket-propelled grenades carried by Communist troops in Vietnam. It was lighter and more manoeuvrable than the M48 Patton tanks also deployed to Southeast Asia, providing better mobility, but this benefit was substantially negated in the jungles of Vietnam as the lighter Sheridan was unable to negotiate dense vegetation easily. The M551s deployed to Europe were also plagued with mechanical difficulties.

Given its obvious drawbacks, by 1978, the U.S. Army phased the Sheridan out of its front-line units. However, the tank remained in service with the 82nd Airborne Division into the mid-1990s. The Sheridan was deployed to Panama and participated in Operation Just Cause in 1989, and later to the Middle East during Operation Desert Shield/Storm, where its vulnerability to enemy tanks limited its use for reconnaissance purposes. Reports vary as to whether the Shillelagh system was ever fired in combat, though such an event may have occurred during Desert Storm.

Some Sheridans remain in use, their silhouettes modified to resemble potential enemy tanks, at the U.S. National Training Centre, in Fort Irwin, California.

Scimitar

Manufactured by the Alvis Company, the FV107 Scimitar is one of a series of light armoured vehicles, including the FV101 Scorpion, intended for reconnaissance, infantry support, and rapid deployment. Its speed and mobility on the battlefield make it ideal for scouting operations.

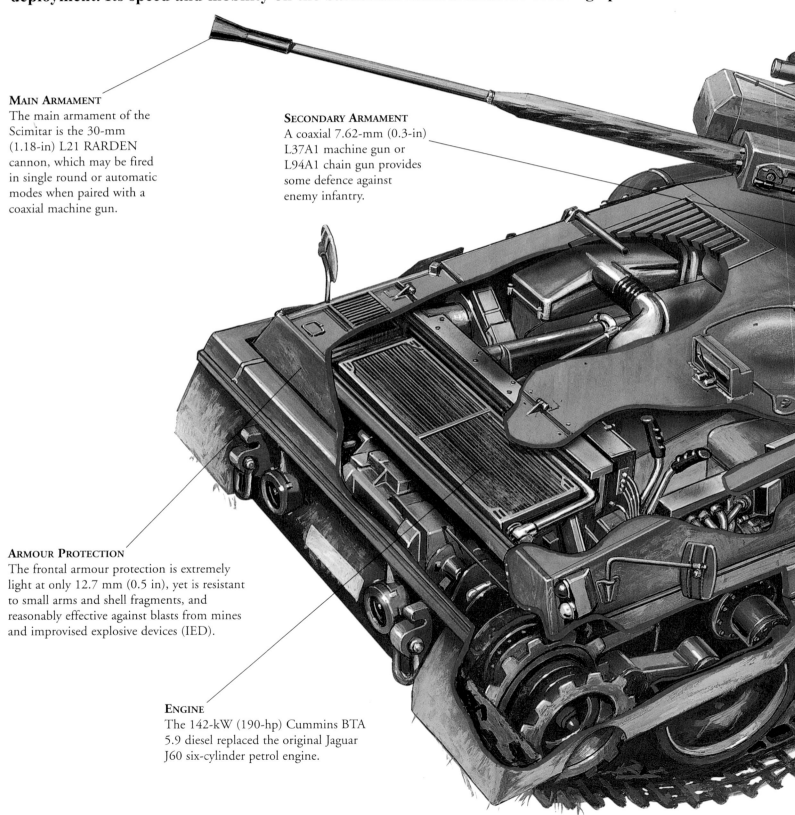

MAIN ARMAMENT
The main armament of the Scimitar is the 30-mm (1.18-in) L21 RARDEN cannon, which may be fired in single round or automatic modes when paired with a coaxial machine gun.

SECONDARY ARMAMENT
A coaxial 7.62-mm (0.3-in) L37A1 machine gun or L94A1 chain gun provides some defence against enemy infantry.

ARMOUR PROTECTION
The frontal armour protection is extremely light at only 12.7 mm (0.5 in), yet is resistant to small arms and shell fragments, and reasonably effective against blasts from mines and improvised explosive devices (IED).

ENGINE
The 142-kW (190-hp) Cummins BTA 5.9 diesel replaced the original Jaguar J60 six-cylinder petrol engine.

OBSERVATION

Five periscopes provide the commander with a 360-degree view of his surroundings, and he can also use an optical gunsight. The gunner sees through two periscopes and both passive and active night sights. The driver's two periscopes are interchangeable with night-vision scopes.

INTERIOR CONFIGURATION

The welded aluminium hull consists of a driver and engine compartment forwards and a fighting compartment, including the turret, to the rear. The driver is seated to the left, while the commander and gunner are positioned inside the aluminium turret, with the commander to the left.

SUSPENSION

The torsion bar suspension includes five wheels with rubber coats, which are efficient both crossing country and on roads

Developed in the late 1960s as one of a family of light reconnaissance vehicles with common automotive components, the Scimitar is somewhat lightly armed compared with its sister vehicle, the FV101 Scorpion, which carries a 76-mm (2.95-in) main weapon.

SCIMITAR – SPECIFICATION

Country of Origin: United Kingdom
Crew: 3
Designer: Alvis
Designed: 1971
In Production: Late 1960s
Manufacturer: Alvis
In Operation: 1974–present
Number Built: Unavailable
Weight: 7.8 tonnes (8.58 tons)

Dimensions:
Length: 4.9 m (15.75 ft)
Width: 2.2 m (7 ft 3 in)
Height: 2.1 m (6 ft 9 in)

Performance:
Speed: 80 km/h (50 mph) (6.4 km/h [4 mph] on water)
Range, Cross-country: 450 km (279.6 miles)
Range, Road: 645 km (400 miles)
Fording Capacity: 1.07 m (3.5 ft)
Maximum Gradient: 30 degrees
Maximum Trench Width: 2.06 m (6.75 ft)
Maximum Vertical Obstacle: 0.5 m (1.66 ft)
Ground Clearance: 0.35 m (1 ft 2.3 in)

Engine:
Powerplant: 1 x Cummins BTA 5.9 diesel 142 kW (190 hp) @ 4750 rpm
Capacity: 4.2 l (1.1 gallons)
Power/weight ratio: 24 bhp/tonne
Suspension: Torsion bar
Fuel Capacity: 425 l (94 gallons)

Armour and Armament:
Armour Type: Rolled/welded toughened aluminium
Main Armament: 1 x 30-mm (1.18-in) L21 RARDEN cannon sabot, HE, and 40 armour-piercing special effects (APSE) rounds
Secondary Armament: 1 x Coaxial 7.62-mm (0.3-in) L37A1 MG. 3000 rounds

Ammunition Types:
High Explosive Incendiary (HEI)
High Explosive (HE)
Armour Piercing (AP)
APSE (Armour Piercing Secondary Effects)
Armour Piercing Discarding Sabot-Tracer (APDS-T)
Additional defence: 2 x 4 barrel smoke launchers.

Gun Control Equipment:
Turret traverse: Electric/manual
Elevation Range: -10 to +35 degrees
Stabilization: Azimuth & elevation
Fire Control System: Computerized, with thermal imaging/laser rangefinder

VARIANT: FV 101 SCORPION

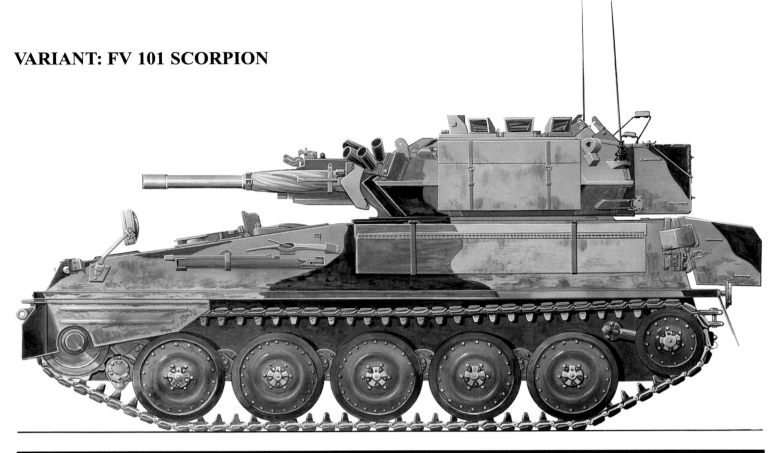

SCIMITAR AND SCORPION

The interior of the FV107 Scimitar is functional with driving/engine and fighting compartments, which allow reasonable movement for its crew of three. The driver steers the vehicle with conventional tillers and pedal brakes, while the commander and gunner are afforded excellent visibility. Although its armour protection is extremely thin at only 12.7 mm (0.5 in), the aluminium construction of both the hull and turret has proven effective against blast, shock waves, and small arms. The addition of appliqué armour enhances survivability on the battlefield, and thermal night-vision imaging allows more effective fire support during nocturnal operations. The FV101 Scorpion (shown here) was the first in a group of seven armoured vehicles manufactured by the Alvis Corporation. It was introduced in 1973 and deployed with British forces during the 1982 Falklands War.

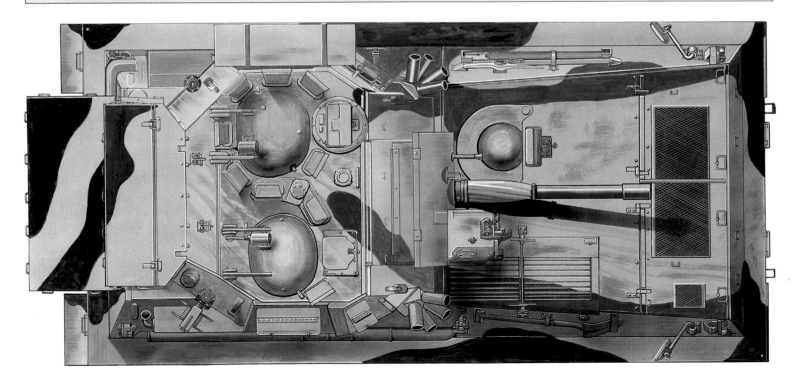

Used for scouting by medium reconnaissance regiments and armoured infantry units, the Scimitar provides added firepower and mobility. With a low ground pressure, it is capable of reaching remote areas of the battlefield where heavier armoured vehicles cannot penetrate.

First deployed in 1970, the FV107 Scimitar was the second in the line of light armoured fighting vehicles designed and manufactured by the Alvis Company beginning in the late 1960s. The Scimitar filled the British Army's requirement for one of several variants that could provide direct fire support for infantry yet have excellent mobility and relatively high speed. Its light weight of only 7 tonnes (8 tons) meant that it could be deployed by air.

While the FV101 Scorpion, the first of the Alvis series, carried a 76-mm (2.95-in) cannon, the FV107 Scimitar is armed with a 30-mm (1.18-in) L21 RARDEN cannonn

Interior view

The Alvis FV107 Scimitar armoured reconnaissance vehicle had a crew of three. It mounted a 30-mm (1.18-in) RARDEN cannon, which could be used as an automatic weapon or fire single rounds.

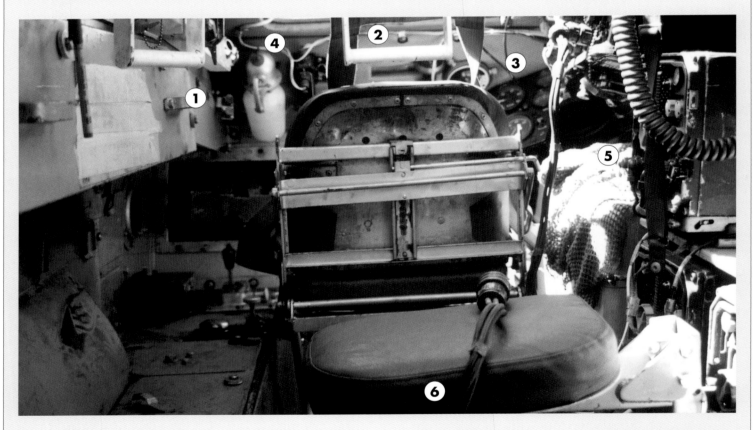

(1) **Hull Armour:** The welded aluminium hull was less than 13 mm (0.5 in) thick, making it susceptible to weapons of heavy calibre.

(2) **Driver's Compartment:** Located inside the hull and to the left of the engine, the driver of the FV107 Scimitar steered the vehicle with a pair of levers.

(3) **Optics:** The driver and other crew were provided image-intensification sights and were protected by an NBC (nuclear, biological, chemical) defence system.

(4) **Operations Systems:** The driver deployed a flotation screen for amphibious operations and maintained communications with the commander and gunner via an intercom.

(5) **Storage Area:** The storage of equipment, provisions, and reserve ammunition was at a premium and all available space was dedicated to this purpose.

(6) **Driver Controls:** The driver was oriented forwards and viewed the terrain ahead through periscopes affixed to the hatch.

An Alvis FV107 Scimitar armoured reconnaissance vehicle crosses a small stream via rapidly deployed bridging equipment. Laser rangefinding equipment is visible, as are banks of smoke grenade launchers attached to each side of the turret.

capable of firing in single shot or automatic mode. Its rate of fire is up to 90 rounds per minute, and 165 rounds may be stored in the relatively spacious aluminium turret. The weapon achieves a muzzle velocity of up to 1200 m (3937 ft) per second, and some of its armour-piercing rounds are capable of penetrating the side armour of larger main battle tanks. Paired with either a coaxial 7.62-mm (0.3-in) L37A1 machine gun or L94A1 chain gun with a rate of fire up to 125 rounds per minute and at least a single smoke grenade launcher, the Scimitar is capable of substantially augmenting standard infantry small arms. It is also poses a credible threat to low-flying enemy aircraft.

SPEED AND PROTECTION

While its armour is relatively thin, the welded aluminium hull is light and may withstand most small-calibre weapons. However, the primary characteristic of the Scimitar, in both offensive and defensive situations, is speed. Early versions were powered by the 4.2 l (1.1 gal) Jaguar J60 petrol engine. However, this was upgraded with the 5.9 l (1.5 gal) Cummins BTA diesel engine, generating 141 kW (190 hp) and a top road speed of 80 km/h (50 mph). The torsion bar suspension, with rubber wheels, is ideal for rapid road movement.

The vehicle's height of just under 2.1 m (7 ft) presents a low silhouette, while the low ground pressure of only 5.1

pounds allows the Scimitar to access difficult terrain, such as loose desert sand, snow-covered tundra, or swamp. Additional external armour provides added protection on some vehicles. The Scimitar is also amphibious, engaging a flotation screen and snorkel apparatus.

A variety of upgrades have been applied to the FV107 without alterations being made to the original vehicle. These include improved communication equipment, the installation of large storage bins within the turret, passive night-vision capability, and additional externally mounted machine guns. For improved target acquisition, laser rangefinding systems have been installed. For the powerplant, improved cooling systems have been fitted, and newer tanks also have automatic fire suppression, a bore evacuator for the 30-mm (1.18-in) cannon, and an auxiliary power generator.

A forced air system allows the FV107 Scimitar to function in adverse environmental conditions, including chemical, biological, radiation, and nuclear combat situations. While locked down, the crew is able to breathe normally for an extended period and prepare hot meals. It is equipped with a hole beneath the commander's seat, which may be used as a toilet.

The Scimitar has been deployed to combat during the Falklands War, the first and second Gulf Wars, the conflicts in Bosnia and Kosovo, and in Afghanistan.

Marder

The first infantry fighting vehicle developed and deployed by a NATO country, the Marder entered service in 1971. It has since been joined by the British Warrior and U.S. Bradley, while retaining its reputation as a highly functional combat support platform.

MAIN ARMAMENT
Mounted outside the turret, the 20-mm (0.79-in) Rheinmetall Rh.202 cannon is fed by three separate belts, allowing the gunner to change ammunition as combat conditions demand. A MILAN anti-tank guided missile system may also be attached to the turret.

INFANTRY ACCESS
Infantry can engage the enemy dismounted or from inside the Marder, firing through two circular firing ports on either side of the hull. Ingress and egress are accomplished through two roof hatches and a ramp door to the rear.

ENGINE
The MTU MB 883 Ea-500 diesel engine delivers 441 kW (600 hp) and a top road speed of 78 km/h (47 mph).

SECONDARY ARMAMENT
A coaxial 7.62-mm (0.3-in) MG3 machine gun was originally complemented by an additional remotely controlled 7.62-mm (0.3-in) gun. This was mounted near the rear of the vehicle but was later removed.

FACTS

- An infrared searchlight and smoke grenade launchers are attached to the Marder turret.

- Composite armour withstands 30-mm (1.18-in) shells, small-arms fire, and shell fragments.

- The Puma infantry fighting vehicle is slated to replace the ageing Marder currently in service.

TURRET
The two-man turret houses the commander and gunner and is situated to the right on top of the hull. Capable of 360-degree traverse, it incorporates periscopes for the commander and gunner, while the gunner also has an optical gunsight, which can be replaced with infrared equipment.

HULL
Based on a tracked chassis first conceived in the early 1960s, the Marder hull is divided into driving and engine compartments forwards and a troop compartment capable of transporting six fully armed combat infantrymen to the rear.

The Marder reflects the German style in armoured warfare, with excellent speed and cross-country mobility, good armour protection, and heavy firepower, including firing ports for mounted combat. The Marder remains an excellent vehicle to this day, matched only by much more recent designs.

RIVAL: AMX 10P

MARDER – SPECIFICATION

Country of Origin: West Germany
Crew: 3 + 7
Designer: Rheinmetall Landsysteme
Designed: 1971
Manufacturer: Rheinmetall Landsysteme
In Production: 1971–75
In Service: 1971–present
Weight: 29.2 tonnes (32.2 tons)

Dimensions:
Length: 6.79 m (22.28 ft)
Width: 3.24 m (10.63 ft)
Height: 2.98 m (9.78 ft)

Performance:
Speed: 78 km/h (47 mph)
Range: 520 km (323 miles)
Ground Clearance: 0.45 m (1.48 ft)

Engine:
Powerplant: 1 x MTU MB 833 Ea-500 diesel engine producing 441 kW (600 hp)
Transmission: RENK HSWL 194
Suspension: Torsion bar
Fuel Capacity: 652 l (172 gallons)

Armour and Armament:
Armour Type: Welded steel, protection up to 20 mm (0.79 in) APDS
Main Armament: 1 x 20-mm (0.79-in) Rheinmetall MK 20 Rh 202 automatic cannon MILAN ATGM launcher
Secondary Armament: 1 x 7.62-mm (0.3-in) MG3 machine gun

Variants:
Marder 1 A1A: As 1 A1 but without any passive night vision equipment. 1112 vehicles upgraded to this standard.
Marder 1 A1A4: Marder A1A with SEM 80/90 cryptographic radios.
Marder 1 A1A2: Marder 1 with A1 turret and A2 chassis.
Marder 1 A1A5: Marder A1A2 with SEM 80/90 cryptographic radios.
Marder 1 A2 (1984–1991): Between 1984–91, all German Marder 1s were upgraded to A2 standard. This included substantial modification of the suspension, fuel tanks, cooling system, and water-jet cleaning system. Additionally, a new sighting system was installed. The infrared searchlight equipment was removed, and all vehicles were fitted with thermal imagers.
Marder 1 A2A1: Marder 1 A2 with SEM 80/90 cryptographic radios.
Marder 1 A3: 1988–98 upgrade.
Marder 1 A4: Marder 1 A3 with SEM 93 cryptographic radio.
Marder 1 A5 (2003–04): Additional anti-mine armour and completely remodelled interior in order to avoid blast and shock injuries to the crew on impact with a mine. Applied to 74 Marder 1 A3s only.

RIVAL: SAURER 4K-4FA-G1

MARDER

The Marder infantry fighting vehicle combines fire support capabilities along with transportation of an infantry squad into combat with armour protection. Its innovative development includes a 20-mm (0.79-in) cannon mounted on top of the turret but external to the turret housing in order to eliminate the build-up of fumes when the weapon is in action. The driver is seated forwards and to the left with the engine compartment on his right, while the commander and gunner occupy the turret directly behind and above the engine. The troop compartment to the rear accommodates six infantrymen seated back to back in groups of three, facing outwards.

MARDER MICV

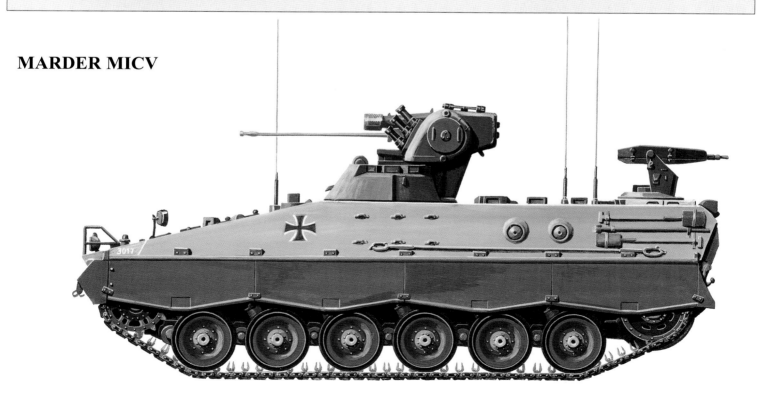

The vehicle's only major drawback is its lack of amphibious capability, although the Marder can ford up to 1.5 m (5 ft) of water without preparation. A conversion package allows the traverse of water up to 2.5 m (8 ft) in depth.

Considered by most observers to be an effective combination of troop carrier and light tank, the German Marder (Marten) was the first infantry fighting vehicle developed by a NATO country. Its combination of mobility, armour protection, and firepower have made it an ideal weapon for close combat support and infantry deployment. The prototype Marder was delivered by Thyssen Henschel in 1966, and more than 3000 were built before production ceased a decade later.

The Marder has been exported to numerous countries, and as it is replaced by the Puma infantry fighting vehicle, which is currently in development, demand for reconditioned

Interior view

The troop compartment of the German Marder infantry fighting vehicle accommodated up to seven fully armed combat soldiers, who could deploy rapidly through a rear exit.

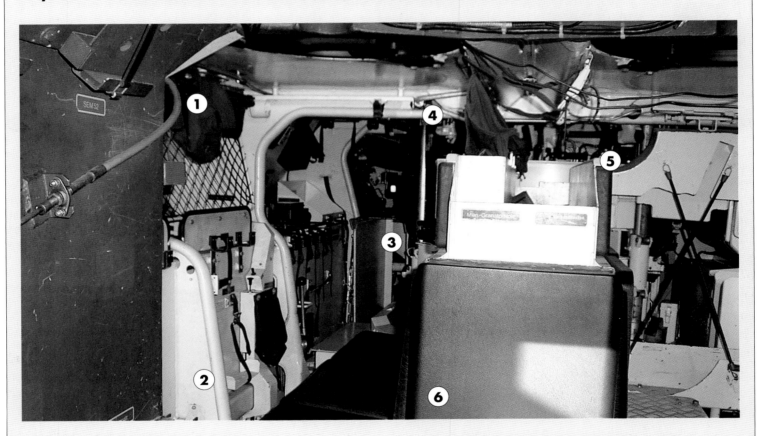

① **Infantry Seating:** Bench seats were arranged in the troop compartment, facing inwards and to the rear and near the exit.

② **Ammunition Storage:** Space for storing ammunition was contained in the vehicle's hull adjacent to the troop seating area.

③ **Forward Access:** The troop compartment and crew areas were separated by an internal bulkhead with communication and movement through a small access space.

④ **Turret Floor:** The two-crew turret was centred on top of the hull and directly above the troop compartment.

⑤ **Weapons Equipment:** Systems related to the servicing of the Marder's weapons system were located inside and below the turret for crew convenience during field operations.

⑥ **Engine Compartment:** Servicing and maintenance of the engine was facilitated from the exterior.

Photographed during training exercises, the driver of the German Marder peers through his hatch, while the two-crew turret and its weapons are clearly visible. Sloping armour and reinforced hulls increase survivability.

Marder vehicles is expected to increase. The excellent reputation of the Marder is accomplished through its design, which was innovative for its day. The 20-mm (0.79-in) Rheinmetall MK 20 Rh.202 automatic cannon is mounted externally on the two-crew turret, allowing fumes to dissipate into the atmosphere. Fed by three separate ammunition belts, the tank is capable of adapting rapidly to engage a variety of targets. The tank is armed with weapons capable of penetrating the armour of most contemporary infantry and reconnaissance vehicles, along with the side and rear armour of some older tanks.

Some Marders have been re-equipped with a more powerful 25-mm (0.98-in) gun, while the option is available to attach a MILAN anti-tank guided missile system to the turret. Secondary armament includes a 7.62-mm (0.3-in) MG3 coaxial machine gun. The driver views the field through three periscopes with the centre one interchangeable with night-vision equipment. The commander utilizes eight periscopes for an excellent field of vision, while the gunner has three periscopes and operates a PERI-Z11 acquisition and targeting system.

Compared to other infantry fighting tanks, the Marder may be disadvantaged in capacity because it carries only six personnel plus a single infantryman in a position behind the driver. However, the 441-kW (600-hp) diesel engine, RENK HSWL 194 transmission, and torsion bar suspension provide excellent mobility, with the vehicle capable of traversing a gradient of 60 per cent. Weighing up to 29 tonnes (32 tons), the Marder is one of the largest, heaviest infantry fighting vehicles in the world.

SERVICE LONGEVITY

The Marder was first meant to be one of a family of armoured vehicles, and variants include conversions to carry the Roland air defence system, a mobile radar apparatus, and a driver training vehicle. Further, the Argentine TAM light tank is based on the Marder chassis. Upgrades to the Marder include the 1A3, with improvements to the sloped armour protection capable of withstanding the 30-mm (1.18-in) shell of the Russian 2A42 cannon mounted by the BMP-2 vehicle, a reinforced suspension and improved transmission, reconfigured turret, and easier access through to the troop compartment. The 1A4 variant includes enhanced radio equipment. The 1A5 offers better protection against mines.

In the summer of 2009, the German army deployed Marder vehicles to Afghanistan in support of infantry fighting the Taliban guerrillas. The Chilean army currently operates Marders that have been retired from service with German forces. Replacement of the Marder with the Puma infantry fighting vehicle is tentatively scheduled to begin in 2011.

AAV7

The primary amphibious transport vehicle of the U.S. Marine Corps, the AAV7 is the most recent in a long line of amphibious tracked vehicles designed to insert combat troops and provide fire and logistical support during an inland or cross-country advance.

MAIN ARMAMENT
The AAV7 is equipped with a M242 Bushmaster 25-mm (0.98-in) chain-fed auto-cannon with 900 rounds.

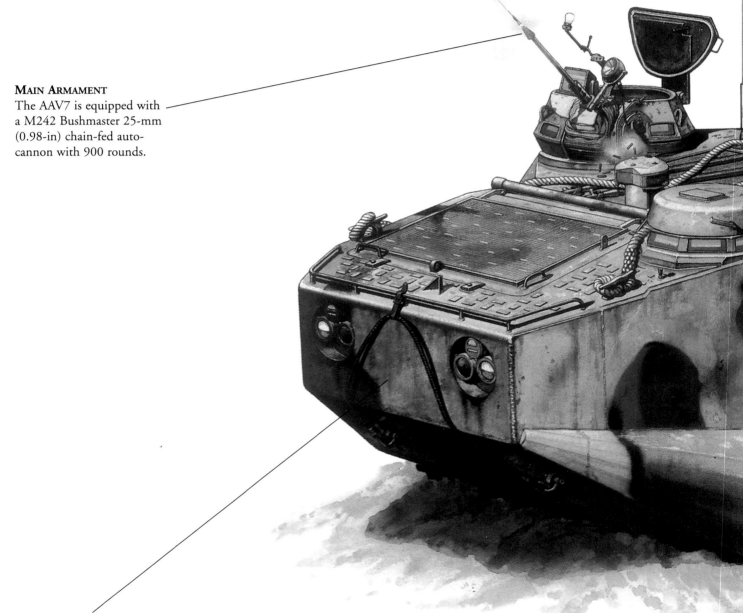

ARMOUR PROTECTION
With up to 45 mm (1.77 in) of protective armour, the AAV7 is lighter than its U.S. Army counterpart, the M2/M3 Bradley Fighting Vehicle, but its capacity is much greater.

- The AAV7 did not initially include NBC (nuclear, biological, chemical) defence capabilities.

- The Expeditionary Fighting Vehicle (EFV) is slated to replace the AAV7 within the next decade.

- The AAV7 is amphibious without modifications in the field to efficiently cross rivers and streams.

CARGO CAPACITY
The AAV7 is capable of carrying its crew of three along with up to 25 combat-ready Marines. In the logistics support role, it is capable of carrying up to 4.5 tonnes (5 tons) of equipment and supplies.

INFANTRY ACCESS
The relatively spacious troop compartment of the AAV7 is accessed through a large ramp door at the rear of the vehicle and a pair of roof hatches. Troops are seated on benches facing inwards along the length of the hull and in the centre.

ENGINE
The General Motors Detroit Diesel 8V53T engine was subsequently replaced by the 300-kW (400-hp) Cummins VT 400 903 turbocharged diesel engine, which also has multi-fuel capability.

DRIVE TRAIN
The FMC Corporation HS-400-3A1 transmission drives the tracked vehicle with six rubber-coated road wheels on either side and a torsion bar suspension.

The primary responsibility of the AAV during an amphibious operation is to spearhead a beach assault. It disembarks from a ship and comes ashore, carrying infantry and supplies to provide a forced entry into the amphibious assault area for the surface assault element.

AAV7 – SPECIFICATION

Country of Origin: USA
Crew: 3 + 25
Designer: FMC Corporation
Manufacturer: FMC Corporation
In Production: 1972–
In Service: 1972–present
Number Built: More than 1800
Weight: 22.8 tonnes (25.1 tons)

Dimensions:
Length: 7.94 m (26 ft)
Width: 3.27 m (10.73 ft)
Height: 3.26 m (10.7 ft)

Performance:
Operational Range: 480 km (300 miles)
Speed, Road: 64 km/h (45 mph)
Speed, Cross-country: 13.5 km/h (8.2 mph)

Powerplant:
Engine: 1 x Detroit Diesel 8V-53T (P-7), Cummins VT 400 903 (P-7A1) 300 kW (400 hp); or VTAC 525 903 391 kW (525 hp) (AAV-7RAM-RS)
Power/weight: 13 kW (18 hp) per tonne
Suspension: Torsion-bar-in-tube (AAV-7A1); torsion bar (AAV-7RAM-RS)

Armour and Armament:
Armour: 45 mm (1.77 in)
Main Armament: 1 x Mk 19 40-mm (1.57-in) automatic grenade launcher (864 rounds) or M242 Bushmaster 25-mm (0.98-in) (900 rounds)

Secondary Armament: 1 x M2HB 12.7-mm (0.5-in) machine gun (1200 rounds)

Operators
United States: Marine Corps – 1311.
Argentina: Infanteria de Marina – 21 x LVTP7s.
Brazil: Corpo de Fuzileiros Navais do Brasil – 13 x AAV-7A1, 9 x LVTP-7A1, 2 x LVTC-7A1 and 2 x LVTR-7A.
Cambodia: Royal Cambodian Navy – 63 x AAVT-7s, including 2 x AAVTC-7, 1x AAVTR-7, 9 x AAVTP-7.
Italy: Esercito Italiano – 35 x LVPT7s, 25 of which have been upgraded to AAV-7A1 standard.
South Korea: Republic of Korea Marine Corps – 162.
Republic of China: Republic of China Marine Corps (Taiwan) – 54.
Spain: Spanish Marines (BRIMAR) – 36.
Thailand: Royal Thai Marine Corps – 24.
Venezuela: Venezuelan Navy – 11 x AAVT-7s (1 x AAVTC-7, 1 x AAVTR-7, 9 x AAVTP-7).
Indonesia: Indonesian Marine Corps – 10 units (LVTP7A1) donated by South Korea.
Greece: Hellenic Army – 100 units to be procured from USMC.

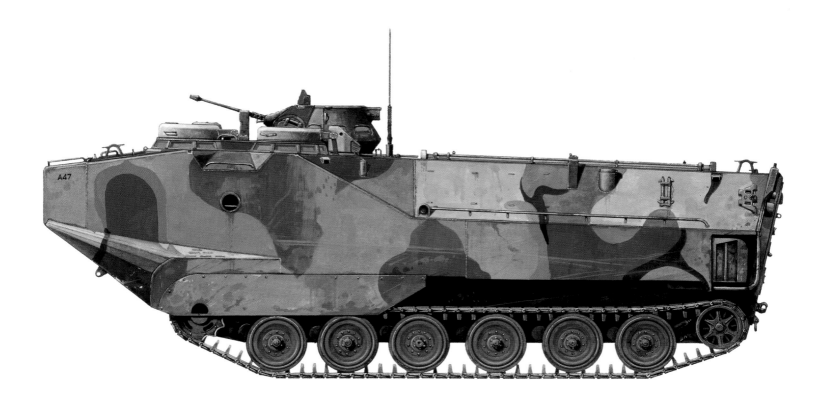

AAV7

The AAV7 is divided into two compartments, with the driver forwards and to the left of the transversely mounted engine, the commander and gunner just behind, and the large troop compartment to the rear. The commander is seated below a cupola equipped with seven vision blocks for an all-around view of the surrounding terrain, while the gunner is seated in the turret directly opposite. The driver utilizes seven vision blocks, while an infrared periscope may be fitted for night vision. The 12.7-mm (0.5-in) machine gun is effective in anti-aircraft defence, while the 40-mm (1.57-in) Mark 19 grenade launcher is a lethal anti-personnel weapon.

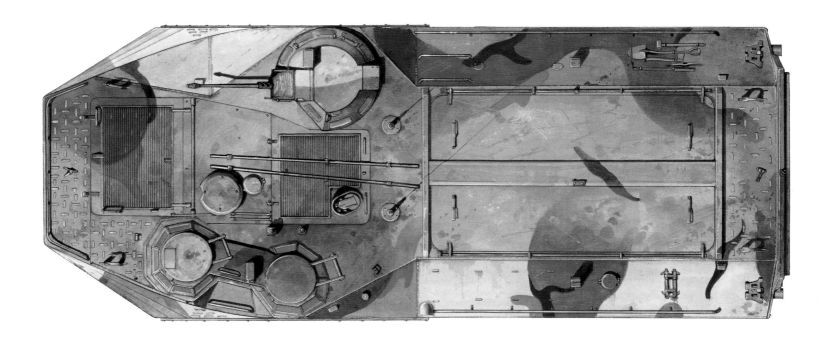

AAVs are deployed during amphibious assaults, during the conduct of river crossings as components of the mechanized task force, and during other special operations ashore. When properly put to use, AAVs are effective in operations after dark, and on a majority of the world's rough terrain.

Amphibious operations in the Pacific theatre during World War II demonstrated the need for a tracked amphibious vehicle capable of delivering combat troops ashore, supporting them with direct fire, and transporting supplies and equipment to combat zones. The AAV7 is, therefore, a direct descendant of early landing craft developed to traverse extensive water, coral reefs, sandy beaches, and other terrain.

During the Vietnam War, the U.S. Marine Corps recognized the deficiencies of its relatively short-range LVTP5 series. In 1964, the Corps issued a directive for the development of a replacement vehicle, and the project was

Interior view

The AAV7 is the front-line cross-country and urban troop transport vehicle of the U.S. Marine Corps and is capable of carrying up to 25 combat-ready marines.

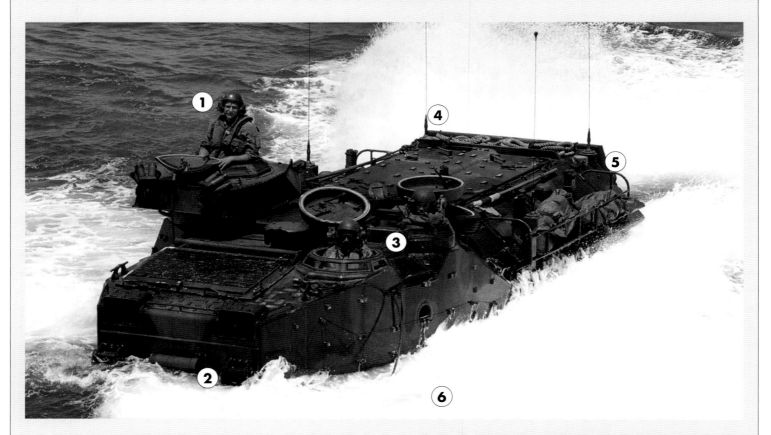

1. **Cupolas:** Multiple cupolas are on the exterior and at least one of these is often equipped with a 12.7-mm (0.5-in) heavy machine gun.

2. **Sloping Hull:** Configured similarly to the bow of a boat, the forwards hull of the AAV7 contributes to the stability of the amphibious vehicle in water.

3. **Viewing Ports:** Prominent in the silhouette are viewing ports and periscopes, which are available for crew to look through while the vehicle is buttoned up.

4. **Communications Gear:** Antennae for the sending and receiving of data for communications equipment are installed at the rear of the troop compartment.

5. **Entry and Exit:** A large ramp facilitates the rapid entry and exit of up to 25 combat-ready marines from the troop compartment.

6. **Water Jets:** A pair of water jets propel the AAV7 through water at approximately 13 km/h (8 mph).

Although the armour protection is limited at 45 mm (1.77 in) and is known to be substantially less than that of the U.S. Army's Bradley Fighting Vehicle, the AAV7 still has much broader capabilities. As many as 25 combat-ready marines can be accommodated on three benches – one along the centre of the compartment and two on the sides of the hull. Access is gained through a ramp, which folds down, as well as two roof hatches. With the central bench removed and the side benches folded, the cargo capacity of the AAV7 is up to 4.5 tonnes (5 tons).

UPGRADES AND IMPROVEMENTS

An extended service life programme was initiated in 1982, upgrading the former LVTP7 to the AAV7A1 configuration. Among the improvements was the installation of a Cummins diesel engine. Electric elevation components for the turret replaced the hydraulics, and an improved torsion bar suspension, smoke grenade launchers, and night vision equipment for the driver were added. In 1987, the Upgunned Weapons Station with the Mk19 40-mm (1.57-in) grenade launcher was added, and along with a 12.7-mm (0.5-in) machine gun, bow planes, magnetic heading systems, and automatic fire suppression capability. By 1992, enhanced appliqué armour had been added. Further upgrades included an improved suspension system and a powerplant similar to the 391-kW (525-hp) engine of the Bradley Fighting Vehicle.

undertaken by FMC Corporation, now a division of BAE Systems' Ground Systems. Two years later, prototypes of a vehicle designated the LVTPX12 were delivered, and by 1971 the first of the new LVTP7 were in service. By 1985, the Marine Corps had changed the vehicle's designation to AAV7 (Amphibious Assault Vehicle).

The AAV7 is constructed of a box-like, watertight welded aluminium hull. It presents a high silhouette, for which the design has been criticized. Shaped like a boat, its bow facilitates movement through water at a speed of 13.5 km/h (8.2 mph), powered by a pair of water jets. On the road and across difficult terrain, its 300-kW (400-hp) Cummins diesel engine powers the AAV7 at speeds of 64 km/h (45 mph).

Variants of the AAV7 include the AAVC7A1 command vehicle and the AAVR7A1 recovery vehicle. There is an option to attach mine-clearing equipment as well.

The AAV7 has been deployed in combat with Argentine forces during the 1982 Falklands War and with U.S. forces in Lebanon, Grenada, the Gulf War, and the invasion of Iraq in 2003. The vehicle is currently deployed with the armed forces of at least a dozen countries, and its service life with the U.S. Marine Corps is expected to extend until at least 2015 when its replacement, the Expeditionary Fighting Vehicle (EFV) is scheduled to be available.

T-72

Developed primarily for the export market and the satellite states of the Warsaw Pact, the T-72 was produced concurrently with the T-64 main battle tank. In some respects, the T-72 was inferior to its companion, which was intended specifically to equip armoured units of the Red Army.

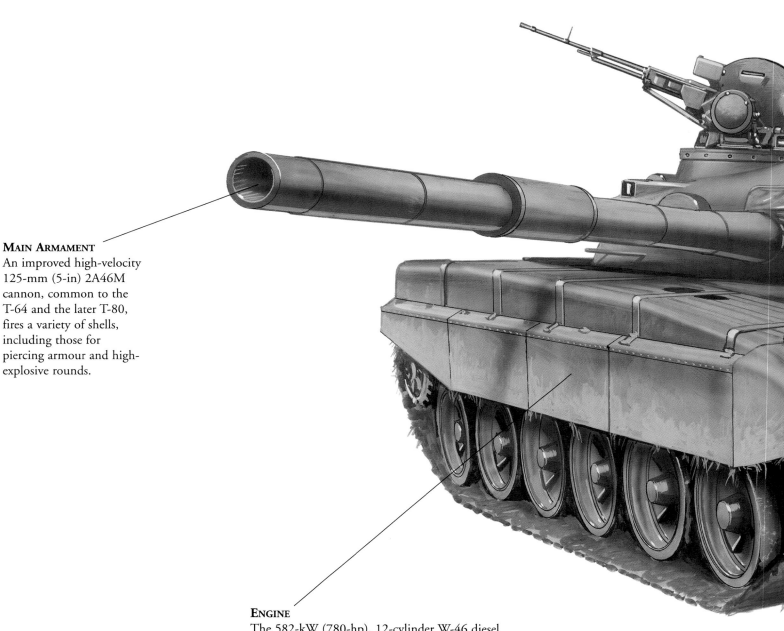

MAIN ARMAMENT
An improved high-velocity 125-mm (5-in) 2A46M cannon, common to the T-64 and the later T-80, fires a variety of shells, including those for piercing armour and high-explosive rounds.

ENGINE
The 582-kW (780-hp), 12-cylinder W-46 diesel engine is also capable of running on benzene and kerosene. Later models were upgraded with a 626-kW (840-hp) engine.

TURRET
Cast from a single piece of steel, the turret of the T-72 retains the characteristic egg shape and is protected to a maximum thickness of 280 mm (11 in) of armour.

CREW COMPARTMENTS
The commander and gunner are seated in the turret to the left and right of the main gun, while the driver's position is forwards and centred in the hull. An automatic loader eliminates the need for a fourth crewman.

SUSPENSION
The torsion bar suspension supports six cast, rubber-coated wheels with a large drive sprocket, four return rollers, and single-pin tracks with rubber bushed pins. Spring-mounted armour plating protects the upper edges of the wheels.

ARMOUR PROTECTION
Consisting of a composite plating of steel, tungsten, ceramic, and plastic, the front glacis of the T-72 is protected with up to 200 mm (7.8 in) of armour. Steel side plates on early models varied in thickness from 50–80 mm (1.96–3.1 in).

Introduced in the early 1970s, the T-72 is not actually a further development of the T-64. Instead, it was a parallel design chosen as a high-production tank complementing the T-64. While the T-64 was deployed only in forwards Soviet units, the T-72 was deployed within the Soviet Union and exported.

T-72A – SPECIFICATION

Country of Origin: Soviet Union
Crew: 3
Designer: Kartsev-Venediktov
Designed: 1967–73
Manufacturer: Uralvagonzavod
Produced: 1971–present
In Service: 1973–present
Number Built: 25,000+
Weight: 41.5 tonnes (45.7 tons)

Dimensions:
Length (gun forward): 9.53 m (31 ft 3 in)
Length (hull): 6.95 m (22 ft 10 in)
Width: 3.59 m (11 ft 9 in)
Height: 2.23 m (7 ft 4 in)

Performance:
Speed: 60 km/h (37 mph)
Operational Range: 460 km (290 miles); 700 km (430 miles) with fuel drums

Powerplant
Engine: 1 x V-12 diesel 582 kW (780 hp)
Power/weight: 14.1 kW (18.8 hp) per tonne
Suspension: Torsion bar
Ground clearance: 0.49 m (19 in)
Fuel capacity: 1200 l (320 gallons)

Armour and Armament:
Armour: 500 mm (20 in) of third-generation composite armour consisting of high-hardness steel, tungsten, and plastic filler with ceramic component
Primary Armament: 1 x 125-mm (4.9-in) 2A46M gun

Secondary Armament: 1 x 7.62-mm (0.3-in) PKT coaxial machine gun, 1 x 12.7-mm (0.5-in) NSVT anti-aircraft machine gun

Variants
T-72 Ural (1973): Original version.
T-72A (1979): Added laser rangefinder and electronic fire control, turret front and top being heavily reinforced with composite armour (nicknamed "Dolly Parton" by U.S. intelligence), provisions for mounting reactive armour, smoke grenade launchers, flipper armour mount on front mudguards, internal changes.
T-72M: Export "Monkey model" version, similar to T-72A but with thinner armour and downgraded weapon systems. Also built in Poland and former Czechoslovakia.
T-72B (1985): New main gun, stabilizer, sights, and fire control, capable of firing 9M119 Svir guided missile, Super Dolly Parton armour including 20 mm (0.79 in) of appliqué armour in the front of hull, improved 626-kW (840-hp) engine.
T-90 (1995): Modernization of the T-72, incorporating technical features of the heavier, more complex T-80. Originally to have been named T-72BU.

The T-72 design has been further developed into the following new models:
Lion of Babylon tank (Iraq)
M-84 (former Yugoslavia)
M-95 Degman (Croatia)
M-2001 (Serbia)
PT-91 Twardy (Poland)
T-90 (Russia)
Tank EX (India)
TR-125 (Romania)

T-72

Characteristically divided into three compartments – driver forwards, fighting section in centre, and engine to the rear – the T-72 perpetuated several attributes of the T-54/55 series, including the inconspicuous silhouette, elliptical turret, and seriously cramped crew accommodations. One significant improvement was the installation of an automatic loader for the powerful 125-mm (5-in) main gun, which allowed the tank to operate with a crew of three. However, the driver's field of vision was somewhat limited with only a single periscope, and contrary to the steering wheel and automatic transmission designs of modern Western tanks, both his hands were fully occupied with a pair of tillers and a manual transmission with seven gears.

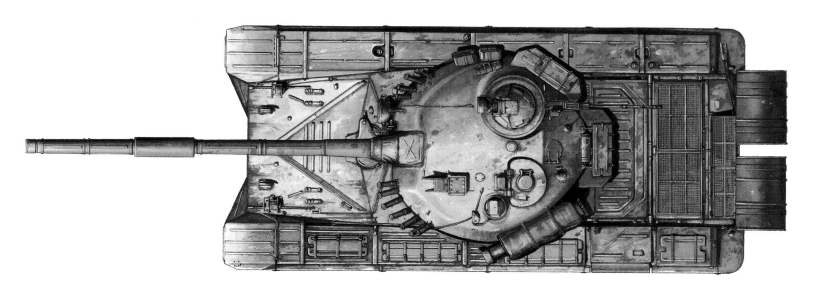

Even though the tank incorporated a wide variety of the features of its predecessors, the T-72 marked the initial Soviet design effort to develop a modern main battle tank, rather than to continue the narrower specifications of heavy and medium tanks.

The T-72 is currently considered superior to the 1960s vintage Western main battle tanks, but inferior to more recent models, especially in protection, crew comfort, and fire control. The T-72 is both cheaper and more conservative than the T-64.

In the late 1960s, the Soviet Union began to develop two main battle tanks. The T-64 included notable improvements over the previous T-54/55 and T-62 designs, as did the T-72. However, the T-64 was intended to equip front-line Red Army units, while the T-72 was intended for use within the Soviet military and for export to Warsaw Pact nations and other Soviet arms customers. Together, the T-64 and T-72 represented the first real innovation in Soviet tank design since the fabled T-34 of World War II.

In the event, the T-64 may have been too innovative to sustain, and production was halted in 1981 after only 5000 were produced. T-72 production has exceeded that number several times, and the tank has been built under licence in several countries. The T-72 entered production in 1971 and is still being manufactured today.

In comparison to the T-62, the most striking advances in the T-72 were a vastly improved diesel engine, the installation of the superb 125-mm (4.9-in) 2A46M smoothbore gun and an automatic loading system, and the introduction of composite armour and better targeting capabilities. The 582-kW (780 hp), 12-cylinder W-46 diesel engine is much quieter than the diesel in the T-62, causing less vibration and generating less smoke. The 125-mm (4.9-in) cannon is capable of penetrating the armour of earlier tanks and contemporary NATO tanks with warhead ammunition of certain shapes. The automatic loading system increases the rate of fire to a maximum of eight rounds per minute, but it has been prone to malfunction. The composite armour is similar to British-developed Chobham armour and effectively triples the protection of homogenous steel at similar thickness.

MODERN EQUIPMENT

The crew of three includes the driver, the gunner (who sits in the turret to the left with both day and night gunsights integrated with laser rangefinding equipment), and the commander, who is seated in the turret to the right beneath a rotating cupola and is equipped with infrared night and optical gunsights along with a back-up stadiametric rangefinder. A 7.62-mm (0.3-in) PKT machine gun is mounted coaxially, while a 12.7-mm (0.5-in) machine gun, pintle-mounted above the commander's hatch, provided defence against aircraft. The original diesel engine was upgraded to a 626-kW (840-hp) diesel in 1985. The T-72 is equipped with NBC (nuclear, biological, chemical) defences, an amphibious package allowing the tank to ford water up to 5.5 m (18 ft) deep, and an anti-radiation liner of lead and foam. Later variants included the T-72M and T-72M1, equipped with advanced passive armour, and the T-72B with the 626-kW (840-hp) diesel engine, improved fire control,

appliqué armour, and guided missile firing capability. The T-72M is built in Poland and the Czech Republic and the T-72M1 is manufactured in Russia.

The combat record of the T-72 includes the fighting in Lebanon in 1982, the 1991 Gulf War, and the 2003 invasion of Iraq. Its reputation is that of an inferior weapon to most tanks employed by the Israeli Defence Force and the Coalition forces that defeated Saddam Hussein's Iraqi army. However, many of the Iraqi tanks were older and had not been sufficiently upgraded. The T-72 remains in service, and a number of countries have ordered them in recent years.

Interior view

The interior of the T-72 main battle tank remained characteristic of previous Soviet tank designs, with limited space and little attention paid to the comfort of the three crew members.

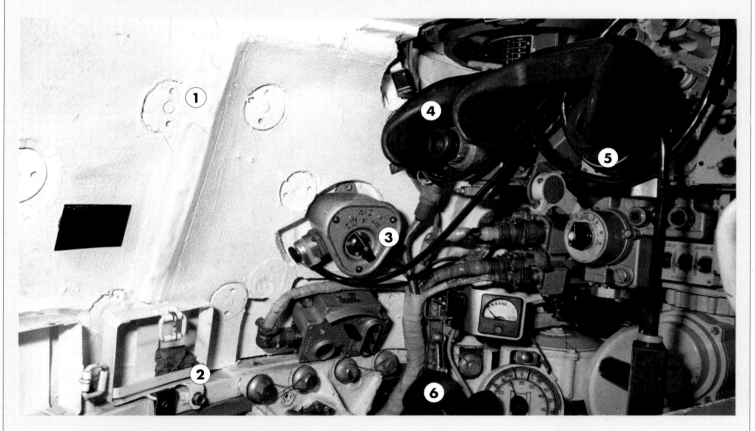

(1) **Turret Armour:** Spall liner material lessened the lethal impact of metal splinters that might cause injury, while the T-72 turret was protected by composite armour.

(2) **Breech Guard:** The gunner was separated from the large breech of the 125-mm (4.9-in) main gun by a steel panel with an attached handle grip.

(3) **Gunner's Intercom:** The gunner maintained internal communications with the other T-72 crewmen via an intercom system.

(4) **Infrared Sights:** The gunner was capable of acquiring potential targets during night operations using large infrared sights mounted at eye level above his seat.

(5) **Daytime Sights:** The day sights and laser rangefinder employed by the T-72 gunner were located to the right of the night-vision equipment.

(6) **Gunner's Controls:** The gunner aimed and fired the main cannon of the T-72 using a series of controls mounted near his seat.

Ratel

The Ratel Infantry Fighting Vehicle forms the basis of a family of armoured vehicles designed and manufactured in South Africa for the country's military. Its variants include platforms for anti-tank, mortar, and direct fire support. A number of Ratel have been exported to other countries.

SECONDARY ARMAMENT
A coaxial 7.62-mm (0.3-in) machine gun is mounted in the turret, while a second machine gun of the same size is attached to a rear cupola above the troop compartment. Some Ratel vehicles include a third 7.62-mm (0.3-in) machine gun attached to the turret.

SUSPENSION
Six run-flat wheels are each powered, and the vehicle is capable of running on four wheels if necessary.

CAPACITY
The Ratel crew of three, including a commander, driver, and gunner, is augmented with up to seven fully armed combat infantrymen, who can be carried in the troop compartment.

MAIN ARMAMENT
The Ratel 20 (shown) mounts a turreted 20-mm (0.79-in) semi-automatic cannon or a 12.7-mm (0.5-in) heavy machine gun for direct fire support, while its variants field such weapons as a 90-mm (3.54-in) cannon, a 60-mm (2.36-in) mortar, or anti-tank guided missiles.

ENGINE
The 210-kW (282-hp) turbocharged, six-cylinder D3256 BTXF diesel engine generates a top speed of 105 km/h (65 mph) on the road and 30 km/h (18 mph) cross country.

ARMOUR PROTECTION
At a maximum of 20 mm (0.79 in), the Ratel's light armour protects against small arms and shell fragments. An additional armour package protects the underside against mines and IEDs (improvised explosive devices).

The South African army pursued a new concept, which was the armoured infantry fighting vehicle. It could carry a powerful gun as well as a squad of troops. Each soldier has their own vision and firing port so they can fight from within the vehicle.

RATEL – SPECIFICATION

Country of Origin: South Africa
Crew: 3 + 7
Designer: Sandcock-Austral
Designed: 1968
Manufacturer: Sandcock-Austral
Produced: 1974–87
In Service: 1978–present
Number Built: More than 1350
Weight: 18.5 tonnes (20.39 tons)

Dimensions:
Length: 7.212 m (23.66 ft)
Width: 2.5 m (8.2 ft)
Height: 2.915 m (9.56 ft)

Performance:
Speed, Road: 105 km/h (65 mph)
Speed, Cross-country: 30 km/h (18.6 mph)
Operational Range: 1000 km (621 miles)
Fording: 1.20 m (3 ft 11 in)
Gradient: 60 degrees
Vertical Obstacle: 0.35 m (1 ft 1.5 in)
Trench: 1.15 m (3 ft 9 in)

Powerplant:
Engine: 1 x D 3256 BTXF 6-cylinder diesel 210 kW (282 hp)
Power/weight: 11.36 kW (15.24 hp) per tonne
Suspension: Wheeled 6x6, 350-mm (13.78-in) clearance

Armour and Armament:
Armour: 20 mm (0.79 in)
Main Armament: 1 x 20-mm (0.79-in) semi-automatic cannon
Secondary Armament: 1 x 7.62-mm (0.3-in) MG (coaxial), 7.62-mm (0.3-in) MG (anti-aircraft), 1 x 7.62-mm (0.3-in) MG (anti-aircraft), 2 x 2 smoke grenade dischargers

Variants:
Ratel 20: Original version, French-designed turret.
Ratel 60: Turret is identical to that of the Eland 60 with a 60-mm (2.36-in) breech-loading mortar.
Ratel 81: No turret, but an 81-mm (3.2-in) mortar is installed in the crew compartment for use as a fire support platform.
Ratel 90: Crew of 3 plus 6 infantry, turret is identical to that of the Eland 90. Primary role: fire support for the Mechanized Battalions.
Ratel 120: 120-mm (4.7-in) mortar carrier. Prototype only.
Ratel Command: Crew of 9 men, two-seater turret with a 12.7-mm (0.5-in) machine gun.
Ratel EAOS: Enhanced Artillery Observation System.
Ratel Maintenance: Set up as a mobile workshop.
Ratel ZT3: New anti-tank turret, with a rack containing 3 anti-tank missiles ready for launch and additional missiles stored within the hull.
Ratel Logistic: 8 x 8 logistic vehicle. Only 2 prototypes were manufactured.

RATEL

RATEL

The South African Ratel was the first wheeled infantry fighting vehicle placed into service. Its mobility provided greater reliability and required less maintenance than tracked vehicles in the rugged, arid terrain of the country's border regions, and it had run-flat wheels and reinforced armour for protection against mines. The driver is located forwards and in the centre of the vehicle with the commander and gunner inside the turret, the troop compartment behind with space for up to seven fully equipped soldiers, and the engine at the rear. The Ratel was also the first infantry fighting vehicle to install a commander's cupola.

The Valkiri multiple rocket launcher was developed in the early 1980s and entered service with the South African National Defense Force in 1982. One interesting feature is that it could be easily disguised as a small canvas-covered truck.

SUPPORT VEHICLE: VALKIRI

The South African army needed new armoured vehicles for conventional warfare operations and to provide more effective support for its tank force. The Ratel programme started in the 1970s after the government had evaluated foreign fighting vehicles and decided to build their own.

In addition, the policy of apartheid in South Africa created its own issues for the nation's military leadership. Embroiled in border wars and in need of modern, efficient military vehicles, the South African army was essentially left to its own devices to develop and manufacture a family of infantry fighting vehicles. An extensive arms embargo curtailed the import of foreign military vehicles, so by the late 1960s the firm of Sandock-Austral had designed and initiated the manufacture of the Ratel.

NATIVE AND NIMBLE
Named after the African honey badger, an animal known for its fighting prowess, the Ratel is a six-wheeled, all-wheel drive, heavily armed fighting vehicle capable of transporting an infantry squad of up to seven combat-ready soldiers. Its main armament ranges from a 12.7-mm (0.5-in) heavy machine gun to anti-tank missiles, a 60-mm (2.36-in) mortar, a 20-mm (0.78-in) semi-automatic cannon, and a 90-mm

(3.54-in) low-velocity gun. Its development began in 1968 after the South African army evaluated the armoured fighting vehicles of several nations and decided to build a vehicle that could not only transport infantry, but also allow them to fight from relative safety and provide direct fire support, engaging enemy armoured personnel carriers, light armoured vehicles, and dug-in positions.

THE FIRST 1000 ARE DELIVERED
The Ratel was produced between 1974–87, with more than 1000 vehicles delivered to the South African army and an unknown number exported. The hull was constructed at the Sandock-Austral facility in Durban and transported to Boksburg by rail for completion. Replacing the ageing British-built Saracen and the locally built Eland armoured cars, the Ratel borrowed some technology from its predecessor, such as the two-man turret, a copy of the one that was used with the Eland 90.

The South African army received the first Ratels in 1977. The vehicle rapidly became a favourite among the soldiers with its heavy armament, reliable wheeled mobility, and relatively smooth ride. The basic version, the Ratel 20, had a crew of three, was powered by a 210-kW (282-hp) diesel engine, and carried its infantry complement in a central troop compartment just forward of the engine. The vehicle is distinguished by its angular hull configuration. Its armour is

Developed in South Africa, the wheeled Ratel infantry fighting vehicle was specifically designed for the open country in which it operated. A rear turret sometimes mounted a machine gun, and viewing ports were placed in the troop compartment.

Interior view

The interior included a two-crew turret forwards, which housed the commander and gunner, who serviced a 20-mm (0.78-in) semi-automatic cannon or a 12.7-mm (0.5-in) machine gun.

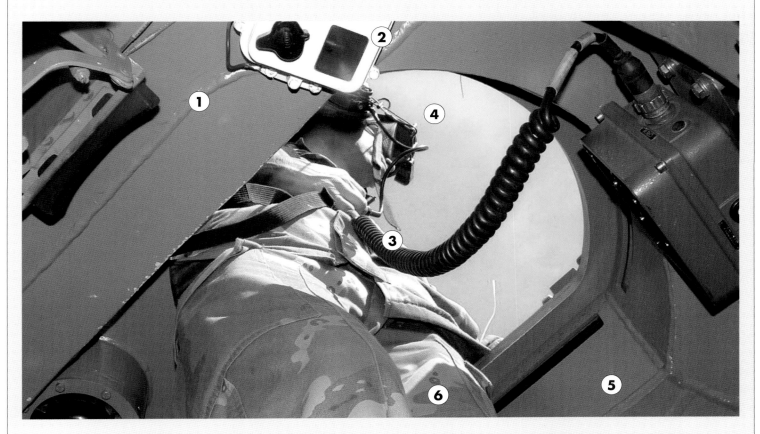

1 Commander's Position: The commander occupied space on the left side of the turret and often rode with the hatch open.

2 Control Switch Box: A switch box for interior lighting or other purposes was located on the ceiling of the Ratel turret within easy reach of commander and crew.

3 Internal Communications: The crew communicated internally via an intercom system with squawk boxes mounted at accessible locations within the vehicle.

4 Communications Gear: The commander's helmet was equipped with voice communications gear.

5 Armour Protection: The light armour of the Ratel, at 20 mm (0.79 in) thick, protected against most small arms and the fragments of heavier-calibre shells.

6 Cupola: With one of two cupolas installed aboard the standard Ratel, the commander's position included several viewing ports for use during combat operations.

thin at only 20 mm (0.79 in), but a steep slope adds protection against small arms and shell splinters. The hull has been reinforced with additional armour to protect against mines. Four firing ports on either side allow the infantry to engage combatants from inside the Ratel.

Access to the vehicle is provided through a driver's hatch on top of the front of the hull, the commander's hatch, which is built into the cupola on top of the turret, an adjacent hatch for the gunner, and eight hatches along the top of the troop compartment. Large doors on either side also provide for swift entrance and exit.

Variants include the Ratel 60, equipped with a turret-mounted 60-mm (2.36-in) mortar, the Ratel 90, fielding the 90-mm (3.54-in) cannon (a licence-built copy of the French GIAT F1), the Ratel ZT3, equipped with 127-mm (5-in) Ingwe anti-tank guided missiles, a command vehicle, an artillery observation version, and a recovery vehicle. The iKlwa is an upgraded Ratel with a more powerful 335-kW (450-hp) diesel engine relocated to the rear of the vehicle.

The Ratel was deployed extensively during the South African border wars in the defence of the country's once-embattled frontier.

Merkava

Designed and built in Israel, the Merkava series has served as the main battle tank of the Israeli Defence Force since the late 1970s. Crew survivability and tactical mobility are hallmarks of the Merkava's design and are readily apparent in its combat record.

SECONDARY ARMAMENT
The Merkava IV is heavily armed with two 7.62-mm (0.3-in) machine guns for defence against enemy infantry and a heavy 12.7-mm (0.5-in) machine gun capable of downing low-flying helicopters. A pop-up 60-mm (2.36-in) mortar tube is located in the turret roof.

MAIN ARMAMENT
The Merkava III and its successor, the Merkava IV, mount the 120-mm (4.7-in) smoothbore guns, upgraded from the 105-mm (4.1-in) L7A3, which armed the earlier models. A semi-automatic loading system is also incorporated.

ARMOUR PROTECTION
Although its armoured strength is classified, it thought to be a combination of an Israeli-built Chobham composite armour and steel. Estimates of its relative thickness, including a pronounced slope, are in excess of 600 mm (24 in).

HEAVY TRACKS
Developed by Israeli engineers, the TSAWS (Tracks, Springs, and Wheels System) is designed to handle the rugged terrain and desert conditions of the Middle East.

INTERNAL LAYOUT
The innovative hull design of the
Merkava places the engine and diesel
fuel tanks in the entire forward section,
while the driver is seated to the left of
the engine. The commander, gunner,
and loader are positioned within the
turret towards the rear of the vehicle.

FACTS

- Merkava translates from the Hebrew as "Chariot."

- The Merkava series is capable of carrying eight infantrymen or three wounded soldiers on stretchers.

- The Merkava IV was introduced in 2004, and more than 500 will eventually be delivered.

ENGINE
The Merkava IV's 1118-kW (1500-hp) V-12 fuel-injection General Dynamics GD833
diesel engine is capable of generating a top road speed of 64 km/h (40 mph), and
substantially upgraded previous Merkava engines.

It was not until 1967 that the Israeli government turned its attention to the creation of a main battle tank. The Merkava combines the best features of American, British, French, and captured Soviet tanks, all of which have been tried and tested extensively in the past.

MERKAVA III

MERKAVA MK 1 – SPECIFICATION

Country of Origin: Israel
Crew: 4
Designer: Israel Military Industries
Designed: 1977
Manufacturer: IDF Ordnance
In Production: 1977–Present (Mk IV)
In Service: Mk 1 1979–82 (MK IV currently in service)
Number Built: Estimated more than 1000
Gross Weight: 55.9 tonnes (61.5 tons)

Dimensions:
Length (hull): 7.45 m (24.4 ft)
Length (gun forward): 8.63 m (28.3 ft)
Width: 3.7 m (12.1 ft)
Overall Height: 2.75 m (9 ft)

Performance:
Maximum Speed: 46 km/h (28.5 mph)
Range, Road: 400 km (245 miles)
Range, Cross-country: 200 km (125 miles)
Ground Pressure: n/a
Fording Capacity: 1.38 m (4.5 ft) (2 m [6.6 ft] with preparation)
Maximum Gradient: 31 degrees
Maximum Trench Width: 3 m (9.8 ft)
Maximum Vertical Obstacle: 0.95 m (3.1 ft)
Suspension Type: Helical springs

Engine:
Powerplant: 1 x Teledyne Continental AVDS-1790-6A V-12 supercharged diesel
Capacity: 29.3 l (6.5 gallons)
Output: 671 kW (900 bhp) @ 2800 rpm
Power/Weight Ratio: 15 bhp/tonne
Fuel Capacity: 900 l (198.2 gallons)

Armament and Armour:
Main Armament: 1 x 105-mm (4.13-in) L43.5 M68. 85 rounds.
Secondary Armament: (Up to) 3 x 7.62-mm (0.3-in) FN-MAG MGs. 10,000 rounds.
Ancillary Armament: 1 x 12.7-mm (0.5-in) Browning M2HB MG in AA mount (optional); 1 x 60-mm (2.36-in) Soltam mortar in rear compartment. 30 rounds.
Armour Type: Homogeneous rolled/welded and cast nickel-steel
Maximum Thickness: n/a

Variants
Mk II: Introduced 1983. Improvements made across all areas.
Mk IIB: Updated fire control system; thermal optics.
Mk IIC: Increased armour protection to top of turret.
Mk IID: Modular Composite Armour on chassis and turret for improved protection.
Mk III: Introduced 1989. 1 x 120-mm (4.7-in) main gun; new transmission system; improved suspension.
Mk 3 "Baz": Introduced 1995. Improved armour protection; indigenous AC system.
Mk 3D: Modular Composite Armour on chassis and turret.
Mk 3D "Dor-Dalet": Improved tracks; R-OWS implementation.
Mk 4: Latest production version.
"Sholef" (Slammer): Self-propelled 155-mm (6.1-in) gun; prototype; never produced.
ARV: Armoured Recovery Vehicle (prototype).
LIC: Based on Mk III "Baz" and Mk IV tanks but converted for urban warfare.
"Tankbulance": With battlefield medical capabilities as well as armament.
Merkava IFV "Namer": Introduced 2008. Merkava ARV "Nemmera": Armoured Recovery Vehicle; two versions with varying crane and winch sizes.

MERKAVA I

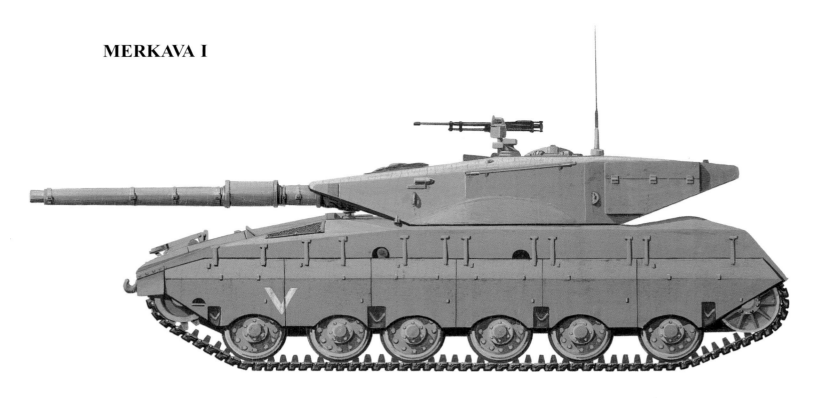

MERKAVA

The Merkava's hull is fashioned from both cast pieces and welded sections, and its unique interior configuration provides enhanced crew survivability. With the engine and diesel fuel tanks positioned forwards, the diesel fuel and substantial engine block provide additional protection to the modular armour in the event of hull penetration. Originally designed to accept either the 105-mm (4.1-in) or 120-mm (4.7-in) gun, the wedge-shaped turret minimizes the tank's silhouette and presents sharply oblique frontal angles. The commander utilizes only a hatch, rather than a cupola, for entry and exit. The Merkava does not incorporate a turret basket. Instead, the floor moves as the turret rotates in target acquisition.

MERKAVA I

The first main battle tank of Israeli design and construction, the Merkava has fared well against enemy armour. However, its urban warfare capabilities have been heavily criticized.

On the premise that only crews assured of maximum protection will boldly exploit armament and mobility, the Merkava's design places primary emphasis on crew survivability, with firepower next, and mobility last. In production since 1977, the Merkava has a radically original configuration.

When Great Britain and France suspended the supply of certain weapons systems following the Six Day War of 1967, the Israeli government was abruptly made aware of its dependence on foreign sources of armament. The Israelis decided to become essentially self-sufficient and develop their own main battle tank as a priority. With the urging of General Israel Tal, a veteran tank commander, the Merkava programme was established in 1968, and by the mid-1970s the first Merkava became operational.

A TANK FOR ISRAEL

Designed by Israeli Military Industries and manufactured by IDF Ordnance, the Merkava entered service in 1979. Its variants have since seen combat in successive campaigns against militant forces in Lebanon.

The design of the hull of the initial model, the Merkava I, was radically configured, with the engine and diesel fuel

tanks forwards for added protection of the crew, turret to the rear, and capacity to serve as a troop carrier or medical evacuation unit in the field. It deployed with the IDF during the 1982 war in Lebanon. The Merkava II, introduced in 1983, was upgraded for urban warfare, and had a redesigned automatic transmission and improved fire control.

The Merkava III entered service late in 1989 and replaced the 105-mm (4.1-in) L7 cannon with the 120-mm (4.7-in) MG251 smoothbore main weapon patterned after the German Rheinmetall 120-mm (4.7-in) design. Further upgrades included a 895-kW (1200-hp) diesel engine, laser rangefinding equipment, improved modular composite armour, and an external telephone for communication with supporting infantry units.

In 1995, the Merkava III was further improved with the BAZ system, which included enhanced fire controls for engaging targets on the move, NBC (nuclear, biological, chemical) defences, and armour upgrades. The Merkava IIID featured better tracks designed by Israeli engineers and manufactured by Caterpillar.

The first operational Merkava IV tanks joined the Israeli Defence Force in 2004, weighing slightly more than the Merkava III at 59 tonnes (65 tons). The latest variant, the Merkava IV, had been in development since 1999. Its primary upgrades included an electrically controlled turret, an enhanced 120-mm (4.7-in) MG253 gun capable of firing a variety of munitions including guided projectiles, and a stabilized fire control system that can acquire moving targets through the use of thermal target sighting and tracking, and night vision enhancements. Paired with a semi-automatic loading system, the main weapon is serviced by a revolving magazine with 10 rounds ready to fire. Total ammunition storage includes 48 rounds of four types.

The Merkava IV powerplant was significantly upgraded to the 1118-kW (1500-hp) General Dynamics GD833 diesel engine, and was also fitted with a warning system to guard against lasers locking onto the vehicle. The Trophy Active

Protection System identifies a threat, determines its likely point of impact, and deploys an appropriate countermeasure. The armour protection standards of the Merkava IV are classified, but the structure of its modular pieces is believed to be state-of-the-art composite material.

The Merkava IV participated in the 2006 Lebanon war against the Hezbollah militia. Its performance has been criticized by some experts as being too vulnerable to anti-tank missiles. Despite such a perspective, the Merkava IV is widely believed to be one of the best main battle tanks in the world, and its crew survivability rate is second to none.

Close-up

The heavily armed and armoured Merkava main battle tank has undergone four major upgrades since its entry into service with the Israeli Defence Force in the early 1980s.

(1) **Machine Guns:** A pair of 7.62-mm (0.3-in) machine guns are mounted to the roof of the Merkava main battle tank turret.

(2) **Modular Armour:** Advanced modular armour protects both the turret and hull of the Merkava and is applied in blocks that can be replaced individually as needed.

(3) **Sighting Equipment:** The Merkava main battle tank is equipped with sophisticated infrared sighting and rangefinding equipment mounted on the turret.

(4) **Viewing Port:** Visibility for the crew was helped by the installation of viewing ports along the exterior of the turret and hull.

(5) **Turret Slope:** The distinctive wedge-shaped turret of the Merkava main battle tank improves armour protection and includes a large rear overhang and bustle rack.

(6) **Main Weapon:** Initially equipped with an 105-mm (4.13-in) L7A3 gun, the tank has been upgunned to a 120-mm (4.72-in) smoothbore weapon in later models.

Leopard 2

Developed in the early 1970s, the Leopard 2 main battle tank was the result of Germany prioritizing the upgrade of the Leopard 1 with technological advances. It was derived through joint research with the U.S., although cooperative effort between the nations collapsed twice.

SECONDARY ARMAMENT
A coaxial 7.62-mm (0.3-in) MG3A1 machine gun is positioned in the turret, while a second 7.62-mm (0.3-in) machine gun is pintle-mounted near the loader's hatch. Banks of smoke grenade launchers are placed on either side of the main gun.

MAIN ARMAMENT
The 120-mm (4.7-in) L55 smoothbore gun developed by Rheinmetall Waffe Munition of Ratingen, Germany, replaced the earlier, shorter-barrelled L44 weapon, increasing muzzle velocity.

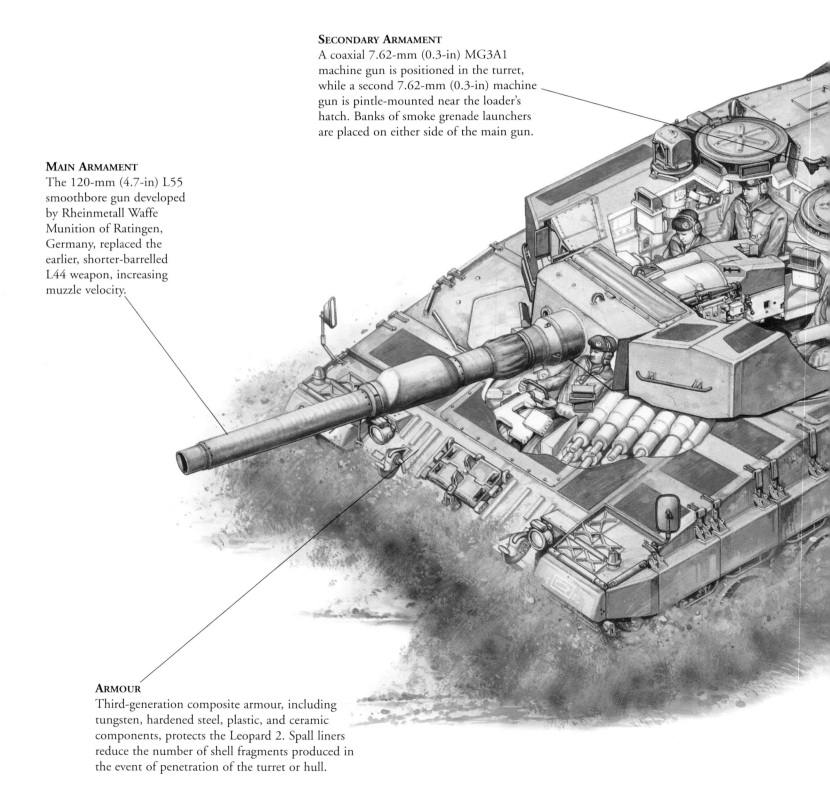

ARMOUR
Third-generation composite armour, including tungsten, hardened steel, plastic, and ceramic components, protects the Leopard 2. Spall liners reduce the number of shell fragments produced in the event of penetration of the turret or hull.

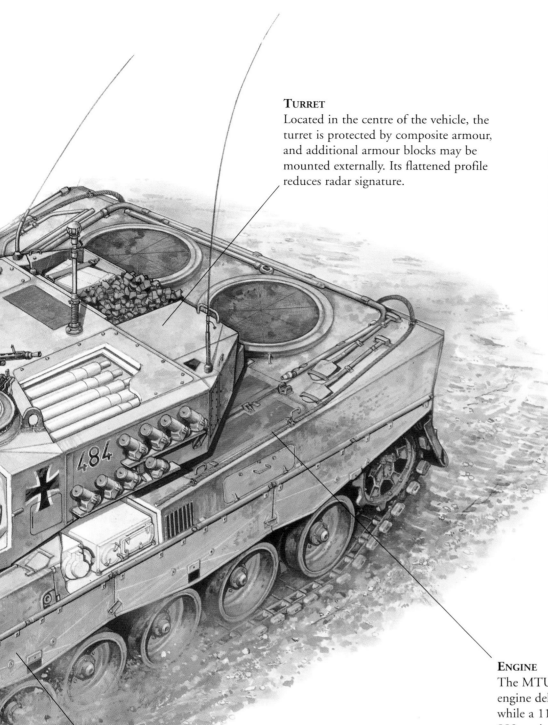

TURRET
Located in the centre of the vehicle, the turret is protected by composite armour, and additional armour blocks may be mounted externally. Its flattened profile reduces radar signature.

ENGINE
The MTU MB 873 Ka-501 diesel engine delivers 1103 kW (1479 hp), while a 1118-kW (1500-hp) MTU MT 883 engine has been used in trials with the EuroPowerPack upgrade. The transmission is the Renk HSWL 354.

HULL CONFIGURATION
Divided into three compartments, the hull includes the driver position forwards, the fighting compartment in the centre, and the engine compartment to the rear, separated by a firewall. The commander, gunner, and loader are positioned inside the turret.

Utilizing Leopard 1 and MBT-70 components, a new vehicle was developed reflecting German tank design priorities, and this became the Leopard 2. Sixteen prototypes were trialled between 1972 and 1974 to test a variety of layouts.

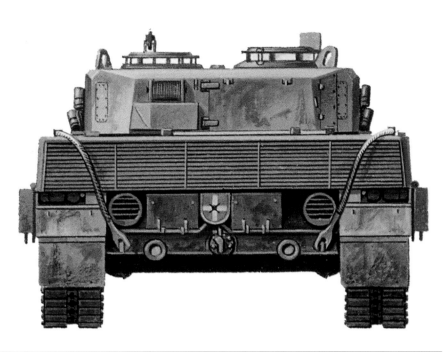

LEOPARD 2 – SPECIFICATION

Country of origin: West Germany
Crew: 4
Designer: Krauss-Maffei
Designed: 1970s
Manufacturer: Krauss-Maffei Wegmann Maschinenbau Kiel
Produced: 1979–present
In Service: 1979–present
Weight: 62.3 tonnes (68.6 tons)

Dimensions:
Length (gun forward): 9.97 m (32.7 ft)
Width: 3.75 m (12.3 ft)
Height: 3 m (9.8 ft)

Performance:
Speed: 72 km/h (45 mph)
Operational Range: 550 km (340 miles)

Engine:
Powerplant: 1 x MTU MB 873 Ka-501 liquid-cooled V-12 twin-turbo diesel engine 1500 PS (1479 hp/1103 kW) at 2600 rpm
Power/weight: 17.7 kW/t (24.1 PS/t)
Transmission: Renk HSWL 354
Suspension: Torsion-bar
Fuel Capacity: 1200 l (317 gallons)

Armour and Armament
Armour Type: 3rd generation composite; including high-hardness steel, tungsten, and plastic filler with ceramic component.
Main Armament: 1 x 120-mm (4.7-in) Rheinmetall L55 smoothbore gun. 42 rounds.

Secondary Armament: 2 x 7.62-mm (0.3-in) MG3A1. 4750 rounds.

Variants
Buffel ARV: Armoured Recovery Vehicle based on the Leopard 2 hull.
Leopard 2A3: 300 vehicles were delivered from December 1984 to December 1985, added new digital SEM 80/90 VHF radios and revised exhaust grills with circular bars.
Leopard 2A4: 370 vehicles were delivered from December 1985 to March 1987. The fire control system was fitted with a digital core in order to use new ammunition. A Deugra fire and explosion suppression system was installed and the return rollers repositioned. Turret protection was also increased.
Leopard 2A5: Narrow "pinched" turret appearance is introduced.
Leopard 2A6: Long-barrelled version of the Leopard 2 using the new Rheinmetall 120-mm (4.7-in)/55-calibre smoothbore gun.
Leopard 2A6EX: Export version.
Leopard 2 AVLB: Bridgelayer.
Leopard 2 Trainer: Driver training vehicle.

LEOPARD 2

Incorporating sophisticated composite armour along with the latest in armament, communications, target acquisition and ranging, and NBC (nuclear, biological, chemical) defence systems, the Leopard 2 main battle tank has been recognized as one of the finest weapons of its kind in the world. The coordination of the commander's and gunner's observation systems enables the tank to function with deadly efficiency in combat. The PERI-R 17 A2 periscope, built by Rheinmetall Defence Electronics, provides the commander with a 360-degree stabilized view of the battlefield both day and night. The gunner is able to transfer his visual image to the commander's monitor, enabling them to share the same field of vision.

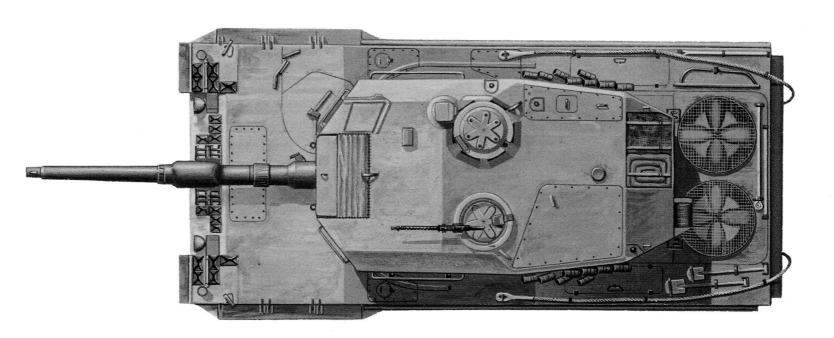

In September 1977, the German Ministry of Defence formally decided to go ahead with plans for the production of 1800 Leopard 2 tanks, which were to be delivered in five batches. From the original group of companies bidding, Krauss-Maffei was chosen as the main contractor and systems manager.

The development of a German-American main battle tank design had begun in the late 1960s as both nations sought to replace their ageing front-line vehicles. The initial result was the MBT-70, a short-lived design that exposed the diverging priorities of the military establishments of the two nations. Ultimately, the Leopard 2 became the German priority, while the U.S. followed through the development of the M1 Abrams. By the mid-1970s, the two nations had once again reached a joint development agreement, and the prototype Leopard 2 was shipped to the U.S. for trials in comparison to the XM-1 Abrams prototype.

Interior view

The interior of the Leopard 2 main battle tank includes an array of electronic, communications, and weapons technology. Although headroom is limited within the turret, the layout is functional.

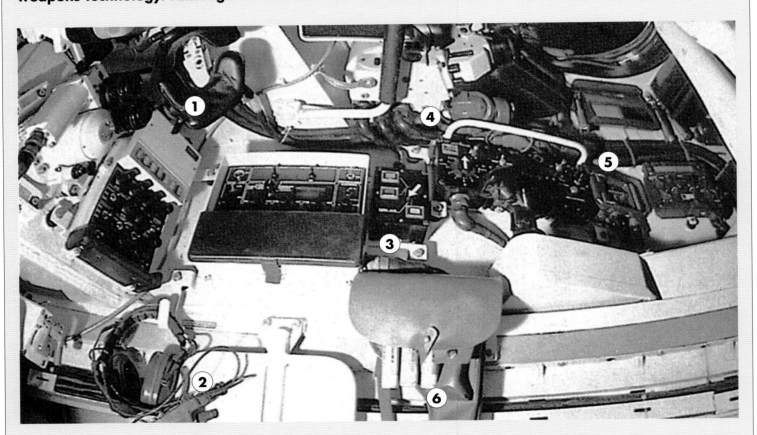

1. **Optical Equipment:** The gunner was equipped with daytime optical and rangefinding equipment along with infrared capabilities for nocturnal combat operations.

2. **Communications Gear:** The internal communications aboard the tank were facilitated by intercoms with headsets and control boxes placed near crew positions.

3. **Gunner's Controls:** The gunner used a variety of controls for traversing the turret and elevating the weapon.

4. **Hand Bar:** The commander used a hand bar to reach his position and steady himself inside the turret.

5. **Commander Position:** Seated high in the turret, the commander could override the operation of the main weapon and direct the vehicle's movement during combat.

6. **Gunner's Position:** Seated on the right side of the hull, forwards and below the commander, the gunner was responsible for the laying and firing of the main weapon.

The ponderous profile of the Leopard 2 main battle tank belies its ability to move rapidly across both open country and difficult terrain. The Leopard 2 has been exported from Germany to several countries.

When U.S. authorities evaluated the performance of the two tanks, they were deemed comparable in several key areas. However, the XM-1 was considered to be the better armoured of the two and, for this reason, the U.S. chose to continue pursuing the Abrams independently. The Germans embarked on full production of the Leopard 2, which entered service in 1979. The tank incorporates numerous advanced systems, including arguably the finest main gun in the world. Designed by Rheinmetall Waffe Munition of Ratingen, Germany, the 120-mm (4.7-in) L55 smoothbore gun extends the calibre of earlier 120-mm (4.7-in) weapons from 44 to 55, providing greater muzzle velocity, range, and enhanced ability to pierce armour. Developed specifically for use with the gun, the LKE 2 DM53 kinetic energy shell of heavy tungsten improves penetration of the target.

ON TARGET

In addition to advanced sighting and target identification for the commander and gunner via their PERI-R 17 A2 periscopes, the commander can use thermal imaging, which is displayed on a monitor inside the turret. The gunner's periscope is slaved to the fire control system, and his thermal imaging view can be shared with the commander. The gunner's sight is the stabilized Rheinmetall EMES 15 with laser rangefinding and Zeiss optronik thermal sights, which are also compatible with the fire control system.

The rangefinding equipment provides up to three range values in as little as four seconds, and the gunner reads the digital range directly from a distance up to 10 km (6.2 miles) and an accuracy within 20 m (66 ft).

Upgrades of the Leopard 2 have been regular through the years, and a current package includes enhancements to the hydraulic system. This eliminates the use of hydraulic fluids in the turret, which reduces noise, power consumption, and operating cost, as well as enhancing reliability.

The primary variants of the original Leopard 2 include the 2A1 with thermal sight for the gunner, modified ammunition racks, and improved fuel filters; the 2A3 with upgraded digital radio equipment; and the 2A4 with an automated fire and explosion suppression system, digital fire control, and improved composite turret armour of titanium and tungsten construction. The Leopard 2A5 included external add-on armour for the turret, spall liners for the interior, all electric turret controls, an improved gun braking system for heavier ammunition and a longer L55 gun, an auxiliary engine, improved mine protection, and air-conditioning.

The Leopard 2 has been deployed with the armed forces of Germany and other nations in Kosovo and Afghanistan, where a Canadian Leopard 2 hit an IED (improvised explosive device). The commander remarked, "It worked as it should." No casualties were sustained.

M1A1 Abrams

The M1 Abrams main battle tank entered service with the U.S. Army in 1980, and a series of upgrades have maintained its combat advantage, as demonstrated during the Gulf War, the invasion of Iraq, and operations in Afghanistan. The M1A1 variant made its debut in 1985.

MAIN ARMAMENT
A re-engineered version of the German 120-mm (4.7-in) Rheinmetall L44 smoothbore gun, designated the M256, serves as the main armament for the M1A1 Abrams. The U.S. gun requires fewer parts than the German model.

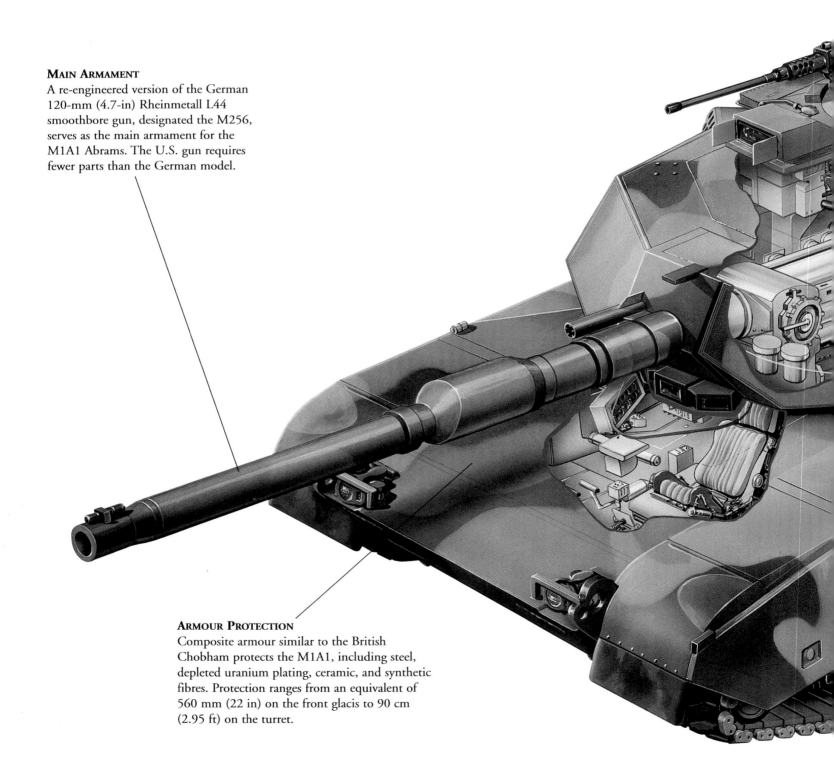

ARMOUR PROTECTION
Composite armour similar to the British Chobham protects the M1A1, including steel, depleted uranium plating, ceramic, and synthetic fibres. Protection ranges from an equivalent of 560 mm (22 in) on the front glacis to 90 cm (2.95 ft) on the turret.

SECONDARY ARMAMENT

A 12.7-mm (0.5-in) M2HB machine gun is attached to the turret adjacent to the commander's hatch, while a coaxial 7.62-mm (0.3-in) M240 machine gun is installed in the turret, and a second M240 is skate-mounted above the loader's hatch.

AMMUNITION STOWAGE

Ammunition is stowed in armoured boxes at the turret rear, separated from crew positions by an armoured bulkhead with its top panels designed to blow outwards.

F A C T S

- The M1 Abrams tank was developed as a replacement for the U.S. Army's M60 Patton.

- More than 8800 M1 and M1A1 tanks have been produced for the U.S., Egypt, Kuwait, and Saudi Arabia.

- Periodic upgrades have enhanced the performance of the Abrams through 30 years of service.

ENGINE

The AGT 1500 gas turbine engine produced by Lycoming Textron provides 1120 Kw (1500 hp) and a top speed of 67 km/h (42 mph) on the road. The engine is reliable and quieter than a contemporary diesel, but high fuel consumption is a logistic challenge.

CREW POSITIONS

The crew of four includes the driver, positioned forwards in a reclining seat, while the commander and gunner are situated to the right, and the loader to the left inside the turret.

The **M1A1 Abrams tank closes with and destroys enemy forces on the integrated battlefield using mobility, firepower, and shock effect. Its attributes make the Abrams tank particularly suitable for attacking or defending against large concentrations of heavy armour forces on a highly lethal battlefield.**

M1A1 ABRAMS – SPECIFICATION

Country of Origin: USA
Crew: 4
Designed: 1972–80
Designer: Chrysler Defense
Manufacturer: Lima Army Tank Plant (1980–present), Detroit Arsenal Tank Plant (1982–96)
In Production: 1980–present
In Service: 1980–present
Number Built: More than 9000
Gross Weight: 57 tonnes (63 tons)

Dimensions:
Length (hull): 7.92 m (26 ft)
Length (gun forward): 9.83 m (32.25 ft)
Width: 3.66 m (12 ft)
Overall Height: 2.89 m (9.5 ft)
Ground Pressure: 0.96 kg/cm²
Fording Capacity: 1.22 m (4 ft) (2.3 m [7.5 ft] with preparation)
Maximum Gradient: 31 degrees
Maximum Trench Width: 2.75 m (12 ft)
Maximum Vertical Obstacle: 1.27 m (4.2 ft)
Suspension Type: Advanced torsion bars

Performance:
Maximum Speed: 67 km/h (42 mph)
Range, Road: 500 km (310 miles)
Range, Cross-country: 300 km (180 miles)

Engine:
Powerplant: 1 x Avco-Lycoming AGT-1500 gas turbine producing 1120 kW (1500 bhp) @ 3000 rpm
Capacity: n/a

Power/Weight Ratio: 17.2 kW (23.1 bhp) per tonne
Fuel Capacity: 1910 l (420.7 gallons)

Armament and Armour:
Main Armament: 1 x 120-mm (4.7-in) L/44 M256. 40 rounds.
Secondary Armament: 2 x 7.62-mm (0.3-in) M240 MGs. 11,000 rounds.
Ancillary Armament: 1 x 12.7-mm (0.5-in) Browning M2HB MG in AA mount. 900 rounds.
Armour Type: Homogeneous rolled/welded nickel steel with composite appliqué to hull and turret front.

Variants
XM1: Experimental model. Nine test-beds produced in 1978.
M1: First production variant. Produced 1979–85.
M1IP: (Improvement Production) Produced briefly in 1984 before the M1A1. Contained upgrades and reconfigurations.
M1A1: Produced 1986–92.
M1A1HC: (Heavy Common) Depleted uranium armour mesh, pressurized NBC system, rear bustle rack for storage, and M256 120-mm (4.7-in) smoothbore cannon.
M1A1-D: (Digital) Digital upgrade for the M1A1HC.
M1A1-AIM: (Abrams Integrated Management) A programme whereby older units are reconditioned to zero-hour conditions; and the tank is improved by adding Forwards-Looking Infra-Red (FLIR) and Far Target Locate sensors, a tank-infantry phone, communications gear, including FBCB2 and Blue Force Tracking, to aid in crew situational awareness, and a thermal sight for the 12.7-mm (0.5-in) machine gun.
M1A1 KVT: (Krasnovian Variant Tank) M1A1s modified to resemble Soviet tanks for use at the National Training Center. Fitted with MILES gear and a Hoffman device.
M1A1M: Export variant ordered by the Iraqi army.

M1A1 ABRAMS

The original M1 Abrams main battle tank entered service three decades ago. Later, during the mid-1980s, the M1A1 enhancement programme was undertaken, including increased armour protection, a nuclear, biological, and chemical (NBC) defence system, a reinforced suspension, and a modified transmission. Another significant modification was the redesign of the turret gun mount and bustle rack. The changes increased the weight of the M1A1 by more than a ton, yet there was no significant decline in performance. The firepower of the M1A1 was significantly improved over its predecessor with the replacement of the 105-mm (4.1-in) M68A1 rifled gun with a modified Rheinmetall L44 smoothbore gun designated the M256.

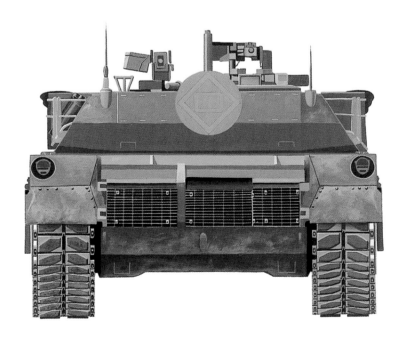

The main battle tank of the U.S. Army, an M1A1 Abrams is shrouded in dust as it rolls forwards on a desert road. Battle-tested during the Gulf War and the invasion of Iraq, the M1A1 dates to the mid-1980s and has seen various upgrades.

During the Gulf War of 1991, only 18 Abrams tanks were taken out of service because of battle damage. Nine were permanent losses; another nine suffered repairable damage, mostly from mines. Not a single Abrams crewman was lost in the conflict while inside the M1A1's armour.

Research and development of a new main battle tank for the U.S. Army and Marine Corps began in the late 1960s and continued after joint ventures with the German government resulted in failure. By 1976, the first prototype M1 Abrams tanks had been delivered, and the tank entered service in 1980. Designed by Chrysler Defense Corporation and manufactured by General Dynamics, the M1 combined firepower, mobility, and survivability. This lethal package ably demonstrated its dominance over Soviet-era battle tanks of the Iraqi army during the 1991 Gulf War and again during the invasion of Iraq in 2003.

The 1120-kW (1500-hp) Lycoming Textron gas turbine engine revolutionized armoured vehicle propulsion, powering the 57-tonne (63-ton) tank at up to 67 km/h (42 mph) on the road and reaching respectable cruising

speed in a matter of a few seconds. The engine has proven reliable in extreme climates and runs considerably quieter than a diesel, so much so that it has earned the nickname "Whispering Death" for the M1.

POWERFUL PUNCH

The M1A1, which was produced beginning in August 1985, introduced the 120-mm (4.7-in) M256 smoothbore gun, a modified version of the highly successful German Rheinmetall L44.

Target acquisition capabilities allow the M1A1 to engage enemy armour often at stand-off distances, locating, ranging, and firing before the opponent can bring its weaponry to bear. The digital fire control computer accepts data from laser rangefinding equipment and calculates the firing solution while accounting for angle measurements, the bend of the barrel itself based on a muzzle reference system. External sensors and a pendulum static cant sensor on the turret provide data on wind velocity and climatic conditions.

Armour protection for the M1 has, since 1988, included depleted uranium encased in steel, which has a much higher density than steel itself, while synthetic fibres, ceramics, and rubber are other components. During the Gulf War, there were recorded incidents of Abrams armour being penetrated by the projectiles of Soviet-made T-72 tanks. Ammunition stowage areas and upper surfaces of the M1A1 are constructed to blow outwards in the event of hull or turret penetration, minimizing the risk of a catastrophic explosion and greatly improving crew survivability.

CREW POSITIONING

Positioned forwards and in the centre of the hull, the driver has the use of three periscopes, one of which may be changed to night vision. His seat reclines to reduce the

profile of the tank. The commander, who is seated to the right inside the turret, is provided with a 360-degree view of the field through six periscopes. The gunner, who also sits to the right inside the turret, utilizes a single-axis GPS-LOS visual system and a Hughes laser rangefinder, which allows the weapon to identify targets with documented kills at ranges greater than 2500 m (8200 ft). The loader, seated to the left on the inside of the turret, is often the second most experienced member of the M1A1 crew and has responsibilities for loading both the main and secondary armament, and searching for air or anti-tank threats.

Interior view

The interior of the M1A1 Abrams includes a three-crew turret, a driver's compartment with a semi-reclining seat, and an engine compartment housing a gas turbine powerplant.

(1) **Breech Block:** The breech of the 120-mm (4.7-in) M256 smoothbore cannon is mounted inside the M1A1 turret.

(2) **Gunner's Controls:** The gunner uses fire control instrumentation and selects ammunition for the M1A1 main weapon, which the tank commander may override.

(3) **Turret Armour:** Composite armour protection is substantial on the M1A1 Abrams main battle tank, ranging up to an equivalent of 900 mm (35 in) in thickness.

(4) **Auxiliary Sight:** Telescopic sights are available for personnel in the event of battle damage or failure of other equipment.

(5) **Commander Position:** The commander uses many sights for the turret-mounted 12.7-mm (0.5-in) machine gun and an optical extension of the gunner's primary sight.

(6) **Turret Basket:** The floor functions as a turret basket, which rotates as the turret traverses to maintain the orientation of the crew to its weaponry and ammunition.

M2 Bradley

A shroud of controversy surrounded the development of the M2 Bradley infantry fighting vehicle, which took more than 15 years to reach deployment from conceptualization. When the Bradley finally entered service in 1981, it excelled in numerous combat situations.

SECONDARY ARMAMENT
A single 7.62-mm (0.3-in) M240C machine gun is mounted coaxially in the turret, while firing ports allowed infantrymen to engage enemy troops from inside the troop compartment of the initial M2 Bradley.

MAIN ARMAMENT
The McDonnell Douglas M242 25-mm (0.98-in) Bushmaster chain gun fires high-explosive rounds and others capable of penetrating the armour of some main battle tanks. The Bradley is also capable of mounting the TOW anti-tank guided missile system.

ENGINE
The early Bradley was powered by a 373-kW (500-hp), eight-cylinder supercharged diesel engine. This powerplant was later upgraded to the 447-kW (600-hp), eight-cylinder Cummins VTA-903T diesel, capable of a top speed of 66 km/h (41 mph) on the road.

INFANTRY ACCESS

Early Bradleys transported up to seven infantrymen, while later models carried six, who exited the vehicle through a roof hatch or rear ramp door.

PERSONNEL CAPACITY

The standard crew of three includes the commander and gunner, who are seated inside the turret, and the driver, who sits forwards and to the left in the hull with the engine on his right. A squad of six fully armed combat infantrymen is transported in the rear compartment.

ARMOUR PROTECTION

The 7017 explosive reactive armour constructed of aluminium alloy provides basic protection against armour-piercing rounds up to 23 mm (0.9 in), while spaced laminate armour and some additional appliqué steel plates add further protection.

The Bradley fighting vehicle is able to close with and destroy enemy forces in support of mounted and dismounted infantry and cavalry combat operations. It has sufficient cross-country mobility to keep up with the Abrams main battle tank.

M2 BRADLEY

M2 BRADLEY – SPECIFICATION

Country of Origin: United States
Crew: 3 + 6 (7 in M2A2 ODS/M2A3)
Manufacturer: BAE Systems Land and Armaments
In Service: 1981–present
Number Built: 4641
Weight: 27.6 tonnes (30.4 tons)

Dimensions:
Length: 6.55 m (21.5 ft)
Width: 3.6 m (11.8 ft)
Height: 2.98 m (9.78 ft)

Performance:
Speed: 66 km/h (41 mph)
Operational Range: 483 km (300 miles)

Engine:
Powerplant: 1 x Cummins VTA-903T 8-cylinder diesel 447 kW (600 hp)
Power/weight: 19.74 hp/tonne
Suspension: Torsion bar

Armour and Armament:
Armour Type: Spaced laminate armour. Front armour protects against 25-mm (0.98-in) APDS from classified distance. Hull base is Aluminium 7017 Explosive Reactive Armour.
Main Armament: 1 x 25-mm (0.98-in) M242 chain gun. 900 rounds
TOW anti-tank missile
7 TOW missiles

Secondary Armament: 1 x 7.62-mm (0.3-in) M240C machine gun. 2200 rounds.

Variants:
M2A1 IFV: Introduced in 1986, the A1 variant included an improved TOW II missile system, a Gas Particulate Filter Units (GPFU) NBC system, and a fire-suppression system. By 1992, the M2A1s had begun being remanufactured to upgraded standards.
M2A2 IFV: Introduced in 1988, the A2 received an improved 447-kW (600-hp) engine with an HMPT-500-3 hydromechanical transmission and improved armour (both passive and the ability to mount explosive reactive armour). The new armour protects the Bradley against 30-mm (1.18-in) APDS rounds and RPGs (or similar anti-armour weapons). Ammunition storage was reorganized.
M2A3 IFV: Introduced in 2000, the A3 upgrades make the Bradley IFV/CFV totally digital.
M2 BSFV: Bradley Stinger Fighting Vehicle air defence system.
M2A2 ODS/ODS-E: "Operation Desert Storm" and "Operation Desert Storm-Engineer" improvements were based on lessons learned in 1991 during the first Gulf War. Improvements included an eye-safe laser rangefinder (ELRF), a tactical navigation system (TACNAV) incorporating the Precision Lightweight GPS Receiver (PLGR) and the Digital Compass Systems (DCS), a missile countermeasure device designed to defeat first-generation wire-guided missiles. Seats in the rear were changed to a bench configuration, greatly improving dismount times.

SUPPORT VEHICLE: STRYKER

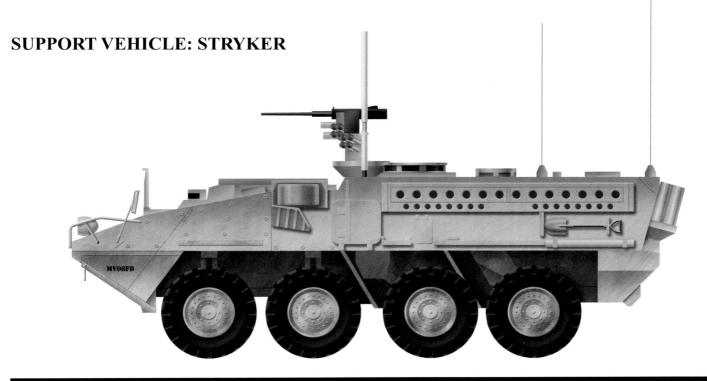

M2 BRADLEY

The costly T-BAT-II (TOW-Bushmaster Armoured Turret-Two Man) turret employed with the initial M2 Bradley infantry fighting vehicle houses the stabilized mount for the M242 25-mm (0.98-in) chain gun, a computerized Integrated Sight Unit (ISU) for both the gun and TOW missile package, thermal imaging equipment, and a seat for the commander, positioned to the right, and for the gunner on the left. The M242 is capable of firing up to 200 rounds per minute. Turning a switch, the gunner chooses armour-piercing or high-explosive shells, fed via an integrated dual system. A collapsible launch rack is installed on the left side of the turret for the TOW anti-tank missiles. The Stryker (illustrated above) entered service with the U.S. Army and became its first armoured fighting vehicle deployed since the M2/M3 Bradley two decades earlier. The Hummer, in service since the 1980s, serves as a small light personnel vehicle and largely replaced the jeep.

SUPPORT VEHICLE: HUMMER

Although the M2 Bradley was 15 years in the making and its detractors roundly criticized early trials, the infantry fighting vehicle and its cavalry counterpart, the M3, have been proven under battlefield conditions.

The Bradley originated in a 1965 U.S. Army requirement for a replacement for the M113 armoured personnel carrier, which is in reality only a "battle taxi" that can move troops under thin protection but lacks the armour, firepower, and mobility needed to manoeuvre with tanks on the battlefield.

The M2 Bradley fighting vehicle entered service with the U.S. Army in 1981. By that time it had already survived controversial issues regarding survivability tests, a delay in development due to the budget and manpower constraints of the Vietnam War, and conflicting perspectives concerning firepower, protection, and mobility.

The army needed to replace the ageing M113 armoured personnel carrier. The M551 Sheridan project had largely been acknowledged as a failure and the M114 scout vehicle was also deemed inadequate. This new tank, named after General Omar Bradley, a hero of World War II, was designed for both infantry and cavalry operations. The vehicle was to transport infantry into combat, provide direct fire support, and maintain the pace of advance with the M1 Abrams main battle tank. Designated M2, the infantry version initially carried a crew of three and had room for seven combat

infantrymen, while the M3 cavalry version transported only two scout infantrymen in addition to the crew. The capacity of the M2 was later reduced to six.

FORMIDABLE FIREPOWER

The 25-mm (0.98-in) M242 chain gun fires high-explosive or armour-piercing shells with cores of dense depleted uranium. Dual remote ammunition selection allows the gunner to engage different types of targets in rapid succession. The M2 Bradley carries 900 25-mm (0.98-in) rounds, while the M3 carries up to 1200. The commander or the gunner can fire the weapon using a duplicate fire control system, which includes a computerized integrated sight unit (ISU) and thermal imaging. The TOW anti-tank guided missile, and later the TOW II, is fired from a twin box launcher attached to the left side of the turret.

The Bradley is amphibious. Early models had a flotation screen, while later variants have an inflatable pontoon. It is propelled through water by track action at 6 km/h (4 mph).

Virtually all early M2 Bradley fighting vehicles have been upgraded through the years. In 1986, the A1 was armed with the improved TOW II missile with an effective range of 4 km (2.5 miles), and other upgrades included a fire suppression system and a nuclear, biological, and chemical defence system utilizing gas particulate filter units.

LATEST TECHNOLOGY AND A HOT MEAL

The lessons learned in the 1991 Gulf War inspired a series of electronic improvements in the ODS (Operation Desert Storm) upgrade to the A2. These included improved laser rangefinding, a tactical navigation system, digital compass and global positioning, countermeasures against missiles, interface with the Force XXI Battle Command Brigade and Below (FBCB2) command system, and thermal imaging for the driver. Bench seating and a heater for meals were installed in the troop compartment. The A3 upgrade included second-generation Forward Looking Infrared Sighting (FLIR), an electro-optical imaging system, advanced fire control software, and other technical upgrades.

The combat record of the M2 Bradley infantry fighting vehicle testifies to its potency. Losses have been minimal, and vulnerability to mines, improvised explosive devices (IED), and rocket-propelled grenades has been addressed. Other vehicles based on the Bradley include air defence and anti-tank platforms and a forward observation fire support version. Research and development of a next-generation infantry fighting vehicle is ongoing, and the successor to the Bradley is expected to debut by 2020.

Interior view

The interior is divided into driver and fighting compartments along with a compartment to transport up to six combat infantrymen.

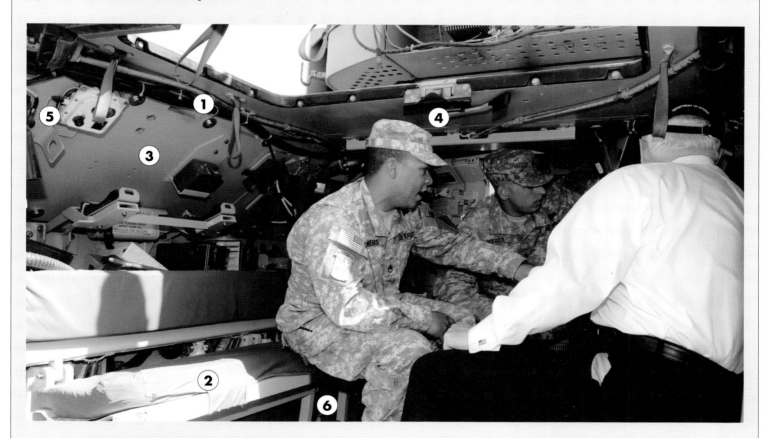

(1) **External Access:** Infantrymen can enter the troop compartment, fire their small arms from it, or load ammunition through a large hatch on top of the hull.

(2) **Seating:** Infantrymen sit on a pair of long benches aligned down the length of the troop compartment.

(3) **Hull Armour:** The thin aluminium alloy armour of the hull is explosive-reactive and provides protection against armour-piercing shells up to 23 mm (0.9 in).

(4) **Forward Access:** The troop compartment is separated from the forward sections by a partition, but movement between the two sections is possible.

(5) **Intercom System:** Communication between the forwards sections and the troop compartment is facilitated by intercom.

(6) **Hull Floor:** To defend against powerful mines and improvised explosive devices, the lower hull of many M2 Bradley infantry fighting vehicles has been reinforced.

Challenger 1

The convergence of political upheaval and technological transition gave rise to the Challenger 1 main battle tank, which bridged the gap between the ageing Chieftain and the modern Challenger 2, the British Army's mainstay of the new millennium.

SECONDARY ARMAMENT
Smoke grenade launchers were attached to the hull in two banks, while a 7.62-mm (0.3-in) LA82 machine gun was mounted coaxially and a 7.62-mm (0.3-in) L37A2 machine gun was mounted on top of the commander's cupola.

ENGINE
The 895-kW (1200-hp) Perkins Engine Company Condor V-12 diesel engine provided the Challenger 1 with a top speed of 60 km/h (37 mph).

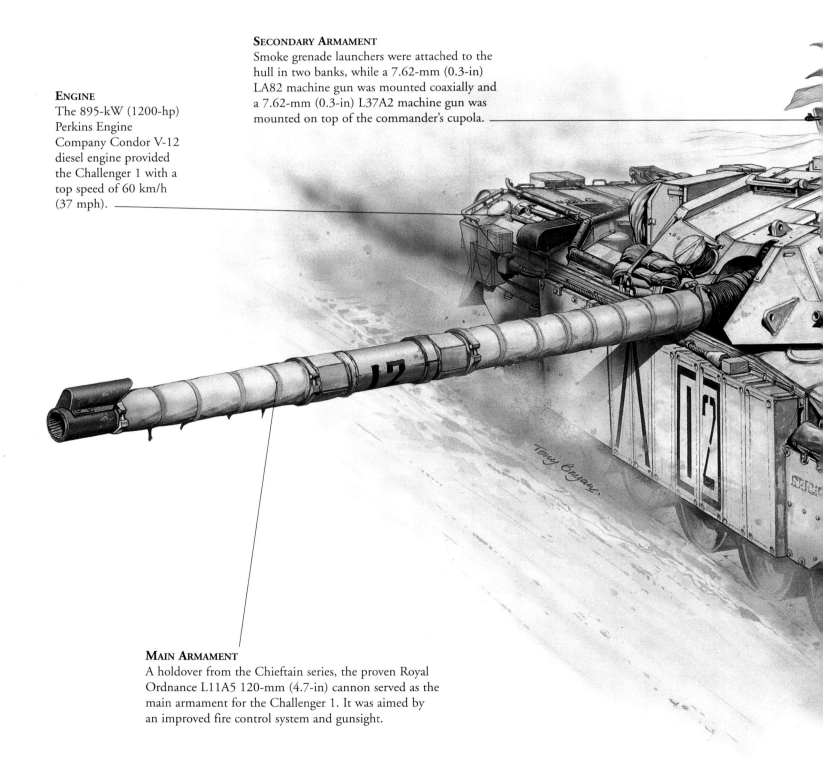

MAIN ARMAMENT
A holdover from the Chieftain series, the proven Royal Ordnance L11A5 120-mm (4.7-in) cannon served as the main armament for the Challenger 1. It was aimed by an improved fire control system and gunsight.

TURRET
The sloped turret housed the commander on the right, the loader to his left, and the gunner ahead and below. Its elongated shape provided ample space for the crew while minimizing the vehicle's silhouette.

F A C T S

- Only 420 Challenger 1 tanks were built during a seven-year period from 1983–90.

- The Jordanian army maintained a large number of Challenger 1 tanks, augmenting older modified Chieftains.

- The failure of a joint venture between Great Britain and Germany contributed to the tank's development.

DRIVER COMPARTMENT
Seated in a reclining position forwards and on the tank's centreline, the driver used a single-piece hatch and could also view the field through a periscope that was interchangeable with a night scope.

SUSPENSION
The hydro-pneumatic suspension supported six aluminium road wheels on each side of the Challenger 1 with idlers, drive sprockets, and a pair of return rollers. Side armour was added for additional defence against roadside bombs and projectiles.

The Challenger 1 was derived from the Shir II, a radically modified version of the Chieftain developed for the Shah of Iran. It was ordered by the British Army as an interim main battle tank after the collapse of an Anglo-German project and the subsequent MTB-80 programme.

CHALLENGER I

CHALLENGER 1 – SPECIFICATION

Country of Origin: United Kingdom
Crew: 4
Designer: Military Vehicles and Engineering Establishment (MVEE)
Designed: Late 1970s–1982
Manufacturer: Royal Ordnance Factories
In Production: 1982–90
In Service: 1983–2000
Number Built: 420
Gross Weight: 62 tonnes (68 tons)

Dimensions:
Length (gun forward): 11.55 m (37.9 ft)
Length (hull): 8.39 m (27.5 ft)
Width: 3.52 m (11.55 ft)
Overall Height: 2.89 m (9.5 ft)

Performance:
Maximum Speed: 60 km/h (37 mph)
Range, Road: n/a
Range, Cross-country: n/a
Ground Pressure: n/a
Fording Capacity: 1.1 m (3.5 ft)
Maximum Gradient: 28 degrees
Maximum Trench Width: 3.15 m (10.33 ft)
Maximum Vertical Obstacle: 0.91 m (3 ft)
Suspension Type: Hydro-pneumatic

Engine:
Powerplant: 1 x Rolls-Royce Condor 12V 1200 V-12 diesel producing 895 kW (1200 bhp) @ 2300 rpm
Capacity: n/a

Power/Weight Ratio: 14.43 kW (19.35 bhp) per tonne
Fuel Capacity: 1800 l (396.5 gallons)

Armament and Armour:
Main: 1 x 120-mm (4.7-in) L/53 L11A5. 64 rounds
Secondary: 2 x 7.62-mm (0.3-in) GPMG MGs. 4000 rounds
Turret Traverse: Electro-hydraulic/manual
Elevation Range: n/a
Stabilization: Elevation and azimuth
Fire Control System: Digital ballistic computer, optical sights laser rangefinder, thermal imaging sights
Armour Type: Chobham composite
Minimum Thickness: n/a
Maximum Thickness: n/a

Variants:
Challenger: Initial series designation until adoption of Challenger 2 into service, thus necessitating a need for the Challenger "1" designation; based on the formerly Iranian export design of the "Shir 2" main battle tank.
Challenger ARV: Armoured Recovery Vehicle.
Challenger Trainer: Driver Training Vehicle with fixed turret.
Challenger Marksman SPAAG: Self-Propelled Anti-Aircraft Challengers fitted with Marksman turret.
"Al Hussein": Jordanian Export Variant sold as refurbished British product.

SUPPORT VEHICLE: AS90 SELF-PROPELLED GUN

CHALLENGER 1, AS90 AND FV432

Although the Challenger 1 was accepted by the British Army in December 1982, several shortcomings remained to be corrected. These included problems with the laser sights, main engine generator drive, and gearbox. The layout of the hull was standard British design with the engine to the rear, fighting compartment located in the centre, and the driving compartment forwards with the driver's seat reclining in order to reduce the overall height of the vehicle to 2.89 m (9.5 ft). The interior was functional, while the introduction of composite Chobham armour, much stronger than conventional steel, provided a tremendous enhancement to survivability.

The AS90 155-mm (6.1-in) self-propelled gun, which entered service in 1992, is another member of the modern armoured fighting vehicle family of the British Army, while the FV432 armoured personnel carrier (below) has remained in service since the 1960s.

SUPPORT VEHICLE: FV432 APC

A vast improvement over the Chieftain, especially in terms of mobility and protection, the Challenger 1 still reflected the British concept of armoured warfare in which tanks are mainly used as anti-tank guns. As a result, the design emphasizes firepower and, above all, protection at the expense of mobility.

The Islamic revolution that had toppled the Shah of Iran in 1979 prompted the cancellation of an order for 1225 Shir 2 main battle tanks from the British Ministry of Defence. Meanwhile, a joint venture between the British and the Federal Republic of Germany aimed at developing a main battle tank in order to standardize the armoured fighting vehicles of NATO countries collapsed. Pondering the question as to what could be done with the Shir 2, the British subsequently embarked on a programme of their own, known as the MBT-80, to produce a new and improved tank design. This, too, proved unsuccessful. Cost overruns in the

Interior view

The interior of the British Challenger 1 main battle tank included space for the storage of 64 projectiles for the main L11A5 120-mm (4.7-in) cannon. Storage areas are located in the hull and turret.

1. **Armour Protection:** The interior has spall liner material to decrease the potential for injury to crewmen from steel splinters.

2. **Ammunition Rack:** Ammunition storage racks prevent damage to high-explosive and armour-piercing shells during transportation.

3. **Armour-Piercing Shell:** This is primarily for use against enemy armoured vehicles, and is one of several types of ammunition that can be selected during combat.

4. **Protective Covers:** Caps protect the tips of armour-piercing shells from damage during movement across country.

5. **Fire Controls:** A number of selector knobs direct the type of ammunition and a range of other factors in target acquisition, such as loading and firing the main weapon.

6. **Storage Box:** Ammunition and other gear are also stored in numerous built-in boxes inside the turret and hull of the Challenger 1 main battle tank.

The Challenger 1 main battle tank was developed somewhat by happenstance, yet the vehicle served with distinction during Operation Desert Storm, destroying a large number of Iraqi tanks and armoured personnel carriers without sustaining any losses.

budget and the continuing advancements in technology spelled doom for the project.

Ultimately, the British defence establishment decided to retool the Shir 2 design to meet the current specifications of the British Army. This was acknowledged all around as a simple, short-term solution to respond to existing requirements. Eventually, a new generation of main battle tanks populated the armoured formations of the British Army. However, it was decided that the interim project would still go forwards. Initially known as the Cheviot, it was renamed the Challenger. While the Challenger became a front-line British tank, it did suffer from mechanical issues, which were to be corrected as quickly as possible, while also incorporating numerous improvements that would be standardized in the future main battle tank design.

ARMOUR AND EXPEDIENCE

The Challenger hull is constructed in traditional British layout with the driver, fighting, and engine compartments front to rear. The driver's seat reclines in order to lower the profile of the vehicle. Sloped at 70 degrees, the ceramic and metal composite Chobham armour, first utilized on the Challenger 1, provided the same protection for the crew of four as 61 cm (24 in) of conventional steel plate, though the exact thickness remains classified information. The proven

L11A5 120-mm (4.7-in) cannon, which utilized separate bagged propellant charges rather than brass casings, was mounted in a spacious sloped turret. Two 7.62-mm (0.3-in) machine guns allowed close defence against enemy infantry.

The GEC Marconi improved fire control system and No. 10 Mk. 1 laser sight were intended to improve accuracy with ballistic sensors that allowed for weather conditions and for vehicle and targets to be acquired even while they were moving. Advanced optics included the commander's No. 15 day sight and Rank Pullin image intensification swap sight, while the gunner's thermal imaging and laser rangefinder equipment were linked to the Marconi system. The powerplant for the Challenger 1 was typically the 895-kW (1200-hp) Perkins Engines Company Condor V-12 diesel or the Rolls-Royce CV 12 diesel with equivalent power.

Although only 420 tanks were built during a brief seven-year period from 1983–90, the Challenger 1 saw action during the first Gulf War and was credited with destroying 300 Iraqi tanks with no losses due to enemy action. Known only as the Challenger until the advent of its replacement, the tank was later designated the Challenger 1 and its improved successor was called the Challenger 2. A large number of Challenger 1 tanks were to be transferred to the Jordanian army as the new Challenger 2 became available with the turn of the century.

M270 MLRS

The Multiple Launch Rocket System (MLRS) introduced saturation firepower and "shoot-and-scoot" capability to the U.S. Army. Its mobility and strike capability against ground targets has proven a formidable combination on the battlefield, engaging a variety of targets.

FIRE CONTROL
Advanced fire control capabilities include the use of a global positioning system.

CREW
The crew of the MLRS, which includes a driver, gunner, and section chief, is capable of firing the system without leaving the protection of the cab, allowing for rapid fire and quick relocation.

ENGINE
A 373-kW (500-hp) Cummins Diesel engine powers the MLRS at up to 64 km/h (40 mph), keeping pace with forward ground units, including the M1 Abrams main battle tank.

MAIN ARMAMENT
The M269 launcher/loader module is capable of firing a variety of rockets against enemy ground targets individually or in a ripple of up to 12 projectiles in less than one minute.

FACTS

- The M270 MLRS chassis is based on the Bradley Fighting Vehicle.

- More than 1300 M270 systems have been constructed since 1980.

- Shaken Iraqi soldiers referred to the M270 as "steel rain" during Operation Desert Storm.

MUNITIONS
MLRS munitions include the M-77 Dual Purpose Improved Conventional Munition grenade or bomblet, Reduced Range Practice Rockets, extended range rockets, and guided rockets included with the long-range U.S. Army Tactical Missile System (ATACMS).

CHASSIS
Designated the M993 Self-Propelled Launcher/Loader, the chassis of the M270 MLRS is a stretched version of the Bradley Fighting Vehicle. Six road wheels are grouped in pairs of two on each side, and the torsion bar suspension cushions the tracked vehicle while traversing rugged terrain.

The MLRS offers manpower savings, massive firepower, and high survivability because of its armored cab and ability to "shoot and scoot." The system operates day and night in all types of weather and can engage and defeat cannon and rocket artillery, air defence concentrations, trucks, light armour, and personnel carriers.

M270 MLRS – SPECIFICATION

Vehicle
Country of Origin: United States
Crew: 3
Designer: Vought Corporation
Designed: 1977
Manufacturer: Lockheed Martin, Diehl BGT Defence
In Production: 1980–2003
In Service: 1983–present
Number Built: 1300
Weight: 24,948 kg (55,000 lb)

Dimensions:
Length: 6.86 m (22.5 ft)
Width: 3.02 m (9 ft 9 in)
Height: 2.6 m (8 ft 5 in)

Performance:
Maximum speed: 64 km/h (40 mph)
Range: 438 km (300 miles)

Engine:
Powerplant: 1 x Cummins VTA-903T V-8 turbocharged diesel producing 373 kW (500 hp) @ 2600 rpm

Armament Capacity:
Rate of fire (rockets): 12 rounds in less than 60 seconds
Rate of fire (missiles): 2 rounds in 20 seconds
Armament load: 12 rockets, two pods with six rockets each, or two missiles, two pods with two missiles each

Standard Rocket: MGM-140 Army Tactical Missile System (ATACMS)

Dimensions:
Length: Approximately 3.96 m (13 ft)
Diameter: Approximately 61 cm (24 in)
Range: More than 165 km (100 miles); (Extended range version: more than 290 km [180 miles])
Propellant: Solid fuel rocket motor
Guidance (Block I ATACMS): Ring laser gyro
Guidance (Block IA, II, IIA): Inertial navigation with GPS
Warheads: Anti-personnel, anti-material, precision anti-armour submunitions and other variants
Load: Two missiles per launcher, two pods with one missile each

Other Rockets and Missiles:
M26: Rocket with 644 M77 Dual-Purpose Improved Conventional Munitions (DPICM) sub-munitions. Range of 32 km (20 miles).
M26A1: Extended Range Rocket (ERR), with range of 45 km (28 miles) and using improved M85 submunitions.
M26A2: As M26A1, but using M77 submunitions.
M27: Completely inert training launch pod/container to allow full loading cycle training.
M28: Training rocket. M26 with three ballast containers and three smoke marking containers.
M28A1: Reduced Range Practice Rocket (RRPR) with blunt nose.
XM29: Rocket with Sense and Destroy Armour (SADARM) submunitions. Not standardized.
M30: Guided MLRS (GMLRS). Precision-guided rocket with range over 60 km (37.3 miles).
XM31: Variant of M30 with a unitary high-explosive warhead.
M39: Army Tactical Missile System (Army TACMS), with range of 97 km (60.3 miles).
XM135: Rocket with binary chemical warhead (VX [nerve agent]). Not standardized.

M270 MLRS

The tracked M993 Self-Propelled Launcher/Loader supports the traversable Launcher/Loader Module carried to the rear of the vehicle. The launcher/loader consists of a large box, armoured against shell splinters and small-arms fire, containing a pair of integral twin-boom cranes used to load and unload the weapons. Two launch pod containers carry six loaded missiles, ready to fire, and each pod is independently controlled. The system is capable of firing rockets independently or in a ripple salvo of 12 in less than one minute. The entire module may be fired, reloaded, and placed back in action in fewer than 10 minutes. A new generation of missiles offers precision-guided accuracy.

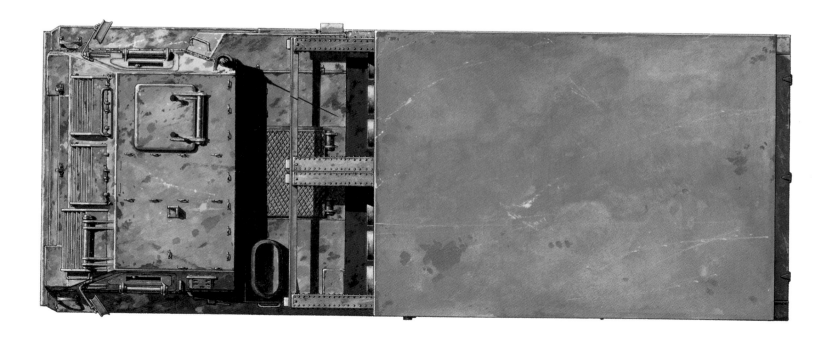

The Multiple Launch Rocket System is a versatile weapon system that supplements traditional cannon artillery by delivering large volumes of firepower in a short time against critical, time-sensitive targets. These targets often include enemy artillery, air defence systems, mechanized units, and personnel.

In something of a departure from the U.S. military establishment's penchant for precision targeting, in the late 1970s the army opted for what was originally a tactical saturation weapon to bring firepower to a concentrated area. The M270 Multiple Launch Rocket System (MLRS) was authorized in 1976, developed by the Vought Corporation, and manufactured by Lockheed Martin and Diehl BGT Defence beginning four years later. Its primary offensive capability was conceived not only as a platform for heavy fire support, but also a "shoot-and-scoot" system, which allows the crew of three to sight, range, and fire the

Interior view

The fire control centre aboard the M270 MLRS includes sophisticated computer controls and targeting equipment, which establish elevation, direction, and flight time to the selected target.

(1) **Communication Gear:** Helmets worn by the crew members include communications equipment to aid efficient operations.

(2) **Selector Switches:** These controlled such activities as the raising and lowering of the missile system, its direction, and other key elements of operation.

(3) **Forward Vision:** During transportation, the crew is able to view the terrain through ports that are protected during the operation of the rocket system.

(4) **Protective Cover:** A protective shield is lowered to diminish the noise and potential danger from small-arms fire.

(5) **Display Monitor:** Information relayed to and from the crew is displayed on a computer monitor visible to those controlling the rocket system.

(6) **Computer Controls:** Data is fed into the onboard targeting system, which then computes the correct firing solution to destroy a distant enemy.

In preparation for distant transport, an M270 MLRS tracked vehicle, its headlights blazing, is guided by a soldier. The M270 mounts the M269 launcher/loader module, which is capable of firing 12 rockets in less than a minute.

weapon rapidly and then relocate before counterbattery fire is able to detect its position and respond.

"SHOOT AND SCOOT"

The combination of firepower and mobility appealed originally to military planners for several reasons. The M270 chassis is based on a stretched version of the M2/M3 Bradley Fighting Vehicle. Designated the M987 Self-Propelled Launcher/Loader (SPLL), the vehicle mounts a Launcher/Loader Module (LLM) with 12 ready-to-fire rockets in two interchangeable pods. Powered by a reliable 373-kW (500-hp) V8 Cummins VTA903 diesel engine, the M270 is capable of a top road speed of 64 km/h (40 mph), enabling it to keep pace with forward infantry and armoured units, including the M1 Abrams main battle tank. The survivability of the M270 is enhanced due to the fact that the three crew members (section leader, gunner, and driver) can operate the weapon without leaving the safety of the armoured cab, as well as its "shoot-and-scoot" capability.

Although the role of the M270 was originally to deliver unguided munitions onto enemy targets, the system's role has evolved into one that is capable of firing precision-guided weapons as well. The standard ammunition package for the M270 includes several options depending on time, target, and mission. The 227-mm (9-in) M26 rocket,

weighing up to 306 kg (675 lb) and 3.95 m (13 ft) in length, delivers, among others, up to 644 M-77 Dual Purpose Conventional Munition grenades or bomblets, while the XM29 is equipped with a SADARM (Sense and Destroy Armour) munition. The M30 precision-guided rocket delivers the M85 cluster bomb submunition, and the M39, which has a tactical range of 97 km (60 miles), delivers the M74 bomblet.

The most significant upgrade to the original M270 system is the M270A1, which includes the capability to fire the munitions of the Army Tactical Missile System (ATACMS) with improvements to the mechanical launch process, fire control, and extended range rockets. Global positioning equipment and meteorological sensors, to an altitude of 100 m (128 ft), assist in accuracy, measuring wind speed prior to launch. The Improved Launcher Mechanical System (ILMS) substantially decreases the time needed for deployment and firing.

The MLRS was highly successful against Iraqi troop concentrations and mobile Scud missile launchers during Operation Desert Storm. Its firepower has earned the nicknames "battlefield buckshot" and the "commander's personal shotgun." The armed forces of at least 20 nations have deployed the M270 MLRS system to date, and it has also been built under licence for several European countries.

Warrior

The Warrior mechanized infantry combat vehicle was developed to facilitate the changing role of the armoured personnel carrier into a fighting support vehicle. Although its development began in 1972, the Warrior did not enter service with the British Army until 1987.

MAIN ARMAMENT
The 30-mm (1.18-in) L21A1 RARDEN cannon fires several different types of ammunition and is capable of penetrating the armour of other infantry fighting vehicles and numerous main battle tanks of an older generation.

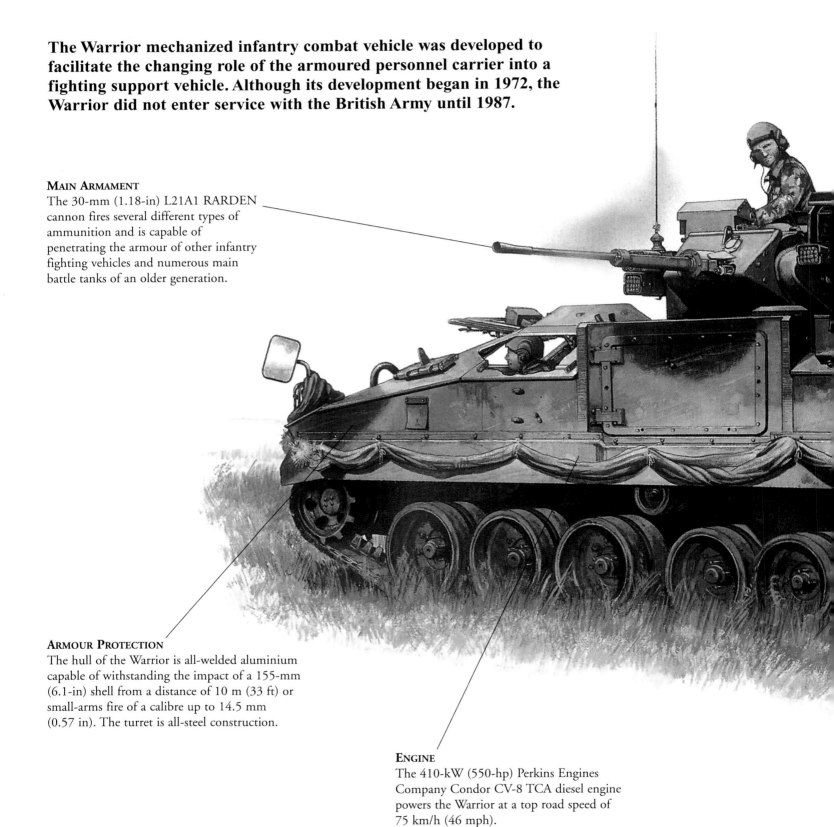

ARMOUR PROTECTION
The hull of the Warrior is all-welded aluminium capable of withstanding the impact of a 155-mm (6.1-in) shell from a distance of 10 m (33 ft) or small-arms fire of a calibre up to 14.5 mm (0.57 in). The turret is all-steel construction.

ENGINE
The 410-kW (550-hp) Perkins Engines Company Condor CV-8 TCA diesel engine powers the Warrior at a top road speed of 75 km/h (46 mph).

SECONDARY ARMAMENT
An L94A1 coaxial 7.62-mm (0.3-in) chain gun, two banks of four smoke grenade launchers, and accommodations for LAW or TOW anti-tank missiles round out the potent offensive capability of the Warrior. A second 7.62-mm (0.3-in) machine gun is also mounted on some vehicles.

FACTS

- The concept for the Warrior infantry fighting vehicle was inspired by the operational achievements of the Soviet BMP.

- Seven years elapsed before the completion of the first Warrior prototype.

- An improvement programme involving several aspects of the Warrior package is currently underway.

SUSPENSION
Six rubber-coated road wheels with the single-pin TR30 track designed by William Cook Defence are supported by a torsion bar suspension. This provides stability during cross-country manoeuvres.

TROOP COMPARTMENT
Situated to the rear of the vehicle, the troop compartment carries seven fully armed infantry, who exit through a powered rear door rather than a descending ramp.

The Warrior was designed to replace the FV432 APC in the 13 mechanized infantry battalions of the 1st, 3rd, and 4th Armoured Divisions of the British Army based in the Federal Republic of Germany. The transition period would last from 1988–94.

WARRIOR

WARRIOR – SPECIFICATION

Country of Origin: United Kingdom
Crew: 3 + 7
Designer: GKN Sankey/GKN Defence
Designed: Late 1970s
Manufacturer: GKN Sankey/BAe Systems
In Production: 1980–95
Number Built: 1000+
Weight: 25.4 tonnes (28 tons)

Dimensions:
Length: 6.3 m (20.7 ft)
Width: 3.03 m (9.94 ft)
Height: 2.8 m (9.19 ft)

Performance:
Speed, Road: 75 km/h (46 mph)
Operational Range: 660 km (410 miles)
Gradient: 60 degrees
Fording: 1.13 m (3 ft 8.5 in)
Vertical Obstacle: 0.75 m (2 ft 6 in)
Trench: 2.5 m (8 ft 2.5 in)

Engine:
Powerplant: 1 x Perkins V-8 Condor diesel producing 410 kW (550 hp)
Suspension: torsion bar

Armour and Armament:
Armour Type: Aluminium and appliqué
Main Armament: 1x 30-mm (1.18-in) L21A1 RARDEN cannon
Secondary Armament: 1 x coaxial 7.62-mm (0.3-in) L94A1 chain gun, 1 x 7.62-mm (0.3-in) machine gun

Variants
FV510: Infantry Section Vehicle. The main version operated by the British Army.
FV511: Infantry Command Vehicle.
FV512: Mechanized Combat Repair Vehicle. Operated by REME detachments in Armoured Infantry battalions. Equipped with a 6.5-tonne (7.16-ton) crane plus power tools. Able to tow a trailer carrying two Warrior power packs.
FV513: Mechanized Recovery Vehicle (Repair). Also operated by REME detachments in Armoured Infantry battalions. It is equipped with a 20-tonne (22.04-ton) winch and 6.5-tonne (7.16-ton) crane plus power tools and is able to tow a trailer carrying two Warrior power packs.
FV 514: Mechanized Artillery Observation Vehicle. Operated by the Royal Artillery as an Artillery Observation Post Vehicle (OPV) and fitted with mast-mounted Man-packable Surveillance and Target Acquisition Radar (MSTAR) and Position and Azimuth Determining System (PADS), with image-intensifying and infrared equipment. The 30-mm (1.18-in) RARDEN cannon is replaced with a dummy weapon, allowing space for the targeting and surveillance equipment.
FV 515: Battery Command Vehicle.
Desert Warrior: An export version adapted for operations in hostile desert conditions. It was fitted with the Delco turret, mounting a stabilized M242 Bushmaster 25-mm (0.98-in) chain gun with coaxial 7.62-mm (0.3-in) chain gun and 2 x Hughes TOW ATGM launchers (one mounted on each side). In 1993, Kuwait purchased 254 Desert Warrior vehicles.
Warrior 2000: A new version developed for the Swiss army that did not enter production, it featured an all-welded aluminium hull, increased armour, digital fire control system, more powerful engine, and a Mark 44 30-mm (1.18-in) cannon.

SUPPORT VEHICLE: BULLDOG (FV432) APC

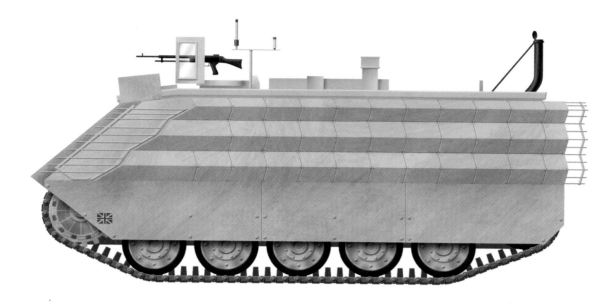

WARRIOR

The interior of the Warrior accommodates a crew of three, with the commander and gunner on the right and left, respectively, inside the turret and the driver forwards with the engine on his right. Unlike other modern infantry fighting vehicles, the passenger compartment of the infantry combat version (shown) does not include firing ports for the seven combat infantrymen, who are carried to the rear of the vehicle. In keeping with British doctrine, infantrymen disembark and fight on foot, while the Warrior provides close support. The soldiers exit the vehicle through a single door, which was modified from an original two-door design in the prototype.

SUPPORT VEHICLE : VIKING (BvS10) APC

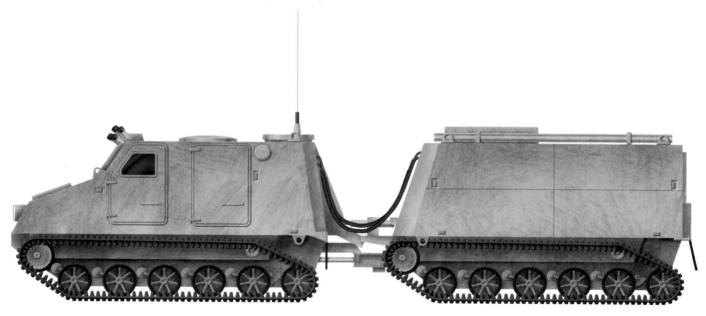

The Warrior was designed with speed and cross-country ability in order to keep pace with the Challenger 2 series of main battle tank for the British Army. Other considerations included fielding a close support combat vehicle that would work with infantry and other armoured units in an offensive assault.

Despite technical difficulties and cost overruns, the Warrior infantry fighting vehicle did develop into a vast improvement over its predecessor, the FV432 Trojan. However, while British engineers first conceived of an improved support vehicle for forwards operations in the early 1970s, actual deployment with British armoured infantry battalions in Western Europe did not occur until 15 years later.

More than 1000 Warriors, including the infantry support section vehicle, and others for command, recovery, artillery observation, desert, and arctic operations, have been produced since the 1980s, and these have seen combat in

Interior view

The troop compartment of the British Warrior infantry fighting vehicle transported a squad of up to seven fully armed combat infantrymen, who exited to the rear of the tank during combat operations.

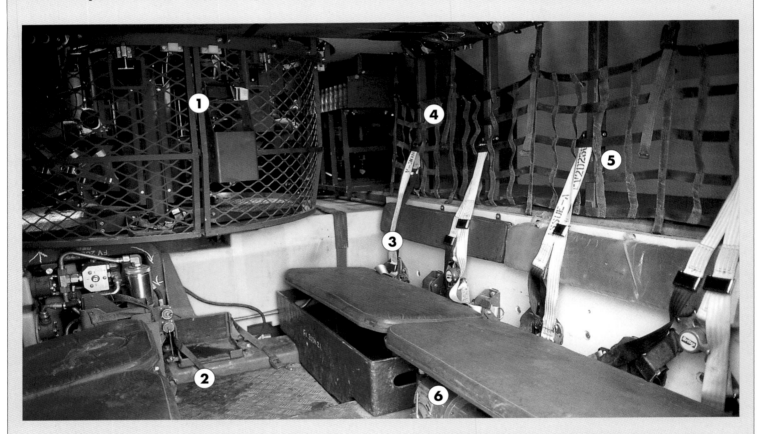

(1) **Weapons Support:** Servicing of the turret-mounted weapons was accomplished within the turret and from below as ammunition and other components were passed.

(2) **Infantry Seating:** Facing inwards, the seating within the Warrior's troop compartment assisted easy entry and exit.

(3) **Armour Protection:** Sacrificing armour protection for speed, the hull was capable of withstanding small-arms fire.

(4) **Engine Compartment:** A thin bulkhead separated the engine compartment from the area carrying troops.

(5) **Storage Space:** Mesh nets were placed along the hull of the troop compartment to maximize storage space for ammunition, infantry gear, and other supplies.

(6) **Hull Floor:** Due to susceptibility to land mines and improved explosive devices (IED), the hulls of many Warriors have been reinforced.

Afghanistan, Iraq, and the Balkans. Heavily armed, the infantry vehicle mounts the 30-mm (1.18-in) RARDEN cannon manufactured by BAE Systems RO Defence Facility, in Nottingham. Both commander and gunner, seated in the steel turret, are equipped with Pilkington Optronics day/night sights. A 7.62-mm (0.3-in) chain gun, and sometimes a second machine gun, provide defence against enemy infantry, while the section variant serves as a platform for either the LAW or TOW anti-tank missile system. A complete nuclear, biological, and chemical (NBC) defence system is included, allowing the occupants to maintain full function for up to 48 hours.

The Warrior powerplant consists of the 410-kW (550-hp) Perkins Engines Company CV-8 TCA diesel engine. Its automatic transmission has four forward and two reverse gears. The suspension is the reliable torsion bar configuration with six rubber-coated wheels and the single pin TR30 track produced by William Cook Defence. Its aluminium and steel armour can withstand small arms, shell fragments, and some cannon fire. In combat areas, it is often upgraded with the addition of appliqué armour. An export version of the Warrior was delivered to the Kuwaiti army in 1994, and the Swiss army ordered a variant, designated the Warrior 2000, in 1998. The original Warrior was developed by GKN Sankey and later manufactured by BAE Systems.

The Warrior section vehicle was never intended to serve as a combat platform for its complement of seven infantrymen, and therefore firing ports were never incorporated into the hull. Its firepower and manoeuvrability compensate for this shortcoming, though, by allowing it to access remote areas to provide direct fire against enemy positions. Its speed and cross-country capability have given it a decided edge in combat. To date, the greatest loss of life involving the Warrior took place during Operation Desert Storm when three vehicles were destroyed by friendly fire from American aircraft, killing nine British soldiers.

CONTINUING ENHANCEMENT

A major improvement initiative for the Warrior has been underway since 2004 with the intention of extending its service life to at least 2025. The project includes the introduction of the General Dynamics UK Bowman tactical communications system along with enhanced night capabilities via the Thales Optronics BGTI (battle group thermal imaging) programme. An improved turret with a 40-mm (1.57-in) stabilized case telescoped weapon system (CTWS) is being installed to British Army specifications under the Manned Turret Integration Programme (MTIP). Such a stabilized weapon will be able to fire with greater accuracy while on the move. Improved protection against improvised explosive devices (IED) is another component of the ugrade. In November 2009, BAE Systems entered a bid for the comprehensive Warrior Capability Sustainment Programme (WCSP).

Raising a cloud of dust, a Warrior infantry fighting vehicle churns forwards across country. Periscopes and viewing ports for the commander and gunner are prominent on top of the vehicle's two-crew turret.

M1A2 Abrams

The 120-mm (4.7-in) smoothbore M256 cannon is a modified version of the Rheinmetall L44 gun, which equipped the German Leopard and other Western main battle tanks. A possible refit to the Rheinmetall 120-mm (4.7-in) L55 gun may occur in the future.

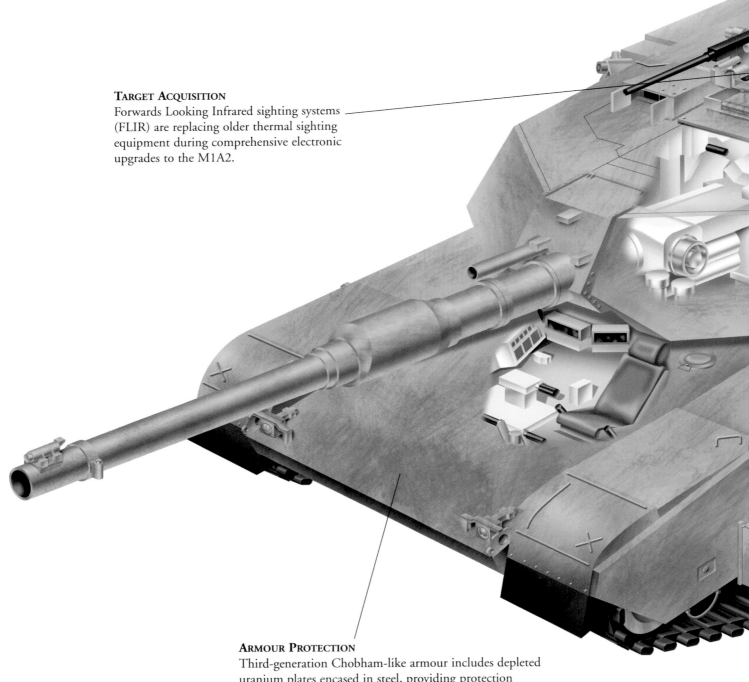

TARGET ACQUISITION
Forwards Looking Infrared sighting systems (FLIR) are replacing older thermal sighting equipment during comprehensive electronic upgrades to the M1A2.

ARMOUR PROTECTION
Third-generation Chobham-like armour includes depleted uranium plates encased in steel, providing protection equivalent to 960 mm (38 in) of rolled homogeneous armour on the turret, 590 mm (23 in) on the glacis, and 650 mm (25.5 in) on the lower front hull.

ENGINE
The AGT 1500 turbine engine provides
1118 kW (1500 hp) for the M1A2 and runs
much more quietly than a diesel. The AGT 1500
has been out of production since 1992, and
initiatives are underway to improve existing
engines and eventually replace the AGT 1500.

EXTERIOR TELEPHONE
A telephone mounted on the hulls of
some M1A2s allows supporting infantry
to communicate with the tank crew while
in the field.

SECONDARY ARMAMENT
A coaxial 7.62-mm (0.3-in) M240 machine
gun is installed in the turret and sighted
along with the main gun, while a second
M240 is skate-mounted above the loader's
hatch and a 12.7-mm (0.5-in) M2HB heavy
machine gun is sited on top of the turret at
the commander's hatch.

FACTS

- Production and upgrades of existing M1s to the M1A2 standard began in 1986.

- The M1A2 includes upgrades to electronics, urban warfare, and other systems.

- The service life of the M1 series of main battle tanks is expected to extend 70 years.

The M1A2 main battle tank is being fielded to armoured battalions and cavalry squadrons of the U.S. Army's heavy force. In lieu of new production, the army began to upgrade approximately 1000 older M1 tanks to the M1A2 configuration.

RIVAL: C1 ARIETE

M1A2 ABRAMS – SPECIFICATION

Country of Origin: United States
Crew: 4
Designer: General Dynamics
Designed: 1986
Manufacturer: General Dynamics (Land Systems Division)
In Production: 1992–present
In Service: 1992–present
Number Built: 77 for the U.S. Army, 315 for Saudi Arabia, and 218 for Kuwait
Weight: 62 tonnes (68 tons)

Dimensions:
Length (gun forward): 9.83 m (32.25 ft)
Width: 3.66 m (12 ft)
Turret Height: 2.37 m (7.79 ft)

Performance:
Maximum speed (road): 67.6 km/h (42 mph)
Maximum speed (cross-country): 54.7 km/h (34 mph)
Range: 426 km (265 miles)
Ground Clearance: 0.48 m (1.58 ft)
Ground Pressure: 15.4 PSI
Obstacle Crossing: 1.07 m (3.5 ft)
Vertical Trench: 2.7 m (9 ft)

Engine:
Powerplant: 1x AGT-1500 turbine engine
Power Rating: 1118 kW (1500 hp)
Power to Weight Ratio: 21.6 hp/tonne
Hydro-kinetic Transmission: 4 speed forward; 2 speed reverse

Armour and Armament:
Armour: Chobham, RH armor, steel encased depleted uranium mesh plating
Main Armament: 1 x 120-mm (4.7-in) M256 smoothbore cannon
Secondary Armament: 1 x 12.7-mm (0.5-in) M2 machine gun; 2 x 7.62-mm (0.3-in) M240 machine guns

Variants
M1A2 (Baseline): Production began in 1992 (77 built for the U.S. and more than 600 M1s upgraded to M1A2, 315 for Saudi Arabia, 218 for Kuwait). The M1A2 offers the tank commander an independent thermal sight and ability to shoot at two targets in rapid sequence without the need to acquire each one sequentially.
M1A2 SEP: (System Enhancement Package) Has upgraded third-generation depleted uranium encased armour with graphite coating (240 newly built, 300 M1A2s upgraded to M1A2SEP for the U.S., 250 for Egypt in 2 Egyptian co-production batches of 125 each).
M1 Grizzly CMV: Combat Mobility Vehicle.
M1 Panther II: Remote Controlled Mine Clearing Vehicle.
M104: Wolverine Heavy Assault Bridge.
M1 Assault Breacher Vehicle: Assault variant for the U.S.M.C. Based upon the M1A1 Abrams chassis, the Assault Breacher Vehicle has a variety of systems installed, such as a full-width mine plough, two linear demolition charges, and a lane-marking system. Reactive armour has been fitted to the vehicle providing additional protection against HEAT-based weapons. The turret has been removed and is replaced by a welded steel superstructure.
M1 Armoured Recovery Vehicle: Only a prototype produced.

RIVAL: TYPE 90

M1A2 ABRAMS

The M1A2 enhancement to the Abrams series of main battle tanks includes the improvements completed with the M1A1, such as an upgrade to the 120-mm (4.7-in) M256 main gun, an improved turret, heavier suspension, nuclear, biological, and chemical (NBC) defences, and better armour protection, with the addition of a commander's independent thermal viewer, weapons station with thermal imager, digital colour terrain map display, thermal imaging gunner sights, enhanced navigational equipment, integrated display and thermal management systems for the driver, and a digital data bus along with radio interface equipment allowing for a shared view of the battlefield among supporting M1A2 tanks.

RIVAL: TYPE 85/90

The primary M1A2 Abrams main battle tank included electronic enhancements to the M1A1 and was in production until 1999. In February 2001, General Dynamics Land Systems was contracted to supply a system enhancement package to many of the M1A2 tanks by 2004.

Building on the proven success of the M1A1 Abrams main battle tank, the M1A2 included significant upgrades to thermal-imaging and computer-based systems. As a result, many of the M1A1 tanks in service were upgraded with the M1A2 package. Perhaps the most significant upgrade came in the form of the two-axis gunner's GPS-LOS primary sight developed by Raytheon, greatly increasing the probability of a first-round hit.

Even as the original M1 entered service in 1980, engineers were at work to upgrade the design, which was destined to become the leading main battle tank in the world

Interior view

The interior incorporates an independent thermal viewer and weapon station for the commander along with improved radio, navigation, and digital data equipment.

(1) **Viewing Ports:** The commander's cupola has ports to assist in surveying the terrain while the tank is buttoned up.

(2) **Spall Liner:** The interior has spall liner material to prevent injury to the crew caused by the impact of a shell on the turret exterior.

(3) **Communications:** Internal communications are maintained by an intercom system. Each crewman is equipped with a headset that incorporates communication gear.

(4) **Hatch:** Above the commander's hatch is a heavy machine gun. A light machine gun is skate-mounted above the loader's hatch.

(5) **Turret Armour:** Third-generation explosive-reactive armour protects the turret of the tank with the equivalent of more than 900 mm (35 in) of armour plating.

(6) **Commander's Position:** The commander of the M1A2 Abrams is positioned above the gunner on the right side of the large, flat turret.

This M1A2 Abrams tank is seen in desert camouflage scheme as its crew takes a well-deserved break during the fighting in Iraq in 2003. The M1A2 compiled an impressive record during the swift military campaign.

following the performance of the M1A1 during the Gulf War of 1991. Upgrades to the M1A2 have increased its overall weight to 62 tonnes (68 tons). This has made it into one of the heaviest main battle tanks in the world, yet its mobility remains uncompromised.

TECHNOLOGY TRANSFER

The SEP programme, initiated with the M1A2 in the late 1990s, includes the installation of second-generation FLIR (Forward Looking Infrared Sighting) equipment to improve recognition and identification of targets, the installation of auxiliary power protected by armour, a thermal management system to maintain a temperature of less than 35°C (95°F) inside the tank to enhance crew performance and reduce the risk of electronics overheating, full-colour map displays with faster data processing, and seamless compatibility with the U.S. Army Force XXI Battle Command, Brigade and Below Programme (FBCB2), a digital battlefield command information system.

Some discussion has taken place surrounding the retirement of the 120-mm (4.7-in) M256 gun and replacing it with the longer-barrelled Rheinmetall 120-mm (4.7-in) L55. However, such a change may never occur. The M256 has proven lethal firing ammunition with a depleted uranium core, achieving kills from distances of 2500 m (2734 yards), apparently with greater success than European main battle tanks firing rounds with tungsten cores from the L55.

Because it is stabilized in two planes, the M256 is capable of accurately firing while on the move.

Another enhancement to the M1A2 is the Tank Urban Survival Kit (TUSK). The kit includes enhanced explosive-reactive armour on the tank's sides and slat armour on its rear to defend against rocket-propelled grenades and other close-in projectiles, upgraded armour plating for external attachment to the side skirts for better protection of the drivetrain and suspension against mines and improvised explosive devices (IED), a gun shield and thermal sight for the loader's 7.62-mm (0.3-in) machine gun, and a modification to allow the commander to fire the 12.7-mm (0.5-in) machine gun from inside the turret. TUSK can be fitted to the M1A2 in the field and includes an external telephone for communication between the tank crew and infantrymen.

A lighter, smaller, and quieter LV100-5 gas turbine engine is currently in development to replace the existing AGT gas turbine powerplant. Developed by Honeywell and General Electric, the engine emits no visible exhaust fumes. Another generation of Abrams, the M1A3, is currently in development. Prototypes should be available for testing by 2014, and the first M1A3 may be deployed by 2017. In addition to the U.S. Army and Marine Corps, the M1 Abrams series serves as the main battle tank of the armed forces of Australia, Egypt, Kuwait, and Saudi Arabia. The Iraqi government is reported to be considering purchasing the Abrams as well.

Leclerc

Developed in the late 1970s, the Leclerc main battle tank replaced the AMX 40 with the French army and brought the nation's armoured force up to date in comparison to its contemporaries, the German Leopard 2 and the U.S. M1 Abrams.

MAIN ARMAMENT
The GIAT 120-mm (4.7-in) CN120-26/52 cannon is longer than that of most other main battle tanks at 52 calibres and is capable of firing standard NATO ammunition.

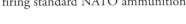

F A C T S

- A total of 862 Leclerc tanks, manufactured by GIAT, later Nexter, were produced between 1990 and 2008.

- The armed forces of France and the United Arab Emirates deploy the main battle tank.

- Initially, four French armoured regiments were equipped with the Leclerc.

ARMOUR PROTECTION
The welded steel turret and hull are further protected with modular armour, which combines steel, Kevlar, and ceramics. Later production models incorporate a combination of tungsten and titanium.

SECONDARY ARMAMENT
Contrary to conventional Western tank
armament, the Leclerc includes a coaxial
12.7-mm (0.5-in) M2HB machine gun, while
a lighter 7.62-mm (0.3-in) machine gun is
turret-mounted for anti-aircraft defence.

AMMUNITION STORAGE
A total of 40 rounds for the main
weapon are carried, one inserted in the
chamber and ready to fire, with a
capacity for 22 in the magazine of the
automatic loading system, and up to 18
in a carousel near the front of the hull.

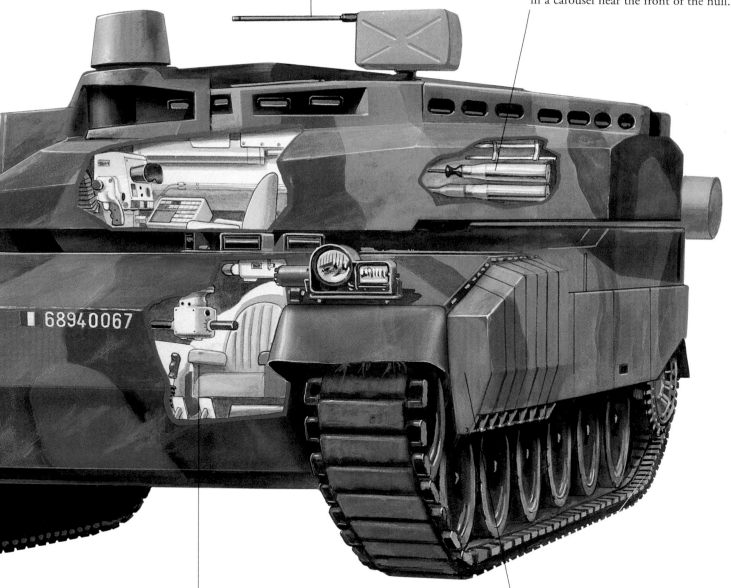

68940067

DRIVER COMPARTMENT
The driver is seated forwards and to the
left in the hull, equipped with three
periscopes, including an OB-60 driver's
sight manufactured by Thales
Optronique with channels for both day
and night vision.

ENGINE
The Leclerc powerplant is the SACM V8X-
1500 hyperbar diesel engine, which
generates 1120 kW (1500 hp). The
Suralmo-Hyperbar high-pressure gas turbine
serves as a supercharger, and the Turbomeca
TM307B auxiliary power unit is installed.

The Leclerc tank is not simply a tank in the widely understood definition of the term: it is in fact a weapons system. As a tank incorporating the products of the most recent technology, it reaches a level of excellence on each traditional quality – mobility, protection, and firepower.

LECLERC

LECLERC – SPECIFICATION

Country of Origin: France
Crew: 3
Designer: GIAT Industries
Designed: 1983–91
Manufacturer: Nexter (GIAT Industries)
In Production: 1991–2008
In Service: 1992–present
Number Built: 862
Gross Weight: 51 tonnes (56 tons)

Dimensions:
Length (hull): 6.88 m (22.6 ft)
Length (gun forwards): 9.87 m (322.4 ft)
Width: 3.71 m (12.2 ft)
Overall Height: 2.46 m (8.1 ft) (to turret roof)

Performance:
Maximum Speed: 70 km/h (43.5 mph)
Range, Road: 550 km (330 miles)
Range, Cross-country: 350 km (210 miles)
Ground Pressure: 0.9 kg/cm^2
Fording Capacity: 1 m (3.3 ft)
Maximum Gradient: 30 degrees
Maximum Trench Width: 3 m (10 ft)
Maximum Vertical Obstacle: 1.25 m (4.1 ft)
Suspension Type: Hydro-pneumatic

Engine:
Powerplant: 1 x SACM V8X-1500 hyperbar diesel producing 1120 kW (1500 bhp) @ 2300 rpm
Capacity: n/a
Power/Weight Ratio: 28.3 bhp/tonne
Fuel Capacity: 1300 l (286 gallons)

Armament and Armour:
Main Armament: 1 x 120-mm (4.7-in) GIAT CN120-26/52
Secondary Armament: 1 x 7.62-mm (0.3-in) MG on turret for anti-aircraft; 1 x 12.7-mm (0.5-in) M2HB MG
Turret Traverse: Electro-hydraulic/manual
Elevation Range: n/a
Stabilization: Elevation and azimuth
Armour Type: n/a

Variants:
Leclerc AZUR: Action en Zone Urbaine, "improve fighting ability in urban environments."
Leclerc EPG: Engin Principal du Génie, "main engineering vehicle" – armoured engineering.
Leclerc DNG: Dépanneur Nouvelle Génération – repair tank.
Leclerc MARS: Moyen Adapté de Remorquage Spécifique – Armoured recovery vehicle.
Leclerc EAU: "Tropicalized" version of the United Arab Emirates fitted with: EuroPowerPack with the MTU 883 diesel engine of 1100 kW (1475 hp); externally mounted auxiliary power unit; remote-controlled mount for 7.62-mm (0.3-in) machine gun, allowing under-armour operation; completely automated driving and turret functions, for use by crew with only basic training; mechanical air-conditioning, to cool the tank without the use of electric current, which could reveal the position of the tank.

SUPPORT VEHICLE: PANHARD VBL SCOUT CAR

LECLERC

In order to avoid many of the problems other nations had experienced with automatic loading systems, the engineers at GIAT Industries and its successor, Nexter, designed the turret of the Leclerc main battle tank around its main weapon, the CN120-26/52 120-mm (4.7-in) cannon and its components. The driver is located in the middle of the hull while the commander and gunner occupy the turret, and either is capable of selecting up to six targets, which may be engaged in as little as 30 seconds. With eight periscopes, the commander also utilizes the HL-70 stabilized panoramic sight manufactured by Safran, while the gunner uses the stabilized SAVAN 20 sight with thermal imaging.

SUPPORT VEHICLE: RENAULT VAB

Draped with camouflage netting to conceal it from detection from the air, a Leclerc main battle tank speeds across a barren landscape. A desert warfare variant of the Leclerc has been developed for service in arid climates.

The French military sought a partnership with a foreign state to limit the cost per unit of building tanks. In response, the United Arab Emirates ordered 436 Leclerc tanks to augment the total of 426 being planned for the French army.

Although discussions surrounding the development of a main battle tank to replace the outmoded AMX 30 dated back to the middle of the 1960s and continued for more than a decade, the pace of development quickened appreciably when a joint venture between the French government and the Federal Republic of Germany failed in late 1982. Because the designers of the two nations were unable to agree on certain fundamental aspects of the project, each embarked on their own individual effort. The French did so after rejecting the purchase of Israeli, German, or U.S. models.

The first prototype of the Leclerc main battle tank appeared in 1989, and production of the vehicle, named for the heroic commander of the Free French 2nd Armoured Division during World War II, began in 1990. At 51 tonnes (56 tons), the Leclerc is lighter than most main battle tanks, and its overall construction is more compact, yielding an excellent power-to-weight ratio. Its 1120-kW (1500-hp),

12-cylinder SACM V8X-1500 hyperbar diesel engine generates a top speed of 71 km/h (44 mph) on the road and is turbocharged with the Suralmo-Hyperbar gas turbine. The Turbomeca TM370B auxiliary power source may be used when the main engine is not engaged. The SESM ESM 500 automatic transmission features five forward and two reverse gears, and the suspension system is hydro-pneumatic. Remarkably, the field replacement of the engine can be completed in as little as 30 minutes.

Although only French-manufactured ammunition is currently in use, the 120-mm (4.7-in) main cannon is compatible with standard NATO ammunition. Firing up to 12 rounds per minute with a purported accuracy of 95 per cent, the weapon is equipped with a thermal sleeve and an automatic compressed-air fume extractor. In addition to the automatic loading system, the gun may be loaded manually from inside or outside the turret.

COMPLEMENTARY SYSTEMS
The FINDERS (Fast Information, Navigation, Decision, and Reporting) system, a Nexter product, includes the designation of targets and mission planning capabilities via a colour map display that can also locate the subject tank, friendly tanks, and hostile vehicles. The Nexter Terminal Integration System

works in concert with the EADS defence electronics system to exchange digitized data received from higher command and transfer information to a computerized map. Digital fire controls permit the ranging of targets at 4 km (2.5 miles) and identification at a distance of 2.5 km (1.5 miles).

Developed jointly by Nexter and Lacroix Tous Artifices, the Galix combat vehicle protection system includes nine 80-mm (3.1-in) grenade launchers attached to the turret and capable of firing smoke, infrared, or fragmentation grenades, while the KBCM defence package consists of missile and laser "paint" warning equipment, and infrared jamming gear.

A TANK FOR THE TROPICS

A tropical variant of the Leclerc was developed for the United Arab Emirates and includes a 1120-kW (1500-hp) MTU 883 V-12 diesel engine and the Renk HSWL295 TM automatic transmission. A package designated Leclerc Battle Management Equipment includes a system similar to FINDERS, and the HL-80 command sight, similar to the French tank's HL-70.

While the Leclerc has yet to see tank-versus-tank combat, it has been deployed with French forces serving under the United Nations flag in Kosovo and Lebanon.

Interior view

The interior of the tank mounts controls for various communications, rangefinding, and targeting equipment, while secondary optical sights are available in the event of battle damage or malfunction.

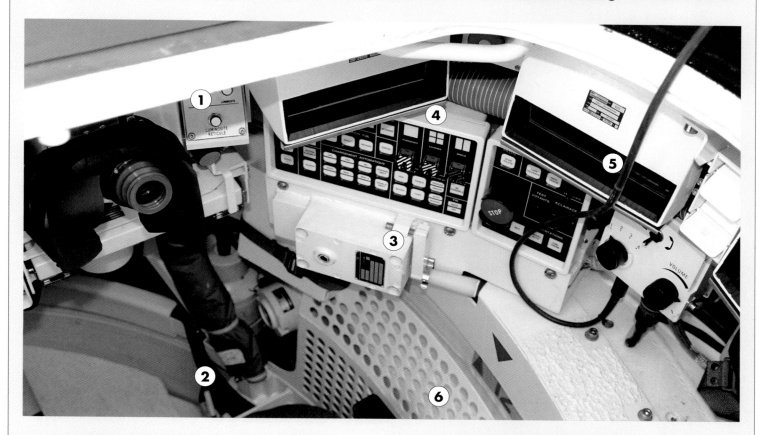

(1) **Gunner's Position:** The gunner's position allows access to fire control, target acquisition, and rangefinding equipment.

(2) **Stabilized Sights:** The stabilized sights of the digital fire control system maintain target identification capabilities even as the vehicle crosses rugged terrain.

(3) **Control Box:** Maintenance and communication links aboard are serviced through access points and housings throughout the interior of the vehicle.

(4) **Fire Control Panel:** The complex fire control system is operated by the gunner in order to acquire targets and lay the main gun of the tank.

(5) **Viewing Ports:** The gunner views the surrounding terrain through a series of viewing ports located within his position.

(6) **Turret Basket:** The turret basket of the Leclerc traverses 360 degrees along with the turret as the crew search for targets in the surrounding area.

T-90

Intended as an interim solution while work progresses on a new generation of main battle tank, the Russian T-90 combines elements of the long-running T-72 and the T-80, which has been the subject of criticism for poor combat performance.

TURRET
The commander and gunner sit inside the rounded turret on the right and left. In 1999, a T-90 with a welded turret adapted from an experimental tank programme appeared along with the cast turret of earlier production tanks.

ENGINE
The 626-kW (840-hp) 12-cylinder Model 84 V-84MS diesel engine powered the initial T-90, while the T-90S, an export variant sold to India, utilizes a 736-kW (1000-hp) 12-cylinder V-92S2 powerplant.

COUNTERMEASURES
The computer-controlled Shtora-1 package includes infrared jamming equipment affixed to the turret, laser warning components, and aerosol grenades to obscure the tank from tracking beams.

SECONDARY ARMAMENT
A 7.62-mm (0.3-in) PKT machine gun is mounted coaxially, and the 12.7-mm (0.5-in) turret-mounted anti-aircraft machine gun may be operated by the commander from inside the tank.

MAIN ARMAMENT
The 125-mm (4.9-in) smoothbore 2A46M, adapted from a powerful anti-tank weapon, continues as the main gun in the T-90, as it has been in the T-72 and T-80.

ARMOUR PROTECTION
Both composite armour consisting of a basic steel shell with layers of plastics and aluminium and the Kontakt-5 explosive-reactive armour (ERA) protect the interior of the T-90.

MISSILE SYSTEM
The 9M119M Refleks anti-tank guided missile is fired with a laser guidance system and is effective against both armour and aircraft.

F A C T S

- The T-90 programme emerged from the Soviet government's desire to maintain factory jobs in two industrial centres.

- The Indian army has purchased and adapted the T-90 in response to Pakistani deployment of the T-80.

- Computerized fire control is still considered to be inferior to Western systems.

The T-90 main battle tank, the most modern tank in the Soviet army arsenal, went into low-level production in 1993 based on a prototype designated as the T-88. Initially seen as an entirely new design, the production model is in fact based on the T-72.

RIVAL: T-80

T–90 – SPECIFICATION

Country of Origin: Russian Federation
Crew: 3
Designer: Vladimir Potkin at Kartsev-Venediktov Design Bureau
Designed: 1992–93
Manufacturer: Uralvagonzavod
In Production: 1993–present
In Service: 1996–present
Number Built: More than 400
Weight: 46.5 tonnes (51.3 tons)

Dimensions:
Length: 9.53 m (31 ft 3 in)
Width: 3.78 m (12 ft 5 in)
Height: 2.22 m (7 ft 3 in)

Performance:
Speed: 60 km/h (37 mph)
Operational Range: 550 km (340 miles)

Engine:
Powerplant: 1 x Model 84 V-84 12-cylinder diesel producing 626 kW (840 hp)
Or 1 x V-92 12-cylinder diesel producing 736 kW (1000 hp)
Or 1 x V-96 12-cylinder diesel producing 919 kW (1250 hp)
Power/weight: 13.5 kW/tonne (18.1 hp/tonne) for Model 84 V-84 12-cylinder diesel engine
15.7 kW/tonne (21.5 hp/tonne) for V-92 12-cylinder diesel engine
19.8 kW/tonne (26.9 hp/tonne) for V-96 12-cylinder diesel engine
Suspension: Torsion bar

Armour and Armament:
Armour: Steel-composite reactive blend version APFSDS: 550 mm (21.6 in) + 250–280 mm (9.8–11 in) with Kontakt-5 = 800–830 mm (31.5–32.7 in); Version HEAT: 650 mm (25.6 in) + 500–700 mm (19.7–27.6 in) with Kontakt-5 = 1150–1350 mm (45.2–53 in)
Main Armament: 1 x 125-mm (4.9-in) smoothbore gun with ATGM capability; mainly 9M119 Svir.
Secondary Armament: 1 x 7.62-mm (0.3-in) coaxial machine gun, 1 x 12.7-mm (0.5-in) anti-aircraft machine gun.

Variants
T-90: Original production model.
T-90K: Command version of the T-90.
T-90E: Export version of T-90.
T-90A: Russian army version with welded turret, V-92S2 engine, and ESSA thermal viewer. Sometimes called T-90 Vladimir.
T-90S: Export version of T-90A. Sometimes called T-90C. Found with two different turret armour arrays.
T-90SK: Command version of the T-90S. Differs in radio and navigation equipment.
T-90S "Bhishma": Modified T-90S in Indian service.
BREM-72: Armoured recovery vehicle.
MTU-90: Bridge-layer tank with MLC50 bridge.
IMR-3: Combat engineer vehicle.
BMR-3: Mine-clearing vehicle.

RIVAL VARIANT: T80BV

T-90

Despite its modernization, the interior of the T-90 continues the Russian trend of close quarters with little thought for crew comfort. The elliptically shaped turret forces the commander and gunner to function under a low ceiling. An automatic loader has reduced the standard Soviet tank crew from four to three, carrying 22 rounds in its carousel, while an additional 21 rounds are stored nearby. The driver compartment is centred in the welded hull, his seat secured to the hull roof to increase survivability in the event of an explosion caused by a mine or improvised explosive device (IED) beneath the vehicle. The T-80BV (above) incorporated Kontakt-1 explosive reactive armour to the T-80 tank, which appeared in the mid-1970s.

T-90

Flying a recognition pennant in Russian colours, this T-90 main battle tank completes a demonstration run. The T-90 was intended as an interim tank eventually to be eclipsed by a new generation of Russian armoured vehicles.

Due to financial woes, the T-90 main battle tank is only present with the Russian ground forces in modest numbers. The cost of each T-90 was estimated recently to be £1.5 million (about $2.3 million), increasing primarily due to the higher cost of raw materials.

The T-90 has been in manufacture since the mid-1990s, and is another in a long line of Soviet (and later Russian) main battle tanks conceived as an interim solution while a new generation of technologically advanced vehicles is being developed. It originated as a project that was to benefit the local economies of two cities that produce tanks, namely Omsk, where the T-80 was built, and Nizhni Tagil, where advanced versions of the T-72 were manufactured.

Eventually, combining the advanced fire control system of the T-80 with the 626-kW (840-hp) diesel engine and Kontakt-5 explosive-reactive armour similar to the British-developed Chobham, the T-90 was placed in production in 1993 with Kartsev-Venediktov as principal designer and manufacturing under the direction of Uralvagonzavod. The T-90 continues to resemble previous Soviet and Russian tank designs with its characteristic low silhouette and elliptical turret. Its 125-mm (4.9-in) 2A46 smoothbore main gun had been proven in previous tank types and was retained with the

capability of firing numerous projectiles, including the Refleks 9M119 AT-11 Sniper laser-guided missile, effective against armour and low-flying aircraft. Secondary armament consists of a 7.62-mm (0.3-in) coaxial machine gun and a turret-mounted 12.7-mm (0.5-in) machine gun for anti-aircraft defence.

The T-90's turret has a distinctive clamshell appearance, exaggerated by the addition of explosive-reactive armour bricks to its exterior. In addition to the Kontakt-5 composite protection, the basic composite armour also protects the turret, while a sophisticated array of countermeasures, designated Shtora-1, or Curtain, further protect the tank against enemy fire. These countermeasures include infrared jamming equipment, laser warning receivers to alert the crew when the tank has been "painted" by opposing laser beams, and aerosol grenades to obscure the vehicle.

CRAMPED QUARTERS

The layout of the tank follows traditional Soviet-style configuration with the driver forwards and centred, the commander seated to the right of the main gun, and the gunner to the left, with the engine compartment to the rear. An automatic loading system has replaced the fourth crewman and provided some relief to the cramped quarters of the T-90 interior, but the problem of crowding persists. The commander, driver, and gunner are equipped with various thermal imaging and laser rangefinding equipment for target acquisition and laying the gun.

An export version of the T-90, designated T-90S, has been sold to the Indian government, and more than 600 have been delivered to date. The T-90S typically is upgraded to a 746-kW (1000-hp) diesel engine but does not include all systems with which the Red Army T-90 is equipped. The Indian government has subsequently sought bids for customized packages to equip the T-90S.

The standard T-90 includes an NBC (nuclear, biological, chemical) defence package, anti-radiation lining, equipment for clearing mines, and a bulldozing capability to dig its own revetment. The driver often performs double duty as a mechanic and must be capable of undertaking basic field repairs. Variants of the T-90 also include the T-90A (nicknamed Vladimir in honour of chief designer Vladimir Potkin) with a welded turret, the Indian export T-90S, the T-90K command tank, and several specialized vehicles for recovery and bridge laying.

The estimated life of the T-90 is approximately 30 years, and it is expected to be replaced by a new Russian main battle tank currently under development.

Close-up

Developed as a temporary solution to the Russian military's need for a main battle tank, the T-90 is expected to be replaced by a substantially altered armoured vehicle in the near future.

(1) **Smoke Grenade Launchers:** Attached to the turret of the T-90, these are capable of independently firing or discharging multiple canisters simultaneously.

(2) **Wide Tracks:** Tracks of extended width provide better traction for the T-90 and increase speed and mobility.

(3) **Armour Panels:** Explosive-reactive armour provides many times the protection of conventional armour plate.

(4) **Countermeasures:** Laser warning receivers and other sophisticated countermeasures warn the crew when the tank is painted by enemy radar equipment.

(5) **Main Weapon:** The T-90 tank mounts a powerful 125-mm (4.9-in) smoothbore gun capable of firing a variety of shells.

(6) **Reinforced Hull:** The hull of the T-90 main battle tank may be reinforced with additional armour to protect against land mines and IEDs.

Challenger 2

Although the Challenger 2 retains the name of its predecessor, less than 5 per cent of the components of the two main battle tanks are compatible. The Challenger 2 is now one of the most reliable and combat-proven tank designs in the world.

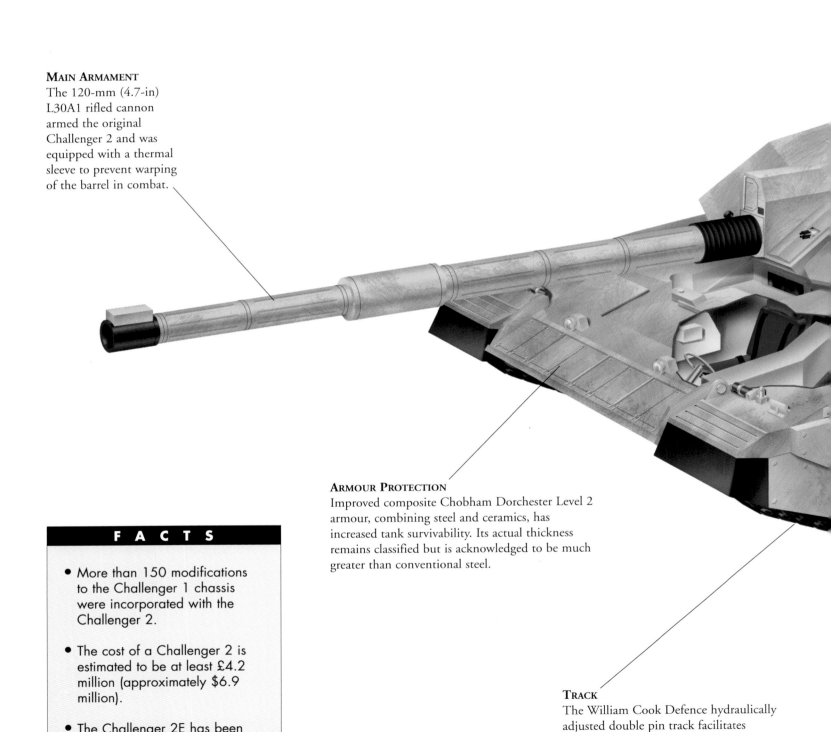

MAIN ARMAMENT
The 120-mm (4.7-in) L30A1 rifled cannon armed the original Challenger 2 and was equipped with a thermal sleeve to prevent warping of the barrel in combat.

ARMOUR PROTECTION
Improved composite Chobham Dorchester Level 2 armour, combining steel and ceramics, has increased tank survivability. Its actual thickness remains classified but is acknowledged to be much greater than conventional steel.

TRACK
The William Cook Defence hydraulically adjusted double pin track facilitates movement across all types of terrain and is serviced with relative ease in the field.

FACTS

- More than 150 modifications to the Challenger 1 chassis were incorporated with the Challenger 2.

- The cost of a Challenger 2 is estimated to be at least £4.2 million (approximately $6.9 million).

- The Challenger 2E has been developed by BAE Systems for the export market.

TARGET ACQUISITION
The commander is provided with a gyrostabilized fully panoramic gunsight with thermal imaging and laser rangefinding, while the gunner's gyrostabilized primary sight, thermal imaging, and laser rangefinding equipment are backed up by a coaxial auxiliary sight.

SECONDARY ARMAMENT
Two machine guns, a Hughes 7.62-mm (0.3-in) L94A EX-34 chain gun mounted coaxially and a 7.62-mm (0.3-in) L37A2 GPMG attached to the loader's hatch, provide close defence and infantry support.

ENGINE
The 890-kW (1200-hp) 12-cylinder Perkins Caterpillar CV12 diesel engine powers a David Brown TN54 epicyclical transmission with six forwards and two reverse gears, and generates a top speed of 59 km/h (37 mph) on the road.

SUSPENSION
The hydrogas variable spring rate suspension provides outstanding stability during road or cross-country manoeuvres.

The Challenger 2 is the first British Army tank since World War II to have been designed, developed, and produced exclusively by a single prime contractor, in this case, BAE Systems Land Systems. Reliability goals were laid down in a fixed-price contract.

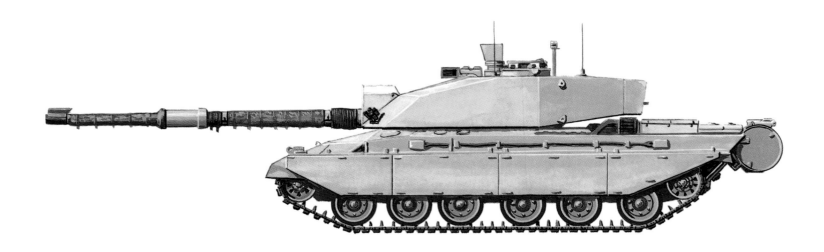

CHALLENGER 2 – SPECIFICATION

Country of Origin: United Kingdom
Crew: 4
Designer: Alvis Vickers
Designed: 1986–91
Manufacturer: Vickers Defence Systems (BAE Systems Land and Armaments)
In Production: 1993–2002
In Service: 1998–present
Number Built: 446
Weight: 62.5 tonnes (68.9 tons)

Dimensions:
Length (hull): 8.3 m (27 ft 3in)
Length (gun forwards): 11.5 m (37 ft 9 in)
Width: 3.5 m (11 ft 6 in)
Width (with appliqué armour): 4.2 m (13 ft 9 in)
Height: 2.5 m (8 ft 2 in)

Performance:
Speed, Road: 59 km/h (37 mph)
Speed, Cross-country: 40 km/h (25 mph)
Operational Range: 450 km (280 miles)

Engine:
Powerplant: 1 x Perkins CV-12 Diesel 890 kW (1200 hp)
Power/weight: 14.2 kW/t19 (0.2 hp/t)
Transmission: David Brown TN54 epicyclic transmission (6 forward, 2 reverse)
Suspension: Hydro-pneumatic

Armour and Armament:
Armour: Chobham/Dorchester Level 2 (classified)

Main Armament: 1 x 120-mm (4.7-in) L30A1 rifled gun. 52 rounds.
Secondary Armament: 1 x Coaxial 7.62-mm (0.3-in) L94A1 EX-34 chain gun, 1 x 7.62-mm (0.3-in) L37A2 commander's cupola machine gun.

Variants
Challenger 2E: Export model with improved cooling system (in service in Oman).
Challenger 2 Trainer: Driver trainer vehicle (base Challenger 2 sans turret).
Challenger 2 Titan: Bridgelayer vehicle. Can carry a single bridge 26 m (85.3 ft) in length or two bridges 12 m (39.4 ft) in length. It can also be fitted with a bulldozer blade.
Challenger 2 Trojan: Battlefield engineering vehicle. Styled as an AVRE for Armoured Vehicle, Royal Engineers in British Army parlance. Designed as a replacement for the Chieftain AVRE (ChAVRE). It uses the Challenger 2 chassis, with an articulated excavator arm and a dozer blade.
CRARRV: (Challenger Armoured Repair and Recovery Vehicle) An armoured recovery vehicle based on the Challenger hull and designed to repair and recover damaged tanks on the battlefield. Instead of armament it is fitted with a main winch, an Atlas crane, a dozer blade, and arc-welding tools.

SUPPORT VEHICLE: ARMOURED STARSTREAK

The interior of the Challenger 2 is similar in design to its predecessor with the diesel engine to the rear, fighting compartment centred, and the driver's position forwards. The commander is seated in the turret to the right with the loader on his left and the gunner in front and below. An automatic loader was abandoned in favour of a fourth crew member to increase 24-hour combat efficiency while reducing the potential for mechanical failure. Along with sophisticated Chobham armour, the turret and hull incorporate stealth technology, an NBC (nuclear, chemical, biological) defence system and state-of-the-art electronics, which are protected against jamming.

The armoured Starstreak (above) is a self-propelled platform for the Starstreak missile system, which is used against helicopters and low-flying aircraft. A variant of the FV101 Scorpion, the Sultan armoured command vehicle (below) entered service with the British Army in the late 1970s.

SUPPORT VEHICLE: SULTAN ARMOURED COMMAND VEHICLE

Deployed with six regiments of the Royal Armoured Corps in the UK and Germany, the Challenger 2 has seen service in Iraq, Bosnia, and Kosovo and exercised in Canada, Oman, and Poland. It has surpassed reliability targets on both trials and on exercises.

Perhaps the most reliable main battle tank in the world, according to its manufacturer, the Challenger 2 has emerged as the primary armoured fighting vehicle of the British Army. Although it was designed around the basic hull and turret configuration of its predecessor, the interim Challenger 1, the Challenger 2 is a remarkably improved, very modern weapon. More than 150 modifications to the older Challenger were incorporated into the Challenger 2, and approximately 5 per cent of the components, primarily automotive, were considered compatible.

Originally ordered from Vickers Defence Systems, the Challenger 2 was being developed as that company became Alvis Vickers, and subsequently evolved to BAE Systems, which incorporated the project into its Land Systems division. The Challenger 2 entered service with the British Army in 1998, and the government of Oman purchased the tank for its defence forces, with export models placed in service three years later.

The 120-mm (4.7-in) L30A1 rifled cannon is operated by a fire control system manufactured by Canada-based Computer Devices Company (CDC), and planned upgrades include navigational enhancements along with a battlefield information control system. Its electro-slag remelting (ESR) construction is equipped with a bore evacuator, coupled with a chromium lining, and insulated with a thermal sleeve for longer barrel life and to prevent warping in combat.

ELECTRONICS AND STEALTH

The CDC and stabilization systems are electronically controlled, and the turret is capable of rotating 360 degrees in nine seconds, completely independent from the hull. Control of the turret and gun are maintained through solid-state electronics rather than more vulnerable hydraulic lines. The turret and hull are both equipped with stealth technology as a defence against radar detection.

By January 2004, the British Ministry of Defence authorized trials for a new main weapon to replace the L30A1 as part of the Challenger Lethality Improvement Programme. The choice was the Rheinmetall L55 smoothbore, made in Germany, which is similar to the main weapon of the German Leopard 2A6 tank. Following the completion of firing trials in 2006, the L55 is expected to be incorporated into the same turret space as the L30 and will allow the Challenger 2 to utilize more effective standardized

The business end of the Challenger 2 main battle tank mounts a 120-mm (4.7-in) gun. Smoke grenade launchers are clearly visible in this photo, as are the twin hatches on top of the turret and its pair of 7.62-mm (0.3-in) machine guns.

Interior view

The Challenger 2 interior incorporates a number of improvements over its predecessor, the Challenger 1, which had been considered an interim solution to the demands of a new British main battle tank.

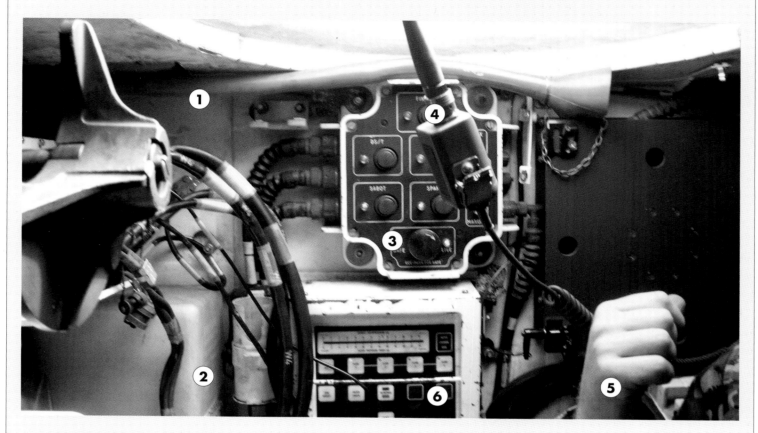

(1) **Spall Liner:** The interior is equipped with a spall liner material that reduces the risk of steel splinters injuring crew.

(2) **Electronic Circuitry:** Thousands of electronic circuits maintain a number of systems on board the tank, including those for target acquisition, rangefinding, and gun laying.

(3) **Control Panel:** Numerous control panels serve the weapons, NBC (nuclear, biological, chemical), fire control, and other systems on board the tank.

(4) **Communications:** Internal communications are maintained via intercom, linked by lines from headsets to central control boxes.

(5) **Commander's Position:** The Challenger 2 commander is situated beneath the turret hatch and provided with controls to lay and fire the main 120-mm (4.7-in) gun.

(6) **Turret Equipment:** The turret houses a series of buttons and gauges that allow the commander to manipulate the orientation of the weapons and direct other crewmen.

NATO 120-mm (4.7-in) ammunition developed in Germany and the United States.

A second generation of Chobham composite armour protects the turret and hull of the Challenger 2, while approximately 450 of the 62.5-tonne (69-ton) tank have been manufactured. The tank's advanced thermal imaging and laser rangefinding are state of the art, and back-up optics are provided in the event of failure or battle damage. The Challenger 2 powerplant is the 890-kW (1200-hp) 12-cylinder Perkins Caterpillar CV-12 diesel engine, while the Challenger 2E, built for export, is equipped with a 1118-kW (1500-hp)

Europack and transversely mounted MTU 883 diesel engine with the HSWL 295TM automatic transmission.

The combat record of the Challenger 2, primarily established during Operation Iraqi Freedom, records only one of its kind destroyed. This was at the hands of another Challenger and was caused by an incident of friendly fire. Two other Challenger 2s have been damaged by improvised explosive devices (IEDs) and the shaped charge of a rocket-propelled grenade. Several reports indicate Challenger 2s had been hit by multiple rocket-propelled grenades and an anti-tank missile and yet sustained no serious damage.

Glossary

AA: Anti-Aircraft

AAVP: Assault Amphibian Vehicle, Personnel. Troop-carrying AAV.

ACRV: Armoured Command and Reconnaissance Vehicle. Command vehicle also used for gathering battlefield intelligence.

Ammunition: A complete unit of fire, consisting of primer, case, propellant and projectile.

APC: Armoured Personnel Carrier. APCs, usually armed with machine guns, generally transport infantry to the battle before the troops dismount to fight on their own.

AT: Anti-Tank. Applied to weapons and weapon systems whose primary function is to destroy heavy armour.

AVLB: Armoured Vehicle-Launched Bridge. Temporary bridge usually laid down by a converted tank chassis.

AVRE: Armoured Vehicle Royal Engineers. British term for combat engineer vehicle.

Barbette: Open gun mounting – normally with front and side protection.

Bore: The interior of the barrel of any firearm, forward of the chamber.

Carrier: Wheeled or tracked armoured vehicle used to transport supplies and ammunition to the front line.

Cartridge: Unit of ammunition, consisting of brass or steel case, primer, propellant and projectile.

Coaxial: Two guns mounted in the same turret or mantlet, rotating together and firing along the same axis.

Cruiser tanks: Prewar and World War II British medium tanks for rapid advance and exploitation after a breakthrough. Fast, lightly armed and armoured, and used by cavalry.

Cupola: Armour plated revolving dome on top of the turret.

Depression: Angle by which a tank's gun can point below the horizontal. Limited by length of gun inside turret, where the gun is mounted in the turret, and the height of the inside of the turret.

Direct fire: Line-of-sight fire directly towards a target, as opposed to indirect fire. Most tanks use direct fire exclusively in battle.

Ditched: A tank is ditched when the trench it is being driven across is too wide or the ground beneath is too soft or waterlogged to allow the tracks to grip.

DP: Dual-purpose. When a weapon is intended for more than one job, or a round of ammunition has more than one effect, it is said to be dual-purpose.

Elevation: Angle by which a tank's gun can point above the horizontal – the greater the angle the greater the range.

Fording: Depth of water which a military vehicle can wade through without flooding engine. Usually quoted as without preparation and with preparation.

GP: General-Purpose

GPMG: General-Purpose Machine Gun. MG used as both infantry LMG and for sustained fire. Variants adapted as coaxial guns for tanks and as anti-aircraft guns on many different kinds of armoured vehicle.

Gradient: Degree of slope up which a tank can travel.

HE: High Explosive

HEAP: High Explosive Anti-Personnel. Dual-purpose HE round which destroys by a combination of blast and anti-personnel effects.

HEAT: High Explosive Anti Tank. Tank round or guided missile with shaped-charge warhead designed to burn through the thickest of armour.

Hull: Main part of armoured vehicle, comprising chassis and superstructure, onto which tracks/wheels and turret are mounted.

Idler: The end wheel of a tracked vehicle. It is not driven, being used to adjust track tension.

IFCS: Integrated Fire Control System. British system developed for the Chieftain tank incorporating target location, rangefinding and gun engagement.

Infantry: As applied to tanks, denoting vehicles used for infantry support and assault. Often applied to slow, heavily armoured vehicles before World War II.

LARS: Light Artillery Rocket System. Multiple rocket system developed for the German Bundeswehr.

Laser: Light Amplification by Stimulated Emission of Radiation. Intense beam of single wavelength light used by the military primarily for rangefinding and target illumination.

LAV: Light Armoured Vehicle. Canadian-built wheeled APC based on a Swiss design and used by the U.S. Marine Corps.

LAW: Light Anti-armour Weapon. Hand-held rocket launcher giving infantry some short-range anti-armour capability.

Light tanks: One of the original classes of tanks. Thinly armoured fast tanks designed primarily for reconnaissance.

LMG: Light Machine Gun. Squad support weapon which can often be fired from the gun ports of infantry fighting vehicles.

LRV: Light Recovery Vehicle

LVT: Landing Vehicle, Tracked. The original amphibious assault vehicles used by the Allies in Europe and the Pacific during World War II. The term continued in use until the 1990s with the LVTP-5 and the LVTP-7, before being replaced by the designation AAV or Assault Amphibian Vehicle.

Machine guns: Rifle-calibre small arms capable of automatic fire, used as primary or secondary armament of armoured vehicles.

MBT: Main Battle Tank. MBTs are the primary tank type of modern armies, and combine characteristics of their medium and heavy tank ancestors.

MCV: Mechanized Combat Vehicle. Another term for IFV.

MG: Machine Gun; also Maschinengewehr (German).

MICV: Mechanized Infantry Combat Vehicle.

MILAN: Missile d'Infantrie Léger Anti-Char (light infantry antitank missile).

Mk.: Mark. used to denote major variants of any military design.

MLRS: Multiple Launch Rocket System. M270 armoured vehicle capable of firing 12 rockets out to a range of more than 30km (19 miles).

MRL: Multiple Rocket Launcher. Launch platform for unguided artillery missiles.

Muzzle brake: Device attached to the gun muzzle to reduce recoil force without seriously limiting muzzle velocity.

Muzzle velocity: Speed of projectile as it leaves the muzzle. Air friction means velocity drops rapidly once in flight.

Ordnance: Military equipment, specifically tube artillery.

Panzerkampfwagen: 'Armoured fighting vehicle' (German). Specifically tracked AFV or tank.

Panzerwagen: 'Armoured vehicle' (German)

Periscope: Optical device which enables viewer to see over obstacles. Enables tank crew to look out while remaining protected.

Rate of fire: Number of rounds which can be fired in a period of time, usually expressed in rounds per minute.

Recoil gear: Connects weapon to cradle by utilizing lugs on the breech ring. Absorbs recoil and has a recuperator which returns the gun to its firing position.

Reconnaissance vehicle: Mobile, lightly armoured vehicle used for gathering battlefield intelligence.

RP: Rocket propelled. Applied to tank ammunition, artillery rounds and antitank grenades.

RPG: Rocket Propelled Grenade Launcher. Soviet-made infantry antitank weapons.

SAM: Surface-to-Air Missile

Semi-automatic: Firearm which fires, extracts, ejects and reloads only once for each pull and release of the trigger.

Schwere: 'Heavy' (German)

Smoothbore: Cannon without rifling, designed to fire unrotated fin-stabilized projectiles.

Snorkel: Breather pipe delivering air to the engines of armoured vehicles; allows vehicle to run submerged.

SOG: Speed Over Ground

SP: Self-Propelled

SPAAG: Self-Propelled Anti-Aircraft Gun system

SPAAM: Self-Propelled Anti-Aircraft Missile system

SPAT: Self-Propelled Anti-Tank system

SPG: Self-Propelled Gun

SPH: Self-Propelled Howitzer

Spring: Part of suspension which absorbs vertical movement when on rough ground. It also enables the driven parts of the suspension to remain in contact with the ground.

Sturmpanzer: Assault armoured vehicle (German). The name given to the first A7V tanks.

Tank destroyer: U.S. Army World War II lightly armoured tracked vehicle armed with a powerful gun. Designed to ambush enemy armour.

Thermal imaging: Sensor system which detects heat generated by targets and projects it as a TV-style image onto a display screen.

Track: Endless belt circling the sprocket, idler, roadwheels and return rollers of a tracked suspension and providing the surface for the wheels to run on.

Transmission: Means by which the power of the engine is converted to rotary movement of wheels or tracks. Transmission can be hydraulic, mechanical, or electrical.

Traverse: The ability of a gun or turret to swing away from the centreline of a vehicle. A fully rotating turret has a traverse of 360 degrees.

Trench: Field fortification which the tank was developed to deal with. Expressed as a distance in feet or metres in a tank's specification, trench indicates the largest gap a tank can cross without being ditched.

Turret: Revolving armoured box mounting a gun. Usually accommodates commander and other crew.

Velocity: The speed of a projectile at any point along its trajectory, usually measured in feet per second or metres per second.

Whippet: World War I term originally describing the first medium tanks, later to describe any light tank.

Index

Picture Credits

Art-Tech/Aerospace: 14, 21, 27, 33, 38, 45, 50, 51, 87, 98, 111, 116, 128, 134, 135, 140, 229, 252, 258, 306, 307, 312

Art-Tech/MARS: 181, 205, 222, 288

BAE Systems: 160

Cody Images: 6, 7, 8, 56, 62, 63, 68, 69, 74, 81, 93, 122, 123, 147, 180, 223, 277, 289, 300

Corbis: 253 (Ronen Zvulun)

John Dovey: 247

Christopher Foss: 246

Hans Halberstadt: 141, 175, 193

Krauss-Maffei Wegmann: 259

Narayan Sengupta: 105

Tank Museum: 15, 20, 26, 32, 39, 44, 75, 80, 86, 92, 99, 110, 129, 146, 169, 199, 204, 210, 241, 276, 313

U.S. Department of Defense: 9, 57, 117, 152, 153, 158, 159, 161, 162, 163, 168, 174, 186, 187, 192, 198, 211, 217, 234, 235, 240, 264, 265, 270, 271, 282, 283, 294, 295

Wikimedia Creative Commons Licence: 104 (George Chernilevsky), 216 (Bachcell), 228 (Caplio G3), 301 (Rama)

All artworks courtesy of Art-Tech/Aerospace, Alcaniz Fresno's S.A. and Amber Books